MILITARY JUSTICE IN THE MODERN AGE

Military justice systems across the world are in a state of transition. These changes are due to a combination of both domestic and international legal pressures. The domestic influences include constitutional principles, bills of rights and the presence of increasingly strong oversight bodies such as parliamentary committees. Military justice has also come under pressure from international law, particularly when applied on operations. The common theme in these many different influences is the growing role of external legal principles and institutions on military justice. This book provides insights from both scholars and practitioners on reforms to military justice in individual countries (including the UK, Canada, the Netherlands and Australia) and in wider regions (for example, South Asia and Latin America). It also analyses the impact of 'civilianisation', the changing nature of operations and the decisions of domestic and international courts on efforts to reform military justice.

ALISON DUXBURY is a Professor at the Melbourne Law School, University of Melbourne, Australia.

MATTHEW GROVES is a Professor of Law at Monash University, Australia.

MILITARY JUSTICE IN THE MODERN AGE

Edited by

ALISON DUXBURY

Melbourne Law School, University of Melbourne

MATTHEW GROVES

Faculty of Law, Monash University

CAMBRIDGE
UNIVERSITY PRESS

CAMBRIDGE
UNIVERSITY PRESS

University Printing House, Cambridge CB2 8BS, United Kingdom

Cambridge University Press is part of the University of Cambridge.

It furthers the University's mission by disseminating knowledge in the pursuit of education, learning and research at the highest international levels of excellence.

www.cambridge.org
Information on this title: www.cambridge.org/9781107042377

First published 2016

A catalogue record for this publication is available from the British Library

Library of Congress Cataloguing in Publication data
Military justice in the modern age / edited by Alison Duxbury and Matthew Groves.
pages cm
Includes index.
ISBN 978-1-107-04237-7
1. Courts-martial and courts of inquiry. 2. Military courts. 3. Military law.
I. Duxbury, Alison, 1970– editor. II. Groves, Matthew, editor.
K4754.M555 2016
343'.01–dc23
2015036056

ISBN 978-1-107-04237-7 Hardback

CONTENTS

CONTRIBUTORS

Ivette Castañeda García holds a bachelor's degree in social sciences from the Pontificia Universidad Catolica del Peru and a Masters in International Studies from Universidad Torcuato Di Tella in Argentina. She has worked in several governmental and non-governmental organisations in Peru, dealing with aspects of military and security issues, such as post-conflict reforms on armed and police forces, human rights and social conflicts. In 2008–2010 Ivette worked in the Latin American Defense and Security Network (RESDAL), an NGO in Argentina. In that role, she worked for a programme called 'Military Justice in Latin America: Disciplinary Codes and Intern Regulations', which involved the systematisation and data analysis of military justice system of sixteen Latin American countries. Castañeda García currently works for the Presidency of the Council of Ministers of Peru.

Christina M. Cerna is a graduate of New York University, Ludwig-Maximilian Universitat, the American University and Columbia University and a former Fulbright scholar. Cerna was Principal Human Rights Specialist at the Inter-American Commission on Human Rights (IACHR) at the headquarters of the Organization of American States (OAS) in Washington, DC, from 1979 to 2011. She conducted research as a Fulbright fellow at the European Court of Human Rights (2000–2001). In 1992–1994 she was seconded by the IACHR to the UN Centre for Human Rights (now the Office of the UN High Commissioner for Human Rights) in Geneva to assist in the preparation of the UN World Conference on Human Rights, held in Vienna in 1993. Cerna has published numerous articles on international human rights law, the inter-American system and public international law. She taught international human rights law as an adjunct for the law schools at George Washington University, Penn State University and, since 2005, at Georgetown University.

Pauline Collins holds a law degree from the University of Adelaide, and Master of Laws and PhD from the University of Queensland. Pauline's

PhD is a comparative study of the civilian courts' jurisprudence in the United Kingdom, the United States and Australia on military matters and the impact on the civil–military relationship. Dr Collins is an associate professor at the University of Southern Queensland, School of Law and Justice. Prior to becoming an academic, she was a legal practitioner in South Australia for ten years, working in general practice, Parliamentary Counsel, the Crown Solicitor's Office and Director of Public Prosecutions. She has published on matters such as industrial relations, alternative dispute resolution, legal education, international law and private military companies.

Paul Cronan is the former Director-General of the Australian Defence Force Legal Service (DGADFLS). In that capacity, he served as the senior military legal advisor to the Chief of the Defence Force and the Secretary of the Department of Defence, and as the principal source of legal advice to the Department of Defence on military legal issues. As the head of the tri-service ADF legal service, Air Commodore Cronan was responsible for the professional oversight and direction of more than 140 permanent and 320 reserve legal officers. Air Commodore Cronan received his Bachelor of Laws and Graduate Diploma in Legal Practice from the Queensland Institute of Technology in 1982 and 1983, respectively, and his Master of International Law from the University of Sydney in 2005.

Alison Duxbury is a professor at the Melbourne Law School. She is also an associate director of the Asia Pacific Centre for Military Law and a member of the Board of Directors of the International Society for Military Law and the Law of War. Dr Duxbury studied law at the University of Melbourne and the University of Cambridge. Her publications include 'The Curious Case of the Australian Military Court' (2010) 10 *Oxford University Commonwealth Law Journal* 155 and *The Participation of States in International Organisations: The Role of Human Rights and Democracy* (Cambridge 2011).

Geoffrey Farmiloe, LLB (Hons) LL.M AFRIN, is a barrister of the Honourable Society of the Inner Temple and a university law lecturer to both undergraduate and postgraduate students. Having previously served in the Royal Navy, he then devoted a large proportion of his life to various aspects of criminal law. His academic research had led him to specialise in military law and the historical development of law within the Royal Navy. He continues to work on the legal aspects of military justice and the laws of armed conflict and has been involved in editing a text on aviation law.

Michael Gibson was, prior to his recent appointment as a military judge, Deputy Judge Advocate General (Military Justice) in the Canadian Forces. He joined the Canadian Forces in 1980. He initially flew as an air navigator in the Royal Canadian Air Force, doing passenger, cargo, VIP and air-to-air refuelling missions. Since becoming a legal officer, he has been prosecution, defence and appellate counsel, and has had significant involvement in recent legislation affecting the military justice system as policy architect, instructing counsel for the drafting of legislation, and as a witness before parliamentary committees. He has also published many articles on international human rights law and the administration of justice by military tribunals.

Matthew Groves is a professor in the Faculty of Law at Monash University, where he teaches administrative and public law. Groves was a member of the Administrative Review Council, which was the peak Australian body that advises the Commonwealth Attorney-General on administrative law issues. Groves has written and edited several books, including Matthew Groves (ed.), *Law and Government in Australia* (Sydney: Federation Press, 2005) and Matthew Groves (ed.), *Modern Australian Administrative Law: Concepts and Context* (Cambridge, 2014). His most well-known work is Mark Aronson and Matthew Groves, *Judicial Review of Administrative Action*, 5th edn (Pyrmont: Thomson Reuters Australia, 2013).

Victor Hansen is a professor of criminal law, criminal procedure, evidence, national security law and prosecutorial ethics at New England Law Boston. Before joining the New England faculty, he served a twenty-year career as an Army JAG Corps officer. His previous assignments include work as a military prosecutor and supervising prosecutor and a military defence attorney and supervisory defence counsel. He also represented Lieutenant General Ricardo Sanchez, during the investigations into detainee abuse at Abu Ghraib prison. Prof Hansen served as an associate professor of law at the Judge Advocate General's Legal Center and School in Charlottesville, Virginia. He is the author of many articles on criminal and military law, and national security issues. Hansen is also a co-author of a treatise titled *Military Crimes and Defenses*, published by Lexis-Nexis.

Chris Jenks is an assistant professor of law and directs the criminal justice clinic at the SMU Dedman School of Law in Dallas, Texas. Prior to joining the law faculty he served for twenty years in the US Army, first as an Infantry officer, serving in Kuwait and Bosnia, and later as a judge advocate, serving in Korea and Iraq. In his last assignment he served as Chief of the International Law Branch at the Office of the Judge Advocate General in the Pentagon. He is a graduate of the United States Military Academy, the University of Arizona College of Law, the Judge Advocate General's Legal Center and School, and Georgetown University Law School. He is currently a PhD candidate at the University of Melbourne in Australia, focusing on the US approach to war crimes investigations and prosecutions. He has published articles and book chapters on international criminal law, human rights law and international humanitarian law.

U.C. Jha served in the Indian Air Force for twenty-four years until retiring in 2001 as Wing Commander. Dr Jha was awarded a PhD in law and governance from Jawaharlal Nehru University, New Delhi. He also holds master's degrees in biological sciences, law, business administration, and defence and strategic studies. He has authored twelve books and published more than sixty articles on subjects relating to military law, environment, human rights and international humanitarian law. He was awarded a visiting fellowship by Jawaharlal Nehru University in 2008–2009. Jha is a visiting faculty member at the Indian Society of International Law, Centre for the United Nations Peacekeeping and United Service Institution of India, New Delhi. He has also worked as Consultant (Legal) for the National Human Rights Commission of India.

Panagiotis Kremmydiotis is the chief judge of the Athens Air Force Military Court. He has been a military judge in the Judicial Corps of the Hellenic Armed Forces since 1984. Kremmydiotis holds graduate law and social-political sciences degrees from the Aristotle University of Thessaloniki, a postgraduate degree from that university on penal law and criminology, and a further LLM from Bristol University on international law. He has delivered seminars and lecture programmes on international humanitarian law, military law, civilian criminal law and procedure at Military Medical School, Medical Personnel School and Military Police School. Kremmydiotis has also published many scholarly articles on military law, criminal law and procedure, human rights and humanitarian law.

Michelle Lesh was a Golda Meir post-doctoral fellow at the Hebrew University of Jerusalem. She worked as a legal assistant to the Turkel

Commission during its second phase. She also provided an expert's paper on the Second Turkel Report to the drones inquiry by the UN Special Rapporteur on counterterrorism and human rights (A/68/389; A/HRC/25/29). Dr Lesh's areas of research include international humanitarian law, international human rights law and the interaction between these bodies of law. Her work currently focuses on the legal controversy over targeted killing as well as the duty to investigate under international law.

Rain Liivoja is a senior lecturer and Branco Weiss Fellow at the Melbourne Law School. He is also Project Director for the Law of Armed Conflict at the Asia Pacific Centre for Military Law and an affiliated research fellow of the Erik Castrén Institute of International Law and Human Rights, University of Helsinki. Dr Liivoja's research focuses on the law of armed conflict, state jurisdiction and comparative military justice. He holds degrees from the University of Tartu and the University of Helsinki.

Ann Lyon is a member of the Faculty of Law at the University of Plymouth in the United Kingdom. Her main area of expertise is British constitutional law but she also researches in military law. Lyon's best-known work on military law is 'Two Swords and Two Standards', which was published in the *Criminal Law Review* in 2005. That article offered the radical thesis that courts which are constituted and operate according to military principles might offer greater procedural protections and observance of rights than equivalent civilian courts.

Rob McLaughlin is an associate professor of law at the Australian National University, and a captain in the RANR. His postings include Director Operations and International Law, Director Naval Legal Service, Strategic Legal Adviser and Fleet Legal Officer. He has served on operations in East Timor and Iraq, and in maritime law enforcement operations. He is a consultant to the United Nations Office on Drugs and Crime and the International Maritime Organization on counter-piracy and maritime crime. Dr McLaughlin holds a PhD from Cambridge University and has published widely on many aspects of military law and operations.

Peter Rowe is an emeritus professor of the Law School at the University of Lancaster in the United Kingdom. He has published widely in various areas of human rights and international law. Rowe is the author of *The Impact of Human Rights Law on the Armed Forces* (Cambridge, 2006). This seminal book examined the growing influence of human rights law on the British armed forces. One of the key conclusions of this book – which is to challenge the widely held assumption that human rights principles weaken effective military organisations and their operations – has profoundly influenced recent scholarship on military law. He has also published many articles on the influence of domestic and international human rights law on soldiers and the military.

John Tarrant is a professor of law at the University of Western Australia. He has published on a wide range of topics including contract, tort, property, corporations law, insolvency law, mining law, international law, practice and procedure and unit trusts. Before becoming an academic, Tarrant held positions in the mining, oil and gas industries as an executive director of Australian and Canadian listed companies.

Aifheli Enos Tshivhase is an associate professor in public law at the Nelson Mandela Metropolitan University (NMMU) and is also Military Law Officer in the reserve force of the South African Air Force, where he carries the rank of Captain. After obtaining an LLM in human rights and democracy in Africa, Dr Tshivhase served as a law clerk to Justice Kate O'Regan of the Constitutional Court of South Africa. He then joined the regular force of the South African National Defence Force in 2002 as a defence counsel, where he started as a lieutenant. After serving in the military for just over two years he joined the University of Cape Town, where he taught, *inter alia*, constitutional law and criminal procedure for nine years. In 2008 he was appointed by the Minister of Justice to serve on the advisory committee of the SA Law Reform Commission, looking into the review of defence legislation to ensure its compliance with the Constitution of South Africa. Aifheli has also had a stint at the University of Johannesburg, where he taught the Bill of Rights and Public International Law in 2013. He is a recipient of the Fox International Fellowship at Yale University in the United States (2009–2010). Aifheli has published on judicial independence of military courts in South Africa and was awarded a PhD in the same field by the University of Cape Town in 2012.

Bas van Hoek is a legal military adviser in the Royal Dutch Air Force. He has been a legal adviser in the Dutch Public Prosecution Service and Head of the Expertise Centre for Military Criminal Law. Before his position at the Public Prosecution Service, Bas was attached to the military legal branch of the Netherlands Royal Army. In that capacity he held various positions in the operational field, including a deployment in Bosnia-Herzegovina and the province of Uruzgan, Afghanistan. Bas is also an adjunct associate professor of military criminal and disciplinary law at the University of Amsterdam. Bas is a member of the editorial board of the *Van den Bosch-bundel*, a commentary on Dutch military criminal and disciplinary law. Bas has published several articles in the *Militair Rechtelijke Tijdschrift* and *The Military Law and the Law of War Review*. He also contributed to the expert report on comparative military justice in the second phase of the Turkel Commission.

Christopher Waters is a professor at the Faculty of Law, University of Windsor, Canada. He joined the Faculty in 2007 and served as Associate Dean from 2009 to 2012. His previous academic post was at the School of Law of the University of Reading. Waters teaches and researches on various aspects of public international law, with an emphasis on international humanitarian law. He has extensive field experience in Eastern Europe and the former Soviet Union. His publications include articles in *Defence Studies* and the *American Journal of International Law*. His latest book is *A Guide to International Law Careers* (with A. Smit, 2014).

FOREWORD

HIS HONOUR JUDGE JEFF BLACKETT

Judge Advocate General of Her Majesty's Armed Forces (UK)

> La guerre! C'est une chose trop grave pour la confier à des militaires.[1]

There are some critics who might pray Clemenceau in aid when they suggest that military justice in the modern age is too serious a matter to be entrusted to the military. On the other hand it has been claimed that the civilianisation of military justice is part of the 'lawfare' or 'legal encirclement' which is hampering operational effectiveness.

There is no doubt that the greatest modern challenge to military justice comes from the pressure to civilianise. Many human rights groups argue that military justice is anachronistic in the modern age, where national citizens who serve in a state's armed forces are entitled to all of the rights and safeguards associated with an independent civilian justice system. And that has been reflected in the various levels of civilianisation of military justice systems around the world. However, it is also acknowledged that the military are distinct from other parts of society and that the work undertaken on a state's behalf requires a separate system of military law.[2]

It is difficult to conceive of an effective armed force, particularly one which deploys in the furtherance of its government's policy, without a separate system of justice or at least a system which acknowledges the unique nature of military service. Appreciating and understanding the military context is essential to the administration of justice in the military in peace or armed conflict or at home or abroad. Peter Rowe deals very succinctly with this issue when he writes, 'It should not be forgotten that the maintenance of discipline within the armed forces is as important in

1 War is too serious a matter to leave to soldiers. As quoted in *Clemenceau and the Third Republic* (1946) by John Hampden Jackson, p. 228; this has also become commonly paraphrased as, war is too important to be left to the generals.

2 House of Commons Select Committee on the Armed Forces Bill, Special Report of Session 2005–2006, Volume 1, Chapter 2.

peacetime as it is during an armed conflict. Military Courts can have as important a role in both situations: human rights bodies and organisations should recognise this role.'

That said, there is always a tension where any element of military business is placed in the hands of civilians. Certainly, civilians generally provide the necessary independence and impartiality which might not otherwise be apparent. But it is also important that those civilians who operate in the system enjoy the confidence of both the military and the general public to ensure military justice is not perceived as a cover-up, on the one hand, or oppression, on the other. In the United Kingdom that civilian oversight is provided by civilian judge advocates who sit in both the civilian and military courts. Most are ex-military but they are selected and trained in exactly the same way as civilian judges. Additionally, the Court Martial was established as a standing court by the Armed Forces Act 2006, rather than the *ad hoc* courts martial which existed before 2009, and this also ensured independent judge advocates are much more involved in case management. This means they, and the military justice system, are able to withstand critical scrutiny as to fairness while still providing a system which supports operational effectiveness.

It is remarkable, but perhaps not unsurprising, that military justice systems around the world, each existing in very different operational and political contexts, are facing similar challenges. In this book Alison Duxbury and Matthew Groves have drawn together a number of expert contributors whose insight is invaluable in examining those challenges. It is an outstanding collection of essays which tackles head-on the civilian–military intersection, drawing on comparisons of several military justice systems, before examining the very important place of military justice within international law. It represents a compendium which will provide a useful reference for future debate. I commend it to all those involved, or interested, in the administration of military justice.

Royal Courts of Justice
UK

ACKNOWLEDGEMENTS

In the last few years, justice mechanisms in the military context have received much media attention. This is particularly apparent in the discussion surrounding the military commissions administered by the United States for detainees in the 'war on terror'. Such military commissions did not offer the full protections provided by the United States' Uniform Code of Military Justice (UCMJ), the statute that governs the trial of the offences, primarily by members of the armed forces of the United States, outlined in the code. While jurisdiction pursuant to the UCMJ permitted the trial of those suspected of violating the law of war, a deliberate choice was made to create an alternative process for people detained in the war on terror.

The aim of this book is not to examine these extraordinary measures (which have been covered in detail elsewhere), but rather to analyse another development, that is, the wide ranging reforms to military justice systems throughout the world that have taken place in the last few decades. In some states these reforms have resulted in adjustments to the existing military justice system, whereas in other states either a completely new system has been proposed or military justice has been incorporated into the civilian justice system. Many of these reforms have been the result of the influence of international law, not least international human rights law. The chapters in this book focus attention on the detail and significance of these reforms, which have rarely been the subject of detailed scholarly analysis.

This book originates in a symposium convened at the Melbourne Law School, University of Melbourne in November 2011, to commemorate ten years since the establishment of the Asia Pacific Centre for Military Law (APCML), a collaborative initiative between the Melbourne Law School and the Australian Defence Force Legal Service. The topic of the symposium was 'Military Justice in the Modern Age' and the aim was to gather both practitioners of military law and academics to discuss some of the challenges faced by military justice systems. This book is based in part on the papers presented at that symposium.

Many people and organisations have assisted us with this project over the years. We would like to thank the Ian Potter Foundation and the Social Justice Initiative and the Australia India Institute at the University of Melbourne, for their generous support for the symposium. We would particularly like to thank the APCML, for supporting and hosting the symposium, and its administrator, Cathy Hutton, for her assistance in organising the event. In the production of the book, we would like to thank Kasia Pawlikowski, a former JD student at the Melbourne Law School, for her excellent research assistance and for her work in formatting the chapters. Our thanks are also extended to Finola O'Sullivan and Richard Woodham at Cambridge University Press.

TABLE OF CASES

TABLE OF TREATIES

1

The reform of military justice

MATTHEW GROVES AND ALISON DUXBURY

At the conclusion of World War I a committee established by the United Kingdom Army Council was tasked with examining the 'law and rules of procedure regulating Military Courts-Martial, both in peace and war, and to make recommendations'.[1] In its 1919 report to Parliament, the committee began by noting the 'enormous expansion of the Army during the European war' and the 'corresponding increase in the number of Courts-Martial'.[2] Sadly, it also stated that the difficulties in dealing with the volume of legal work were exacerbated by the fact that 'so many of the regular officers who were familiar with military law' were lost in the first few months of the war.[3] The need for reinforcements 'rendered it impossible to devote much attention to the legal side of the training of new officers'.[4] The committee was of the opinion that given the difficult circumstances, as a whole, the work of courts martial during the war was 'well done',[5] although it made a number of recommendations for future improvements. Such recommendations included redrafting the Army's disciplinary code to remove repetition and overlapping provisions and the appointment of trained legal advisers with experience in military discipline to assist in a number of matters, such as the work of courts martial and legal education.[6] The committee commented on a range of matters, including the distinction between courts martial held on active service and in times of peace, the difficulties in ensuring justice

[1] *Report of the Committee Constituted by the Army Council to Enquire into the Law and Rules of Procedure Regulating Military Courts-Martial* (London, HMSO, 1919) at 2 ('Report of Committee').

[2] Ibid., at 3. There were 252,773 courts martial for the entire war. [3] Ibid. [4] Ibid.

[5] Ibid. In a separate report, H. Bottomley (MP), Major Lowther (MP) and Stephen Walsh (MP) were more critical of aspects of the court-martial system, commenting that legal aid (in the form of a friend, solicitor or counsel) should be provided and that a 'competent judicial tribunal' should hear appeals in cases where a death sentence had been pronounced: ibid., at 14.

[6] Ibid., at 3–4.

while on operations, particularly where troops were in proximity to the enemy, and the rights of soldiers when charged with offences.

In the (nearly) one hundred years since this report was written, the military justice system in the United Kingdom has been subject to a number of different reform efforts, not least due to the entry into force of the European Convention on Human Rights (ECHR) in 1953 and the adoption of the Human Rights Act 1998 (UK). Such reforms are not limited to the armed forces of the United Kingdom. As the chapters in this book demonstrate, military justice systems throughout the world, whether they are separate from the civilian justice system, as in the United Kingdom, or a part of that system, are in a state of transition. This book examines both the domestic and international influences on these transitions in military justice and discusses two important questions: first, in what way(s) has military justice been changing throughout the world; and second, why is military justice in a state of transition?

Before considering some of the common themes explored in this book, it is important to reflect on the use of the term 'military justice' in this context. 'Military justice' in this book is used broadly to refer to the systems which states have put in place to regulate both disciplinary and criminal offences by members of their armed forces. In some states, separate regimes (including distinct courts or courts martial) have been established to deal with violations committed by members of the armed forces and civilians who are associated with the military. Such violations may include offences against the ordinary civilian criminal law as well as specific offences only known to the military (e.g. disobeying a superior order). In other situations, states deal with these offences within their ordinary civilian criminal justice systems. The chapters in this book examine not only the mechanisms that investigate and hear the more serious offences but also those procedures designed to deal with infractions arising at the lower end of the spectrum (often managed as summary matters within defence forces).[7] Some practitioners and commentators prefer to use the term 'military discipline' rather than 'military justice' to describe such systems. This is in order to highlight the fact that legal instruments and institutions dealing with members of the armed forces are primarily designed to maintain discipline. This point is emphasised in Chapter 13 by Cronan, an air commodore in the Australian Defence Force, when he notes that military discipline is designed to promote certain behaviours, such as obedience to lawful

[7] For an analysis of summary procedures see Chapter 17 by Aifheli Enos Tshivhase.

orders, which are required to ensure that the military's objectives are met. The underlying point of his analysis is that the rules contained within a military justice or discipline system operate to guide and inform the military personnel to which they apply.

Whether the terminology of 'military justice' or 'military discipline' is adopted, the changes explored in this book have been the result of a combination of domestic and international influences. Some changes can be attributed to the 'war on terror' but many have a much longer history, as is demonstrated by the recommendations contained in the report to the UK Parliament in 1919. Some striking examples of change, specifically in the laws of war, can be drawn from US history, where the first comprehensive attempt to document the laws of war was made during the American Civil War. This was achieved by the *Lieber Code*, the instructions to the Union forces of the United States in the American Civil War, which took a 'seminal step' in providing a 'detailed codification and exposition of the laws of war'.[8] This early attempt of the United States to codify the laws of war both assumed and explained a concept of military justice to which military commanders and their soldiers were subject. The promulgation of this code during the Civil War demonstrates that in the United States, as in the United Kingdom, momentous wars sharpened the legal and political focus on the laws of war and, in turn, on military justice. Military justice in the United States underwent enormous reforms after World War II, driven by widespread dissatisfaction by former members of the military who complained of the arbitrary and arcane nature of military justice. These complaints led to a wholesale revision of military justice in the United States and the adoption of the Uniform Code of Military Justice (the UCMJ), which was arguably based on similar principles to the American Civil Rights movement in that it sought to provide greater rights to a part of society that had previously been denied them. Ironically, in recent times the UCMJ has been the subject of much the same complaints that led to its own creation, although wholesale reform seems unlikely.[9]

One of the common themes that emerges in the reforms that have been adopted (and in some cases rejected) in various states is the question

[8] Stephen C. Neff, *War and the Law of Nations: A General History* (New York, Cambridge University Press, 2005), p. 186.

[9] The most significant review of the UCMJ was the 'Cox Commission': Honorable Walter T. Cox III, *Report of the Commission on the 50th Anniversary of the Uniform Code of Military Justice* (2001). A summary of its report is located on the website of the National Institute of Military Justice: www.nimj.org.

whether military justice should be a part of, or separate from, the civilian justice system. As demonstrated in this collection, views on this fundamental issue differ dramatically between legal systems and commentators. Changes in military justice that result in the adoption of civilian elements or attributes are often referred to as 'civilianisation', or potentially 'lawfare' when the involvement of civilian institutions and norms is seen as interference.[10] The term is not exclusively directed to military justice, but the increasing influence of civilian justice norms and civilian courts on the military has been viewed as the sharp edge of civilianisation because such structures impose a strong form of civilian oversight upon the military. Many argue that this oversight conceals a subtle but far-reaching challenge to the autonomy of the military and the internal command structure that lies at the heart of an effective military force. In Chapter 6 Hansen examines reforms to military justice in light of the commander's unique responsibility to ensure compliance with the laws of war. He argues that '[r]eforms to military justice should not undermine the commander's authority and responsibility to ensure law of war compliance'.[11] The perceived threat civilianisation may pose is that it enables soldiers to question the decisions and authority of their commanders by recourse to external legal norms. Chapter 4 by Collins (which examines whether the judiciary has showed deference – or otherwise – to military institutions in their decisions), Chapter 7 by McLaughlin (which discusses the question whether the command power is susceptible to judicial review) and Chapter 2 by Rowe (which argues that properly constituted military courts have an important role in times of peace and armed conflict) demonstrate that such recourse also includes challenges to the structures of domestic military justice systems.[12]

'Lawfare' is the more recent and weaponised successor to civilianisation.[13] Lawfare does not refer to the modernisation of military law or

[10] An alternative term to civilianisation is 'juridification', which refers more particularly to the effect of external judicial oversight upon the military. See, e.g., G.R. Rubin, 'United Kingdom Military Law: Autonomy, Civilianisation, Juridification' (2002) 65 *Modern Law Review*, p. 36; Anthony Forster, 'British Judicial Engagement and the Juridification of the Armed Forces' (2012) 88 *International Affairs*, p. 283.

[11] See Chapter 3. [12] See Chapters 2, 4, 14.

[13] The notion of lawfare was popularised by Charles Dunlap Jr but has been traced to Australia some twenty-five years earlier. See Christopher Waters, 'Beyond Lawfare: Juridical Oversight of Western Militaries' (2009) 46 *Alberta Law Review*, pp. 885, 890 (fn 27), citing John Carlson and Neville Yeomans, 'Whither Goeth the Law – Humanity or Barbarity' in Margaret Smith and David Crossley (eds.), *The Way Out: Radical Alternatives in Australia* (Melbourne, Lansdowne Press, 1975).

military justice *per se* but instead to the suggested adverse effect that the use of law to control the military may have on its ability to fulfil its combat function. Lawfare was originally used to describe 'the use of law as a weapon of war'[14] – invariably by one's adversaries – but is now applied to the more subtle circumstances 'where law can create the same or similar *effects* as those ordinarily sought from conventional warmaking approaches'.[15] The evolving conception of 'lawfare' makes clear that no single term can adequately capture the different forces that operate within and outside military justice. However, the very notion of lawfare highlights that the 'justice' component of 'military justice' is contested. In Chapter 3 Waters leaves little doubt that the level of civilian legal oversight of the military remains less than civilian political oversight, but he also makes a strong case for the evolution of civilian oversight in a form that remains conscious of the particular character and role of the military. Waters' conclusions are consistent with the scholar who popularised the notion of lawfare, Charles Dunlap Jr, who has recently adopted a more subtle approach to the concept, conceiving of lawfare as a 'strategy of using – or misusing – law as a substitute for traditional military means to achieve an operational objective'.[16] This more refined approach conceives of lawfare as a supplementary weapon, available to both sides in a conflict. Dunlap argues that this more neutral approach to lawfare is not a new gloss because

> the term was always intended to be ideologically *neutral*, that is, harking back to the original characterization of lawfare as simply another kind of weapon, one that is produced, metaphorically speaking, by beating law books into swords. Although the analogy is imperfect, the point is that a weapon can be used for good or bad purposes, depending upon the mindset of those who wield it. Much the same can be said about the law.[17]

Dunlap also conceded that lawfare must be available to one's enemies and mounted a defence of that possibility as follows:

[14] Charles J. Dunlap Jr, 'Law and Military Interventions: Preserving Humanitarian Values in 21st Century Conflicts' (Humanitarian Challenges in Military Intervention workshop paper, Carr Centre for Human Rights, John F. Kennedy School of Government, Harvard University, Working Paper, 2001) at 5: www.hks.harvard.edu/cchrp/pdf/publications_pdf/nshr/Vol_1_Nov2001_DunlapMeilingerOwen.pdf.

[15] Charles J. Dunlap Jr, 'Does Lawfare Need an Apologia?' (2012) 43 *Case Western Reserve Journal of International Law*, pp. 121, 122.

[16] Charles J. Dunlap Jr, 'Lawfare Today: A Perspective' (2008) 3 *Yale Journal of International Affairs*, p. 146, at 146.

[17] Dunlap, above n. 15, at 122 (citations omitted).

> Just because the law is available, for example, to the most evil of criminals who may avail themselves of its protections from time to time does not mean that the law acquires the attributes of the criminal. Nor does it mean, incidentally, that those lawyers who assist such persons in securing their legal rights necessarily share their malevolent intent.

It merely means that law – at least ideally – has established norms that, on balance, best serve society as a whole even when it has the effect of protecting people that many find odious and even dangerous. Overall, however, it is indisputable that the public enjoys enormous benefits from the social order that law creates – notwithstanding that occasionally evildoers determined to disrupt that social order are among those who profit from the rights and liberties the law produces and protects.[18] This reasoning proceeds on the assumption that the chief beneficiaries of lawfare are those who make up the very society that has promulgated the law and those beneficiaries include the military forces of that society. This proposition leads to a further conclusion: while the military and civilian may be distinct, they are not, and indeed cannot be, separate. The same is true of military and civilian life more generally. A military force and its members are drawn from society and may exist and operate distinctly from that society, but they are not and cannot be separate from that wider society.[19]

This book is designed to capture these influences by first examining the civilian–military intersection and the influence of civilianisation as described above. This includes (in Part I) civilian oversight of the military (Chapter 3), the relationship between military justice and the civilian courts (Chapter 4), the impact of civilianisation on military administrative law (Chapter 7) and the prospect of civilians being subject to military justice (Chapter 5). Part I also provides a critical account of the potential impact of civilianisation on military courts (Chapter 2) and analyses the role of the military commander in military justice systems (Chapter 6). What is revealing in the accounts of military justice in this book is that although the influence of civilianisation is pervasive across legal systems, this does not mean that there is a common response to this push for greater civilian involvement. As Dahl, the former attorney general for the Armed Forces in Norway, remarked at an expert consultation on human

[18] Ibid.

[19] Although the classic work of Clode suggests that there was a long period in which military and civilian life were in many respects almost wholly separate: Charles M. Clode, *Military Forces of the Crown: Their Administration and Government*, 2nd revised edn (London, John Murray, 1874).

rights considerations in military tribunals convened by the Office of the High Commissioner for Human Rights in 2015, in some countries military justice is conducted by courts martial convened for individual cases and in others it is conducted through the civilian courts. There are also a number of other variations, including standing military courts or civilian courts with specialised military expertise, with practices altering depending on whether it is a time of war or peace.[20] As is stated by Rowe, '[M]ilitary courts or tribunals come in various shapes and sizes'.[21] These differences have meant that countries have dealt with the influence of civilian laws and institutions on their military justice systems in a variety of different ways.

The laws and institutions which have influenced the reform of military justice systems can be broadly grouped into two sources: domestic and international law. The domestic influences upon military justice include constitutional principles, charters or bills of rights and the rise of oversight bodies such as parliamentary committees and specialist Ombudsmen.[22] The domestic legal requirements of military justice systems are increasingly flavoured by international legal instruments and principles. Consequently, military justice has also come under pressure from international law (including both international humanitarian law and international human rights law) particularly when applied on operations. Part II of this collection focuses on a number of domestic military justice systems to determine the way in which domestic and international legal principles have influenced their historical development. Van Hoek's analysis of the Netherlands in Chapter 11 provides a detailed account of a twenty-five-year legislative process which led to a 'civil swing' in the military justice system. Castañeda's discussion (Chapter 10) of selected military justice systems in Latin America demonstrates the way in which the restoration of democracy has sparked a debate on the role and place of military justice systems in national society. The potential domestic (and international) influences are also clear in Lesh's examination of Israel's investigative processes and the report of the Turkel Commission (Chapter 12).

Whereas the influence of international humanitarian law on military action and institutions is well accepted, the involvement of international human rights law and human rights bodies is more controversial. A 2015

[20] United Nations High Commissioner for Human Rights, Summary of the Discussions held during the Expert Consultation on the Administration of Justice through Military Tribunals and the Role of the Integral Judicial System in Combating Human Rights Violations, A/HRC/28/32 (29 January 2015), p. 4.

[21] See Chapter 2. [22] See Chapters 2 and 4.

report by a UK think tank, Policy Exchange, entitled *Clearing the Fog of Law* examines recent litigation concerning British military action in Iraq and Afghanistan and suggests that the European Court of Human Rights (ECtHR) 'is supplanting and undermining the older and far more suitable body of International Humanitarian Law'.[23] The report has been criticised for overstating the extent of the alleged problem of judicial oversight (suggested in the subtitle to the report – 'Saving our armed forces from defeat by judicial diktat') and oversimplifying the relationship between the extraterritorial application of human rights law and international humanitarian law.[24] Whether the influence of international human rights principles and institutions is to be welcomed or not, there is no doubt that it is becoming more pervasive. This is true of the application of international human rights principles on operations and also the influence of human rights law, particularly the right to a fair trial, on military justice systems. For example, Lyon and Farmiloe discuss the impact of the decisions of the ECtHR on the military justice system in the United Kingdom in Chapter 8. International human rights law, and its influence on reform of military justice throughout the world, is also the central theme of a number of chapters in Part III, including Chapters 15 and 16 by Kremmydiotis and Cerna, respectively. Kremmydiotis examines a diverse range of reforms across the world and the way in which international standards have influenced these reforms. Cerna provides a detailed analysis of the decisions in the inter-American system of human rights and their influence on military justice systems in Latin America. Much of the jurisprudence in this area is on the operation of courts martial and military courts (dealing with the more serious offences); however, Tshivhase's analysis in Chapter 17 also examines the future of military summary trials in the light of the jurisprudence of the ECtHR. Such an analysis is timely given that although discussion of reforms to military justices tends to focus on the trial of more serious offences, most matters are dealt with at the lower level.[25] Tshivhase argues that such trials should be maintained, given their

[23] Richard Ekins, Jonathan Morgan, and Tom Tugendhat, 'Clearing the Fog of Law – Saving Our Armed Forces from Defeat by Judicial Diktat' in *Policy Exchange* (London, Policy Exchange, 2015), p. 9.

[24] See Eirik Bjorge, 'The Fogmachine of War: A Comment on "Clearing the Fog of Law"' *EJIL: Talk!* (13 April 2015) www.ejiltalk.org/the-fogmachine-of-war-a-comment-on-the-report-clearing-the-fog-of-law/.

[25] For example, in 2013 in the Australian Defence Force forty-two trials were held by courts martial (General and Restricted) and Defence Force magistrates, 1403 trials were held before summary authorities and 5383 minor infringements were dealt with by discipline

importance to military discipline, but that the influence of human rights law means that reform is inevitable.

Despite the undoubted influence of human rights principles on many military justice systems, not all countries accept the direct effect of international human rights law in their legal systems. As is demonstrated by Tarrant's analysis of Australia's military justice system in Chapter 14, the extent to which international human rights principles may directly impact on domestic structures depends on the reception and incorporation of international law into a national legal system. But this does not mean that international human rights law has not been discussed in the context of changes to Australia's military justice system. As is highlighted by Cronan (Chapter 13) in his examination of the Australian system, human rights provisions (including the European Convention on Human Rights and the International Covenant on Civil and Political Rights) and cases have been referenced in reviews of Australia's military justice system.[26] Jha's account of military justice in South Asia (Chapter 9) also reveals that a number of countries have not been subject to the same drive to reform on the basis of international human rights law.

One issue in the human rights discussions and jurisprudence that has proved particularly problematic is the trial of civilians by military courts or tribunals. Recommendations of the expert consultation convened by the Office of the High Commissioner for Human Rights contained reference to General Comment 32 of the Human Rights Committee in which the committee stated that 'civilians should not be subject to the jurisdiction of military courts except in exceptional circumstances'.[27] In Latin America the jurisprudence of the inter-American Human Rights system has displayed a complete antipathy for civilians being tried in military courts, as demonstrated by the cases examined by Cerna and Liivoja (Chapters 16 and 5). However, the ECtHR has not adopted a complete ban against such a possibility. The differences in approach can be explained by the very different historical factors which have led to reforms to military justice in Latin America, as recounted in Castañeda García's analysis of reforms to military justice in Latin America in Chapter 10. Liivoja highlights that there are both practical and policy reasons why a particular group of civilians, those who travel with the armed forces as 'associated civilians', should be subject to military

officers: see Judge Advocate General, *Defence Force Discipline Act 1982 – Report for the period 1 January to 31 December 2013* (2014) Annexes A–N.

[26] See Chapter 13. [27] See above n. 20, 16.

jurisdiction in certain situations. Liivoja argues that military justice systems possess the legal structures and expertise to provide effective legal oversight and accountability over these associated civilians, including private contractors. Consequently, as is recognised by the UN Special Rapporteur on the independence of judges and lawyers, there may be situations where civilians who travel with the armed forces on operations can and should be subject to military jurisdiction.[28]

The position of civilians who travel with defence forces when they are deployed overseas also highlights one of the other questions that arises throughout this collection: should the type of trial (and the trial institution) be dependent on whether an offence is committed in times of peace or war/at home or on operations? It is often claimed that the exceptional circumstances in which military justice must sometimes be dispensed render civilian institutions inappropriate to the task of enforcing discipline (or justice), particularly when the military is deployed overseas. Gibson succinctly makes this point in his discussion of military justice in operational settings in Chapter 19, when he states that '[S]eparate military justice systems exist because of the needs of armed forces to effectively fulfil their mission of defending the state and their parent societies.'[29] However, the approach to this issue is by no means universal. Van Hoek's discussion (in Chapter 11) of the 'civil swing' in the Netherlands demonstrates that military justice can be administered via the civilian court system. Civilian courts may also be involved in other stages of a trial process – for example, in some countries the civilian courts hear appeals from military courts or tribunals.[30] The analysis by Castañeda García of military justice in Latin America also highlights the way in which reform of military justice in certain countries has led to the incorporation of civilian elements in response to the military's role in dictatorships and the use of military courts to try civilians in the past (Chapter 10). For example, military justice in Argentina is now administered through the civilian criminal code with an ordinary jury hearing cases involving the military in times of peace and war.[31] These innovations demonstrate that not all legal systems regard civilian courts as inappropriate forums to hear cases against military personnel, even during armed conflicts.

There is no doubt that the 'sharp end' of military justice – the way in which it does and should function when armed forces are in operational environments – is an important issue – not only to ensure the rights of defence force members but also to ensure that justice is seen to be done

[28] See Chapter 5. [29] See Chapter 19. [30] See Chapter 15. [31] See Chapter 10.

by civilians living in operational environments.[32] Chapters 18 and 19, by Jenks and Gibson, respectively, in Part III examine different aspects of military justice in operational settings. Gibson traces the role of military justice in operational settings, particularly peacekeeping missions and situations of transitional justice. He argues that it is necessary for states to provide appropriate jurisdiction and resources to military justice systems to enable them to fulfil such missions. Jenks focuses on the practice of the United States in charging service members with specific offences under the UCMJ rather than law of war violations or war crimes when on operations. Together with analyses by Kremmydiotis, Cerna and Tshivhase, in Chapters 15, 16 and 17, respectively, the other chapters in Part III demonstrate that international law provides an important lens through which to view the practices of military justice systems. These chapters are clearly not the last word on the interplay between international and domestic law in military justice, as exemplified by the recent decision of the ECHR in *Jaloud* v. *Netherlands*[33] discussed by both Collins and van Hoek in Chapters 4 and 11, respectively.

The analyses provided in this book demonstrate that, despite the passage of years and the very different types of operations in existence since the armistice that ended World War I, the concerns articulated in the 1919 report remain in sharp focus during contemporary debates about reforms to military justice. At the conclusion of World War I such concerns included the differences between military justice in times of war and peace, the difficulties in implementing full judicial guarantees during military operations, the desirability of access to the civilian justice system, and the rights of service members particularly when subject to the most severe penalties (which, in World War I, included the death sentence).[34] The reforms to military justice prompted by the development of international human rights law since World War II arose from similar sentiments to those expressed by three members of the 1919 Committee (in the context of the application of the death penalty), who reasoned that[35]

> whilst the efficiency of the fighting forces and the exigencies and abnormal conditions of war may render many departures from ordinary legal

[32] Dahl has commented that '[W]hen soldiers committed crimes against local civilians whom they were supposed to protect, putting the accused on an airplane for prosecution at home did not make a good impression.' Quoted in United Nations High Commissioner for Human Rights, above n. 20, p. 4.

[33] European Court of Human Rights, Grand Chamber, Application No. 47708/08, 20 November 2014.

[34] *Report of the Committee*, above n. 1, at 2. [35] Ibid., at 14.

> procedures inevitable, and justify the vesting in offices of exceptional disciplinary and other powers, no man joining the army should forfeit the right of an appeal for his life to a competent judicial tribunal.

That concern was expressed almost a century ago and draws attention to an enduring question in military justice. How much can the special nature of the military and its activities justify departures from the normal protections of the law? In 1919 that question was thought to be one about the rights of soldiers – it is now accepted as one affecting soldiers, their enemies and citizens, including civilians in war zones. The importance of a military justice system to maintaining military discipline, the independence of procedures for investigations and summary procedures and courts martial, the need for military justice systems to be able to deal with offences in times of peace, as well as on operations, is made clear throughout this collection. The different approaches taken by jurisdictions examined also demonstrate that, while many themes and problems may be common to all military justice systems, the methods of meeting those challenges are not.

This collection aims to contribute to the ongoing discussion about the desirability and processes of reform to military justice systems. As the report of 1919 demonstrates, this is not a new conversation, but one that has raised similar issues over the decades, albeit using different terminology. The enduring problems that remain in some of the central concepts of military justice provide an important reason for carefully documenting new practices and relevant legal principles. The military's role in novel missions, for example international peacekeeping missions and transitional justice regimes, examined by Gibson, provides another reason for carefully documenting new practices and relevant legal principles. No doubt, in the next few years as we commemorate the centenary of World War I there will be many discussions of aspects of military life, which will draw on the experiences of those who served in that war. Military justice systems will inevitably be a part of those discussions.[36] The laws to which military forces and their commanders and members are subject provide an important source of moral and legal legitimacy to military forces and their operations. Given this fact, continued debates and conversations about the rationales, roles and functions of military justice systems are not new, nor are they to be feared, but rather they should be welcomed.

[36] For example, in October 2014 'The Flanders Field Conference' was convened by the International Society for Military Law and the Law of War in Ypres, Belgium, to discuss lessons learned from the past and contemporary challenges in military law and international humanitarian law.

PART I

The civilian–military intersection

2

How well do international human rights bodies understand military courts?

PETER ROWE

I Introduction

Military courts have not always received a good press. They are frequently perceived as being inferior to civilian courts in their ability to provide a forum for a fair trial, or they are seen as 'courts' subject to manipulation by senior officers of the armed forces or by the government of the day. Yet both international humanitarian law (IHL)[1] and international human rights law (IHRL) recognise their existence. In the former body of law military courts are given specific tasks to perform whilst in the latter their very existence has been called into question to the extent that the Sub-Commission (of the Commission on Human Rights) on the Promotion and Protection of Human Rights concluded in 2002 that there was 'a growing consensus on the need to limit the role of military tribunals, or even [to] abolish them'.[2]

This chapter will argue that those charged with the task of considering and drafting international norms, whether in the form of a treaty or 'soft law', or those interpreting existing law should be clear as to what constitutes a military court, the different purposes to which such courts are employed and the unique nature of each state's military court. Sadly, some or all of these basic concepts do not seem to have been understood fully, particularly,

[1] IHL requires armed forces to possess an 'internal disciplinary system': see Protocol Additional to the Geneva Conventions of 12 August 1949, and Relating to the Protection of Victims of International Armed Conflicts, 8 June 1977, in force 7 December 1978, 1125 UNTS 3, art. 43. In addition, IHL recognises that an occupying power may try civilians in occupied territory by 'properly constituted, non-political military courts': Geneva Convention Relative to the Protection of Civilian Persons in Time of War of 12 August 1949, in force 21 October 1950, 75 UNTS 287, art. 66. The issue of a military court established by an occupying state is discussed in Section V.

[2] Louis Joinet, *Issue of the Administration of Justice through Military Tribunals*, E/CN.4/Sub.2/2002/4, (UN Sub-Commission on the Promotion and Protection of Human Rights, 9 July 2002), p. 3.

by some human rights bodies and organisations. It is also important to exercise caution when speaking of *international* human rights law in relation to military courts in general. Military courts can vary as much as the countries in which they are established. The problems faced by the Inter-American Court or Commission are, on the facts, often quite different from those faced, for instance, by the European Court of Human Rights. Their decisions in relation to military courts will reflect these differences.

II Military courts are not uniform

Military courts[3] play an essential role in times of peace as well as in times of armed conflict as a means of enforcing discipline and professionalism within a state's armed forces.[4] States will normally train their young men (and sometimes, women) to use high-powered lethal weapons. Moreover, a level of aggression, unlike in civilian employment, is an aim of this training. If high standards of discipline are not maintained within units of the armed forces, the most serious of all crimes can be committed easily, principally against civilians. Within a democratic state, the armed forces will normally possess more physical power than any other of its agents. It is clearly in the interests of governments and citizens, where the armed forces are called upon to use force, either within the state itself or abroad, that this is carried out within, and not outside, the relevant areas of law applicable to the situation.

In armed conflict the enforcement of principles of IHL by military courts is likely to be much more effective than enforcement by

[3] It is common for military commanders to possess statutory power to impose a range of punishments on their subordinates for breaches of discipline. Such action cannot be considered to be the decision of a court or tribunal or, indeed, judicial in any way. It is, however, misleading to accept the position that disciplinary punishments (which can be imposed by a military commander on subordinates) are quite distinct from criminal punishments (where an independent and impartial tribunal is required). The nature of a disciplinary punishment may be considered to be equal in severity to a criminal punishment. In this case it should be imposed only by a court or tribunal (whether a military or a civilian court). See *Engel* v. *The Netherlands* (1979) 1 EHRR 647 at [82].

[4] The Geneva Conventions 1949, common art. 3(1)(d), appears to envisage both parties to a non-international armed conflict using courts to enforce discipline. For discussion of the difficulties involved in the use of courts by non-state organised armed groups, see Anne-Marie La Rosa and Carolin Wuerzner, 'Armed Groups, Sanctions and the Implementation of International Humanitarian Law' (2008) 90(870) *International Review of the Red Cross*, p. 327 at 339–40; Jonathan Somer, 'Jungle Justice: Passing Sentence on the Equality of Belligerents in Non-International Armed Conflict' (2007) 89(867) *International Review of the Red Cross*, p. 655 at 670. Were such courts to be established, they would be considered to be military courts on the basis of the discussion in the following text.

international courts or tribunals. First, military courts are more likely to deal with the ordinary soldier, while international courts or tribunals have tended to concentrate on commanders.[5] Second, military courts (particularly in their preliminary processes) can operate relatively quickly, providing much needed deterrence at unit level.[6] Third, military courts can also provide a range of lesser military breaches and penalties to deal with situations where proof beyond reasonable doubt of a very serious crime is likely to prove to be difficult. Fourth, an early investigation of alleged misconduct during the course of an armed conflict can normally, in practical terms, only be carried out by military personnel, particularly where the alleged offence is committed by one or more members of the armed forces engaged in military operations abroad. Finally, press or other media[7] publicity of an incident can cause a state to act very quickly to show that it is able and willing to deal with any allegations of misconduct during the course of military operations.

The principle of complementarity contained in the Rome Statute of the International Criminal Court[8] is likely to produce reliance on trial, for one of the crimes within the jurisdiction of the Court, before a military court, especially where the alleged crime has been committed abroad. This could give military courts a new lease of life since states which are party to that statute will need to demonstrate that their trial processes (whether civilian or military) were conducted before courts exhibiting the appropriate degree of independence and impartiality to deny admissibility to the International Criminal Court.[9] Therefore, it cannot be argued that 'the sole justification for the existence of military tribunals has to do with the practical eventualities, such as those related to peacekeeping operations or extra-territorial situations'.[10] This ignores the

[5] See, for example, various accounts of US court-martial proceedings in (2007) 100 *American Journal of International Law*, p. 478; (2008) 101 *American Journal of International Law*, p. 494; (2009) 103 *American Journal of International Law*, p. 358; and for UK courts-martial cases, see The Aitken Report: An Investigation into Cases of Deliberate Abuse and Unlawful Killing in Iraq in 2003 and 2004 (London, Ministry of Defence, 25 January 2008) http://mod.uk/NR/rdonlyres/7AC894D3-1430-4AD1-911F-8210C3342CC5/0/aitken_rep.pdf.

[6] This aspect of military justice is examined in detail in Tshivhase, Chapter 17.

[7] A number of cases have come to light through soldiers taking their own photographs, particularly in recent times on their mobile phones.

[8] Rome Statute of the International Criminal Court, 17 July 1998, in force 1 July 2002, 2187 UNTS 90 (Rome Statute).

[9] Ibid., art. 17(2)(c).

[10] Emmanuel Decaux, *Issue of the Administration of Justice through Military Tribunals*, E/CN.4/Sub.2/2005/9 (UN Sub-Commission on the Promotion and Protection of Human

essential requirement of maintaining military discipline during armed conflict, riots or disturbances in which the armed forces are engaged and also in peacetime training.

Not all states, however, are alike or indeed similar. They vary due to historical and legal development, their national law, foreign policy ambitions, the nature of their armed forces and their relationship with the government. In relation to the latter point, Kyle and Reiter wrote that 'the stronger the military in relation to the government, the more likely and the more capable the military is to resist reform of military courts'.[11] Some states will find a role for their armed forces only where the state itself is attacked, others will be prepared to contribute units to UN peacekeeping forces or, following a UN Security Council resolution, take part in military operations. Some, but not all, states may use their armed forces within their own territory to assist civilian organisations following a natural disaster, to destroy illegally grown narcotics or to defeat those who would seriously challenge the government in one way or another.

At present military courts operate mainly to try members of the armed forces for breaches of military discipline. In some states, and in some circumstances, civilians may also be charged before these courts.[12] Therefore, 'military courts' cannot be seen as a homogenous type of trial process. The format and powers of each state's military courts are *sui generis*. In some states military courts can try offences against that state's criminal law. In others, the jurisdiction of military courts is restricted to breaches purely of the military code. Some states may grant their military courts the jurisdiction to try members of their armed forces for acts committed whilst serving abroad, while other states may not so provide. Various combinations of these practices are, of course, possible. It is, however, the usual practice for such courts to be established by statute. In democratic states, therefore, they will be established through the relevant parliamentary process.[13]

Rights, 2 June 2005) [59]. For comment on this, see Report of the Expert Meeting on Human Rights and the Administration of Justice by Military Tribunals (Brasilia, 2007) www.law.yale.edu/The_Brasilia_Report.pdf.

11 Brett J. Kyle and Andrew G. Reiter, 'Dictating Justice: Human Rights and Military Courts in Latin America' (2012) 38(1) *Armed Forces & Society*, p. 27 at 34.

12 The difficulties surrounding this possibility are examined in Liivoja, 'Trying civilian contractors in military courts: a necessary evil?', Chapter 5.

13 In addition, the ordinary courts may have the power to declare that parliament has acted outside the constitution of the state. See *Lane* v. *Morrison* (2009) 239 CLR 230, in which

These variations make attempts to formulate a norm of international law intended to apply to all military courts difficult. In the same way, efforts to describe the role of military courts within a particular state run grave risks of inaccuracy, first because the role of military courts must be seen within the context of the whole legal processes of that state and second, because a state can change the law relating to its military courts at any time. Finally, there is always a considerable risk of inaccuracy if a non-national law specialist attempts to summarise the law of a state with which he or she is unfamiliar.

Military courts have practical problems over and above those faced by the ordinary civilian criminal process, many of which arise from the cultural environment and hierarchical nature of the military. A significant problem is the possibility that soldiers, who could be witnesses to an alleged crime (or military offence), conspire to give misleading or false evidence out of a misguided sense of loyalty to a colleague facing an investigation or trial.[14] Another problem is that the hierarchical structure of the armed forces in many states can give rise to the risk (or at least the perceived risk) of command interference with the independence of military justice, through either the investigation or the trial processes. Linked with this is the risk of impunity, particularly of senior military officers where they are able to control the whole military court system. Not all states will exhibit these problems, either singly or in combination, whilst a number will have taken steps to prevent some or all of them.

III What is a 'military court'?

When military personnel purport to convene a court, some basic questions arise. What is the nature of a 'court' of law? Does a body become a 'court' merely because the law establishing it describes it as such or as a tribunal? Although described as a 'court martial' in the early twentieth century, the bodies composed solely of military officers in the martial law

the High Court of Australia declared the statutory provisions creating the Australian Military Court to be invalid when set against the Australian Constitution.

14 Charles M. Clode's classic account argued that a soldier was especially loyal to his commanders because a soldier 'gives himself up wholly to his superior Officer in religion, politics, civil relations, loyalty, internal and external behaviour. He wears his clothes, cuts his hair, holds his person, and regulates his step and action at the command of Officers': Charles M. Clode, *The Administration of Justice Under Military and Martial Law* (London, John Murray, 1872), p. 14. It is now widely acknowledged that modern soldiers typically feel the strongest loyalty to their fellow comrades rather than to their commanding officers.

cases convened by the United Kingdom during the Boer War and the uprising in parts of what is now the Republic of Ireland during 1916–1920 to try civilians were not considered to be 'courts'.[15] They were 'but a body of military officers entrusted by the commanding officer with the duty of inquiring into certain alleged breaches of his commands contained in the Proclamation [of martial law], and of advising him as to the manner in which he should deal with the offences'.[16] Even at the time they could be distinguished from courts martial comprising the same military individuals and convened to try serving members of the British Army for offences against military law.[17] Apart from the status of the accused, the latter courts were established by statute, whereas the former were recognised by the common law as being an executive, rather than a judicial, process.

We have seen that merely describing a deliberating body as a 'court' does not, necessarily, make it such.[18] In similar vein, a 'kangaroo court' is more akin to an unusual marsupial than it is to a 'court'. What distinguishes such a body from a court is that the latter must be established by law to apply the law[19] and to make decisions binding on the parties. It will

[15] *Tilonko* v. *Attorney-General of the Colony of Natal (Court Martial)* [1907] AC 93 at 94. The Earl of Halsbury, LC stated, 'if there is war, there is a right to repel force by force, but it is found convenient and decorous, from time to time, to authorize what are called "Courts" to administer punishments ... but to make these proceedings of so-called "Courts-martial", administering summary justice under the supervision of a military commander, analogous to the regular proceedings of Courts of justice is quite illusory.' This view was supported in *Re Clifford* [1921] 2 AC 570 at 581.

[16] *Re Clifford* [1921] 2 AC 570 at 581 (Viscount Cave).

[17] In *R* v. *Governor of Lewes Prison* [1917] 2 KB 254 the petitioner was tried by a field general court martial since the Defence of the Realm (Consolidation) Act 1914 (UK) declared that a civilian charged under that Act was to be treated 'as if he were a person subject to military law'. For the same offence, a British soldier would have been tried before the same type of court martial.

[18] This was a central finding of the High Court of Australia that the Australian Military Court was unconstitutional in *Lane* v. *Morrison* (2009) 239 CLR 230. The High Court held that a statutory designation of the Australian Military Court was a superior court of record did not determine the constitutional question of whether it was in fact validly constituted according to the requirements of the exercise of judicial power. In other words, calling an institution a court did not make it one.

[19] British military courts for the trial of former enemy individuals in respect of war crimes committed during World War II were established by the Crown under the royal prerogative (without an Act of Parliament) in June 1945, as regulations for the Trial of War Criminals. The courts sat in areas of Germany then under occupation or control by UK armed forces. They applied the procedure of a field general court martial *mutatis mutandis* 'as if the accused were persons subject to military law charged with having committed offences on active service', Royal Warrant – Regulations for the Trial of War Criminals 0160/2498 A.O. 81/1945 (18 June 1945) art. 3. For the background, see

usually provide some form of appeal from its decisions to another court. A court is also expected[20] to be independent from the executive and those called upon to make decisions must act impartially (discussed later).

There are significant differences among states as to the way in which their ordinary criminal courts arrive at a verdict. In some states, the trial judge gives directions on the law, with a jury of lay individuals deciding the issue of guilt or innocence. In others, a single judge or a bench of trial judges combine both roles, whilst in other states, decisions as to guilt or innocence are made by the judge(s) along with one or more lay persons. Military courts, as a group, are not immune from such variations as to the fact-finding process. International law, whether in the form of IHL or IHRL, does not take a view on which method of decision-making in a criminal trial is to be preferred. Instead, these branches of international law concern themselves with basic structural issues such as whether the court is 'regularly constituted, respecting the generally recognised principles of regular judicial procedure',[21] or whether the tribunal is 'competent', 'independent and impartial'.[22]

In the military context the personnel comprising the court within a particular state are *sui generis*, not only compared with a state's civilian judicial system but also amongst the processes established by other states. Thus, the judge may, or may not, be a civilian judicial figure; he or she may be a qualified lawyer serving in the armed forces or be a civilian lawyer. It will be assumed, for the purpose of this chapter, that the 'judge' is someone with legal qualifications sufficient to hold judicial office within the state. Where the role of the judge is separated from those who decide guilt or innocence, the 'jury' is likely to consist of a number of

A.P.V. Rogers, 'War Crimes Trials under the Royal Warrant: British Practice 1945–1949' (1990) 39(4) *International and Comparative Law Quarterly*, p. 780. *Quaere* whether UK law would permit the establishment of a court by royal prerogative to sit within the United Kingdom.

20 See, for example, the International Covenant on Civil and Political Rights, 16 December 1966, in force 23 March 1976, 999 UNTS 171, art. 14; Convention for the Protection of Human Rights and Fundamental Freedoms, 4 November 1950, in force 3 September 1953, 213 UNTS 221, art. 6. (European Convention on Human Rights).

21 Protocol Additional to the Geneva Conventions of 12 August 1949, and Relating to the Protection of Victims of International Armed Conflicts, 8 June 1977, in force 7 December 1978, 1125 UNTS 3, art. 75 (Additional Protocol I); Geneva Conventions, common art. 3; Protocol Additional to the Geneva Conventions of 12 August 1949, and Relating to the Protection of Victims of Non-International Armed Conflicts, 8 June 1977, in force 7 December 1978, 1125 UNTS 609, art. 6 (Additional Protocol II). See also the Rome Statute, art. 17(2).

22 International Covenant on Civil and Political Rights, art. 14.

military officers, one or more non-commissioned officers, or a civilian alongside military members.

Military courts or tribunals come in various shapes and sizes. The membership of a military court may be composed solely of military officers in uniform with military officers acting as the advocates, all assisted by military personnel as administrators. The court may be located within a military compound whether open to the public or not and guarded by military personnel. Such courts are likely to be composed of military officers[23] acting as a 'jury' with a civilian or military judge, or the military officers may be advised on the law by a civilian lawyer. Military courts may sit outside the normal civilian judicial structures within a state. There may be limited links to the civilian judicial system through judicial review or appeal. It is not uncommon for military courts to form a part of the general military bureaucracy of a state, leaving open the perception of possible command influence over the pre-trial and the trial processes.

These are relatively easy structures to discern as military courts. The position is not so clear, however, where military members have equal status with civilian members in a court. Does the presence of the former make the whole court a military court? Were, for instance, the International Military Tribunal at Nuremberg and the International Military Tribunal (Far East) *military* courts, as their name suggests, due to the presence of a military officer as the judge from the USSR?[24]

In some states the term 'military' court is avoided and replaced with the term, 'security' court or 'national safety' court,[25] where one or more 'military judges' form part of the membership of the court. Does the presence of a 'military judge' make that court a 'military court'? The Grand Chamber of the European Court of Human Rights has taken the

[23] In many states, commissioned officers will have achieved a level of education higher than the average of the general population. In some states non-commissioned officers may serve in a military court. An example is the case of warrant officers, Armed Forces Act 2006 (UK) s. 156.

[24] Robert Cryer and Neil Boister, *Documents on the Tokyo International Military Tribunal* (Oxford, Oxford University Press, 2008), pp. lii–lv; Kevin Jon Heller, *The Nuremberg Military Tribunals and the Origins of International Criminal Law* (Oxford, Oxford University Press, 2011), p. 39.

[25] The National Safety Court in the Kingdom of Bahrain 'convicted 21 defendants for inciting hatred, carrying out violence and attempting to overthrow the elected government' in 2011. It comprised two civilian judges and a military judge, 'Bahrain defends court's decision for convicting 21 saboteurs and thugs', 24×7 News, 24 June 2011, http://twentyfoursevennews.com/?p=9939.

view that it does not, although the presence of such an individual gives the perception of a lack of independence and impartiality, with the result that such individuals should not be appointed. In *Ocalan* v. *Turkey*,[26] a case involving a trial before the National Security Court in Turkey, there was no analysis of whether the court, comprising a president, one civilian judge and one military judge,[27] had to be unanimous. If not, the other judges could not only ignore the views of the 'military judge', but could also give the appearance of being able to do so. It is difficult to imagine that the mere presence of a military judge could 'allow [the independent and impartial president of the court and the civilian judge] to be unduly influenced by considerations that had nothing to do with the nature of the case' as the Grand Chamber concluded.[28] The removal of military judges from a national security court, as Turkey did in 1999, can be justified more easily on policy grounds than on the basis that the mere presence of a military judge can 'contaminate' a civilian court. If this line of reasoning is followed, it could leave open the possibility of challenging an appeal court, which hears appeals from a military court, where in that appeal court one or more military judges sit alongside a majority of civilian judges.[29]

IV The independence and impartiality of military courts

It cannot be assumed that military courts will be independent or that their members will be impartial when deciding individual cases, since

[26] (2005) 41 EHRR 955. See also *Incal* v. *Turkey* (1998) 29 EHRR 449 at [67]–[72] (*Incal*). A number of later cases against Turkey make the same points. Both these cases involved the trial of a civilian.

[27] The military judge had to be appointed from 'judges and prosecutors of the first rank', *Ocalan* v. *Turkey* (2005) 41 EHRR 955 at [52] (*Ocalan*). The military judge is described as a 'a regular army officer belonging to the military legal service': [113]. A substitute civilian and a substitute military judge were also to be appointed at the same time. The military judge was removed from the composition of the national security court in 1999: [52].

[28] *Ocalan* v. *Turkey* (2005) 41 EHRR 955 at [113]. This is quite different from the situation where judges recuse themselves on the grounds that they have a personal interest in a particular case or know one of the parties or witnesses.

[29] In Spain 'since 1987 the jurisdiction of the last degree [in military justice cases] has been the Military Chamber of the Supreme Court, composed of four civilian judges (including the president) and four military judges, who, in order to ensure their independence, are given legal status similar to that of retirement and can no longer be reinstated in the armed forces': Joinet, above n. 2, pp. 14–15. This would suggest that the lack of independence found by the European Court of Human Rights in *Ocalan* and *Incal* could have been based on a perceived lack of independence rather than on the status of the military judge of the court.

they are all employed directly by an executive arm of government. Necessary firewalls have to be built into the process to ensure that an outside observer could have no 'legitimate reason to fear that a particular court lacked independence or impartiality'.[30] These requirements are not easy to achieve within the military context. The relationship between employer and employed within the armed forces is unlike that in other professions.[31] It is built upon a hierarchy providing for the punishment (in some form) or retraining of subordinates who fail to obey their military superiors.

It is not sufficient for a state to claim that its military courts operate within the structures established by national law if these courts do in fact, or are perceived to, lack competence,[32] independence and impartiality.[33] The court and its military members must be separated from the normal military command structures. The military command must be removed from the decision to convene a military court, to prosecute, to appoint the court members and to assess the performance of court members (whether through remuneration levels or otherwise). They should not be able to interfere with the judicial processes involved, whether at the pre-trial, trial or post-trial stages.[34] Where the judge in a military court is a civilian, such issues do not arise.[35] A judge in a military court must be answerable solely to the civilian judicial structure and be seen to be separated structurally and socially from the military command system. There is clearly a further risk, where a military court permits defendants

[30] *Martin* v. *United Kingdom* (2006) 44 EHRR 31. In English law a similar principle applies: see Lord Steyn, *Lawal* v. *Northern Spirit Ltd* [2003] ICR 856 at [14], who commented that 'public perception of the possibility of unconscious bias is the key'.

[31] See *Kalac* v. *Turkey* (1999) 27 EHRR 552 at [28].

[32] Unlike the International Covenant on Civil and Political Rights, art. 14, this requirement is not set out in the European Convention on Human Rights but it must be implied. The presence in a military court of a qualified lawyer whose legal advice must be followed by the members of the court, who themselves are not lawyers, would suffice for this requirement if the function of those other members is to determine guilt or innocence on the basis of that legal advice. In carrying out this function these other members act in a way similar to a jury or other lay members in criminal trials held in many countries.

[33] See *Findlay* v. *United Kingdom* (1997) 24 EHRR 221; *Egyptian Initiative for Personal Rights and Interrights* v. *Arab Republic of Egypt*, Case 334/06, African Commission on Human and Peoples' Rights (2011) [200].

[34] See *Martin* v. *United Kingdom* (2006) 44 EHRR 31 at [41]–[42]. See also *Findlay* v. *United Kingdom* (1997) 24 EHRR 221; *Cooper* v. *United Kingdom* (2004) 39 EHRR 8; *Grieves* v. *United Kingdom* (2004) 39 EHRR 2 at [69]–[91]; *R* v. *Generaux* (1992) 88 DLR (4th) 110.

[35] Compare, for example, *Cooper* v. *United Kingdom* (2004) 39 EHRR 8, where there was a civilian judge, with *Grieves* v. *United Kingdom* (2004) 39 EHRR 2, where the judge was a serving naval officer but qualified as a lawyer. See discussion in Chapter 8.

to be represented only by assigned military lawyers of a rank junior to that of the officers sitting on a military court, that the defendant will be unable to obtain independent legal advice and advocacy.[36]

It is equally important that these requirements of competence, independence and impartiality should exist also at the investigation and charging stages. It is likely to be easier for a senior officer to interfere with the pre-trial stages rather than with the proceedings of a military court. The structural independence and integrity of military courts can be undermined if the same qualities are absent from pre-trial procedures. Detailed investigations of fact will be required to establish the actual and perceived nature of pre-trial, trial and post-trial processes should any human rights body examine the compatibility of a state's military court with international human rights standards.

In order to meet these requirements it is not sufficient for a state to argue that its national law provides for an appeal to a civilian court that complies with the relevant principles. Some appeal courts may be comprised solely of civilian judges whilst others will contain a combination of civilian and military judges. There will be no issue where the appeal court is comprised of civilian judges, but where they are joined by one or more military judges it may be questioned whether they meet the necessary criteria. Some states may not provide any appeal[37] from a military court on the basis that military courts essentially enforce discipline and any right of appeal could have the effect of weakening discipline. Moreover, it might be argued that art. 14(5) of the International Covenant on Civil and Political Rights, which includes a requirement that criminal convictions have to be reviewable by a 'higher tribunal according to law', only refers to an appeal for persons 'convicted of a crime' and not to a person found to have committed a military offence.[38] Whilst a number of states provide some form of appeal to a military person found to have committed a military offence, the position of the civilian tried by a military court is quite different. A civilian can only be tried for a criminal offence and an appeal to an independent and impartial tribunal should be available.

[36] See, for example, African Commission on Human and Peoples' Rights, *218/98: Civil Liberties Organisation, Legal Defence Centre, Legal Defence and Assistance Project/Nigeria* (7 May 2001), at [31].

[37] They may, however, provide some form of administrative review of the military court proceedings. Compare the Decaux, above n. 10, Principle 16: 'in all cases where military tribunals exist, their authority should be limited to ruling in the first instance'.

[38] A military offence might, in reality, have the same characteristics as a criminal offence, *Engel* v. *The Netherlands* (1979) 1 EHRR 647. See n. 3.

certainly if the state is a party to the International Covenant on Civil and Political Rights.[39]

V The arguments against military courts

Military courts are often contrasted with civilian courts generally or civilian courts within the same state. However, military courts conduct their proceedings in a manner and with personnel often quite different from a civilian court in the same state. Consequently, a criticism of a military court for a particular practice is not a criticism of a military court as such if exactly the same point could be made against the civilian courts of the same state. Criticism of a military court system can only be seen objectively where that criticism is based on sound principles. Military courts will often attract more interest from senior members of a government than will the workings of the civilian courts. This is because they are perceived as important to the armed forces and, in consequence, significant to the security of the state. It is for this reason that a number of states have entered a reservation to the European Convention on Human Rights so as to exclude their armed forces discipline systems from the scope of the Convention.[40]

In practical terms military courts are most vulnerable to challenge from a human rights body on the ground that the court is (or is perceived to be) not independent of the executive arm of government. It is also of concern where senior military officers can influence, directly or indirectly, the investigation, the charging stages or the trial itself. The

[39] See, for example, HRC, Concluding Observations of the Human Rights Committee on Spain, UN Doc CCPR/C/79/Add.61 (3 April 1996), at [19], which draws attention to the obligations of states under art. 14(5) of the International Covenant on Civil and Political Rights. See also *Egyptian Initiative for Personal Rights and Interrights* v. *Arab Republic of Egypt*, Case 334/06, African Commission on Human and Peoples' Rights (2011) [203]; Statement by the African Commission on Human and Peoples' Rights on the Trial and Sentencing of Twenty-five Sahrawi Civilians by a Military Court in Morocco, 23 February 2013. The same issues will arise, as discussed earlier, where the appeal court has amongst its members one or more military judges.

[40] In referring to arts. 5 and 6 France declared on ratification that 'those articles shall not hinder the application of the provisions governing the system of discipline in the armed forces'. Azerbaijan, Czech Republic, Slovakia and Spain have made similar reservations, whilst Armenia, Moldova, Portugal, Russia and Ukraine have entered reservations to art. 5 in respect of their armed forces. France also entered a reservation to arts. 9 and 14 of the International Covenant on Civil and Political Rights 1966 to the effect that 'these articles cannot impede enforcement of the rules pertaining to the discipline regime in the armies'. It would appear that no other states have made any similar reservation or declaration.

European Court of Human Rights has been particularly active in deciding applications brought against a number of states in relation to their military court structures.[41] It is unlikely that any other human rights body would dissent from these views. It is therefore argued that compliance with the Court's decisions by all states, whether members of the Council of Europe or not, would ensure that their military justice systems would possess a sufficient degree of independence from the executive arm of government so as to satisfy any human rights body.

In reality, problems with military courts cannot necessarily be solved by this relatively simple suggestion. The adequacy of all law is tested most keenly where the stakes are the highest. This can be seen particularly where the state is confronted by an internal armed conflict, or even a situation falling short of an armed conflict, and where its armed forces are deployed to maintain order. Depending on the threat to the state, the seriousness of the disorder and the scale of casualties suffered by soldiers, it becomes a relatively short step from arresting suspects to inflicting on them humiliating, degrading treatment, torture or causing their disappearance. It also becomes a short step to treating rioters as 'subversives' or 'terrorists'. Where there is evidence to suggest that soldiers have violated the criminal law in their treatment of detainees, the civilian courts are likely to be seen (at least externally) as the most appropriate forum for any trial. Indeed, it has been argued that military courts should not be used to try soldiers charged with human rights breaches.[42] Such a conclusion calls for analysis.

It is not easy to see why military courts should be excluded from dealing with human rights abuses merely because it is a military rather than a civilian court. If the military court, along with its investigation and charging procedures, is independent from the organs of government and it arrives at its decisions impartially, its quality, as a court, must be equal to that of a civilian court able to display the same qualities.[43] The issue will only arise where the military court has exclusive jurisdiction over

[41] See *Engel* v. *The Netherlands* (1979) 1 EHRR 647 and the cases referred to in n. 34.

[42] Sometimes this refers to 'gross' human rights breaches; at other times the adjective is deleted. See, for example, Decaux, above n. 10, Principle 8; *Rosendo Cantú* v. *Mexico* [2010] Inter-Am Court HR (ser C) No. 216, at [161]; *Radilla-Pacheco* v. *Mexico* [2009] Inter-Am Court HR (ser L) No. 209, at [274].

[43] This is likely to be the case in states with strong democratic control of their armed forces if a conviction of a criminal offence by a military court is a bar to proceedings before a civilian court on the same charge. It is worthy of note that the International Covenant for the Protection of All Persons from Enforced Disappearance 2006 does not impose any restriction on the use of military courts. Compare the Inter-American Convention on

such cases, as the risk of impunity for serious crimes will be greatest in this situation. It is difficult to justify exclusive military jurisdiction merely because the accused is a soldier. There may be situations where this is appropriate (such as where two soldiers fight each other in barracks) but it will generally be inappropriate if the victim of an alleged crime is a civilian. Where a military court possesses concurrent jurisdiction with a civilian court that avenue exists for the trial of soldiers providing there is an independent mechanism for allocating cases to the one system or the other. Concurrent jurisdiction may not, however, be an option if a soldier is accused of a criminal offence committed outside the state's territory during military operations and where only that soldier's military court possesses jurisdiction in such circumstances.[44]

Where a criminal case, which may also be seen as serious human rights breach, against a soldier is brought before a military court following serious disorder, considerable problems remain. On the one hand, some may see this trial by a military court as being in the interests of the soldier or commanders, who may wish to conceal their part in the situation or to downplay the seriousness of the alleged crime. Others may see that it is in the interests of the military to hold the trial in a military court as such courts have the chance of being able to punish severely the soldier concerned, to isolate him or her from the armed forces as a whole by describing the soldier as a 'bad apple' and thus restore the public image of the armed forces. A truly independent and impartial military court should be able to see through conflicting perceptions and deliver objective justice.

It may, however, be argued that the conclusion in the last paragraph is no more than a counsel of perfection. What if civilian witnesses called to give evidence against the accused would face risks to their own security

Forced Disappearance of Persons, 9 June 1994, in force 28 March 1996, 33 ILM 1429, art. IX and note the reservation of Mexico, which purported to retain military jurisdiction where a member of its armed forces commits 'an illicit act [forced disappearance] while on duty'. This reservation was declared by the Inter-American Court of Human Rights to be incompatible with the objects and purposes of the Convention. See *Radilla-Pachecho* v. *Mexico* [2009] Inter-Am Court HR (ser L) No. 209, at [311]–[312]. The basis of this decision is that a military court is unable to provide an independent and impartial tribunal, a conclusion which this chapter challenges.

44 This will arise where a status of forces agreement (or memorandum of understanding) between the territorial and the sending states gives exclusive jurisdiction to the latter. This is common in UN peacekeeping missions. See generally, Zsuzsanna Deen-Racsmány 'The Amended UN Memorandum of Understanding: A New Incentive for States to Discipline and Prosecute Military Members of National Peacekeeping Contingents' (2011) 16(2) *Journal of Conflict & Security Law*, p. 321 at 352.

from members of the armed forces after the trial? Whilst this may be a fact of life, a military court, like a civilian one, could adopt measures to prevent witnesses being identified. This is a practice followed, for instance, by the International Criminal Tribunal for the Former Yugoslavia (ICTY).[45] It cannot be argued that military courts should never hear cases against soldiers for 'human rights' breaches[46] merely because civilian witnesses might be put at risk.

Whether an investigation is conducted by the civilian or by the military authorities, problems of gathering evidence will exist in a more acute form than in an ordinary criminal investigation. If soldiers are unwilling to give evidence against their colleagues or civilians are unwilling to come forward, it does not matter who is carrying out the investigation. The ability of the military process to bring a charge against a soldier for failing to carry out a duty or failing to carry out an order have no equivalent in a civilian justice system. Such charges, if brought honestly, may show that in reality the prosecution must have taken the view that a successful prosecution for the more serious offence, which the facts might suggest, would be unlikely.[47]

A further issue needs to be aired where a criminal (or a military) offence is alleged against a soldier. A senior commander of the armed forces can require, or offer the opportunity to, a more junior officer to resign to avoid military court proceedings. If there is credible evidence against that officer, the offer of a resignation is clearly an abuse of the judicial system and not of the military court system as the officer could still be tried if the civilian courts have concurrent jurisdiction. It is, however, inescapable that an officer would normally avoid trial on a

45 International Criminal Tribunal for the Former Yugoslavia, Rules of Procedure and Evidence, Doc No IT/32/Rev.49 (22 May 2013), r. 75.

46 This phrase is included with quotation marks not to detract from the seriousness of alleged conduct by soldiers but to reflect the fact that it is unlikely that they will be charged with such an offence. It is more likely that they will be charged with various forms of assault or a form of homicide within the normal criminal law.

47 It should not be overlooked that a career soldier convicted by a military court may be demoted and dismissed from the armed forces. See, for example, (2007) 100 *American Journal of International Law*, p. 478; (2008) 101 *American Journal of International Law*, p. 494, where senior officers were subjected to court-martial proceedings or were disciplined otherwise. In one case a 'Lt Col Commanding the Soldiers' [Who Were Subject to Court-Martial Proceedings] Battalion Was Relieved of His Command'; (2009) 103 *American Journal of International Law*, p. 358 at 359. The loss of potential pension rights as a result could be very substantial. It is not sufficient, therefore, to consider only the actual punishment imposed by the military court on the soldier.

purely military offence if he or she had resigned from the armed forces.[48]

There is, without doubt, support for the view that civilians should never be prosecuted before military courts.[49] It is, however, difficult to see why this should be the case in all circumstances. It cannot be that civilians, unlike volunteer soldiers, have not consented to being tried by a military court. Conscripted soldiers have no real opportunity to withhold their consent to this form of trial unless it is accepted that their decision not to assert that they are a conscientious objector to military service serves to establish their consent to military trial. Further, if a military court is able to exhibit the necessary qualities of independence and impartiality as a civilian court, there is no logical basis for drawing a distinction between the two systems to the extent that a civilian should only be tried by the latter. The principle that all individuals are equal before the law would also suggest that both court systems are able to treat citizens equally.

It is recognised, however, that in certain circumstances, the trial by military court of civilians should not take place. This is where the state has transferred criminal jurisdiction from the ordinary criminal courts to military courts without good reason, for example, if the state expects its military courts to lack the independence and impartiality of a court and thus to serve its purposes, rather than the interests of justice. If this is the case then there can be no justification for the state's transfer of jurisdiction. But the motives of the state in doing this may be *bona fide*. Consequently, it is necessary to enquire why a state has transferred criminal jurisdiction over civilians to its military courts rather than merely accept the principle that civilians should never be tried by military courts. Indeed, the European Court of Human Rights does not exclude the possibility that a military court could nevertheless be compliant with the Convention when trying a civilian.[50] It is important that the 'existence of such jurisdiction [in national law] should be subjected to particularly careful scrutiny, since only in very exceptional circumstances could the determination of criminal charges against civilians in such courts be held compatible with Article 6'.[51] A state would have to show

48 Some states provide a liability to military law process for a particular period of time after a person has left military service, but only for offences committed whilst serving.

49 See discussion in Liivoja and Cerna in Chapters 5 and 16.

50 *Martin* v. *United Kingdom* (2006) 44 EHRR 31, at 44.

51 Ibid. See also the views of the Human Rights Committee in HRC, *Madani* v. *Algeria*, UN Doc CCPR/C/89/D/1172/2003 (21 June 2007), at [8.7].

'compelling reasons [for doing so] in each specific case', and not merely that national legislation had 'allocate[d] certain categories of offence to military courts *in abstracto*'.[52]

A state may be able to justify the allocation of criminal cases to a military court where the defendant falls into a particular group of individuals. Thus, national legislation may enable civilians employed by, or with some real connection to, the armed forces serving abroad to be tried by a military court.[53] This will usually be as an alternative to the jurisdiction of the territorial state. This was the situation in *Martin* v. *United Kingdom*[54] where the son of a British soldier serving in Germany was tried by a British court martial on a charge of the murder of a civilian. This case is not therefore any authority for the proposition that the European Court of Human Rights has set its face against the trial of a civilian by a military court. At least one other case of a civilian being tried by a British court martial abroad has been reported since the *Martin* case. This involved two British civilian contractors convicted in 2010 by a British court martial in England for offences of assault committed whilst they were employed by British forces in Iraq.[55]

It cannot be doubted that a state has the power under IHL to establish a military court in territory that it occupies for the trial of protected persons.[56] By their very nature such individuals will be civilians. With

[52] Ibid. The Court also required that the justification should be on a 'clear and foreseeable legal basis'. The phrase 'in each specific case' cannot mean a particular criminal offence against a particular defendant since this would introduce arbitrariness into the selection of the court. It must mean that there is an obligation on the state to justify why national legislation permitted a class of defendant (of whom the applicant is one) to be tried by a military court for one or more classes of offence.

[53] The arguments in favour of the legislation which enables this to occur are set out in *R* v. *Martin* [1997] AC 917 at 935 (Lord Hope).

[54] (2006) 44 EHRR 31. According to English law, the applicant was subject to military jurisdiction whilst residing with his father, a British soldier serving in Germany. Under the NATO Status of Forces Agreement 1951 (as supplemented by a later agreement), the German authorities also possessed jurisdiction to try the applicant 'but they had waived it': [12], [21]. See discussion in Chapter 5.

[55] See 'Two civilians jailed by court martial for vicious armed attack on good Samaritan in Iraq', Overseas Civilian Contractors, 12 October 2010, http://civiliancontractors.wordpress.com/tag/uk-court-martial/.

[56] Geneva Convention IV, art. 66, which refers to the occupying Power's 'properly constituted, non-political military courts'. The occupying state must ensure a 'regular trial', art. 71, before 'an impartial and regularly constituted court respecting the generally recognised principles of regular judicial procedure', Additional Protocol I, art. 75(4). It will amount to a grave breach of Geneva Convention IV if a protected person is 'wilfully' deprived 'of the rights of fair and regular trial prescribed in the present Convention', art. 147.

the obligation on the occupying state to 'maintain the orderly government of the territory',[57] the establishment of a military court may be the only real option, particularly where the normal institutions of criminal justice are unable to operate. Any argument that tends to suggest that the trial of civilians before a military court by an occupying state is acceptable but that it is not acceptable, even in very limited circumstances, to try a civilian by a military court in peacetime fails to recognise that the law of human rights may apply in both situations. The key factor is not the categorisation of the court and the defendant but whether such a court is compliant with the principles of competence, independence and impartiality. This will require a detailed analysis of the specific investigation, charging and trial processes of the military court concerned.

It is not necessary for one state to occupy another for military courts or tribunals to be established to determine issues involving individuals who may (or may not) be civilians. Where a 'doubt arises' as to whether an individual captured by opposing armed forces during an international armed conflict is entitled to prisoner of war status, the issue is required to be determined by a 'competent tribunal'.[58] Since this tribunal is likely to be composed solely of military personnel, particularly where the detaining state is conducting military operations abroad, [59] it must be considered to be a military court, despite the fact that its jurisdiction is limited to one specific status issue. Whether the individual is considered to be a civilian at the start of the process or only if found not to be entitled to prisoner of war status,[60] a military tribunal could well be making decisions on civilians.

57 Geneva Convention IV, art. 66. See generally Yoram Dinstein, *The International Law of Belligerent Occupation* (Cambridge University Press, 2009), p. 136 *et seq.*, who draws attention to the fact that Israeli soldiers are tried by their own military court system and not by the military courts set up to deal with protected persons. He also points out that the latter courts may have concurrent jurisdiction with the local courts. This may occur where the period of occupation is a lengthy one.

58 Geneva Convention III, art. 5; Additional Protocol I, art. 45(1). See also the 'appropriate court or administrative board designated by the Detaining Power' established for the reconsideration of internment decisions, Geneva Convention IV, art. 43.

59 See generally, Michael R. Gibson, 'International Human Rights Law and the Administration of Justice through Military Tribunals: Preserving Utility while Precluding Impunity' (2008) 4 *Journal of International Law and International Relations*, p. 1 at 16. Compare the position where the individual is captured within the territory of the detaining state, when the issue may be decided by the civilian courts since anyone not entitled to prisoner of war status will be liable for the crimes committed on the territory of that state, *Osman Bib Haji Mohamed Ali* v. *Public Prosecutor* [1969] 1 AC 430; *Public Prosecutor* v. *Oie Hee Koi* [1968] AC 829; *Military Prosecutor* v. *Kassem* (1971) 42 ILR 470.

60 This depends upon the interpretation of the relevant Articles cited in n. 56 and the significance of the presumption stated to arise in art. 45.

Indeed, if a military court is not suitable for the trial of a civilian, it is not suitable for the trial of a soldier, whether or not a volunteer member of the armed forces. There is no logic in human rights bodies accepting that a soldier can be tried by a military court for a breach of military law merely because the individual defendant is a soldier and not a civilian. The punishments available to military courts when convicting a soldier of a military law offence can be quite severe. In some cases there will be no equivalent criminal law offence but in others there could be. Thus, a military offence of 'fighting'[61] another soldier could equally well amount to a criminal offence of assault. A soldier charged with the military offence before a military court is just as much in need of a fair trial as a civilian tried by a civilian court. There may be circumstances where the soldier should be punished for this offence more severely than the civilian for the analogous criminal offence. The need to maintain a high degree of discipline within the armed forces is designed to protect not only other soldiers but, perhaps more importantly, civilians who come into contact with soldiers, particularly during an armed conflict. The issue should be the nature of a military court and not the classification of those tried before such a court.

VI Conclusion

Rather than arguing that military courts are *ipso facto* unable to achieve international standards of trial rights for those who appear before them, human rights bodies and organisations should be cautious when considering such courts in a universal context. It has been argued that the military courts of each state will vary in their structure, composition and jurisdiction. A view that treats all military courts in the same way is as misguided as a principle that purports to argue that because some motor cars do not have seat belts no motor cars should have them.

Many human rights bodies and organisations are, of course, concerned with military courts in a particular state. When considering such courts, they must grapple with the detailed issues of whether the state's military

[61] For example, see Armed Forces Act 2006 (UK) s. 21 (fighting or threatening behaviour); National Defence Act, RSC 1985, c N-5, s. 77 (offences related to operations); Uniform Code of Military Justice, 10 USC § 928 (2010). Offences such as conduct to the prejudice of good order and discipline or where military courts have jurisdiction to try members of the armed forces for criminal offences all add to the range of charges that may be brought against soldiers. See generally, 'East Timor: The Courts-Martial' (1992) 4 News from Asia Watch 1, www.hrw.org/sites/default/files/reports/INDONESI926.PDF.

courts comply with the generally accepted norms of fair trial. This may involve detailed research work, which cannot be avoided through too ready an acceptance of the mantra that 'civilians should not be tried by military courts'. The key issue, it is argued, is whether the military court of a particular state, along with the investigation and charging stages, is actually (and perceived to be) competent, independent and impartial and is established by the national law. In deciding whether it is so established, there is no alternative to a thorough analysis of a particular court. This has been the methodology adopted by the European Court of Human Rights[62] where the issue has arisen.

To assist with this analysis, human rights bodies and organisations might be encouraged to adopt no more than a presumption of fact, namely, that military courts are not competent, independent and impartial. It should be for the individual state to rebut this presumption.[63] The advantage of this approach is that it will be for the state concerned, with its detailed knowledge of its own military court structure, to establish the facts and the national law applying to these courts. This is preferable to the current position which requires human rights bodies or organisations to attempt to undertake the same analysis from a distance, both geographically and in terms of a detailed understanding of the legal background of the particular military court. Where the state fails to justify the trial of a civilian by a military court or to show that its military courts are independent and impartial, this should not, however, relieve a human rights body of its own investigations.[64]

62 See also the approach of the African Commission on Human and Peoples' Rights, above n. 36, at [44], 'the military tribunal [in this particular situation] fails the independence test'. The Commission has not, however, spoken with one voice on this issue, see African Commission on Human and Peoples' Rights, *206/97: Centre for Free Speech/Nigeria* (1–15 November 1999), at [15], where it is stated that the 'Special Military Tribunal, presided over by a serving military officer ... whose membership also included some serving military officers. This is in violation of the provisions of art. 7 of the Charter [African Charter on Human and Peoples' Rights, 1981] and Principle 5 of the UN Basic principles [on the Independence of the Judiciary, 1985].'

63 Compare, however, the comment by the African Commission on Human and Peoples' Rights in *218/98* that 'a military tribunal *per se* is not offensive to the rights in the Charter *nor does it imply an unfair or unjust process*' (emphasis added), African Commission on Human and Peoples' Rights, above n. 36, at [44]. The problem, as argued earlier, is that it is too easy to draw a conclusion that military courts do give rise to such an implication. The suggested approach would establish no more than a presumption of fact which could be rebutted.

64 Compare HRC, *Madani* v. *Algeria*, UN Doc CCPR/C/89/D/1172/2003 (21 June 2007), at [8.7]: 'the State party's failure to demonstrate the need to rely on a military court in this case means that the Committee need not examine whether the military court, as a matter of fact, afforded the full guarantees of article 14'.

Concentration should also be placed on tackling the issue of exclusive jurisdiction over soldiers by military courts. Such a situation tends to convey, at least, the impression of a lack of independence of the military legal system from investigation to trial processes. At worst it can lead to impunity, particularly of commanders. The importance of maintaining military discipline, ultimately through military courts, in armed conflicts or in situations falling below this level of intensity of action must not be underestimated. Where this is achieved, civilians who take no part in a conflict will be the largest group of beneficiaries. But it should not be forgotten that the maintenance of discipline within the armed forces is as important in peacetime as it is during an armed conflict. Military courts can have as important a role in both situations; human rights bodies and organisations should recognise this role.

3

Democratic oversight through courts and tribunals

CHRISTOPHER WATERS

I Introduction

Oversight of the military by the executive is a core principle of governance in the West. While there are issues in terms of whether militaries 'work or shirk' in the face of political direction they do not like, Western states do not face the outright usurpation of democratically elected executives by their armed forces.[1] However, other aspects of complete democratic oversight over the military – namely from the legislative and judicial branches of government – remain weak, to varying degrees, in Western and non-Western states alike. Legislative oversight, which can involve both fight and not-to-fight decisions, as well as planning and policy matters, is beyond the scope of this chapter, but appears to be on the rise; there is at least a sense of what good practice in this area looks like.[2] Curiously, a third plank of democratic oversight of the military, oversight by legal institutions, remains contested – or often neglected – terrain.[3] This chapter explores the potential of this contested third plank to complete the democratic oversight circle.

For over a decade, judicial or quasi-judicial scrutiny has been resisted by numerous politicians and military leaders as constituting 'lawfare' or one of its variants, such as 'legal-encirclement'. Even where not labelled as lawfare, discussions concerning legal scrutiny have been coloured by

1 On the 'work or shirk' question, see Peter Feaver, 'Crisis as Shirking: An Agency Theory Explanation of the Souring of American Civil – Military Relations' (1998) 24 *Armed Forces & Society*, p. 407.

2 There is also a well-developed literature on the subject; see, for example, Marina Caparini and Philipp Fluri, 'Introduction: The Relevance of Democratic Control and Reform of the Security Sector' in Hans Born, Marina Caparini and Philipp Fluri (eds.), *Security Sector Reform and Democracy in Transitional Societies* (Baden-Baden, Nomos Verlagsgesellschaft, 2002).

3 An additional, non-state plank of democratic oversight comes from civil society.

hyperbole regarding the role of civilian (and sometimes military) lawyers and the constraining role that legal institutions may have on operational effectiveness. At the same time, there are good reasons to move beyond the hyperbole to a reasoned discussion of the appropriate nature of legal scrutiny by civilian courts and tribunals over the armed forces.

This chapter has three sections. Section II sets out the nature of current efforts to provide legal scrutiny over the armed forces. Section III suggests that the seeming thick web of scrutiny is in fact fragile and fragmented, and that any recent advances in legal scrutiny have been incremental. In short, I argue that the lawfare-as-threat paradigm is dead on any objective reading. Sections IV and V outline why the time is ripe to engage in a mature conversation about the necessity of constructing appropriate civilian legal oversight mechanisms. This conversation is not designed to civilianise the armed forces – or even their justice systems – beyond recognition. Between civilianisation for its own sake and military hostility to outside scrutiny, there is an appropriate space for civilian, democratic oversight of the armed forces through courts and tribunals.

II The 'web' of civilian legal scrutiny

In a fully functioning democracy, the military and other security agencies 'provid[e] security for the good of a democratic society – via the reform and subordination of security institutions to democratically mandated civilians and an independent judiciary'.[4] Democratic oversight is seen as a crucial component of good governance and accountability in the security sector, especially when human security, and not only traditional state-centred security, is brought into the mix. There is some soft law support for the notion that democratic oversight is an 'established international norm' and that judicial scrutiny has a role to play in this oversight.[5] For example, the Council of Europe's Parliamentary Assembly has stated:

> 6. Government measures must be both lawful and legitimate. Consequently, some form of democratic supervision is required, the essence of which must be carried out by parliament. The judiciary, in

[4] Eden Cole, Kerstin Eppert and Katrin Kinzelbach (eds.), *Public Oversight of the Security Sector: A Handbook for Civil Society Organizations* (United Nations Development Programme, 2008) at 12 www.dcaf.ch/Publications/Public-Oversight-of-the-Security-Sector.

[5] Ibid., at 11.

> turn, plays a crucial role because it can punish any misuse of exceptional measures in which there may be a risk of human rights violations . . .
>
> 7. Democratic supervision makes use of a series of specific tools intended to ensure the political accountability and transparency of the security sector. These instruments include constitutional principles, legal rules and institutional and logistical provisions, as well as more general activities aimed at fostering good relations between the various parts of the security sector on the one hand, and the political powers (the executive, legislative and judiciary) . . . on the other.[6]

However, even if we accept that democratic oversight is an established norm, two caveats are required. First, it is widely accepted that implementation of the democratic oversight norm is a major challenge.[7] Second, the role of the judiciary in this oversight is often ignored or downplayed in the focus on oversight by the executive and legislative branches of government.[8] Thus the question arises: how much judicial or legal oversight exists at present?

At first blush there is a thick, multi-layered web of civilian legal scrutiny over the armed forces. This apparent web can be broken down into the institutional sources of legal scrutiny and the seeming unpredictability and variance of this scrutiny over space, time and legal regimes.

A *Sources of scrutiny*

As a preliminary point, it should be noted that by 'legal' scrutiny I refer to both judicial and quasi-judicial institutions and not only the third branch of government. Although courts and tribunals are distinguishable along several axes – for example, independence, method of appointment and expertise – they can be treated together for present purposes.[9] First, there

[6] Council of Europe Parliamentary Assembly, *Recommendation 1713 on Democratic Oversight of the Security Sector in Member States* (23 June 2005). See also Promoting and Consolidating Democracy, GA Res 55/96 UN GAOR, 3rd Comm 55th Sess, UN Doc A/RES/55/96 (4 December 2000).

[7] Cole, Eppert and Kinzelbach, above n. 4, at 12.

[8] See, for example, Hans Born, 'Democratic Oversight of the Security Sector. What Does It Mean?', Working Paper Series 9 (Geneva, DCAF, 2002), at 3 www.iskran.ru/cd_data/disk2/rr/005.pdf: 'Oversight should be carried out by the elected political authorities such as parliamentarians and cabinet ministers.' See Chapter 4.

[9] They are also grouped together by some scholars of democratic oversight of the security sector. See, for example, Ian Leigh, 'Executive, Legislative and Judicial Oversight and Guidance over the Security Sector' in Eden Cole, Kerstin Eppert and Katrin Kinzelbach (eds.), above n. 4, at 31.

may be overlapping jurisdiction between courts and tribunals over the same facts or individuals arising out of military action or inaction. Second, the courts play a supervisory role over tribunals in terms of jurisdiction and natural justice. Third, in terms of military perceptions that civilian lawyers in authority unnecessarily 'meddle' in military affairs, no sharp line can be drawn between courts and tribunals.[10]

1 Judicial scrutiny

Judicial scrutiny includes oversight by domestic, regional and international courts. While several jurisdictions have seen wholesale legislative efforts to modernise and civilianise (I return to this problematic term below) their military justice systems, domestic courts in some jurisdictions have not been shy about requiring further changes. The Canadian case of *R* v. *Généreux*,[11] is a paradigmatic example of civilian judges forcing the civilianisation of parallel military justice systems. In that case, the Supreme Court of Canada held that judicial independence guarantees applied to military judges under the Canadian Charter of Rights and Freedoms and advanced the security of tenure for these judges. That decision did not, however, require that military judges' appointments be made until retirement. The *Généreux* requirements were expanded in 2011, when Canada's Court Martial Appeal Court (comprising civilian judges cross-appointed from the regular court system) ruled in *R* v. *LeBlanc*[12] that military judges must be given full security of tenure, as renewable terms of five years were unconstitutional. The Court stated that the roles of civilian and military judges had become 'intrinsically comparable' and that military judges should have full security of tenure until retirement, like their civilian counterparts.[13] Moving beyond military justice systems – and this is where the issue becomes more controversial – domestic civilian courts have also been used to test the actions of their militaries abroad. For example, the detainee policies of both Canada (arising from its activities in Afghanistan) and the United States (in the Guantánamo Bay cases) have been questioned by rights groups in the anti-terrorism context.[14]

[10] I examine soldiers' perceptions in Christopher Waters, 'Is the Military Legally Encircled?' (2008) 8 *Defence Studies*, p. 26.

[11] [1992] 1 SCR 259 (*Généreux*). [12] [2011] CMAC 2 at [17]. [13] Ibid.,

[14] *Attorney General of Canada* v. *Amnesty International Canada* [2009] FC 918 (*Amnesty*); *Hamdan* v. *Rumsfeld*, 548 US 557 (2006).

Regional courts have similarly tested military justice systems against civilian benchmarks and have been used as a testing ground for the legality of military operations. The most developed jurisprudence comes from the European Court of Human Rights' (ECtHR) application of the European Convention on Human Rights (ECHR) to the military.[15] 'First phase' decisions from the ECtHR have resulted in a major impact on military justice systems. For example, in a series of cases against the United Kingdom beginning with *Findlay*, the ECtHR has required wide-ranging changes to the procedures of British courts martial, bringing them closer to their civilian counterparts.[16] 'Second phase' ECtHR scrutiny extends the European legal space to encompass Council of Europe states' actions beyond the continent. The clear trend has been towards greater scrutiny outside the European juridical space. For example, in the 2011 landmark decision in *Al-Skeini* v. *United Kingdom*[17] the Grand Chamber held that the responsibility of the UK to maintain security in Basra in 2003–2004 included an obligation to uphold the ECHR, including the need to conduct an independent investigation into the deaths of civilians at the hands of British soldiers under art. 2 (right to life).[18] The jurisprudence of the Inter-American Court of Human Rights has also considerably narrowed the scope of military jurisdiction – for example, requiring that civilians be tried only by civilian courts – and reduced the chances for impunity for soldiers accused of crimes against civilians.[19]

While the International Court of Justice (ICJ) has not decided cases on the fairness of military justice systems *per se*, it has reviewed military action on human rights and humanitarian law grounds. Its *Wall* Advisory Opinion is an obvious example.[20] By contrast, the International Criminal Court (ICC) has jurisdiction in some instances to scrutinise military action, but also military justice systems, directly. With respect to the latter point, the Rome Statute's admissibility provisions stipulate that the Court may inquire into a state's ability and

15 Convention for the Protection of Human Rights and Fundamental Freedoms, 4 November 1950, in force 3 September 1953, as amended by Protocol 14 to the Convention for the Protection of Human Rights and Fundamental Freedoms, 13 May 2004, CETS no. 194, in force 1 June 2010, 213 UNTS 221.

16 *Findlay* v. *UK* [1997] 24 EHRR 221. See further Peter Rowe, *The Impact of Human Rights Law on Armed Forces* (New York, Cambridge University Press, 2006).

17 (2011) 53 EHRR 18. 18 See Chapter 4.

19 See *Lori Berenson-Mejía* v. *Peru* [1998] Inter-Am Court HR (Ser C) No. 119 and *Radilla-Pachecho* v. *Mexico* [2009] Inter-Am Court HR (Ser L) No. 209. See Chapters 5 and 16.

20 *Legal Consequences of the Construction of a Wall in the Occupied Palestinian Territory (Advisory Opinion)* [2004] ICJ Rep. 136.

willingness to genuinely investigate or prosecute a crime. In determining unwillingness, the court must determine whether domestic proceedings are being conducted 'independently or impartially'.[21] These admissibility criteria create self-imposed pressure on states wishing to avoid ICC interference to ensure that their military justice systems are up to scratch.

2 Quasi-judicial scrutiny

The civilian administrative bodies that exercise legal scrutiny over militaries can be divided into three categories: administrative tribunals, ombudsmen and other non-adjudicative forums such as inquiries and inquests.

A prime example of an administrative tribunal which exercises quasi-judicial scrutiny of the armed forces is the Canadian Military Police Complaints Commission (MPCC), created in 1999. This civilian tribunal conducts investigations into allegations of misconduct or interference in the work of the Canadian Forces military police. It may hold public interest hearings in addition to responding to specific complaints. Recent matters before the MPCC include an accusation of improper investigation into a soldier's on-base suicide[22] and, as discussed below, a public interest inquiry into the role of Canadian Military Police (MP) in transferring Afghan detainees to Afghan national authorities in whose hands, it was alleged, some were tortured or ill-treated.

The first military ombudsman was established in Norway in 1952. Following Canada's Somalia scandal and resulting reorganisation of the Canadian Forces, a military ombudsman was appointed in 1998.[23] While the Canadian Forces Ombudsman does not have the jurisdiction to investigate judicial decision-making, he or she has jurisdiction over a wide range of possible abuses of authority, including delays in the administration of the Code of Service Discipline.[24] The Ombudsman's office is independent of the chain of command and has wide investigative powers. As with most ombudsmen, the Canadian Forces Ombudsman does not

21 Rome Statute of the International Criminal Court, 17 July 1998, in force 1 July 2002, 2187 UNTS 90 art. 17(2)(c).

22 Military Police Complaints Commission, 'Military Police Complaints Commission Hearing into Fynes complaint begins March 27, 2012' (22 March 2012) www.mpcc-cppm.gc.ca/400/media/2012-03-22-eng.aspx.

23 Government of Canada, *Ombudsman: About Us* (National Defence and Canadian Forces Ombudsman, 26 August 2013) www.ombudsman.forces.gc.ca/en/about-us.page.

24 Government of Canada, *Ministerial Directives* (National Defence and Canadian Forces Ombudsman, 26 August 2013) www.ombudsman.forces.gc.ca/en/ombudsman-about-us/ministerial-directives.page.

have determinative powers but can make authoritative recommendations. The Canadian Ombudsman reports to the Minister of Defence, but not, despite urged reforms, Parliament.[25] Many European countries now also have a separate military ombudsman. Other countries' ombudsmen of general jurisdiction may also have jurisdiction over military or veteran affairs. The EU Ombudsman will also entertain complaints from soldiers deployed on EU missions after exhausting domestic remedies. The creation of an Ombudsman for the armed forces in South Africa in 2011 suggests that the model is spreading beyond Western nations.[26]

In terms of other non-adjudicative forums, there is no shortage of domestic, regional and international inquiries, or calls for such inquiries, over military action. Examples of civilian domestic inquiries include the 2011 Gage Inquiry into Baha Mousa's death and the 2012 DLA Phillips Fox inquiry into allegations of 'sexual and other abuse – such as bullying, harassment and intimidation' in the Australian Defence Force over a span of decades.[27] In the UK, coroner inquests have investigated matters such as death from friendly fire and unsatisfactory kit.[28] Inquiries have also originated in a variety of international and regional organisations. Examples include the Goldstone Inquiry of 2009 into the Gaza conflict commissioned by the UN Human Rights Commission and – in a first for this regional organisation – the European Union's Inquiry into the conduct of Georgian and Russian military forces during their 2008 war.[29] Some inquiries are 'internationalised', with both international and international commission members, such as Israel's Turkel Inquiry into the 2010 Gaza Flotilla Raid and the Gaza Blockade.[30] These inquiries

[25] Antonio Lamer, *The First Independent Review by the Right Honourable Antonio Lamer of the Provisions and Operation of Bill C-25, An Act to amend the National Defence Act and to make Consequential Amendments to Other Acts* (Military Grievances External Review Committee, 3 September 2003) www.cfgb-cgfc.gc.ca/documents/lamer-eng.pdf.

[26] On the growth of Ombudsmen for the Armed Forces, see generally *Comparative Perspective of Ombudsman Institutions for the Armed Forces* (Geneva, Centre for the Democratic Control of Armed Forces) www.dcaf.ch/Publications/Comparative-Perspective-of-Ombudsman-Institutions-for-the-Armed-Forces.

[27] 'Report of the Review of Allegations of Sexual and Other Abuse in Defence' *ABC News*, 14 June 2012 www.abc.net.au/news/2012-06-14/dla-piper-investigation-executive-summary/4071664.

[28] See, for example, *R (Smith)* v. *Oxfordshire Assistant Deputy Coroner* [2011] 1 AC 1.

[29] *Report of the UN Fact Finding Mission on the Gaza Conflict*, UN HRCOR, 12th Sess, UN Doc A/HRC/12/48 (23 September 2009); European Union, *Independent International Fact-Finding Mission on the Conflict in Georgia* (September 2009) www.ceiig.ch/Report.html.

[30] The Turkel Commission, *The Public Commission to Examine the Maritime Incident of 31 May 2010* www.turkel-committee.gov.il/files/wordocs/8808report-eng.pdf.

have arisen in the context of a growing body of doctrine on the way in which an independent and competent investigation should be organised.[31]

B Scrutiny across space, time and legal regimes

Having established that there are multiple sites of civilian judicial and quasi-judicial scrutiny of the armed forces, it should also be pointed out that this scrutiny may be perceived not only as 'legal encirclement' but also as 'legal ambush'. The manner in which legal process unfolds is seen as unpredictable across a variety of civilian legal contexts.[32] In the military context, given the scale and breadth of operations, it appears even more unpredictable. It is certainly true that civilian legal challenges to military action can operate across a wide space–time continuum. Some examples of time lags between the events under scrutiny and the culmination of a legal process illustrate this point: in 2010 the Bloody Sunday Inquiry reported on the actions of British soldiers in Northern Ireland in 1972;[33] in 2011 the Dutch Court of Appeal addressed the actions of Dutchbat at Srebrenica in 1995;[34] and, in 2012 the ICJ dealt with claims for redress over German military action in World War II.[35]

In addition, militaries face what may seem to be a bewildering legal pluralism. At the domestic level, rights-based constitutions provide not only fair trial rights, but also a range of relevant rights, including freedom of religion[36] and equality.[37] Classical constitutional issues in the form of the separation of powers may also impact on military justice, as the

[31] See Jacob Turkel, *Examination of the Israeli Mechanisms for Examining and Investigating Allegations of Violations of the Laws of Armed Conflict – 'The Investigation Policy' Part II*, www.turkel-committee.com/content-157-c.html.

[32] Murray S. Levin, 'Learning about the Unpredictability of Litigation through a Mock Jury Exercise' (2008) 16 *Journal of Legal Studies Education*, p. 272.

[33] *Report of the Bloody Sunday Inquiry* (The National Archives) http://webarchive.nationalarchives.gov.uk/20101015151734/bloody-sunday-inquiry.org/.

[34] Tom Dannebaum, 'The Hague Court of Appeal on Dutchbat at Srebrenica Part 1: A Narrow Finding on the Responsibilities of Peacekeepers' *EJIL:* Talk! (25 October 2011) www.ejiltalk.org/the-hague-court-of-appeal-on-dutchbat-at-srebrenica-part-1-a-narrow-finding-on-the-responsibilities-of-peacekeepers/. *Nuhanović* v. *The Netherlands* 200.020.174/01 [2011]. This decision was affirmed by the Supreme Court of the Netherlands on 6 September 2013.

[35] *Jurisdictional Immunities of the State (Germany* v. *Italy: Greece Intervening)* [2012] ICJ Rep 1.

[36] See, for example, *Goldman* v. *Weinberger* 475 US 503 (1986), where the US Supreme Court ruled that a Jewish soldier could not wear a kippa. The US military has subsequently softened its stance: Uniform Code of Military Justice, 10 USC § 774 (2006).

[37] See, for example, *Smith & Grady* v. *United Kingdom* (1999) 29 EHRR 493.

demise of the Australian Military Court demonstrates. In 2009 the High Court of Australia held that the military court fell between the cracks of the judicial and defence powers under the Constitution and declared the legislation establishing the court to be invalid.[38] Quasi-constitutional human rights statutes can also have an impact, as can ordinary legislation or regulation on matters such as health and safety and employment.[39] Internationally, we have the parallel and overlapping regimes of international humanitarian law (IHL) and international human rights law. While the core of IHL is binding globally, international human rights standards are regionally more disparate. Adding further complexity, regional human rights courts have incorporated IHL into their jurisprudence. Finally, international criminal law maps on to grave abuses of human rights and IHL. The mixing of these international legal regimes poses theoretical and operational uncertainties.[40]

III Death of the lawfare paradigm

Where does this range of legal activity leave us? For some, the notion of lawfare captures the overreaching web of sources of civilian scrutiny and civilianisation. Lawfare proponents argue that the operational effectiveness of traditional militaries is being hampered by legal actions and overregulation. Charles Dunlap, the US Air Force JAG officer widely credited with coining the term, wrote in 2001:

> Is warfare turning into lawfare? In other words, is international law undercutting the ability of the U.S. to conduct effective military interventions? Is it becoming a vehicle to exploit American values in ways that actually increase risks to civilians? In short, is law becoming more of the problem in modem war instead of part of the solution?[41]

38 *Lane* v. *Morrison* (2009) 239 CLR 230. See Alison Duxbury, 'The Curious Case of the Australian Military Court' (2010) *Oxford University Commonwealth Law Journal*, p. 10, at 155.

39 For a list of seventeen pieces of legislation which the Canadian Forces view as relevant to their task, see Government of Canada, *Laws Defining the Framework of Rights and Obligations in Canada* (National Defence and Canadian Armed Forces, 7 July 2013) www.forces.gc.ca/en/about/legislation.page.

40 See Robin Geiss and Michael Siegrist, 'Has the Armed Conflict in Afghanistan Affected the Rules on the Conduct of Hostilities?' (2011) 93 *International Review of the Red Cross*, p. 40.

41 Charles J. Dunlap Jr, 'Law and Military Interventions: Preserving Humanitarian Values in 21st Century Conflicts' (Paper presented at Humanitarian Challenges in Military Intervention, Cambridge, 29 November 2001) www.hks.harvard.edu/cchrp/Web%20Working%20Papers/Use%20of%20Force/Dunlap2001.pdf.

The term 'lawfare' continues to hold currency within traditional scholarship and now the blogosphere.[42] In Britain and other common law countries, the term is less frequently used, but the sentiments it encapsulates are readily found, albeit with more muted tones. For example, several former chiefs of defence staff have expressed dismay about the 'legal encirclement' or 'legal siege' of the British armed forces. Admiral Lord Boyce, Chief of Defence Staff at the time of the 2003 Iraq invasion, has been a vocal critic of the perceived encroachment of law and the perceived harm to operational effectiveness. He stated in the House of Lords:

> The Armed Forces are under legal siege ... They are being pushed by people schooled not in operations but only in political correctness. They are being pushed to a time when they will fail in an operation because the commanding officer's authority and his command chain has been compromised with tortuous rules not relevant to fighting and where his instinct to be daring and innovative is being buried under the threat of liabilities and hounded out by those who have no concept of what is required to fight and win.[43]

More recently, the French military has echoed similar concerns about the over-legalisation (judiciarisation) of military action and the resultant inhibitions to risk taking by commanders.[44] However, for the reasons outlined below, I suggest that the lawfare/legal encirclement paradigms are of limited utility.[45]

A Civilian influence is necessary, not new

Civilian legal influence is not new but rather an ongoing process since at least the seventeenth century, when the English Parliament began limiting the king's prerogative over military affairs.[46] Historical perspective

[42] See the special issue of the *Case Western Reserve Journal of International Law*, 'Lawfare!' (2011) 43 *Case Western Reserve Journal of International Law*, p. 1 and *Lawfare: Hard National Security Choices* www.lawfareblog.com.

[43] See United Kingdom, *Parliamentary Debates*, House of Lords, 2005, vol. 673, col. 1236.

[44] See Jean-Michel Baillat, 'Le contexte juridique des opérations militaires' (2012) 754 *Revue Défense Nationale*, p. 104.

[45] I critique lawfare in greater detail in Christopher Waters, 'Beyond Lawfare: Juridical Oversight of Western Militaries' (2009) 46 *Alberta Law Review*, p. 885.

[46] William Winthrop, *Military Law and Precedents* (Boston, Little, Brown, and Company, 1896), vol. II, p. 1446; British History Online, *1688: An Act for Punishing Officers or Soldiers Who Shall Mutiny or Desert Their Majestyes Service* www.british-history.ac.uk/report.aspx?compid=46291. The ongoing civil-military justice interaction is explored in more depth, in Waters, above n. 45.

aside, no matter what sociological theory of civil–military relations one takes, a gap between military and civilian values cannot become a chasm in any healthy society or its security sector. Indeed, with delays and military adaptations, the armed forces keep up with societal and cultural changes, whether such changes relate to haircuts or rights discourse. More concretely, Western armed forces have generally not been on the receiving end of legislative changes but rather have initiated and even drafted their own legislation. In the United Kingdom for example, each of the three services was represented in the last legislative drafting process.[47] In Canada, recent changes have often been driven by the JAG.[48]

B *International Humanitarian Law is fundamentally permissive*

International Humanitarian Law, the body of law governing the military's central activity of combat, remains fundamentally permissive. The principle of military necessity is not codified in the 1949 Geneva Conventions or the 1977 Protocols but is a core principle of IHL. It was defined in the 'Hostage Case' as follows: 'Military necessity permits a belligerent, subject to the laws of war, to apply any amount and kind of force to compel the complete submission of the enemy with the least possible expenditure of time, life and money.'[49] While it would be wrong to suggest that there is no objective analysis possible when applying the military necessity principle in a proportionality analysis during targeting, that there is a degree of nebulousness cannot be denied. As Gary Solis notes, 'Sometimes, military necessity is invoked when military convenience is closer to truth.'[50] More charitably, it can at least be said with respect to balancing military necessity with the principle of distinction during targeting that the 'reasonable military commander' is given some margin of discretion in determining what is proportional.[51]

[47] See Ministry of Defence, *An Overview of the Service Justice System and the Armed Forces Act*, at http://webarchive.nationalarchives.gov.uk.

[48] See National Defence, *Annual Report of the Judge Advocate General to the Minister of National Defence on the Administration of Military Justice in the Canadian Forces: A Review from 1 April 2009 to 31 March 2010*, www.forces.gc.ca/en/about-reports-pubs-military-law-annual-2009-10/index.page.

[49] *United States* v. *Wilhelm List* et al., XI TWC 1253–54 (1948).

[50] Gary Solis, *The Law of Armed Conflict* (New York, Cambridge University Press, 2010), p. 264.

[51] Geiss and Siegrist, 'Has the Armed Conflict in Afghanistan Affected the Rules on the Conduct of Hostilities?', above, n, 40, p. 33.

C Courts deferential to core military activity

Domestic courts have shown themselves to be fundamentally deferential to the military's core activities. This deference is true with respect to deaths and detention of foreigners during military operations, but also, albeit to a lesser extent, when these operations result in the death of the sending state's own soldiers in combat. *In R (Smith)* v. *Secretary of State for Defence*[52] the UK Supreme Court was asked to decide whether the ECHR was breached over the failure to provide a proper investigation into a soldier's heat – stroke death in Iraq. In language that reveals him to be an ardent supporter of the military, Lord Roger stated,

> Any suggestion that the death of a soldier in combat conditions points to some breach by the United Kingdom of his Article 2 right to life is not only to mistake but – much worse – to devalue what our soldiers do . . . While steps can be taken, by training and by providing suitable armour, to give our troops some measure of protection against these hostile attacks, that protection can never be complete. Deaths and injuries are inevitable . . . To suggest that these deaths and injuries can always, or even usually be seen as the result of some failure to protect the soldiers, whether by their immediate companions or by more senior officers of generals or ministers, is to depreciate the bravery of the men and women who face these dangers.[53]

Regional human rights courts have tended to exercise more scrutiny over the military actions than their national counterparts.[54] But while there are relevant courts in Europe and the Americas, not all Western countries are subject to the jurisdiction of regional rights bodies. For example, Australia and New Zealand are not subject to a regional rights body and, while Canada and the United States are member states of the Organization of American States, neither is subject to the jurisdiction of the Inter-American Court of Human Rights. Regional human rights protection therefore remains a patchwork.

D Administrative legal oversight may be muzzled

Even when formal administrative law structures provide scrutiny of the armed forces, these often lack independence and effectiveness. Canada is

[52] [2011] 1 AC 1.

[53] *R (Smith)* v. *Oxfordshire Assistant Deputy Coroner* [2011] 1 AC 1 at [122]–[124]. See Chapter 4.

[54] Consider the reversal by the European Court of Human Rights of the House of Lords' decision in *Al-Skeini* v. *United Kingdom* (2011) 53 ECHR 18.

generally thought of as a model of civilian scrutiny given the innovations established following the Somalia debacle. For example, there appear to be few equivalents to Canada's MPCC, although some ombudsmen have jurisdiction over MP activity. However, the role of the MPCC has been diminished by governments and courts, highlighting the vulnerability of administrative tribunals generally and especially with respect to security matters.[55] In attempting to investigate complaints that the Provost Marshall had transferred detainees to Afghan custody, knowing that there was a real risk of torture in Afghan prisons, and that Canadian MPs had failed to investigate the Canadian commanders' orders to make these transfers, the Commission was met with government stonewalling. This resistance took the form of refusal to provide documentation to the MPCC, refusal to re-appoint the MPCC's chair upon the expiration of his term, delay in appointing a new chair and the appointment of a new chair (one who lacks legal training) by cabinet decision in the middle of a public interest investigation which would potentially implicate the very same government in wrongdoing. Laverne Jacobs explains:

> The fact that the government of the day was both in charge of the appointment and removal process for members of the MPCC and concurrently appearing as a party before the MPCC, cast doubt over the neutrality of Cabinet in replacing Mr. Tinsley. Even if cabinet's actions were legal under the enabling legislation, a reasonable person who takes into account the battle that the MPCC has had to obtain the relevant documents from the government party, including being taken on judicial review, may have a reasonable apprehension of bias.[56]

As well as attempting to stymie the MPCC both administratively and through judicial review over documentary disclosure, the government successfully narrowed the scope of the Commission's investigation through the courts. In *Canada (Attorney General)* v. *Amnesty International Canada*,[57] the government asked the Federal Court of Canada to quash the Commission's inquiry into the 'detainee complaint' and to limit the scope of the 'investigation complaint' which might impugn government policy generally. In agreeing with the government on the detainee complaint, the court held that the capture or detention of

[55] See, for example, Laverne Jacobs, 'A Wavering Commitment? Administrative Independence and Collaborative Governance in Ontario's Adjudicative Tribunals Accountability Legislation' (2010) 28(2) *Windsor Yearbook of Access to Justice*, p. 285; Lorne Sossin, 'The Puzzle of Independence for Administrative Bodies' (2009) 26 *National Journal of Constitutional Law*, p. 1.

[56] Jacobs, above n. 55, at 302. [57] [2010] 4 FCR 182 (*Amnesty*).

insurgents in Afghanistan were not policing functions for present purposes, as this battlefield action arises out of 'established military custom or practice'.[58] In other words, the MPs' role in capturing and holding insurgents was the soldiering part of their dual military/police function. The court also upheld the government's submission on the investigation complaint, holding that the Commission's inquiry must restrict itself to what the Military Police knew or could have known given the extent they were privy to operational decision-making.[59]

In light of its restricted inquiry and the actual knowledge of the MPs involved, the Commission made no findings of wrongdoing on the part of the individual MP officers implicated by the complaints. However, in its report of 27 June 2012, the Commission took the extraordinary step of detailing the government's efforts to stymie its investigation with respect to documentary disclosure and access to witnesses.[60] The Commission said:

> With the Commission's decision to conduct public interest hearings in March 2008, and through to November 2009, the doors were basically slammed shut on document disclosure. The Commission did not receive a single, new document from the Government throughout that time period despite many requests. Many excuses were given for this approximately 21 month dry spell in document production and none were very convincing from the Commission's perspective.[61]

Summing up its scathing views of government action over documentary disclosure, access to witnesses and a general attitude of stonewalling by the government and its legal counsel, the Commission noted a historical parallel, namely government roadblocks to the Somalia Inquiry almost two decades prior. The Commission called for decision-makers to:

> Review the process section of this Report in detail to understand the full extent to which the actions described above severely impeded the Commission's ability to carry out the mandate prescribed to it by Parliament. The Complainants, the subjects, the Department of National Defence, and the public would have been much better served by a more transparent and cooperative approach. The Commission holds out the hope that future public interest investigations and hearings will be

[58] See ibid., at [85]. [59] Ibid., [Order].

[60] Military Police Complaints Commission, *Commission's Final Report – MPCC 2008-042 – Concerning a Complaint by Amnesty International Canada and British Columbia Civil Liberties Association*, MPCC www.mpcc-cppm.gc.ca/300/afghan/2012-06-27-eng.aspx#toc (*MPCC Commission's Final Report*).

[61] Ibid.

> carried out in the spirit of cooperation and respect that the public has a right to expect.[62]

E Predictability reconsidered

An irony of many of the high-profile legal claims against militaries – and the subsequent lawfare backlash – is that such claims are generally predictable and avoidable. Of course it would be facile to think that there could be no vexatious or grasping claims. However, there is a literature on predicting litigation in various industries – from nursing homes to patents[63] – and all industries seek to reduce legal risk. Various branches in the military – in the US Army by Installation Management Command for example – attempt to minimise risks of litigation, as do of course competent JAG offices practising preventative law. Unfortunately, the failure to reduce risk often lies at the highest levels of operational command. Canada's transfer of detainees is a case in point. The Judge Advocate General, Brig.-Gen. Ken Watkin, in a leaked memo to the Chief of Defence Staff and others, wrote that

> Military commanders who know, or are criminally negligent in failing to know, that a transferred detainee would be subjected to such abuse have the obligation to take all necessary and reasonable measures within their power to prevent or repress the commission of such abuse. They may also be subject to criminal liability for failing to submit the matter to competent authorities for investigation and prosecution.[64]

While to date there have been no conclusive, independent findings on what Canadian commanders and politicians knew or did not know,[65] it is clear that the issue was a live one and that earlier steps could have been taken to ensure that related torture, litigation and public relations risks were mitigated. Steps were undertaken by the Canadian Forces – including the

62 Ibid.

63 See Christopher Johnson et al., 'Factors Predicting Lawsuits against Nursing Homes in Florida 1997–2001' (2004) 44 *The Gerontologist*, p. 339 and Colleen Chien, 'Predicting Patent Litigation' (2011) 90 *Texas Law Review*, p. 283.

64 Richard J. Brennan, 'Military Told to Heed Abuse Claims' *The Star*, 25 February 2010 www.thestar.com/news/canada/afghanmission/article/771198-military-told-to-heed-abuse-claims.

65 'After Latest Report on Afghan Detainees, the Same Questions Remain' *The Globe and Mail*, 2 July 2012 www.theglobeandmail.com/commentary/editorials/after-latest-report-on-afghan-detainees-the-same-questions-remain/article4382067/.

suspension of transfers[66] and the strengthening of the detainee transfer agreement[67] – but these reactive steps could have been avoided through preventative legal measures in the first instance.[68] Preventative measures include action or advice by units within the military who are sometimes shut out of operational decision-making at the highest levels, notably JAGs or Military Police. To return to the Canadian MPCC report into the Afghan detainees transfer, the Commission found that MPs had been 'siloed' away from operational information potentially relevant to their policing functions.[69] With proper consultation and information flow, Canada's MPs may have been able to take a more active role in ensuring that any detainee transfers were carried out in a legal, transparent manner and that subsequent litigation risks would have been mitigated or contained.

IV Is civilianisation the answer?

Given the weakness of the lawfare paradigm, is greater civilianisation the way forward?[70] It is not. First, military justice serves a specific need. There are distinct military justice systems which are fair, of limited jurisdiction and supportive of discipline and operational effectiveness.[71] As Michael Gibson states, 'military justice systems, when properly constituted, play a crucial role in the preservation and promotion of the rule of law, both domestically and in the context of international

66 'Canadian Forces Release Statistics on Afghanistan Detainees', 2 September 2011 www.afghanistan.gc.ca/canada-afghanistan/news-nouvelles/2010/2010_09_22b.aspx?lang=eng&view=d.

67 Ian Austen, 'Canada and Afghanistan Reach Accord on How to Treat Detainees' *The New York Times*, 4 May 2007 www.nytimes.com/2007/05/04/world/americas/04canada.html.

68 On preventative lawyering generally see Trevor Farrow, 'Dispute Resolution, Access to Civil Justice and Legal Education' (2005) 42 *Alberta Law Review*, p. 741.

69 Military Police Complaints Commission, *Commission's Final Report – MPCC 2008-042 – Concerning a Complaint by Amnesty International Canada and British Columbia Civil Liberties Association*, MPCC, www.mpcc-cppm.gc.ca/alt_format/300/afghan/2012-06-27-eng.pdf. Interestingly, the Commission contrasted the Canadian MPs' role with the more engaged role for the British MPs in transferring detainees and monitoring these detainees post-transfer, as detailed in *R (Maya Evans) v. Secretary of State for Defence* [2010] EWHC 1445 (Admin).

70 On the various strains of civilianisation, and perceptions of civilianisation, see Matthew Groves and Alison Duxbury, Chapter 1.

71 And where so constituted there is nothing inherently 'anti-human rights' about such a system. As the European Court of Human Rights put it in *Engel* v. *Netherlands* (1979) 1 EHRR 647 at 59, 'each State is competent to organise its own system of military discipline and enjoys in the matter a certain margin of appreciation'.

peacekeeping and peacemaking operations'.[72] For countries with recent troubled experience with military tribunals – Egypt before and after the Arab Spring – it may well be that the jurisdiction of these tribunals should be removed, even if they will need to be constituted again in the future on a more solid legal footing. But for states where the principle of civilian control is more firmly established – including where, for example, civilian appellate courts sit above a military law structure – a distinct system of military justice answers a real need.

Second, civilianisation does not mean more rule of law compliance. For example, it was the US military – led by Judge Advocate General officers – which pressed for compliance with international humanitarian law and domestic constitutional law in the face of opposition by civilian masters during the Bush Administration. As a 2007 article in *Harper's Magazine* stated:

> The American court-martial system has long been something that Americans could be proud of. And more than anything this is thanks to the diligent work and professionalism of the uniformed lawyers who make that system work, the JAG corps. Within two years of its arrival in Washington, the Bush Administration began to take a crow bar to the American military justice system. They wanted a new process in Guantánamo, and they had no position for justice in it. And they wanted the military lawyers to be their frontmen. As a senior JAG officer explained to me in West Point this fall: 'They never asked us for our advice on how to do this. They *instructed* us what to do. And we did the best we could to give their designs at least some modicum of justice. But nobody is happy with the product.' In fact over the last years we have seen a steady parade of JAG officers on the public stage protesting what has been done – a demolition derby of traditional values and procedures.[73]

Third, civilianisation does not lead necessarily to fairer or more human rights compliant results, as the fate of the Australian Military Court (AMC) reveals. As noted earlier, the High Court of Australia decided that the new AMC was unconstitutional, even though it was more independent of the chain of command than the system of courts martial and Defence Force magistrates it replaced.[74] In a 'neither fish nor fowl' decision, the High Court held that the AMC was too independent to be a

[72] Michael R. Gibson, 'International Human Rights Law and the Administration of Justice Through Military Tribunals: Preserving Utility While Precluding Impunity' (2008) 4 *Journal of International Law and International Relations*, p. 5.

[73] Scott Horton, 'Undermining Military Justice' *Harper's Magazine*, 11 December 2011 www.harpers.org/archive/2007/12/hbc-90001896.

[74] *Lane* v. *Morrison* (2009) 239 CLR 230.

military tribunal established under the Commonwealth's defence power but did not meet the Chapter III constitutional requirements of a civilian court either. As Alison Duxbury puts it: 'The final paradox in Australia's military justice system is that a court designed to meet the requirements of independence and impartiality was unconstitutional, whereas a system that raises issues of compliance with human rights principles is compatible with the Constitution.'[75]

V Beyond lawfare and civilianisation?

Georges Clemenceau said, perhaps apocryphally, that 'military justice is to justice like military music is to music'. As someone who – in the face of family discontent – likes martial music, I have never quite understood this simile to be a negative one. I suggest in this section that a balanced approach to civilian legal oversight is possible. What is needed is democratic scrutiny and oversight of the military through legal institutions rather than civilianisation of military justice. In other words, it is possible to move beyond the extremes of those who would abolish distinct systems of military justice as a matter of principle and those in militaries or governments who reflexively resist external scrutiny or legalisation of military action.

The time is right for a reasonable conversation about what sort of civilian oversight – rather than civilianisation per se – would be suitable. There is now a developed literature on the legal aspects of democratic oversight to accompany the literature on civilian oversight through the executive and legislative branches.[76] Importantly, much of this literature takes a socio-legal approach, drawing on military sociology among other disciplines. This has been accompanied by a body of case law on extra-territorial supervision of military action from Strasbourg and other regional rights bodies (with most countries outside of those regimes lagging far behind); a move to greater transparency (some of it forced) from the militaries about the operation of their justice systems;[77] a

[75] Duxbury, above n. 38, at 182.

[76] See Rowe, above n. 16; Gerry Rubin, 'United Kingdom Military Law: Autonomy, Civilianisation, Juridification' (2002) 65 *Modern Law Review*, p. 36; Duxbury, above n. 38, at 182.

[77] On transparency over courts martial in the UK, for example, see Richard Norton-Taylor and Rob Evans, 'Ministry of Defence Agrees to More Openness on Courts Martial' *The Guardian*, 6 December 2011 www.guardian.co.uk/uk/2011/dec/05/ministry-of-defence-courts-martial.

convergence of strategic and legal thinking on what is required to be successful in a counter-insurgency context (IHL/Human Rights respecting armies have a better chance of winning hearts and minds);[78] and several reports into the legal failings of Western militaries both in the war against terror generally and with respect to military justice in particular.[79]

The 2006 'Decaux Principles' offer a useful, if neglected, starting point with respect to the relationship between military justice and courts.[80] The Decaux Principles, drafted under the auspices of the Sub-Commission for the Promotion and Protection of Human Rights, are intended to ensure compliance with universally accepted rights standards by military justice systems. They address the establishment and authority of military tribunals, the scope of application of law, the jurisdiction of military tribunals, fair trials and impartiality. There are a few contentious points in the principles;[81] overall, however, there has been little opposition to the core of the principles by the military or the military's usual critics. For the purpose of the current discussion, Principle 20 (on transparent reviews of codes of military justice) is pertinent:

> Codes of military justice should be subject to periodic systematic review, conducted in an independent and transparent manner, so as to ensure that the authority of military tribunals corresponds to strict functional necessity, without encroaching on the jurisdiction that can and should belong to ordinary civil courts. ... [T]his periodic review should ensure that military justice is appropriate and effective in relation to its practical justification. It would also embody the fully democratic nature of an institution that must be accountable for its operations to the authorities and all citizens. In this way, the fundamental discussion concerning the

[78] See calls for strict legal compliance in the US Army/Marine Corps Counter Insurgency Field Manual, US Army Combined Arms Center http://usacac.army.mil/cac2/coin/repository/FM_3-24.pdf.

[79] Department of Defence, *The Effectiveness of Australia's Military Justice System* (Senate Committee Report, 2005), p. 101 www.defence.gov.au/mjs/docs/mji_government_response_4oct052.pdf. Lord Butler of Brockwell, *Review of Intelligence on Weapons of Mass Destruction* (The National Archives) www.archive2.official-documents.co.uk/document/deps/hc/hc898/898.pdf.

[80] *Draft Principles Governing the Administration of Justice Through Military Tribunals*, UN ECOSOCOR, 66th Sess, Supp No. 11(d), UN Doc E/CN.4/2006/58 (2006). Interest in the Decaux Principles was briefly rekindled in 2013 by the recommendation of Special Rapporteur Knaul that the Principles be formally adopted by the Human Rights Council; see UN GA, *Report of the Special Rapporteur on the Independence of Judges and Lawyers*, UN GA A/68/285 (7 August 2013).

[81] See Chapter 5.

existence of military justice as such can be conducted in a completely transparent way in a democratic society.

While courts are central to democratic oversight, quasi-judicial administrative institutions also play an important role in filling the legal basket of full democratic oversight. The role of administrative law bodies in military oversight has not been a focus of sustained scholarship or international policy attention, and there is scope here for further work.[82] It should be noted that military ombudsmen have received some attention,[83] but there is scope for adjudicative and other non-adjudicative administrative bodies (especially if they are able to develop a real, and not merely notional, body of expertise) to play an important function in military oversight. Other jurisdictions may find it helpful to examine the role of the Canadian MPCC, which appears to have few counterparts in other countries. Although some military ombudsmen have jurisdiction over MPs, by definition they do not have the extensive powers of a dedicated, independent tribunal which mirrors the growing importance of civilian police oversight bodies.[84] Increased independence and increased government transparency and openness are preconditions to meeting the full potential of administrative bodies with respect to military oversight. Here broader reform trends in administrative law should be examined by lawyers with an interest in democratic oversight of the military.[85]

VI Conclusion

After the hyperbole of lawfare and legal encirclement and some serious failings with rule of law compliance in the war on terror, we may be ready to think seriously about the requirements for genuine democratic oversight of the armed forces. This chapter suggests that while executive oversight of the armed forces is strong in Western countries, and legislative oversight on the rise, oversight by legal institutions (both judicial and administrative) has lagged behind in terms of analysis and practice.

82 Recent exceptions in the Canadian context include analysis of the Military Police Complaints Commission, see, for example, Jacobs, above n. 55, at 285; Sossin, above n. 55, at 1.

83 See *Comparative Perspective of Ombudsman Institutions for the Armed Forces*, above n. 26.

84 See Peter Finn, *Citizen Review of Police: Approaches and Implementation*, US Department of Justice http://nacole.org/sites/default/files/184430.pdf.

85 See, for example, Jacobs, above n. 55, 285; Sossin, above n. 55, at 1.

While at first glance there is a thick web of scrutiny by courts, tribunals and non-adjudicative administrative bodies over the military, the scrutiny currently provided by these institutions is uneven and generally fragile. Among the other factors at play is that courts have been overly deferential to the military and that the administrative bodies which do exist have been subject to interference from the executive. In looking to complete the democratic oversight circle, the chapter suggests a greater role for legal institutions in scrutinising military justice and military action. But this expanded role should not be adopted with the aim of civilianising military justice or operational practices simply for civilianisation's sake.

4

The civil courts' challenge to military justice and its impact on the civil–military relationship

PAULINE COLLINS

War is too important to be left either to the generals or the politicians. It must be the people's business.[1]

I Introduction

Civil–military relations theory establishes a clear preference for civilian control over the military. Carl von Clausewitz was an early proponent of this theory, stating: '[p]olicy is the guiding intelligence and war only the instrument . . . No other possibility exists, then, than to subordinate the military . . . to the political.'[2] However, there is very little agreement on the way in which that arrangement can be achieved or, indeed, the operation of the civil–military relationship more generally. Matthew Groves argues that '[i]t is possible that the absence of a settled body of doctrine reflects a wider lack of knowledge about the societal relationship between civilians and the military in modern society.'[3]

The solution of liberal thinkers is to separate military and civilian power to ensure accountability to the people.[4] The analysis of the civil–military dynamic is constrained by an assumption that 'civil' means the executive, and possibly, legislative arms of government, but rarely the judicial arm. This approach lacks any explanation of the constitutional role of the judiciary in defining and managing the civil–military

[1] David M. Kennedy, 'The Best Army We Can Buy' *New York Times*, 25 July 2005 www.nytimes.com/2005/07/25/opinion/25kennedy.html.

[2] Michael Howard and Peter Paret (eds.), *Carl von Clausewitz on War* (Princeton, Princeton University Press, 1989), p. 706.

[3] Matthew Groves, 'The Civilianisation of Australian Military Law' (2005) 28 *University of New South Wales Law Journal*, p. 364, at 366.

[4] James Burk, 'The Logic of Crisis and Civil – Military Relations Theory: A Comment on Desch, Feaver, and Daubner' (1998) 24 *Armed Forces & Society*, p. 455.

relationship and invites the question: what role do the courts play in the civil–military relationship?

This chapter argues that the judiciary is an essential institutional organ assisting with the control of the military. Any undue deference by the courts to the military leads the judiciary to abstain from its proper role of constitutional oversight over all organs of government. Michael Gilbert has expressed this point in strong terms, '[j]udicial oversight is one form of civilian control over the military; abrogating this responsibility is to return power to the military hierarchy that is not meant to be theirs.'[5]

This chapter examines the jurisprudence of the British civilian courts governing deference towards the military. What consequences do national courts' decisions have for the civil–military relationship? Where is the line between the political and the legal, the justiciable and the non-justiciable? What is the impact of the United Kingdom's ratification of the European Convention on Human Rights[6] (ECHR) and its decision to bring rights home through the Human Rights Act 1998 (UK) (HR Act) on the courts' decision-making on military matters? Have human rights developments emboldened judges, or does the deferential approach remain bounded by principles of parliamentary sovereignty and the separation of powers?

II The civil–military 'legal' relationship

The deference of the judicial arm to the military has historically been strong and may account for the absence of a coherent theory on the judicial role in civil–military relations.[7] Older cases have held that the constitutional separation of powers dictates that military decisions are for the legislative and executive arm. This preference by the courts, to absent themselves from oversight of the military, arguably reduces the effectiveness of their constitutional role. Lord Bingham acknowledged that the courts decide where along the political – judicial line a particular matter will sit, observing that: '[t]he more purely political (in a broad or narrow

[5] See Michael Gilbert, 'Military and the Federal Judiciary: An Unexplored Part of the Civil – Military Relations Triangle' (1997–1998) 8 *The United States Air Force Academy Journal of Legal Studies*, p. 197, at 197 'Without an actual, meaningful presence of the judiciary as a leg of the civil – military triangle, the triangle is incomplete and collapses.'

[6] Convention for the Protection of Human Rights and Fundamental Freedoms, Rome, 4 November 1950, in force 3 December 1953, 213 UNTS 222.

[7] David Jenkins, 'Judicial Review under a British War Powers Act' (2010) 43 *Vanderbilt Journal of Transnational Law*, p. 610.

sense) the question is, the more appropriate it would be for political resolution, the less likely it is to be an appropriate matter for judicial decision . . . It is the function of political and not judicial bodies to resolve political questions.'[8]

Questions about the extent to which British courts should venture into the political arena have come into sharp focus since the commencement of the HR Act. More particularly, some scholars have argued that the Act has signalled a new constitutional settlement between the executive government and the courts.[9] Continued adherence to the jurisprudence on the 'separateness' of the military could place the judiciary and the military out of step with this development.[10] Further, the nature and role of standing militaries is changing. They are different from the 'civilian armies' of World War II; they are now volunteer professional militaries,[11] increasingly outsourcing many roles. They are no longer confined to defending the national territory but encompass multinational forces and peacekeeping roles.[12] The term 'military' needs reassessing to avoid the distortions in current civil–military relations theories, which take as unchallenged the classic concept of national defence personnel as citizen-soldiers. Richard Wells notes that the US and, it is suggested, the UK, courts are lagging behind the reality of civil–military relations and the redundancy of maintaining separateness when he states 'only one major policy making institution still bases its policies on this premise, and that is the . . . Supreme Court . . . This doctrine of separatism . . . is based upon a conception of civil–military relations that has become antique to the point of caricature.'[13]

[8] *A* v. *Secretary of State for the Home Department* [2005] 2 AC 68, at [29]. See also *Orloff* v. *Willoughby* 345 US 83, at 93–94 (1953) (Jackson J).

[9] An influential expression of this argument is Jeffrey Jowell, 'Parliamentary Sovereignty under the New Constitutional Hypothesis' (2006) *Public Law*, p. 562.

[10] See, for example, Peter Rowe, 'The Soldier as a Citizen in Uniform: A Reappraisal' (2007) 7 *N.Z. Armed Forces Law Review*, p. 1; Diane H. Mazur, 'Rehnquist's Vietnam: Constitutional Separatism and the Stealth Advance of Martial Law' (2002) 77 *Indiana Law Journal*, p. 701.

[11] The UK introduced an all-volunteer force in 1963.

[12] Glen Segell, 'The Nation-State, Nationalism, and Civil – Military Relations Theory' in Constantine P. Danopoulos, Dhirendra Vajpeyi, and Amir Bar-or (eds.), *Civil – Military Relations, Nation-Building, and National Identity* (Westport, CT, Praeger Publishers, 2004), p. 51.

[13] Richard Wells, 'The Theory of Concordance in Civil/Military Relations: A Commentary' (1996) 23 *Armed Forces & Society*, p. 269. See also, Mazur, 'Rehnquist's Vietnam', above n. 10.

Deference by the courts can conflict with the demand for judicial oversight required by the ECHR, and now HR Act. The UK courts have to grapple with the implementation of human rights in armed conflicts within a national order, which attempts to honour the separation of powers.[14] Considering these matters, the question arises: does the approach of the UK courts in dealing with the military and human rights concerns have consequences for civil–military relations theory?

III The UK courts' approach to military issues

The following cases demonstrate the various ways in which the UK courts have addressed issues surrounding the military, whether it is the extra-territorial application of human rights law to soldiers or their alleged victims, or decisions to go to war. As a starting point, the UK courts have adopted a deferential approach. However, while the orthodox position on separation of powers is followed, there are a number of strong dissenters indicating a possible change in attitude on the justiciability of military issues.[15] The application of justiciability is complex as it depends on the subject matter reviewed, rather than a discernible general principle.[16] The conduct of foreign affairs,[17] national security[18] and defence[19] remain the domain of the executive, but inexorably the courts are making

[14] See Peter Rowe, 'Military Misconduct During International Armed Operations: "Bad Apples" or Systemic Failure?' (2008) 13 *Journal of Conflict & Security Law*, p. 165.

[15] *R (Smith)* v. *Oxfordshire Assistant Deputy Coroner* [2011] 1 AC 1, at [137] (Baroness Hale), and [195] (Mance LJ) (*Smith* v. *Oxfordshire* (SC)) 'there is nothing that makes the Convention impossible or inappropriate of application to the relationship between the state and its armed forces as it exists in relation to overseas operations'.

[16] See, for example, *R (Abbasi)* v. *Secretary of State for Foreign and Commonwealth Affairs* [2003] UKHRR 76 (*Abbasi*). See further, Charlotte Kilroy, 'R. (On the Application of Abbasi) v Secretary of State for Foreign and Commonwealth Affairs: Reviewing the Prerogative' (2003) 2 *European Human Rights Law Review*, p. 222.

[17] See *Abbasi* [2003] UKHRR 76; *R (Al-Rawi)* v. *Secretary of State for Foreign and Commonwealth Affairs* [2006] EWHC 972 (Admin); *Rahmatullah* v. *Secretary of State for Foreign and Commonwealth Affairs and Secretary of State for Defence* [2012] 1 WLR 1492 (*Rahmatullah* (CA)); *Secretary of State for Foreign and Commonwealth Affairs* v. *Rahmatullah* [2013] 1 AC 614 (*Rahmatullah* (SC)); *R (Khan)* v. *Secretary of State for Foreign and Commonwealth Affairs* [2012] EWHC 3728 (Admin).

[18] See, for example, *The Campaign for Nuclear Disarmament* v. *Prime Minister of the United Kingdom* [2002] EWHC 2759 (QB) (*Nuclear Disarmament*); But *cf.* *R (Bancoult)* v. *Secretary of State for Foreign and Commonwealth Affairs* [2008] UKHL 61; *R (Binyam Mohamed)* v. *Secretary of State for Foreign and Commonwealth Affairs* [2009] EWHC 152 (Admin); *J1* v. *Secretary of State* [2013] EWCA Civ 279.

[19] See, for example, *Nuclear Disarmament* [2002] EWHC 2759 (QB); *R (Al-Haq)* v. *Secretary of State for Foreign and Commonwealth Affairs* [2009] EWHC 1910 (Admin);

inroads into government actions. The distinction is often a fine one in which the courts will refuse to examine questions of foreign or international relations, but they will examine the conduct of the executive against its international obligations.[20] The exercise of the prerogative has not been immune from judicial review since the House of Lords case of *Council of Civil Service Unions* v. *Minister for the Civil Service*.[21] Significantly, human rights issues have been present in many cases.[22]

The foreign affairs prerogative regarding the right to go to war is itself challenged by the courts' obligation to determine whether legislation is in conflict with human rights obligations. While the power to declare war is considered the sacred domain of the executive, even this issue has not been declared beyond judicial question.[23] The legal consequences of a decision to go to war may give rise to issues that the courts will consider.[24] However, the reluctance of the courts to use the new power apparently given to them by the HR Act remains strong and the consequence of that reluctance is demonstrated in the following cases.

A *Human rights and the UK military operating extraterritorially*

The extraterritorial reach of the HR Act and the ECHR was the central concern in *R (Al-Skeini)* v. *Secretary of State for Defence*.[25] The case

Mohammed v. *Ministry of Defence; Qasim and Others* v. *Secretary of State* [2014] EWHC 1369 (QB) (*Mohammed* v. *Ministry of Defence*).

20 See, for example, *Al-Jedda* v. *Secretary of State for the Home Department* [2012] EWCA Civ 358 (*Al-Jedda* CA); *Mohammed* v. *Ministry of Defence* [2014] EWHC 1369 (QB).

21 [1985] AC 374.

22 Dominic McGoldrick, 'The Boundaries of Justiciability' (2010) 59(4) *International & Comparative Law Quarterly*, p. 981, at 983. See *J1* v. *Secretary of State* [2013] EWCA Civ 279; *Kennedy* v. *Charity Commission* [2015] 1 AC 455, at [52].

23 Ibid., McGoldrick at 1017; *Nuclear Disarmament* [2002] EWHC 2759 (QB); *R (Gentle)* v. *Prime Minister* [2008] 1 AC 1356 (*Gentle*); *R* v. *Jones* [2007] 1 AC 136.

24 See, for example, *Abbasi* [2003] UKHRR 76. See further *Kuwait Airways Corporation* v. *Iraqi Airways Company* [2002] 2 WLR 1353, at [135]–[149] (Hope LJ); *R (Al-Jedda)* v. *Secretary of State for Defence* [2008] 1 AC 332, at [71]; *Mohammed* v. *Ministry of Defence* [2014] EWHC 1369 (QB); *Hassan* v. *United Kingdom* (European Court of Human Rights, Grand Chamber, Application No. 29750/09, 16 September 2014).

25 [2008] 1 AC 153 (*Al-Skeini* (HL)). See further, *Jaloud* v. *The Netherlands* (European Court of Human Rights, Grand Chamber, Application No. 47708/08, 20 November 2014) reaffirmed *Al-Skeini* (GC) and the extra-territorial application of the Convention based on the factual context (occupier status not being relevant), in regards to the shooting of an Iraqi citizen at a vehicle checkpoint. The Court found the Netherlands, through its full command control over its armed forces personnel, had sufficient control over the checkpoint to bring the applicant within the Convention's jurisdiction. Further,

exemplifies the role civilian courts play in the civil–military relationship. The families of the Iraqi victims were seeking a public investigation into the death of their relatives pursuant to art. 2 of the ECHR. Six matters involving civilian deaths during the occupation of Iraq by the United Kingdom were put forward as test cases.[26] One of the matters concerned a civilian shot in crossfire, although it was not clear who fired the shot. In four matters it was accepted that the victims were shot by members of the British armed forces, but factual disputes remained.[27] The sixth matter involved an incident on 14 September 2003, where an Iraqi civilian, Baha Mousa, and eight others were arrested and taken to a UK military base. Over thirty-six hours they underwent 'appalling maltreatment', using 'banned conditioning techniques', including hooding, stress positions, lack of sleep and food, and bound hands. These techniques were said to maintain the 'shock of capture'.[28] Mousa sustained ninety-three injuries and died.

The United Kingdom accepted that it was an occupying power over Southeast Iraq from 1 May 2003 to 28 June 2004 and therefore the law of occupation applied at the time.[29] The question the courts had to consider was whether the ECHR applied when deaths occur during an occupation of a non-contracting party to the Convention by agents of a contracting party (its military). Article 1 of the ECHR provides that contracting parties are bound to 'secure to everyone within their jurisdiction the rights and freedoms defined in section 1 of this Convention'.[30]

The UK national courts from the Divisional Court to the House of Lords showed a reluctance to interfere in military operations. They

the Netherlands had breached procedural obligations in relation to the conduct of an art. 2 investigation.

26 Other cases include *R (Mousa)* v. *Secretary of State for Defence* [2011] EWCA Civ 1334; *R (Mousa)* v. *Secretary of State for Defence* [2010] EWHC 1823 (Admin); *R (Mousa)* v. *Secretary of State for Defence* [2010] EWHC 3304 (Admin) ('*Mousa*'); *R (Mousa)* v. *Secretary of State for Defence* [2012] HRLR 6 ('*Mousa No.2*'); *R (Mousa)* (No.2) v *Secretary of State for Defence* [2013] EWHC 1412 (Admin).

27 *R (Al-Skeini)* v. *Secretary of State for Defence* [2008] 1 AC 153, at [93] (Carswell LJ) (*Al-Skeini* (HL)).

28 See *The Report of the Baha Mousa Public Inquiry*, HC 1452-I (8 September 2011) vol. 1, pt. 1, ch. 2 [1.36] (*BMPI*).

29 President Bush declared the hostilities that began on 20 March 2003 at an end in early May 2003.

30 Convention for the Protection of Human Rights and Fundamental Freedoms, Rome, 4 November 1950, in force 3 December 1953, 213 UNTS 222, art. 1.

adopted a restrictive approach to human rights law (HRL) although each court had different justifications. The Grand Chamber of the European Court of Human Rights (ECtHR) was critical of the UK *Al-Skeini* judgment. In the Grand Chamber HRL concerns prevailed over state and military interests.

The Divisional Court in *Al-Skeini* v. *Secretary of State for Defence*[31] held that the ECHR and the HR Act applied to Mousa, but not the other deceased victims. The Court considered that in relation to Mousa, the United Kingdom's procedural duties in art. 2 of the ECHR had been breached and, if the HR Act had been applicable, would have been breached in the other five cases. The government's arguments had two aspects. First, the procedural obligations to hold a public inquiry pursuant to the ECHR did not include Iraqi deaths as the Convention did not apply outside member states of the Council of Europe. Second, the HR Act could not be applied beyond the territorial limits of the United Kingdom. Thus, the question arose whether the ECHR applied to the United Kingdom's actions in Iraq.

After an extensive review of the ECtHR jurisprudence on art. 1, the Divisional Court followed the decision of *Banković* v. *Belgium*[32] in which the Grand Chamber held that 'jurisdiction' is 'essentially territorial'.[33] The Divisional Court gave a narrow reading to the exceptions to this proposition. They considered the exceptions under 'state agent authority' (SAA) and 'effective control of an area' (ECA) and concluded that the exceptions had effectively been collapsed into just ECA.[34]

The Mousa matter was held to be within jurisdiction, as at the time of his death he was 'in premises controlled by British forces analogous to diplomatic or consular premises, vessels flying the British flag and aircraft registered in the UK',[35] presumably on the grounds that the base was a limited quasi-territory of the United Kingdom. Underpinning this reading was a belief that the ECHR's rights and obligations could not be 'divided and tailored' to suit circumstances and that *Banković* had limited the application of the Convention to Council of Europe legal space.[36]

31 *R (Al-Skeini)* v. *Secretary of State for Defence* [2004] EWHC 2911 (*Al-Skeini* (DC)).

32 (2001) 11 BHRC 435 (*Banković*). 33 Ibid., at [61].

34 *Al-Skeini* (DC) [2004] EWHC 2911, at [257], [259], [270] (Rix LJ and Forbes J).

35 *R (Al-Skeini)* v. *Secretary of State for Defence* [2008] AC 153, at [97] (Carswell L J). The Secretary of State conceded Mousa was within UK jurisdiction.

36 *Al-Skeini* (DC) [2004] EWHC 2911, at [259] (Rix LJ and Forbes J).

The Court of Appeal affirmed the Divisional Court decision but adopted different reasons. It considered the exceptions of SAA and ECA in a more expansive manner.[37] The Court held that the ECHR applied where a Contracting Party:

> had *effective control of the territory* of another State, ... *irrespective of whether the area in question came within the territory of one of the States' Parties to the European Convention* or not. In principle, therefore, the Convention was capable of being applied to the population of that part of Iraq occupied by the UK, *provided* that the UK had had *effective control of that part of Iraq at the relevant time.*[38]

A problem arose in the way in which the Court interpreted effective control. It found, subjectively, that the United Kingdom did not have effective control due to the volatile circumstances in post-combat operations in Iraq, with little or no control over a barely functioning administration system.[39] The Court considered the ECtHR jurisprudence on SAA, accepting that where agents of the state exercise 'authority' over an individual, they are subject to the ECHR.[40] This included a situation like Mousa's, most likely from the moment he was arrested. The Court of Appeal did not, however, extend the 'authority and control' exception to the five other Iraqi deaths.[41] Brooke LJ accepted that both SAA and ECA exceptions were valid but read the ECA exception as limiting the applicability of SAA.[42]

Lord Justice Sedley expressed doubts but did not dissent because he found no endorsement in the ECtHR's jurisprudence. Sedley LJ nevertheless considered that 'effective control' did not require a high degree of control necessary to apply the full range of the Convention rights. Sedley LJ stated, '[e]ven if British forces in South East Iraq had lacked any real control over what happened from hour to hour, the one thing which they did control was their own recourse to legal force'.[43]

[37] *R (Al-Skeini)* v. *Secretary of State for Defence* [2005] EWCA Civ 1609, at [80]–[81] (Brooke LJ) (*Al-Skeini* (CA)).

[38] Ibid., at [80]–[81] (Brooke LJ). (emphasis added).

[39] Ibid., at [124] (Brooke LJ).

[40] Ibid., at [107]–[111] (Brooke LJ).

[41] Ibid., at [110] (Brooke LJ) 'If troops deliberately and effectively restrict someone's liberty he is under their control. This did not happen in any of these five cases.'

[42] Ibid., at [82]–[83] (Brooke LJ), Richards LJ considered such a difficult question should be left for the House of Lords [210].

[43] Ibid., at [197] Sedley LJ added that '... it sits ill in the mouth of a state which has helped to displace and dismantle by force another nation's civil authority to plead that, as an occupying power, it has so little control that it cannot be responsible for securing the

The House of Lords[44] dismissed the Secretary of State's appeal against the extraterritorial application of the HR Act regarding Mousa and dismissed the appeals of the five other claimants, confirming the lower Court's decision. Lord Bingham considered that s 6 of the HR Act did not have a coextensive jurisdiction with the ECHR based on the presumption that, unless expressly stated, UK legislation does not operate extraterritorially. The remaining judges disagreed with Lord Bingham[45] and considered the HR Act operated coextensively with the ECHR (not least because to limit it extraterritorially would defeat the purpose of 'bringing rights home').[46] After review of the cases the Court chose to follow, as had the lower courts, *Banković*, which was considered the watershed authority on art. 1.[47]

The House of Lords did not wish to develop conflicting case law with the ECHR on the reach of the Convention. Further, as the Convention rights could not be 'divided and tailored', Rodger LJ concluded that jurisdiction 'can arise only where the contracting state has such effective control of the territory of another state that it could secure to everyone in the territory all the rights and freedoms in section 1 of the Convention'.[48] In other words the HR Act, while coextensive with the Convention, was limited to the territory of the United Kingdom and excluded citizens of non-contracting State parties, (e.g. Iraq), except Mousa who was considered to be within jurisdiction on the narrow basis established by the Divisional Court.[49]

population's basic rights' [194]. See also *Al-Skeini* v. *United Kingdom* (2011) 53 EHRR 18, at [13] (Bonello J).

44 *R (Al-Skeini)* v. *Secretary of State for Defence* [2008] 1 AC 153. The court martial *R* v. *Payne*, General Court Martial (2006), Charge Sheet (19 July 2005) www.publications.parliament.uk/pa/ld200506/ldlwa/50719ws1.pdf while the matter was before the House of Lords. Judge Advocate McKinnon ruled Mendonca, Crowcroft and Fallon had no case to answer. Stacey's charge was dismissed, as were two charges against Payne. Peebles and Davies were found not guilty at court martial. Payne pleaded guilty to one offence.

45 *Al-Skeini* (HL) [2008] 1 AC 153, at [95] (Carswell LJ), the two issues were '(a) whether the HR Act applies to acts or omissions of the state agencies ... outside the territorial boundaries of the UK (b) if so, whether the deceased persons were within the jurisdiction of the UK'.

46 Ibid., at [58] (Rodger LJ); [138]–[139] (Brown LJ), the purpose of the HR Act legislation was for the UK courts to have greater control over the application of rights; But *cf. Al-Skeini* (CA) [2004] EWHC 2911, at [302] (Rix LJ & Forbes J) 'It is hard to say that the 1998 Act was designed to bring rights home in [the case of the five Iraqi applicants], for the UK is in no way their home: in their case, it is not their rights which are brought home, but the UK's responsibilities.'

47 *Al-Skeini* (HL) [2008] 1 AC 153, at [108] (Brown LJ).

48 Ibid., at [79] (Rodger LJ).

49 Ibid., at [132] (Brown LJ).

The Grand Chamber in *Al-Skeini*[50] rejected the UK Courts' decisions on the application of the ECHR. The Grand Chamber unanimously found that the United Kingdom as an Occupying Power in the immediate aftermath of invasion had to comply with the Convention and that the deceased Iraqi citizens therefore fell within jurisdiction.[51] The Grand Chamber considered that UK soldiers:

> engaged in security operations in Basra during the period in question, *exercised authority and control over individuals killed in the course of such security operations*, so as to establish a jurisdictional link between the deceased and the UK for the purposes of Article 1 of the Convention. [52]

The Grand Chamber rejected a key point that had been accepted by the UK courts, namely that the British did not have actual factual control over many events upon which the cases were founded. Judge Bonello in his separate concurring opinion in the Grand Chamber forcefully stated:

> the UK went a long and eloquent way in its attempt to establish that it did not exercise jurisdiction over the area assigned to it. It just stopped short of sharing with the Court who did. Who was the mysterious, faceless rival which, instead of it, exercised executive, legislative and judicial authority for three years and more over the area delegated to the UK.[53]

In *Al-Skeini* three British courts reached the same outcome in relation to the non-application of human rights extraterritorially for alleged victims of military actions. While some may see it as a concern about the limits of the courts' jurisdiction, the courts' judgments show a persistent preference for the military and executive over and above the human rights of the individual. This approach has resulted in consequences for UK soldiers and their human rights. After the UK courts in *Al-Skeini* deemed the ECHR was not applicable, the next question was whether the application of this reasoning applied to soldiers while serving in Iraq.

[50] *Al-Skeini* v. *United Kingdom* (2011) 53 EHRR 18 (*Al-Skeini* (GC)). See further, *Jaloud* v. *The Netherlands* (European Court of Human Rights, Grand Chamber, Application No. 47708/08, 20 November 2014).

[51] Five applicants received €17,000 each for the failure to investigate their relatives' deaths, and €50,000 each for costs.

[52] *Al-Skeini* (GC) (2011) 53 EHRR 18, at [149] (emphasis added).

[53] Ibid., at [34].

B *The human rights of soldiers – are the UK courts changing their deferential approach?*

The following cases reflect a line of UK jurisprudence demonstrating an expanding trend in the reach of human rights requirements in matters involving defence and the military. *Al-Skeini* has influenced the courts when considering the treatment of soldiers. This change has been recent and currently the scales are still tipped in favour of a deferential approach. In *R (Gentle)* v. *Prime Minister* (*Gentle*),[54] the Court took a deferential approach to an application for an art. 2 investigation into the deaths of two UK soldiers who died in Iraq. The application was dismissed at all levels of the UK courts, as it required a determination of the lawfulness of the executive's decision to invade Iraq.[55] Lord Bingham stated:

> the Convention was not intended to deal with the question of *jus ad bellum* and whether military action was appropriate, noting '... the restraint traditionally shown by the courts in ruling on what has been called high policy – peace and war.'[56]

The Court of Appeal was similarly reluctant, stating:

> Absent the Convention, the starting point is the proposition that issues relating to the conduct of international relations and military operations outside the UK are not justiciable ... they are governed by international and not domestic law.[57]

Baroness Hale in *Gentle* indicated the beginnings of unease by raising 'just war' principles, and acknowledging it would nevertheless be useful to determine whether the decision to invade Iraq was lawful:

> If the use of force was lawful, it would be of some comfort to know that their sons had died in a just cause. If it was not, there might at least be some public acknowledgement and attribution of responsibility and lessons learned for the future.[58]

[54] [2008] AC 1356, at [1] (Bingham LJ) 'Fusilier ... Gentle ... was killed by a roadside bomb on 28 June 2004. Trooper ... Clarke was ... killed by "friendly fire" on 25 March 2003.'

[55] *Gentle* [2008] AC 1356, at [6]. [56] Ibid., at [8].

[57] *R (Gentle)* v. *Prime Minister* [2006] EWCA Civ 1689, at [26]: 'the Convention respects ... the principle that there remain some areas which are essentially matters for the executive and not the courts' [75].

[58] *Gentle* [2008] AC 1356, at [53] (Baroness Hale) and further [50]: 'A state which expects its soldiers to obey their orders irrespective of their own views on the lawfulness of those

The question of the applicability of the HR Act to soldiers operating extraterritorially arose again in *R (Smith)* v. *Oxfordshire Assistant Deputy Coroner*.[59] Private Jason Smith died of heatstroke on a UK military base in Iraq in 2003 and, after a quashed coronial inquest, his mother sought an inquiry into her son's death pursuant to art. 2 of the ECHR.[60] The Ministry of Defence (MoD) conceded, based on *Al-Skeini*, that Private Smith was within jurisdiction. However, an advisory opinion was sought on whether Private Smith would have been within the United Kingdom's jurisdiction had he not died on the base. In approaching the hypothetical question, the lower courts applied the personal jurisdiction model from the ECHR case law to find that, by virtue of being in the UK military, Private Smith, no matter where he was in Iraq, was within the UK's authority and control, and accordingly within its jurisdiction.[61] The Court highlighted an absurdity in the *Al-Skeini* cases:

> *There is no sensible reason for not holding that there is a sufficient link between the soldier as victim and the UK whether he is at a base or not.*[62]

The Supreme Court provided its advisory determination despite the concern of some judges.[63] The Court held that the HR Act did not apply to soldiers 'beyond the wire' and so treated UK soldiers and Iraqi civilians alike.[64]

The issue came before the UK Court of Appeal[65] and the Supreme Court[66] in *Smith* v. *Ministry of Defence.* The claims relate to incidents in which UK soldiers were killed or injured in Iraq 'beyond the wire' due to

orders should, it seems to me, owe a correlative duty to its soldiers to ensure that those orders are lawful.'

59 [2011] 1 AC 1. 60 Ibid., at [1] (Phillips LJ).

61 *R (Smith)* v. *Oxfordshire Assistant Deputy Coroner* [2009] 3 WLR 1099, at [52] (*Smith* v. *Oxfordshire* (CA)), at [60] (Sir Anthony Clarke MR) the question of jurisdiction was not decided in *Gentle*.

62 Ibid., at [30] (Sir Anthony Clarke MR) (emphasis added).

63 *R (Smith)* v. *Oxfordshire Assistant Deputy Coroner* [2011] 1 AC 1, at [2] (Phillips LJ); [159] (Mance LJ). Three judges expressed concern at providing an advisory opinion at [129] (Walker LJ); [135] [135] (Lady Hale), and [220] (Collins LJ) (*Smith* v. *Oxfordshire* (SC)).

64 *Pritchard* v. *The United Kingdom* (European Court of Human Rights, Fourth Section, Application No. 1573/11, 18 March 2014) was lodged on 20 December 2010. The case concerned the application of the ECHR to soldiers 'beyond the wire' but was removed from the list following a friendly settlement on 18 March 2014.

65 [2012] EWCA Civ 1365 (CA) (19 October 2012) (*Smith* (CA)).

66 [2014] AC 52 (*Smith (No. 2)*).

either faulty equipment, or poor training and command.[67] The claimants in *Smith* conceded that, as the death or injury occurred on the battlefield, based on *Al-Skeini* it was outside the ECHR's jurisdiction. However, they argued that as decisions regarding pre-deployment training and choice of equipment occurred on British territory, they were within jurisdiction based on the reasoning in *Soering* v. *United Kingdom*.[68] In *Soering* the ECtHR held that the United Kingdom was responsible for a decision made within jurisdiction, which may cause breach of an individual's Convention rights outside its jurisdiction.[69] The MoD argued that there was no breach of art. 2 or a claim in negligence.[70] First, they argued that control of military operations and the procurement or use of military equipment, like training, are issues of a political and military nature.[71] Second, at common law, the doctrine of combat immunity applied, and the claims in tort were not 'fair, just and reasonable' within the *Caparo* principle of negligence.[72] Third, they argued, based on *Al-Skeini*, that the death or injury occurred outside art. 1 jurisdiction.[73]

Some of the same Supreme Court judges in *Smith (No. 2)* had previously in *Smith* v. *Oxfordshire* adopted divergent positions demonstrating varying degrees of deference. While the majority in *Smith* v. *Oxfordshire* stood by the classic position, confirming that the ECHR does not apply to the armed forces as matters of armed conflict are non-justiciable,[74] three Law Lords took an opposing position as demonstrated by Lord Kerr:

> I do not believe that the fear of tactical decisions taken in the field by military commanders being subject to painstaking dissection by the courts is justified or that it should deter this court from declaring that when our government commits our armed forces to wars in foreign territories, it cannot deny them the protection that the Convention affords.[75]

67 *Smith* v. *Ministry of Defence* [2011] EWHC 1676 (QB) (30 June 2011), at [1], [3] (Owen LJ) (*Smith* (QB)). The claims fell in two categories, The Snatch Land Rover claims and The Challenger claims.

68 (European Court of Human Rights, Plenary, Application No. 14038/88, 7 July 1989) (*Soering*).

69 *Smith* (QB) [2011] EWHC 1676 (QB) (30 June 2011), at [46] (Owen LJ) limited *Soering* to its facts.

70 Ibid.; [2012] EWCA Civ 1365 (CA) (19 October 2012); *Smith (No. 2)* [2014] AC 52.

71 Ibid., at [6] (Owen LJ).

72 *Smith (No. 2)* [2014] AC 52, at [169] (Carnwath LJ).

73 Ibid., at [45]–[50] (Hope LJ); *R (Al-Skeini)* v. *Secretary of State for Defence* [2008] 1 AC 153.

74 *Smith* v. *Oxfordshire* (SC) [2011] 1 AC 1, at [308] (Collins LJ).

75 Ibid., at [339] (Kerr LJ); [195] (Mance LJ) and [136] (Hale LJ). Both Kerr LJ and Hale LJ were in the majority in *Smith (No. 2)* [2014] AC 52, Mance LJ was in dissent.

The Court of Appeal in *Smith* side-stepped any determination that the advisory opinion in *Smith* v. *Oxfordshire*[76] was binding.[77] Given the opportunity to resolve the seeming difference between *Al-Skeini* (HL) and *Al-Skeini* (GC), the Court of Appeal gave a narrow reading to *Al-Skeini* (GC) limiting the ECHR's application to control over civilians such as in internment situations, and not (unlike the Court of Appeal in *Smith* v. *Oxfordshire*)[78] control over soldiers based on *ratione personae.*[79] The Court of Appeal avoided the potential confrontation between the UK and Strasburg courts by distinguishing between soldiers and civilians. Thus, *Al-Skeini* (GC) was considered not to be in conflict with *Smith* v. *Oxfordshire*[80] decided prior to *Al-Skeini* (GC). Moses LJ in *Smith* (CA) observed that not only were there 'good policy reasons for not'[81] extending Convention jurisdiction to the armed forces operating beyond their base, but issues relating to armed hostilities are essentially non-justiciable.[82]

On appeal, in *Smith (No. 2)*, the Supreme Court changed direction, unanimously accepting that the art. 1 jurisdiction does extend to UK soldiers extraterritorially securing the protection of art. 2, the right to life for soldiers operating 'beyond the wire'.[83]

Reluctance to intrude into the military domain based on ECHR rights is not as strong when the courts consider liability under tort law. Here the UK courts do not generally shy away from consideration of military matters. Owen J in *Smith* (Divisional Court) was not impressed with the MoD's arguments and held 'that there is no basis for holding that in principle claims for personal injury or death of members of the armed forces in combat are not justiciable'.[84] This was confirmed in both *Smith* (CA) and *Smith (No. 2)* with the Courts affirming the inapplicability of

76 *Smith* v. *Oxfordshire* (SC) [2011] 1 AC 1, at [60] (Phillips LJ).

77 *Smith* (CA) [2012] EWCA Civ 1365 (CA) (13 August 2013), at [16] (Moses LJ).

78 *Smith* v. *Oxfordshire* (CA) [2009] 3 WLR 1099, at [30] (Sir Anthony Clarke MR).

79 *Smith* (CA) [2012] EWCA Civ 1365 (CA) (13 August 2013), at [26]–[30] (Moses LJ) 'The soldiers did not fall within the scope of the United Kingdom's Convention jurisprudence. That conclusion makes it unnecessary to resolve the detailed and lengthy debate as to the extent of the substantive obligations . . . implicit within Article 2' [32].

80 *Smith* v. *Oxfordshire* (SC) [2011] 1 AC 1.

81 *Smith* (CA) [2012] EWCA Civ 1365 (CA) (13 August 2013), at [20] (Moses LJ) citing *Smith* v. *Oxfordshire* (SC) [2011] 1 AC 1, at [52]–[60] (Phillips LJ), [91], [104] (Hope LJ).

82 *Smith* (CA) [2012] EWCA Civ 1365 (CA) (13 August 2013) (CA), at [20] (Moses LJ) referring to *Smith* v. *Oxfordshire* (SC) [2011] 1 AC 1, at [125], [127] (Roger LJ) and [308] (Collins LJ).

83 *Smith (No. 2)* [2014] AC 52, at [55] (Hope LJ).

84 *Smith* (QB) [2011] EWHC 1676 (QB) (30 June 2011), at [96] (Owen LJ).

the defence of combat immunity in non-active operation situations, and that questions of fair, just and reasonable application of the law of negligence require evidence to be heard on the question of fact in order for it to be determined at trial.[85]

Turning the tide somewhat, consideration of combat immunity was addressed recently in *R (Long)* v. *Secretary of State for Defence.*[86] In this matter, the mother of a soldier killed along with five others by an armed mob in Iraq on 24 June 2003 sought judicial review requiring the Secretary of State to hold an independent investigation that satisfied art. 2 of the ECHR. The matter had been through numerous internal military enquiries and a coronial inquest. At issue for the claimant, Mrs Long, was the desire to hold accountable someone in the chain of command for negligent observance of a command order that patrols should always carry an Iridium satellite telephone. This case therefore fell under the positive obligation within art. 2 that required the state to protect the lives of its armed force members, as opposed to the other substantive obligation under art. 2 dealing with the unlawful taking of life by state agents. Justice Leggatt deferred to military operational necessity[87] and considered that the impact of subjecting military command to '[t]he process of investigating and litigating such claims . . . would involve a heavy burden of time and resources.'[88] Combat immunity is a public policy, Leggatt J asserted, in which the community accepts that there are circumstances, such as in military operations, where to impose a legal duty of care to avoid negligent actions would be unfair if it gave rise to actions in civilian courts.[89]

Overall, these cases confirm that UK courts, for the most part, take a deferential approach to the military. Despite *Smith (No. 2)* showing a less deferential attitude, the Court recommended great caution, suggesting there would be little likelihood that the claimants could prove a breach of the implied positive obligation under art. 2(1) of the ECHR given the wide discretion that should be accorded the military in the planning and conduct of its operations.[90] However, the cases also demonstrate that some judges are more inclined to intrude further into military matters

[85] *Smith* (CA) [2012] EWCA Civ 1365 (CA) (19 October 2012), at [37], [55], [62] (Moses LJ). *Smith (No. 2)* [2014] AC 52, at [95], [98] (Hope LJ). But *cf. Smith (No. 2)* [2014] AC 52, the dissenting opinions on the applicability of the law of negligence in military contexts [136] (Mance LJ), [156] (Carnwath LJ).

[86] *R (Long)* v. *Secretary of State for Defence* [2014] EWHC 2391 (Admin).

[87] Ibid., at [80]–[84] (Leggatt J). [88] Ibid., at [79]. [89] Ibid., at [77]–[78].

[90] *Smith (No. 2)* [2014] AC 52, at [81] (Hope L).

than previously. The human rights concerns arising from military actions over detainees in the Iraq and Afghanistan wars have particularly challenged the UK courts.

C The UK courts' response to detainees during war

A number of cases dealing with detainees, particularly those held outside conflict zones, have implications for the courts' future preparedness to hold the executive accountable. Although an extensive review of the cases is not undertaken here, it appears that cases on detainees are expanding the scope and intensity of judicial oversight and thus civilian interaction with, or control over, the military. The UK courts have used a number of devices including the application of administrative law principles, the enforcement of habeas corpus writs and even international law in their attempts to ensure executive action regarding the treatment of detainees in the Iraq and Afghanistan conflicts is within the rule of law.[91] In *Mohammed* v. *Ministry of Defence; Qasim and others* v. *Secretary of State*[92] the Court ruled that MoD was liable to compensate Afghanis who had been detained unlawfully 'in pursuit of military objectives which went beyond the legal powers available in the UK'.[93] In reaching this decision, the Court rejected MoD claims that the *lex specialis* was IHL and that HRL, such as art. 5 of the ECHR, was qualified by IHL.[94] The Grand Chamber of the ECtHR in *Hassan* v. *United Kingdom*[95] confirmed the interrelation of IHL and HRL, in particular as regards the right to liberty in an international armed conflict. These decisions demonstrate that the door is opening to judicial consideration of issues traditionally considered immune from review, even matters of high policy relating to war and defence.[96] They also, however,

[91] See, for example, *R (Abbasi)* v. *Secretary of State for Foreign and Commonwealth Affairs* [2003] UKHRR 76, at [64], [106] (Phillips LJ). See Stephanie Palmer, 'Arbitrary Detention in Guantanamo Bay: Legal Limbo in the Land of the Free' (2003) 62(1) *Cambridge Law Journal*, p. 6, at 7. See also the related case of *R (Al-Rawi)* v. *Secretary of State for Foreign and Commonwealth Affairs* [2008] QB 289; *R (Maya Evans)* v. *Secretary of State for Defence* [2010] EWHC 1445 (Admin).

[92] *Mohammed* v. *Ministry of Defence* [2014] EWHC 1369 (QB).

[93] Ibid., at [424] (Leggatt J). [94] Ibid., at [288]–[292].

[95] *Hassan* v. *United Kingdom* (European Court of Human Rights, Grand Chamber, Application No. 29750/09, 16 September 2014).

[96] McGoldrick, 'The Boundaries of Justiciability', above n. 22. See, for example, *R (Al-Saadoon)* v. *Secretary of State for Defence* [2010] QB 486; *R (Hassan)* v. *Secretary of State for Defence* [2009] EWHC 309 (Admin); *Hassan* v. *United Kingdom* (European Court of Human Rights, Grand Chamber, Application No. 29750/09, 16 September 2014); *Ismail* v. *Secretary of State for Defence* [2013] EWHC 3032 (Admin); *R (Mousa)* v. *Secretary of State for Defence (No. 2)*

demonstrate the limits of courts when attempting to hold the executive to account. For example, the act of state doctrine (limiting judicial oversight of another government's actions within its own territory)[97] may prevent the courts adjudicating on the actions of the armed forces when participating in a multinational force. Such actions may include detention of civilians, but the question arises whether bars to the exercise of jurisdiction operate when the rights of detainees are violated.[98] In *Mohammed* v. *Secretary of State for Defence* Leggatt J stated:

> The question whether UK armed forces acted lawfully under Afghan law in detaining SM is plainly justiciable. It does not require determination of any matter a court is unsuited to deal with. Quite the opposite.[99]

Cases have signalled that the prerogative cannot operate as a veil to hide fundamental human rights abuses even if foreign state action is involved. In *Rahmatullah* v. *Secretary of State for Foreign and Commonwealth Affairs*[100] the Court of Appeal considered an application for habeas corpus. The appellant, a Pakistani national, was handed over to the United States by the British after his capture in Iraq and transferred to Afghanistan, without the United Kingdom's knowledge. In 2010, the United States determined that the applicant was not a threat and could be released to Pakistan. However, he remained in detention in Afghanistan. The applicant contended that, due to the provisions of a Memorandum of Understanding between the United Kingdom and the United States, the applicant was sufficiently in the control of the UK government to support the issue of the writ of habeas corpus. However, the government argued that if the writ was issued, it would require the United Kingdom to make a request to a foreign sovereign power, which would be 'inappropriate and futile'.[101] The Court of Appeal reasoned that the doubt and

[2013] EWHC 1412 (Admin); *Al-Sadoon v. Secretary of State for Defence* (2015) EWHC 715 (Admin) (*Al-Saadoon*).

[97] See, for example, W. Harrison Moore, *Act of State in English Law* (London, John Murray, Albemarle Street, 1906).

[98] See, for example, *Al-Jedda* (CA) [2012] EWCA Civ 358 (CA) (29 March 2012); *R* (*Gentle*) v. *Prime Minister* [2008] AC 1356; *R (Al-Skeini)* v. *Secretary of State for Defence* [2008] AC 153; *Mohammed* v. *Ministry of Defence* [2014] EWHC 1369 (QB), at [383], [395], [397] (Leggatt J); *Hassan* v. *United Kingdom* (European Court of Human Rights, Grand Chamber, Application No. 29750/09, 16 September 2014).

[99] *Mohammed* v. *Ministry of Defence* [2014] EWHC 1369 (QB), at [381] (Leggatt J).

[100] [2011] EWCA Civ 1540; [2012] EWCA Civ 182 (CA); *Secretary of State for Foreign and Commonwealth Affairs* v. *Rahmatullah* [2013] 1 AC 614 (*Rahmatullah* (SC)).

[101] *Rahmatullah* v. *Secretary of State for Foreign and Commonwealth Affairs* [2011] EWCA Civ 1540 (CA), at [21] (Neuberger MR).

uncertainty around whether the Secretaries of State had lost control of the appellant was sufficient to justify an order for habeas corpus.[102] Crucially, the Court found that the writ should not be withheld on the basis of diplomatic relations or the possibility of entering forbidden areas such as foreign policy.[103]

The overtures of the British authorities following the issue of the writ were rebuffed by the US government, which refused to release the applicant. Lord Neuberger MR subsequently conceded that the writ did not result in the 'body' being brought before the Court but concluded that the writ was not a 'pointless exercise ... it performed its minimum function of requiring the UK Government to account for its responsibility for the applicant's detention, and to attempt to get him released'.[104] Neuberger MR suggested that this demonstrated the role of the courts in ensuring 'that the executive complies, as far as it can, with its legal duties to individuals, in particular when they are detained'.[105] He also acknowledged that the court 'as a domestic tribunal ... cannot go beyond its jurisdiction, and that jurisdiction does not extend to the US military authorities in Afghanistan'.[106] The Supreme Court affirmed the refusal of the writ but two judges strongly dissented and considered that notwithstanding 'the polite diplomatic' letter from the United States, a further request from the United Kingdom was demanded to answer the question of control.[107] Such reasoning demonstrates a reach into sacred territory and the protective function of habeas corpus.

Despite cases demonstrating an increasing preparedness to investigate matters concerning the military, it is likely that the courts will follow the deferential approach for some time yet. *Al-Skeini* demonstrates that when the UK courts have considered the interests of the military against human rights obligations, their deferential stance has consequences for the civil–military relationship. Not only does it escalate the cost, with further court proceedings and inquiries, but it can give rise to damaging public perceptions of the military, widening the civil–military gap.[108] Instead of the MoD fighting *Al-Skeini* all the way to the ECtHR,

102 *Rahmatullah* CA [2011] EWCA Civ 1540. 103 Ibid., at [47]–[48] (Neuberger MR).

104 *Rahmatullah* v. *Secretary of State for Foreign and Commonwealth Affairs* [2012] EWCA 182 (CA), at [17] (Neuberger MR).

105 Ibid., at [17]. 106 Ibid.

107 *Rahmatullah* (SC) [2013] 1 AC 614 (SC), at [107] (Phillips LJ), [115] (Reed LJ) raised a concern but reserved their opinion, [129]–[131] (Lady Hale and Carnwath LJ).

108 Peter D. Feaver and Richard H. Kohn (eds.), *Soldiers and Civilians. The Civil – Military Gap and American National Security* (Cambridge, MA, MIT Press, 2001).

encouraged by the position of the UK courts, the art. 2 investigations could have occurred in a much timelier and less controversial manner. The resources, costs and angst may have been prevented if the UK courts had decided, as the ECtHR ultimately did, in favour of the application of the ECHR to the Iraqi civilians.

IV Consequences for civil–military relations

The demand of civil–military theory, that civilians control the military, extends to the role of the civilian courts. When the courts adopt a deferential position, they can risk shirking their duty of judicial superintendence. The UK civil courts' approach towards the ECHR's extraterritorial operation has contributed to the uncertainty in response to a military discipline system that does not address adequately the acts of its soldiers. This may well damage the civil–military relationship.

Colonel Jorge Mendonca (the most senior military member implicated in Mousa's death) has written about the impact the perceptions of the military by the UK public has had on the morale of the British forces:

> your return seems at best to be a matter of supreme indifference to the public ... You are expected to disappear quietly from view ... Increasingly, it seems that we soldiers serve a nation that considers us an embarrassment that simply doesn't want to know about us.[109]

In such a situation, the civil–military covenant is damaged, with veterans suffering depression at the end of their service[110] and the public disapproving of the state's war involvement.[111] With innumerable inquiries and yet little foreseeable change, one can conclude that when the UK courts treat the military with deference, the military has no motivation to change.

109 Colonel Jorge Mendonca, 'If We No Longer Respect Our Fighting Men and Women, the Future of Britain Itself Is in Peril' (3 October 2007) *Daily Mail* (London), www.dailymail.co.uk/news/article-485306/If-longer-respect-fighting-men-women-future-Britain-peril.html.

110 A. Iversen et al., 'What Happens to UK Veterans when They Leave the Armed Forces?' (2005) 15(2) *European Journal of Public Health*, p. 175. See also Professor Hew Strachan et al., 'Report of the Task Force on the Military Covenant' (MoD, September 2010).

111 Helen McCartney, 'The Military Covenant and the Civil – Military Contract in Britain' (2010) 86(2) *International Affairs*, p. 411, at 415: 'ICM poll ... found only 25 per cent of the public support current British involvement in Afghanistan and a tiny 20 per cent supported the war in Iraq.' See also Anthony Forster, 'The Military Covenant and British Civil – Military Relations: Letting the Genie Out of the Bottle' (2012) 38 *Armed Forces & Society*, p. 273.

This resistance is evident in military actions surrounding the Iraq Historic Allegations Team (IHAT), which was set up to inquire into the allegations of incidents of abuse of Iraqis between 2003 and 2008.[112] IHAT, an internal inquiry mechanism, has been criticised for lacking independence.[113] This lack of independence has been tested before the courts. Initially at the Divisional Court level, the IHAT investigation was held to satisfy the requirements of a Convention art. 3 independent investigation.[114] This decision was successfully appealed to the Court of Appeal, in November 2011, with the Court finding that the IHAT team could not be 'perceived' to be sufficiently independent (hierarchically, institutionally and practically) to satisfy the requirements of an art. 3 investigation.[115] The Court of Appeal in *Mousa* stated:

> it is impossible to avoid the conclusion that IHAT lacks the requisite independence . . . the Provost Branch members of IHAT are participants in investigating allegations which, if true, occurred at a time when Provost Branch members were plainly involved in matters surrounding the detention and internment of suspected persons in Iraq[116]

The government response to the Court of Appeal's decision took over three months and involved removing the Royal Military Police members from the team and placing the Navy's Provost Marshal in charge. This limited response, demonstrating resistance by the government and the military, did not satisfy the defendants, who have sought an independent judicial inquiry.[117] In 2013 the Divisional Court QB *R (Mousa)* v. *Secretary of State for Defence (No 2)*[118] appointed a designated Judge, Leggatt J, to oversee inquisitorial-type inquiries that would satisfy an art. 2 investigation, while not incurring unreasonable resource demands

[112] See, for example, Eileen Kersey, 'UK High Court Independent Inquiry: Iraqis Claim Abuse' (29 January 2013) *Digital Journal*, www.digitaljournal.com/article/342363.

[113] *R (Mousa)* v. *Secretary of State for Defence* [2011] EWCA Civ 1334, at [16]–[17] (Kay LJ) (*Mousa* (CA)); *R (Mousa)* v. *Secretary of State for Defence* [2012] HRLR 6; *R (Mousa)* v. *Secretary of State for Defence (No. 2)* [2013] EWHC 2941 (Admin).

[114] *R (Mousa)* v. *Secretary of State for Defence* [2010] EWHC 3304 (Admin). Article 3 (the prohibition of torture) imposes an obligation on a state to carry out an independent and effective investigation when torture is alleged to have occurred within its jurisdiction. See further, *Al-Saadoon*, at [20],[199] (Leggatt J).

[115] *Mousa* (CA) [2011] EWCA Civ 1334, at [38] (Kay LJ).

[116] Ibid., at [36].

[117] *R (Mousa)* v. *Secretary of State for Defence* [2012] HRLR 6. See further, European Center for Constitutional and Human Rights and Public Interest Lawyers, 'Communication to the Office of the Prosecutor of the International Criminal Court. The Responsibility of Officials of the United Kingdom for War Crimes Involving Systematic Detainee Abuse in Iraq from 2003–2008' (2014) (10 January).

[118] *R (Mousa)* v. *Secretary of State for Defence (No. 2)* [2013] EWHC 2941 (Admin).

and further costs. In so doing, the court required the Secretary of State to be accountable for resumption of art. 3 investigations within the year.[119] The IHAT investigation, it has been suggested, is likely to reach anywhere between £50m and £100m and not end before 2016.[120]

Certainly, the courts appear to be finding their way in this new territory of human rights and its significance for the civil–military relationship. The decision by the House of Lords in *Al-Skeini* led to the Secretary of State for Defence providing a public inquiry into the death of Mousa and changes to the MoD policy on questioning and interrogation techniques.[121] Due to the Grand Chamber's decision in *Al-Skeini* the UK has had to consider possible further inquiries and prosecutions.[122] Despite the inquiries, there is still no 'root and branch' resolution of the issues raised by *Al-Skeini*. The six acquitted defendants in the Mousa court martial considered their lives and careers destroyed. The MoD perceived that the inquiries had undermined its ability to do its job, by diminishing the regard for the defence force and undermining morale and operational ability.[123] The victims' families felt they had to struggle to obtain justice over a long period with no one successfully prosecuted. Organisations such as the ICRC and Amnesty International were concerned with the actions of the Coalition Provisional Authority and their lack of responsiveness.[124] The overall inadequacies of both the legal and political responses call into question the entire civil–military relationship.

The resistance by the military to the investigations and the increased civilian court and public oversight that is required by the HR Act and the

119 Ibid., at [47] (John Thomas J).

120 See Sean Rayment and David Barrett, '£57m and Rising: The Cost of Inquiries into British "War Crimes"' *The Telegraph UK*, 25 August 2012 www.telegraph.co.uk/news/uknews/defence/9499330/57m-and-rising-the-cost-of-inquiries-into-British-war-crimes.html; Angus Crawford, 'Iraq Historic Allegations Team Probe "Is a Shambles"' (2011) *BBC News UK* www.bbc.co.uk/news/uk/-13757766.

121 *BMPI*, above n. 28: Over three years: 388 potential witnesses, 277 witnesses called, 10,600 documents and 115 sitting days at a cost of £13 million not including MoD costs. Sir William Gage delivered the final report containing 73 recommendations and a table of names linked with actions that could lead to further charges. See *R (Hussein)* v. *Secretary of State for Defence* [2104] EWCA Civ 1087.

122 For example, *Al Sweady* Inquiry commenced 25 November 2009 and finalised 17 December 2014 www.alsweadyinq; Caroline Hawley, 'Al-Sweady Inquiry Opens in UK into Deaths of Iraqis' *BBC News*, 2013 www.bbc.co.uk/news/uk-21651416; the Iraq Inquiry also known as *The Chilcot Inquiry* www.iraqinquiry.org.uk/.

123 Mendonca, above n. 109; *BMPI*, above n. 28: Colonel Mendonca stated the battalion felt like it had been 'left holding the ring with precious few resources and absolutely no plan above the battle group level'. [234].

124 Amnesty International, *Iraq Memorandum on Concerns Relating to Law and Order*, 22 July 2003 www.amnesty.org/en/library/info/MDE14/157/2003/en.

ECHR has developed a significant tension between the judicial and executive arms of government. In 2000, the Army released a document entitled *Soldiering: The Military Covenant.*[125] This document was a response to perceived challenges to its underlying *raison d'être*, with the military feeling inadequately appreciated.[126] Certainly, it aroused long overdue public debate about the state of the civil–military relationship in the United Kingdom. The Covenant aimed to set out the army's perspective of its role in a society where the all-volunteer force means many citizens have lost touch with the military. It also appears to reinforce the traditional view that the military is entitled to specialised and different treatment. Anthony Forster and Helen McCartney,[127] however, argue the Iraq/Afghanistan wars have overtaken the debate, reducing the Covenant to evidence of a military out of touch with the values of the society it is meant to defend.[128]

The rise of HRL requires the military that accept a closer alignment with values that reflect the broader society.[129] As a consequence of *Al – Skeini* the MoD changed its policy on questioning and interrogation techniques. The new policy has been subjected to court scrutiny to test its legality, with the court observing video evidence of interrogations.[130] In these circumstances it may no longer be appropriate for the military to maintain its existence as a 'separate society' demanding deferential treatment. Certainly, the courts have had to grapple with the tension between the ideal of deference towards the military and the new demands to uphold human rights.

The UK judiciary is showing a gradual shift to greater assertiveness, leading to allegations of judicial sovereignty and interventionist courts.[131] Some have welcomed at least one arm of government

125 See Ministry of Defence, *Soldiering: The Military Covenant*, vol. 5 (2000). http://webarchive.nationalarchives.gov.uk/20121026065214/http://www.mod.uk/NR/rdonlyres/4E9E2014-5CE6-43F2-AE28-B6C5FA90B68F/0/Armed_Forces_ Covenant.pdf.

126 Mendonca, above n. 109.

127 See further, Forster, above n. 111 and McCartney, above n 111.

128 Ibid. See generally, Darren Denning, 'In Pursuit of British Public Support for the Next War' (Master's Thesis, National Defense University Norfolk Virginia Joint Advanced Warfighting School, 2011).

129 Charles Dunlap Jr, *Law and Military Interventions: Preserving Military Values in 21st Century Conflicts*, Working Paper, (Cambridge, MA, Harvard University Carr Center, 2001), p. 133.

130 *R (Hussein)* v. *Secretary of State for Defence* [2014] EWCA Civ 1087.

131 See, for example, Anne-Marie Slaughter, 'A Brave New Judicial World' in Michael Ignatieff (ed.), *American Exceptionalism and Human Rights* (Princeton, NJ, Princeton University Press, 2005), p. 275.

exercising its role to provide an independent check on the decision to go to war.[132] There is a perception amongst the public that the government must justify its decision to adopt military intervention.[133] The executive government has been held to account in a way that it did not anticipate at the time of going to war in Afghanistan or Iraq, instead relying on conceptions of the sovereignty of Parliament and national security prerogatives. It did not seem to occur to the executive that the demands of HRL would change anything.[134] The Court of Appeal in *Mousa* alluded to this demand:

> It sometimes seems that part of the choreography of public accountability in this country is the clamour for a public inquiry into suspected wrongdoing by agents of the state. Usually the ministerial decision to order or to refuse such an inquiry is a matter of discretion. However, where the suspected wrongdoing involves breaches of Articles 2 and/or 3 of the [Convention], the investigatory obligation of those provisions is engaged.[135]

Some writers have labelled it 'lawfare'.[136] That term may be derogatory but many acknowledge that 'while lawfare may not eliminate human conflict, it can sometimes humanize that conflict by substituting juridical warfare for the more deadly variety'.[137]

132 See, for example, Jane E. Stromseth, 'Pursuing Accountability for Atrocities after Conflict: What Impact on Building the Rule of Law?' (2007) 38 *Georgetown Journal of International Law*, p. 251.

133 Phil Shiner, 'Comments: A Coverup of Torture, Racism and Complicity in War Crimes. The Evidence of British Abuse and Killing of Iraqi Civilians is Part of an Iceberg of Disgrace which Demands a Public Inquiry' *The Guardian* (London), Monday 23 April 2007 www.guardian.co.uk/commentisfree/2007/apr/23/iraq.iraq; McCartney, above n. 111, at 414. See *R (Maya Evans)* v. *Secretary of State for Defence* [2010] EWHC 1445 (Admin).

134 McGoldrick, 'The Boundaries of Justiciability', above n. 22.

135 *R (Mousa)* v. *Secretary of State for Defence* [2011] EWCA Civ 1334, at [1] (Kay LJ).

136 See, for example, Charles J. Dunlap, 'Commentary, Lawfare Today: A Perspective' (2008) 3 *Yale Journal of International Affairs*, p. 146. See generally, UK, *Defence Committee – Twelfth Report: UK Armed Forces Personnel and the Legal Framework for Future Operations* (26 March 2014) www.publications.parliament.uk/pa/cm201314/cmselect/cmdfence/931/93102.htm; Dunlap popularised the term but accepts the law can still limit human suffering in war and operate as a positive good, at 146–47. Thomas Tugendhat and Laura Croft, *The Fog of Law. An Introduction to the Legal Erosion of British Fighting Power* (London, Policy Exchange, 2013); See also *Smith* v. *Ministry of Defence* [2014] AC 52, at [100] (Hope LJ); [150] (Mance LJ).

137 Harvey Rishikof, 'Juridical Warfare: The Neglected Legal Instrument' (2008) 48 *Joint Force Quarterly*, p. 11, at 12.

V Conclusion

The approach of the UK courts to the demands of HRL and the changing role of the military demonstrates a need to reassess the role that the third arm of government – the courts – play in civil–military relations.[138] The evolving role of the military in modern times challenges the traditional link between civil and military societal values. The citizen–soldier and sovereign state connection is broken when national military forces defend globalised values rather than national borders.

If the judicial arm unduly defers to the elected arm, it may abrogate its duty to the rule of law and the protection of rights. *Al-Skeini* demonstrates the concern of the UK courts to limit Convention rights so as not to affect military operations, using jurisdiction, as the legal justification for this purpose. This case caused difficulties in subsequent cases such as *Smith* v. *Oxfordshire.* In *Smith (No. 2)* the Supreme Court reversed its position reached three years earlier. *Al-Skeini* demonstrates that failure to consider the requirement that the civil is to dominate the military, for instance through preference for human rights over military necessity, has significant consequences. This includes potential damage to the military reputation, thus widening the civil–military gap.

While the courts have authority from rule of law principles, their legitimacy comes from their independence from the other institutions of government. This separation of powers ensures mutual respect for the position of each arm of government but requires that respect to be carefully balanced. It cannot be left unchecked in one area – such as the military. The challenge is for the military, political and judicial institutions to engage in a fresh civil–military vision in this new world of human rights law.

[138] Groves, above n. 3, at 364–65.

5

Trying civilian contractors in military courts: a necessary evil?

RAIN LIIVOJA

I Nature of the problem

Many states have established military courts to deal with offences committed by members of the armed forces. The allocation of jurisdiction between such courts and ordinary civilian courts can be a precarious constitutional law exercise as the reason for creating military courts has often been the desire to place a premium on military expediency at the expense of fair trial rights. Particularly problematic has been the choice made by some states to subject civilians under some circumstances to the jurisdiction of military courts.

During the last half a century, international human rights bodies have been critical of military justice systems, leading many states to a process of civilianisation. Some states have abolished military courts altogether. Others have retained separate military justice systems but introduced civilian elements, by appointing civilian judges or judge advocates, subordinating the prosecution service to civilian authorities, and creating avenues of appeal to ordinary civilian courts. Some states have limited the jurisdiction of military courts to purely disciplinary or duty-related offences. This process has also entailed placing restraints on the exercise of military jurisdiction over civilians. This trend has, however, been less pronounced with respect to a particular group of civilians, namely those deploying with or accompanying the armed forces overseas (associated civilians). Some states have in fact sought to expand the competence of their military justice systems to deal with associated civilians.

While the issue of subjecting associated civilians to military justice is not new to military law, it has attracted special attention twice in modern history. The first occasion was in the aftermath of World War II when the Allied forces became quasi-permanently stationed abroad, accompanied by their family members. Some states enacted legislation to bring these dependants within the jurisdictional reach of their military courts because that was seen as preferable to trials in local courts. The increased use of private military contractors by NATO countries in the Yugoslavian conflict, and more recently by members of the 'coalitions of the willing' in Iraq and Afghanistan, has led to the re-emergence of this problem in another guise. Sometimes fuelled by the impotence of civilian law enforcement authorities to deal with serious crimes committed by contractor personnel on military operations, legislators have sought to extend, reiterate or consolidate the jurisdiction of military courts. In some states, notably the United States, the possibility of trying civilians in military courts has led to constitutional challenges. Such trials also raise issues under international human rights law.

Although the criticisms levelled against military justice systems concerning fair trial guarantees when dealing with military personnel also apply in relation to any potential civilian defendant, there are additional concerns. This chapter examines these concerns in the context of several international human rights treaty regimes. The chapter begins by providing a sampling of national arrangements subjecting associated civilians to military justice systems and considers the UN Draft Principles Governing the Administration of Justice. The chapter argues that international human rights law does not prohibit the trial of civilians in military tribunals but it restricts the circumstances in which such trials can occur and establishes the principles by which they may operate.

II Application of military law to associated civilians

Arrangements subjecting associated civilians to military law appear to be more usual in common law countries. They can be traced back to a common ancestor in the mid-eighteenth century English Articles of War[1] and they have survived partly because common law countries generally exercise very limited extraterritorial jurisdiction over their nationals. That said, military jurisdiction over associated civilians is not unknown in continental legal systems: in France, for example, 'members of the armed forces and persons who follow them on the basis of authorisation' have been subject to military justice.[2] The following analysis

[1] Articles of War 1747 (England), s. XIV, cited in Frederick Bernays Wiener, *Civilians under Military Justice: The British Practice since 1689, Especially in North America* (Chicago, IL, University of Chicago Press, 1967), p. 22.

[2] Code de Justice Militaire (Noveau) [(New) Code of Military Justice] 8 July 1965 (France) art. 121–1.

examines the situation in three common law countries – the United States, the United Kingdom and Australia. These examples illustrate well the slight differences in the way in which military jurisdiction over civilians can be established even among states that have a similar legal tradition and common roots of military justice.

A United States

The Uniform Code of Military Justice (UCMJ), which governs all American military personnel, was amended in 2006[3] so that it applied '[i]n time of declared war or a contingency operation, [to] persons serving with or accompanying an armed force in the field'.[4] So far, only one case, *United States* v. *Ali*, has made its way through the US military justice system under this provision. In 2008, a military judge convicted Mr Alaa 'Alex' Mohammad Ali, a contractor to the US Army, of stabbing a colleague in Iraq. The US Army Court of Criminal Appeals and the US Court of Appeals for the Armed Forces upheld the conviction.[5]

The central constitutional problem in such cases is that the Sixth Amendment to the US Constitution guarantees a right to trial by a jury of peers.[6] In the military justice system, cases of similar gravity are tried by a court martial, with a military judge sitting alone or with a panel made up of service members, rather than a traditional jury. While the Constitution allows a trial without a jury in 'cases arising in the land or naval forces',[7] the Supreme Court had previously held that cases concerning associated civilians do not arise *in* the forces, and these civilians cannot be denied a jury trial on that basis.[8] However, the Supreme Court

[3] John Warner National Defense Authorization Act for Fiscal Year 2007, 17 October 2006 (US), Pub. L. 109-364, 120 Stat. 2083, s. 552.

[4] Uniform Code of Military Justice, 10 USC §§ 801–946, art. 2(a)(10) (2010).

[5] *United States* v. *Ali* 70 MJ 514 (Army Court of Criminal Appeals, 2011); *United States* v. *Ali* 71 MJ 256 (Court of Appeals for the Armed Forces, 2012).

[6] United States Constitution amend VI art. III, § 2. [7] Ibid., amend VIII.

[8] *Reid* v. *Covert* 354 US 1 (1960) (the wives of two service members convicted at court martial of killing their husbands, stationed respectively in England and Japan); *Kinsella* v. *Singleton* 361 US 234 (1960) (soldier's wife stationed in peacetime Germany charged with involuntary manslaughter in consequence of the death of one of her children); *Grisham* v. *Hagan* 361 US 278 (1960) (army civilian employee attached to an army base in peacetime France prosecuted for premeditated murder but found guilty of the lesser included offence of unpremeditated murder); *McElroy* v. *US ex rel. Guagliardo* 361 US 281 (1960) (civilian employee of the Air Force, performing the duties of an electrical lineman, convicted by court martial at the Nouasseur Air Depot near Casablanca, Morocco, of larceny and conspiracy to commit larceny from the Depot).

had also accepted the possibility of trying by court martial civilians who in time of war accompany the forces in the field.[9] That left an uncertainty as to whether a 'contingency operation' mentioned in the current text of the UCMJ would satisfy this test.

In *United States* v. *Ali*, the US Court of Appeals for the Armed Forces held that the Fifth and Sixth Amendments of the Constitution were inapplicable to Ali, a non-citizen tried outside the United States, and that whatever rights he had were met through the court-martial process.[10] In May 2013, the US Supreme Court denied review.[11] That means civilian non-citizens can be constitutionally subjected to trial by courts martial overseas under the UCMJ.

B United Kingdom

In the United Kingdom, the Armed Forces Act 2006 (UK) (which entered into force in 2009) applies to several categories of civilians who serve with or accompany Her Majesty's forces abroad.[12] A similar arrangement existed under the three service discipline Acts that were adopted in the 1950s.[13] Additionally, the Armed Forces Act 2006 (UK) empowers certain military commanders under specific circumstances to make persons identified by name or by description subject to the Act.[14] In the process leading to the adoption of the Act, this section was viewed as a useful device for dealing with contractor personnel.

Approximately two to three civilians are prosecuted every year in the UK court martial system.[15] To put this in perspective, the total number of court martial trials in the UK is just under 500 per year.[16] The cases with civilian defendants tend to fall into two categories.[17] The first involves offences that have become time-barred in the country where

[9] *Reid* v. *Covert* 354 US 1 (1960) (Black J): 'Article 2(10) of the UCMJ ... provides that in *time of war* persons serving with or accompanying the armed forces in the field are subject to court-martial and military law. We believe that Art. 2(10) sets forth the maximum historically recognized extent of military jurisdiction over civilians under the concept of "in the field".'

[10] 71 MJ 256 (Court of Appeals for the Armed Forces, 2012) at 268.

[11] *United States* v. *Ali* 569 US __ (US Supreme Court, 13 May 2013).

[12] Armed Forces Act 2006 (UK) c. 52, sch. 15, ss. 1–6, 8–10.

[13] Army Act 1955 (UK) c. 18, s. 209; Air Force Act *1955* (UK) c. 19, s. 209; Naval Discipline Act 1957 (UK) c. 53, ss. 117–18.

[14] Armed Forces Act 2006 (UK) sch. 15, s. 7.

[15] Personal communications from Judge Hunter, the Vice-Judge Advocate General, to the author (23 April 2012 and 11 December 2015).

[16] Service Prosecuting Authority, *Annual Report 2014/2015* (2015), p. 13.

[17] This information derives from personal communication from Judge Hunter, above n. 15.

they were committed and in practice mostly involve allegations of rape or sexual offences against children. The second category comprises matters that could be tried by a court in the country where the offence was committed but where it is considered more practical and sensible, for example for language reasons, to try them in a British court.

The most notable trial of an associated civilian by court martial in recent history was *R* v. *Martin*.[18] Mr Alan Martin, the son of a British service member stationed in Germany, was suspected of having murdered a young woman working for the British Forces in Germany. Germany waived jurisdiction and Mr Martin was convicted by a court martial in May 1995. This case led to a challenge before the European Court of Human Rights (ECtHR), ultimately leading to changes in the composition of courts martial convened to deal with civilians. The court-martial panel – though not quite a jury, as it may convict by simple majority – is now made up of civil servants, and the only military personnel involved in the trial are the court usher and the assistant prosecutor.[19]

A more recent case, *R* v. *McMahon and Kelly*,[20] dealt with contractor personnel. In August 2007, an incident occurred in a bar within the UK Contingency Operating Base in Basrah, Iraq.[21] Messrs Sean McMahon and James Kelly, employees of Turner Facilities Management, a contractor to the British Army, had to be physically restrained by other patrons during an argument with the barman and were removed from the bar. McMahon and Kelly later sought out one of the persons who had restrained them, another employee of Turner, and brutally attacked him with a baton and a knife. In October 2010, a court martial convicted both men of unlawful and malicious wounding with intent to cause bodily harm, and sentenced them to imprisonment.

C *Australia*

In Australia, the Defence Force Discipline Act 1982 (Cth) applies to (and the jurisdiction of courts martial covers) service members and

18 [1998] AC 917 (HL). 19 Personal communication from Judge Hunter, above n. 15.

20 (Court Martial, Judge Hunter, 27–30 September, and 1 and 11 October 2010) (copy on file with the author).

21 Transcript of Proceedings, *R* v. *McMahon and Kelly* (Court Martial, Judge Hunter, 27–30 September, and 1 and 11 October 2010) (copy on file with the author); Ian Key, 'Court Martial Jails Two Scots Civilians over Attack in Iraq' *The Express*, 13 October 2010, p. 27.

'defence civilians'. The latter are persons who meet two criteria: first, they must accompany, by due authorisation, a part of the defence force outside Australia (or on operations against the enemy in Australia); second, they must have consented, in writing, to subject themselves to the discipline of the defence force.[22] This mechanism for designating persons as defence civilians is used routinely.[23] Australian military lawyers particularly like to mention a concert that was held in December 1999 for Australian forces deployed to East Timor as part of the INTERFET peacekeeping operation. The artists were made 'defence civilians' while in East Timor. Technicians from Telstra, a large Australian telecommunications and media company, were also designated as defence civilians on the same operation. Although a number of people have been made defence civilians, none appears to have been prosecuted under the Defence Force Discipline Act 1982 (Cth).[24]

III Draft Principles Governing the Administration of Justice through Military Tribunals

The question of whether military tribunals should have any jurisdiction over civilians has been on the agenda of the UN Sub-Commission on the Promotion and Protection of Human Rights for many years. In 2005, a special rapporteur, Professor Emmanuel Decaux of the University Pantheon-Assas Paris II, submitted his report on the matter to the Sub-Commission.[25] At the core of this report were a set of Draft Principles Governing the Administration of Justice through Military Tribunals. Draft Principle 5 suggests that:

> Military courts should, in principle, have no jurisdiction to try civilians. In all circumstances, the State shall ensure that civilians accused of a criminal offence of any nature are tried by civilian courts.

22 Defence Force Discipline Act 1982 (Cth) s. 3(1) (definition of 'defence civilian').

23 Conversation of the author with Australian Department of Defence lawyers, 28 August, 13 September and 3 November 2011."

24 MAJGEN Ian Westwood, Chief Judge Advocate of Australia, could not recall any trials of defence civilians under the Act: personal communication to the author (9 December 2015).

25 Emmanuel Decaux, Special Rapporteur, 'Issue of the Administration of Justice through Military Tribunals' 57th Sess, UN Doc. E/CN.4/Sub.2/2005/9 (16 June 2005); Emmanuel Decaux, Special Rapporteur, 'Issue of the Administration of Justice through Military Tribunals', 62nd Sess, UN Doc. E/CN.4/2006/58 (13 January 2006).

Unless the words 'in principle' can be read as a qualifier, this statement does not accurately reflect international law.[26] The special rapporteur's commentary on Draft Principle 5 refers to the practice of the UN Human Rights Committee, and notes that '[m]any thematic or country rapporteurs have also taken a very strong position in favour of military tribunals' lack of authority to try civilians'.[27] The special rapporteur claims that the jurisprudence of the European Court of Human Rights and the Inter-American Court and Commission of Human Rights is 'unanimous on this point'.[28] However, the practice reveals no unanimity between human rights bodies on a general principle that military tribunals are absolutely precluded from exercising jurisdiction over civilians.

IV Human rights treaty regimes

Different human rights treaty bodies[29] hold divergent views on the compatibility of military trials of civilians with their respective human rights instruments. While there is a degree of convergence between the practice of these bodies, particularly over the last decade, the different rationales relied upon nonetheless create a somewhat disjointed picture. The relevant conclusions of the treaty bodies are, moreover, intertwined with their views on military justice more generally, which can make it difficult to separate the part of the jurisprudence that pertains specifically to the trial of civilians. In this section, I briefly explain the jurisprudence of the American, European and UN systems on the human rights issues involved in conducting trials of civilians before courts that have at least one military member.

A American Convention on Human Rights

The strongest support for Draft Principle 5 can be found in the Inter-American system. The Inter-American Court and Commission have taken an unambiguous position that the trial of civilians by military

26 A number of other Draft Principles are similarly problematic. See Michael R. Gibson, 'International Human Rights Law and the Administration of Justice through Military Tribunals: Preserving Utility While Precluding Impunity' (2008) 4 *Journal of International Law & International Relations*, p. 1.

27 Decaux, above n. 25, at [20]. 28 Ibid.

29 I use 'treaty bodies' as a shorthand for international entities assigned to monitor the application of particular treaties, including experts' committees and commissions, as well as courts.

courts is incompatible with the American Convention on Human Rights.[30] The nail on which this jurisprudence hangs is art. 8(1) of the Convention, which provides that:

> Every person has the right to a hearing, with due guarantees and within a reasonable time, by a competent, independent, and impartial tribunal, previously established by law, in the substantiation of any accusation of a criminal nature made against him or for the determination of his rights and obligations of a civil, labor, fiscal, or any other nature.

While this starting point has remained unchanged, the manner in which trials of civilians by military courts have been said to violate this right has changed over time,[31] and the views of the Commission and the Court have become more robust.

In 1982 the Commission recommended that Colombia adopt new legislation to 'either eliminate or, if this is not possible, limit military trials of civilians to crimes that truly affect state security'.[32] In 1985 the Commission noted somewhat more tersely that in Chile the 'widespread and virtually routine intervention of peacetime military courts in the consideration of a very broad category of acts necessarily constitutes an abuse of the purposes for which they are envisaged'.[33]

In the 1990s, the Commission became more outspoken and secured the support of the Court. Much of this occurred against the background of the situation in Peru. In the 1980s and 1990s, the Túpac Amaru Revolutionary Movement (*Movimiento Revolucionario Túpac Amaru*, MRTA) carried out a series of terrorist acts in Peru. In 1992, President Fujimori executed a 'self-coup'. Among other things, he issued two decrees, criminalising, respectively, 'terrorism' and 'treason', the latter being a sort of an aggravated form of terrorism.[34] The offence of 'treason' fell exclusively within the jurisdiction of military courts. In 1993, the constitution was amended to permit military trials of civilians for the crimes of terrorism and treason.[35]

[30] American Convention on Human Rights, San José, 22 November 1969, in force 18 July 1978, 1144 UNTS 123 (ACHR).

[31] See Jeanine Bucherer, *Die Vereinbarkeit von Militärgerichten mit dem Recht auf ein faires Verfahren gemäß Art. 6 Abs. 1 EMRK, Art. 8 Abs. 1 AMRK und Art. 14 Abs. 1 des UN-Paktes über bürgerliche und politische Rechte* (Berlin, Springer, 2005), pp. 82–91, 115–34.

[32] Inter-American Commission of Human Rights, 'Report on the Situation of Human Rights in the Republic of Colombia', OEA/Ser.L/V/II.53 doc. 22 (30 June 1981), Recommendations, at [7(c)].

[33] Inter-American Commission of Human Rights, 'Report on the Situation of Human Rights in Chile', OEA/Ser.L/V/II.66 doc. 17 (9 September 1985), ch. VIII, at [143].

[34] Decree Law No. 25,475 (5 May 1992) (terrorism) and Decree Law No. 25,659 (treason).

[35] *Constitution* (Peru, 31 December 1993) art. 173.

A number of individuals were arrested, detained, tried and punished in accordance with this legal framework for various degrees of alleged collaboration with MRTA. This raised several human rights issues which were extensively litigated in the Inter-American Court and Commission: the definition of the offences, and particularly the line between them, was found to be so unclear as to violate the principle of legality (art. 9); the procedure utilised by the military courts did not live up to the Convention standards in terms of fair trial guarantees (art. 8); and the conditions of detention violated the right to humane treatment (art. 5).[36]

Importantly for present purposes, the Commission also expressed its views as to whether trial by a military court – quite aside from all its specific procedural shortcomings – was compatible with the Convention. In 1993, the Commission noted that:

> [b]y placing civilians under the jurisdiction of the military courts, [the Treason Law] is patently contrary to the rights and guarantees protected under articles 8 [right to fair trial] and 25 [right to judicial protection] of the American Convention, specifically the right to a hearing by a competent, independent and impartial tribunal. The military court is a special and purely functional court designed to maintain discipline in the military and police and ought therefore to apply exclusively to those forces.[37]

The Commission explained further that:

> It is the job of the Armed Forces to combat the terrorists by engaging the irregular armed groups militarily, as is their primary role in the campaign against subversion. The armed forces, however, overstep their natural role when they prosecute civilians accused of belonging to subversive groups, as this function is the proper purview of the judiciary. Furthermore, there are some serious and legitimate doubts about the impartiality of a military court in such cases, as the court would be both judge and prosecutor.[38]

In its 1998 *Annual Report*, the Commission reminded all member states that:

> their citizens must be judged pursuant to ordinary law and justice and by their natural judges. Thus, civilians should not be subject to Military

[36] See, in particular, *Castillo Petruzzi et al.* v. *Peru* [1999] Inter-Am Court HR (ser C) No. 52; *Cantoral Benavides* v. *Peru* [2000] Inter-Am Court HR (ser C) No. 69; *Lori Berenson Mejía* v. *Peru* [2004] Inter-Am Court HR (ser C) No. 199.

[37] Inter-American Commission of Human Rights, 'Annual Report 1993', OEA/Ser.L/V/II.85 doc. 9 rev. (11 February 1994), ch. IV, Peru, s. IV.

[38] Ibid.

> Tribunals. Military justice has merely a disciplinary nature and can only be used to try armed forces personnel in active service for misdemeanors or offenses pertaining to their function.[39]

The Commission took a similar approach when arguing cases before the Court, suggesting that the trial of civilians by military courts violated the right to trial by a 'natural and competent judge' (*juez natural y competente*)[40] or simply a 'natural judge' (*juez natural*).[41] According to the Commission, this principle 'means that judicial competence can be neither derogated nor removed; in other words, absolute adherence to the law is required and judicial competence may not be arbitrarily altered'.[42] In the Commission's view, the term 'treason' in Peru was used to 'cloak this arbitrary mutation in the guise of legality' and to displace the jurisdiction of the 'natural judge'.[43] In the 2007 case of *Loayza Tamayo*, the Court did not see the need to engage with this type of argument, as in that case the military tribunal had, in the Court's view, exceeded its competence as a matter of domestic law – acted formally *ultra vires* – and was thus manifestly not a 'competent court'.[44] However, two years later, in *Castillo Petruzzi*, the Court explicitly picked up the Commission's line of reasoning, holding that 'allowing military courts to try civilians accused of treason, means that the natural judge is precluded from hearing these cases'.[45]

This approach is not without problems. The concept of a natural judge is not an invention of the Commission or the Court – it is recognised in many domestic legal systems.[46] But it seems to have a particularly Ibero-American pedigree. Indeed, in the (official) English versions of the judgments cited, it gets lost in translation: in its place, one finds the rather cumbersome phrase 'competent, independent and impartial tribunal previously established by law'.[47] Yet the notion of 'natural judge' seems

39 Inter-American Commission of Human Rights, 'Annual Report 1998', OEA/Ser.L/V/II.102 doc. 6 rev. (16 April 1999), ch. VII, at [1].

40 See the views of the Commission as cited by the Court in *Loayza-Tamayo* v. *Peru* [1997] Inter-Am Court HR (ser C) No. 33 at [37(a)].

41 See the views of the Commission as cited by the Court in *Castillo Petruzzi et al.* v. *Peru* [1999] Inter-Am Court HR (ser C) No. 52 at [125(f)]; *Lori Berenson Mejía* v. *Peru* [2004] Inter-Am Court HR (ser C) No. 199 at [129.1(h)].

42 Cited in *Castillo Petruzzi et al.* v. *Peru* [1999] Inter-Am Court HR (ser C) No. 52 at [125(f)].

43 Ibid.

44 *Loayza-Tamayo* v. *Peru* [1997] Inter-Am Court HR (ser C) No. 33 at [61].

45 *Castillo Petruzzi et al.* v. *Peru* [1999] Inter-Am Court HR (ser C) No. 52 at [128]. See also *Lori Berenson Mejía* v. *Peru* [2004] Inter-Am Court HR (ser C) No. 199 at [141] and discussion in by Cerna in Chapter 16.

46 Cf. Bucherer above n. 31, pp. 119–20.

47 *Castillo Petruzzi et al.* v. *Peru* [1999] Inter-Am Court HR (ser C) No. 52 at [114(c)], [125(c)], [128], [161].

to transcend all these requirements: it is not about meeting certain procedural criteria, or even the benchmarks of independence and impartiality, but implies, for the lack of a better word, 'appropriateness'. Unsurprisingly, commentators have questioned whether this concept can be readily transposed internationally, especially without discussion as to its meaning.[48]

Finally, mention should be made of an *obiter dictum* in *Durand and Ugarte*,[49] a case that dealt with military jurisdiction over common crimes committed by service members. The Court said:

> In a democratic Government of Laws the penal military jurisdiction shall have a restrictive and exceptional scope and shall lead to the protection of special juridical interests, related to the functions assigned by law to the military forces. Consequently, civilians must be excluded from the military jurisdiction scope and only the military shall be judged by commission of crime or offenses that by its own nature attempt against legally protected interests of military order.[50]

Thus, the Court has not only grounded its views regarding the impermissibility of military trials of civilians in the notion of 'natural judge' but has also considered such trials to be incompatible with the proper role of the armed forces in a democratic society.

B International Covenant on Civil and Political Rights

Article 14(1) of the International Covenant on Civil and Political Rights[51] provides that:

> All persons shall be equal before the courts and tribunals. In the determination of any criminal charge against him, or of his rights and obligations in a suit at law, everyone shall be entitled to a fair and public hearing by a competent, independent and impartial tribunal established by law.

In the 1970s and 1980s, in a series of cases against Uruguay, the Human Rights Committee viewed military trials of civilians through the lens of the requirements of independence and impartiality.[52] However, in the

48 Cf. Bucherer, above n. 31, pp. 119–20. 49 (2000) Inter-Am Court HR (ser C) No. 68.

50 *Durand and Ugarte* v. *Peru* (2000) Inter-Am Court HR (ser C) No. 68, at [117]. See also Federico Andreu-Guzmán, *Military Jurisdiction and International Law: Military Courts and Gross Human Rights Violations* (Geneva, International Commission of Jurists, 2004), p. 118 et seq.

51 International Covenant on Civil and Political Rights, 16 December 1966, in force 23 March 1976, 999 UNTS 171 (ICCPR).

52 Bucherer, above n. 31, pp. 138–40.

1982 case of *Fals Borda*, the Committee refused to find a violation of art. 14 on the basis of the military character of the tribunal alone.[53] The Committee did not view trials of civilians by a military court to be in violation of art. 14 as such, but resorted to an assessment of the features of the particular tribunal.[54] One commentator has speculated that the Committee's approach might have been different had it not found a violation of other provisions of the Covenant – in this instance arts 9(3) and 9(4) on the right to liberty and security of person – as it seems to be the practice of the Committee 'not to push' the analysis in cases where it has found a violation on other grounds.[55]

The Committee consolidated its views in General Comment No. 13 where it explained that although 'the Covenant does not prohibit [military or special courts], nevertheless the conditions which it lays down clearly indicate that the trying of civilians by such courts should be very exceptional and take place under conditions which genuinely afford the full guarantees stipulated in article 14'.[56] While the Committee indicated that military trials of civilians ought to be 'very exceptional', the gist of its position was related to the particular procedural guarantees. A decade later, in *Polay Campos* v. *Peru*, the Committee also turned to independence and impartiality of a military court rather than the nature of the court *per se*.[57] Similarly, when dealing with the country report of Peru in 1996, the Committee's main concern was the independence and impartiality of the court.[58]

The approach appears to have changed somewhat in the following year. While considering the report of Lebanon, the Committee noted the procedural shortcomings of military courts. But its recommendation was not primarily aimed at procedural improvements; rather it suggested that:

[53] Human Rights Committee, *Views: Communication No 46/1978*, UN Doc CCPR/C/16/D/46/1979 (27 July 1982) at [13.3] (*Fals Borda et al.* v. *Colombia*)

[54] Bucherer, above n. 31, p. 141; Sangeeta Shah, 'The Human Rights Committee and Military Trials of Civilians: *Madani v Algeria*' (2008) 8 *Human Rights Law Review*, p. 139, at 145.

[55] Evelyne Schmid, 'A Few Comments on a Comment: The UN Human Rights Committee's General Comment No. 32 on Article 14 of the ICCPR and the Question of Civilians Tried by Military Courts' (2010) 14 *International Journal of Human Rights*, p. 1058, at 1062.

[56] Human Rights Committee, *General Comment No: 13 Equality before the Courts and the Right to a Fair and Public Hearing by an Independent Court Established by Law (Article 14)* UN Doc. HRI/GEN/1/Rev.9 (13 April 1984) 184 at [4].

[57] Human Rights Committee, *Views: Communication No 577/1994*, 61st sess, UN Doc CCPR/C/61/D/577/1994 (9 January 1998) (*Polay Campos* v. *Peru*).

[58] Human Rights Committee, *Preliminary Observations: Peru*, UN Doc CCPR/C/79/Add.67 (25 July 1996) at [12].

> [t]he State party should review the jurisdiction of the military courts and transfer the competence of military courts, in all trials concerning civilians and in all cases concerning the violation of human rights by members of the military, to the ordinary courts.[59]

When considering the situation in other states later that year, the Committee observed that in Slovenia 'civilians may be tried by military courts in certain cases' and, without much further analysis, recommended a change in the law 'so as to prohibit the trial of civilians by military tribunals in any circumstances'.[60] In 1999, the wording became stronger when the Committee observed that 'the continuing jurisdiction of Chilean military courts to try civilians does not comply with article 14 of the Covenant'.[61] The Committee also recommended that Poland amend or repeal legislation which provided military courts jurisdiction to try civilians, noting that 'the Committee does not accept that this practice is justified by the convenience of the military court dealing with every person who may have taken some part in an offence primarily committed by a member of the armed forces'.[62] Thus, the Committee suggested that it was in a position to accept or reject arguments advanced by states justifying the existence of military jurisdiction over civilians.

The Committee developed that position in further cases. The 2003 case of *Kurbanov* v. *Tajikistan* concerned a trial before the Military Chamber of the Supreme Court of Tajikistan of a civilian for murder. The Committee considered that '[i]n the absence of any information by the State party to justify a trial before a military court . . . the trial and death sentence against . . . a civilian . . . did not meet the requirements of article 14, paragraph 1'.[63] The Committee took a broadly similar approach in a pair of cases decided in 2007, *Madani* v. *Algeria*[64] and *Benhadj* v. *Algeria*.[65] Madani and Benhadj were the leaders of the Islamic

[59] Human Rights Committee, *Concluding Observations: Lebanon*, UN Doc CCPR/C/79/Add.78 (1 April 1997) at [14].

[60] Human Rights Committee, *Concluding Observations: Slovakia*, UN Doc CCPR/C/79/Add.79 (4 August 1997) at [20].

[61] Human Rights Committee, *Concluding Observations: Chile*, UN Doc CCPR/C/79/Add.104 (30 March 1999) at [9].

[62] Human Rights Committee, *Concluding Observations: Poland*, UN Doc. CCPR/C/79/Add.110 (29 July 1999), [21].

[63] Human Rights Committee, *Views: Communication No 1096/2002*, 79th sess, UN Doc CCPR/C/79/D/1096/2002 (12 November 2003) (*Kurbanov* v. *Tajikistan*) at [2.2]–[2.3].

[64] Human Rights Committee, *Views: Communication No 1172/2003*, 89th sess, UN Doc CCPR/C/89/D/1172/2003 (21 June 2007) (*Madani* v. *Algeria*).

[65] Human Rights Committee, *Views: Communication No 1173/2003*, 90th sess, UN Doc. CCPR/C/90/D/1173/2003 (20 July 2007) (*Benhadj* v. *Algeria*).

Salvation Front (*Front Islamique du Salut*, FIS), which in 1991 had organised demonstrations against the new electoral laws in Algeria and called for a general strike. Both men were charged with 'jeopardising State security and the smooth operation of the national economy', tried by a military court, and sentenced to twelve years of 'rigorous imprisonment'.[66] In *Madani*, the Committee held that

> It is incumbent on a State party that does try civilians before military courts to justify the practice. The Committee considers that the State party must demonstrate, with regard to the specific class of individuals at issue, that the regular civilian courts are unable to undertake the trials, that other alternative forms of special or high-security civilian courts are inadequate to the task and that recourse to military courts is unavoidable. The State party must further demonstrate how military courts ensure the full protection of the rights of the accused pursuant to article 14.[67]

The language in *Benhadj* was almost identical.[68]

The Committee appears to have extrapolated from the phrase 'very exceptional' contained in General Comment No. 13 an obligation on the state to prove the necessity of resorting to military courts.[69] Moreover, in *Madani* and *Benhadj*, the Committee took the view that a state's failure to demonstrate the need to rely on a military court for the trial of a civilian discloses a violation of article 14, such that the Committee 'need not examine whether the military court, as a matter of fact, afforded the full guarantees of article 14'.[70] Two members of the Committee disagreed, however, arguing that the Committee had overstepped its authority by requiring the state to justify its choice of courts, and conversely neglected to do what it was supposed to do, namely to examine on the facts whether the tribunal in question afforded the guarantees stipulated in art. 14.[71]

[66] Human Rights Committee, *Views: Communication No 1172/2003*, 89th sess, UN Doc CCPR/C/89/D/1172/2003 (21 June 2007) (*Madani* v. *Algeria*).

[67] *Madani* v. *Algeria*, UN Doc CCPR/C/89/D/1172/2003 at [8.7].

[68] *Benhadj* v. *Algeria*, UN Doc. CCPR/C/90/D/1173/2003 at [8.8].

[69] Schmid, above n. 55, at 1063.

[70] *Madani* v. *Algeria*, UN Doc CCPR/C/89/D/1172/2003 at [8.7]; *Benhadj* v. *Algeria*, UN Doc. CCPR/C/90/D/1173/2003 at [8.8].

[71] *Madani* v. *Algeria*, UN Doc CCPR/C/89/D/1172/2003, Dissenting Opinion by Committee Member Mr. Abdelfattah Amor, and Individual Opinion of Committee Member Mr. Ahmed T. Khalil; *Benhadj* v. *Algeria*, UN Doc. CCPR/C/90/D/1173/2003, Individual Opinion of Committee Member Mr. Abdelfattah Amor, and Individual Opinion of Committee Member Mr. Ahmed T. Khalil.

In 2007 the Committee adopted General Comment No. 32, replacing General Comment No. 13. The trial of civilians in military courts was reportedly 'one of the most contentious issues confronted in the negotiation of the [new General Comment]'.[72] In the text of the new document, the Committee admits that the Covenant 'does not prohibit the trial of civilians in military or special courts', as long as such trials comply with the fair trial guarantees of the Covenant.[73] Nonetheless, the Committee 'notes that the trial of civilians in military or special courts may raise serious problems as far as the equitable, impartial and independent administration of justice is concerned'.[74]

In its subsequent practice, the Committee has not faltered from the approach developed in *Madani* and *Benhadj*. Thus, in *Akwanga* v. *Cameroon*, which concerned the serious mistreatment of a political activist by the Cameroonian military authorities and his subsequent trial by a military court, the Committee again found a violation of article 14 because the state had 'not shown why recourse to a military court was required'; an examination of any actual fair trial guarantees afforded by the court was deemed unnecessary.[75] In this instance, however, there was some disagreement within the Committee as to whether there was a need to go further. One member took the view that 'the Committee should take steps to correct the notion that military courts may try civilians; its current position [being] completely out of step with modern standards of international human rights protection and with the most enlightened doctrine on the subject'.[76] A group of six members, for their part, deemed it necessary to reaffirm that 'military courts should not in principle have jurisdiction to try civilians', thus echoing Draft Principle 5, and that states must explain 'the compelling reasons or exceptional circumstances' that force them to depart from that principle.[77]

[72] Schmid, above n. 55, at 1058.

[73] Human Rights Committee, *General Comment No 32 Right to Equality before Courts and Tribunals and to a Fair Trial (Article 14)* UN Doc CCPR/C/GC/32 (23 August 2007) at [22] (footnotes omitted).

[74] Ibid., (footnotes omitted).

[75] Human Rights Committee, *Views: Communication No 1813/2008*, 101st sess, UN Doc CCPR/C/101/D/1831/2008 (22 March 2011) (*Akwanga* v. *Cameroon*) at [7.5]

[76] Ibid., Indvidual Opinion of Committee Member Mr. Fabián Omar Salvioli at [9].

[77] Ibid., Individual Opinion of Committee Members Ms. Christine Chanet, Mr. Ahmad Amin Fathalla, Ms. Zonke Zanele Majodina, Ms. Iulia Moţoc, Sir Nigel Rodley and Ms. Margo Waterval.

C European Convention on Human Rights

In Europe military trials of civilians have been evaluated in the light of Article 6(1) of the European Convention on Human Rights,[78] which provides that:

> In the determination of his civil rights and obligations or of any criminal charge against him, everyone is entitled to a fair and public hearing within a reasonable time by an independent and impartial tribunal established by law.

The bulk of the relevant case law – with one particularly noteworthy exception to be discussed below – consists of cases brought against Turkey. Under the 1982 Constitution, Turkey introduced a system of National Security Courts to try persons for crimes against the security of the state and certain other offences. These courts sat as a panel of three judges, one of them a serving military officer.

In 1994, the Commission noted in *Mitap and Müftüoglu* v. *Turkey* that '[t]his type of procedure is ... likely to raise questions regarding the concept of an impartial and independent tribunal within the meaning of Article 6 of the Convention'.[79] The Court did not, however, pronounce on this point as it deemed this aspect of the particular application to be outside its jurisdiction *ratione temporis*.[80]

However, in 1998, the Court freely ventilated its views on the matter. In *Incal* v. *Turkey*,[81] the Grand Chamber examined the status of the sole military judge and noted a number of constitutional safeguards designed to secure his or her independence and impartiality.[82] However, it also noted that (a) the judge remained a member of the armed forces, which in turn took its orders from the executive; (b) the judge remained subject to military discipline and assessment reports; (c) decisions pertaining to the appointment of the judge were to a great extent taken by the executive; (d) the judge did not have tenure.[83] Assessing, in this light, the position of the National Security Court as a whole, the Grand Chamber turned its attention to appearance: whether there was 'a legitimate reason to fear'

[78] Convention for the Protection of Human Rights and Fundamental Freedoms, Rome, 4 November 1950, in force 3 September 1953, 213 UNTS 222 (ECHR).

[79] *Mitap and Müftüoglu* v. *Turkey* (European Court of Human Rights, Chamber, Application No. 15530/89 and 15531/89, 8 December 1994 [1996] II Reports of Judgments and Decisions 415, at [94].

[80] Ibid., at [26].

[81] *Incal* v. *Turkey* (European Court of Human Rights, Grand Chamber, Application No. 22678/93, 9 June 1998).

[82] Ibid., at [67]. [83] Ibid., at [68].

that the court lacked independence or impartiality.[84] In this respect, the Grand Chamber thought that 'the standpoint of the accused is important without being decisive' and '[w]hat is decisive is whether his doubts can be held to be objectively justified'.[85] Applying this test to the particular case, the Grand Chamber concluded that, because of the participation of a military judge, 'the applicant could legitimately fear that . . . [the court] might allow itself to be unduly influenced by considerations which had nothing to do with the nature of the case'.[86] On that basis the Grand Chamber held that the applicant had 'legitimate cause to doubt the independence and impartiality' of the court, resulting in a violation of art. 6(1).[87]

The logic of *Incal* is not without difficulties. The Grand Chamber found a violation of art. 6(1) by 12 votes to 8. The judges in the minority expressed doubts as to the inferior standing of the military judge as compared to the civilian counterparts. Moreover, as regards 'appearances', they noted that 'in view of the constitutional safeguards enjoyed by military judges, doubts about their independence and impartiality cannot be regarded as objectively justified'.[88]

But, for better or for worse, the Court followed the reasons of *Incal* in a large number of subsequent cases.[89] And, in the 2005 case of *Öcalan* – well known in international law circles for its jurisdictional implications – the Court found that the replacement of the military judge mid-way through the proceedings was insufficient to cure the deficiency.[90]

84 Ibid., at [71]. 85 Ibid. 86 Ibid., at [72]. 87 Ibid., at [73].

88 Ibid., Joint Partly Dissenting Opinion of Judges Thór Vilhjálmsson, Gölcüklü, Matscher, Foighel, Sir John Freeland, Lopes Rocha, Wildhaber and Gotchev.

89 *Çiraklar* v. *Turkey* (European Court of Human Rights, Chamber, Application No. 19601/92, 28 October 1998), at [40]; *Gerger* v. *Turkey* (European Court of Human Rights, Grand Chamber, Application No. 2419/94, 8 July 1999); *Sürek and Özdemir* v. *Turkey* (European Court of Human Rights, Grand Chamber, Application No. 23927/94 and 24277/94, 8 July 1999); *Sürek* v. *Turkey (No. 1)* (European Court of Human Rights, Grand Chamber, Application No. 26682/95, 8 July 1999); *Sürek* v. *Turkey (No. 2)* (European Court of Human Rights, Grand Chamber, Application No. 24122/94, 8 July 1999), *Sürek* v. *Turkey (No. 3)* (European Court of Human Rights, Grand Chamber, Application No. 24735/94, 8 July 1999); *Sürek* v. *Turkey (No. 4)* (European Court of Human Rights, Grand Chamber, Application No. 24762/94, 8 July 1999); *Okçuoğlu* v. *Turkey* (European Court of Human Rights, Grand Chamber, Application No. 24246/94, 8 July 1999); *Başkaya and Okçuoğlu* v. *Turkey* (European Court of Human Rights, Grand Chamber, Application No. 23536/94 and 24408/94, 8 July 1999); *Karataş* v. *Turkey* (European Court of Human Rights, Grand Chamber, Application No. 23168/94, 8 July 1999); *Ülger* v. *Turkey* (European Court of Human Rights, Application No. 57250/00, 29 July 2004).

90 *Öcalan* v. *Turkey* (European Court of Human Rights, Grand Chamber, Application No. 46221/99, 12 May 2005) at [117]–[118].

In the 2006 case of *Ergin* v. *Turkey*, concerning the trial of a civilian for incitement to evade military service before a full-fledged military court, the Court recalled its earlier case law and noted that the arguments made in connection with courts having a single military judge applied *a fortiori* in case of a court made up entirely of military personnel.[91] Curiously, however, the Court admitted 'that it cannot be contended that the Convention absolutely excludes the jurisdiction of military courts to try cases in which civilians are implicated' but 'only in very exceptional circumstances could the determination of criminal charges against civilians in such courts be held to be compatible with Article 6'.[92]

The Court drew support from case law of the Inter-American Court and the Human Rights Committee, as well as Principle 5 in the Draft Principles Governing the Administration of Justice through Military Tribunals.[93] It then made three relevant observations. First, the Court noted 'the particular position occupied by the army in the constitutional order of democratic States, which must be limited to the field of national security' and that 'judicial power is in principle an attribute of civil society'.[94] This is similar to references made by the Inter-American Court in *Durand and Ugarte* to 'a democratic Government of Laws' and 'the functions assigned by law to the military forces'.[95] Second, the Court held that '[t]he power of military criminal justice should not extend to civilians unless there are compelling reasons justifying such a situation, and if so only on a clear and foreseeable legal basis' and that 'the existence of such reasons must be substantiated in each specific case'.[96] This echoes the recent thinking of the Human Rights Committee, as expressed in General Comment No. 32.[97] Finally, the Court observed that 'situations in which a military court has jurisdiction to try a civilian for acts against the armed forces may give rise to reasonable doubts about such a court's objective impartiality' in that there may be insufficient distance between one party to the proceedings and the court itself.[98] The Court clearly had in mind some kind of a violation of the *nemo iudex in causa sua* principle – the armed forces would act, as it were, both as the

[91] *Ergin* v. *Turkey (No. 6)* (European Court of Human Rights, Application No. 47533/99, 4 May 2006), at [43]–[44].
[92] Ibid., at [44]. [93] Ibid., at [45] read in conjunction with [20]–[25]. [94] Ibid., at [46].
[95] *Durand and Ugarte* v. *Peru* (2000) Inter-Am Court HR (ser C) No. 68, at [117].
[96] *Ergin* v. *Turkey (No. 6)* (Application No. 47533/99), at [47].
[97] See text accompanying n. 73 above.
[98] *Ergin* v. *Turkey (No. 6)* (Application No. 47533/99), at [49].

judge and the prosecutor in a particular case. A similar point was made by the inter-American Commission in its 1993 *Annual Report*.[99]

Thus, the Court hedged its bets. It no longer relied exclusively on the 'appearance' of independence and impartiality, but also made use of the functional and equality of arms arguments found in the case law of the inter-American system and, like the Human Rights Committee, insisted on a justification. While a comparative approach is commendable in principle, the plausibility of the outcome depends on the merits of the jurisprudence examined by the Court. As has been briefly noted above, the approaches of the inter-American system and the Human Rights Committee have problems of their own.

One final case from the European Court of Human Rights, *Martin* v. *UK*,[100] bears mentioning in this context. Indeed it is the only instance, as far as I am aware, where a human rights treaty body has considered the position of an 'associated civilian', that is, a civilian deployed with or otherwise accompanying the armed forces abroad. Chronologically, *Martin* is also the most recent of the European Court's judgments considered here, having been handed down some six months after *Ergin*. This case arose from the military trial of the son of a British service member in Germany. What made the case particularly troubling was that Mr Martin was seventeen years old at the time and, having been temporarily detained in the United Kingdom, was returned to Germany to stand trial before a court martial. The Court found a violation of art. 6(1) of the ECHR as a result of an assessment of the composition, structure and procedure of the court martial.[101] While the Court had 'considerable doubts' as to whether the circumstances 'were sufficiently "compelling" to justify the trial of a civilian before a military tribunal', it did not pronounce upon the point.[102]

D Synthesis

Assessing the compatibility of military trials of associated civilians with human rights law in the light of the foregoing is a difficult exercise. Human rights treaty bodies have seldom been faced with that category of civilians and their approach to civilians more generally has hardly been uniform.

[99] See text accompanying n. 38 above.

[100] *Martin* v. *United Kingdom* (European Court of Human Rights, Application No. 40426/98, 24 October 2006).

[101] Ibid., at [46]–[54]. [102] Ibid., at [45].

It is clear that a state party to the American Convention is completely precluded from trying civilians before military courts. As regards states that have to face the ECtHR and/or the Human Rights Committee, the situation is somewhat different. Broadly speaking, a two-pronged test has been established. A military trial of a civilian is only permitted if (a) it is necessary and justified in the particular case by 'objective and serious reasons' (HRCtte) or 'compelling reasons' (ECtHR) (commentators have referred to this as the 'justification test'), and (b) the court and the trial meet all the fair trial guarantees established by the relevant human rights treaty (standards test).[103] Moreover, with respect to the justification test, the burden of proof lies squarely with the state.

The standards test is, of course, beyond reproach as a matter of principle. It is at the core of the right to a fair trial as guaranteed by human rights instruments. In the context of military courts, however, two points are worth making. First, treaty bodies arguably apply stricter requirements of independence and impartiality on military courts than civilian courts,[104] whether in the context of trying service members or civilians. For example, the eight dissenting judges in *Incal* seemed concerned with the Court's use of such standards to discredit the military judge that even the civilian judges might not necessarily meet.[105] Second, the heavy reliance on mere appearance and the readiness to see the presence of a military judge, without further, as a legitimate threat, appears to be grounded more in preconceived ideas than in an objective assessment. There have been instances in the practice of the Turkish National Security Court where the military judge has either joined one of the civilian colleagues to form a majority in an acquittal, or voted for a more lenient sentence than either of the civilian colleagues,[106] suggesting that there is little basis for the quasi-presumption that a military judge is more likely to convict.

The justification test is a far more complicated matter. Eminent scholars have suggested that the determining factor should be the standards test as 'there is no reason in principle why, if [sufficient] safeguards are taken . . . a military court . . . cannot be an independent and impartial tribunal'.[107] Others, however, argue that while the clear enunciation of

[103] Shah, above n. 54, at 146; Schmid, above n. 55, at 1062.

[104] Ann Lyon, 'Two Swords and Two Standards' (2005) *Criminal Law Review*, p. 850.

[105] Ibid., Joint Partly Dissenting Opinion of Judges Thór Vilhjálmsson, Gölcüklü, Matscher, Foighel, Sir John Freeland, Lopes Rocha, Wildhaber and Gotchev.

[106] Bucherer, above n. 31, pp. 71–72.

[107] Peter Rowe, *The Impact of Human Rights Law on Armed Forces* (Cambridge, Cambridge University Press, 2006), p. 101.

the justification test by the Human Rights Committee is a novel development, it is one that is in line with its previous practice.[108]

The problem is not so much the justification test itself but the failure to articulate its legal basis. The ECtHR has only fleetingly touched upon a potential rationale for the test, noting that civilians 'might find themselves in a significantly different position from that of citizens tried by the ordinary courts'.[109] But the Court has failed to substantiate this argument by any references to the non-discrimination clause in art. 14 of the Convention.

The situation with respect to the ICCPR is even more peculiar. Article 14(1) begins with a statement that '[a]ll persons shall be equal before the courts and tribunals'. General Comment No. 32 explains that:

> equality before courts and tribunals . . . requires that similar cases are dealt with in similar proceedings. If, for example, exceptional criminal procedures or specially constituted courts or tribunals apply in the determination of certain categories of cases, objective and reasonable grounds must be provided to justify the distinction.[110]

Yet, the problem of civilians before military courts remains disconnected from this principle in both the case law and the General Comment. The few commentators who have critically examined the jurisprudence of the treaty bodies have also noted the role potentially played by the principle of equality, and some have scolded the treaty bodies for not being clearer that their views are partially based on concerns for equal treatment.[111]

V Assessment

What then of trials of associated civilians before military courts? Are there any reasons for such trials that would outweigh the potential deviation from the principle of equality before courts? There appear to be a number of practical and policy considerations that, in combination, may be sufficiently compelling.

108 Shah, above n. 54, at 146; Schmid, above n. 55, at 1063–64.

109 *Ergin* v. *Turkey (No. 6)* (Application No. 47533/99), at [48].

110 Human Rights Committee, *General Comment No 32*, UN Doc CCPR/C/GC/32, at [14].

111 Daniel Moeckli, *Human Rights and Non-Discrimination in the 'War on Terror'* (Oxford, Oxford University Press, 2008), p. 134; Shah, above n. 54, at 149 (noting that, in *Madani*, 'the Committee failed to justify its approach in terms of *both* equality before the courts and the equitable, impartial and independent administration of justice'). Schmid, above n. 55, at 1064–65.

(a) Military courts may have broader competence to deal with offences committed abroad. Especially in common law countries, the broad extraterritorial jurisdiction that might be necessary to deal with the misconduct of associated civilians may be lacking under ordinary criminal law. Even for continental law countries that generally claim jurisdiction over the conduct of their nationals abroad, associated civilians may be a challenge as they may not be nationals of that state, or there might be procedural impediments for exercising jurisdiction that do not exist with respect to military personnel. Extraterritorial jurisdiction over associated civilians as a matter of international law is an extension of extraterritorial jurisdiction over military personnel,[112] rather than nationals in general. That said, there is nothing in principle to prevent such jurisdiction from being conferred on civilian courts.

(b) Military criminal law often provides for offences that do not exist under civilian law. Admittedly, not all of offences under military law are capable of being committed by civilians. However, some provisions prove invaluable in dealing with the misconduct of associated civilians abroad. In particular, military law generally allows for the prosecution of acts that contravene standing orders (general orders).[113] Such orders permit, for example, the commander of a forward operating base to tailor the military code of conduct to the circumstances prevailing on the ground.[114] But again there is nothing that would prevent the violation of such orders from being proscribed under civilian criminal law.

(c) Military courts can be more easily deployed. The courts of common law countries rely to a greater extent on oral testimony than their counterparts in countries with a continental tradition. In common law countries, it may therefore be seen as imperative to hold the trial of an associated civilian overseas and a military court would be better suited for that purpose. While this is a crucial argument for many proponents of military courts, there are a few points that can be made in opposition. First, it is not impossible for a civilian court to sit

112 Rain Liivoja, 'Service Jurisdiction in International Law' (2010) 11 *Melbourne Journal of International Law* at 309.

113 Armed Forces Act 2006 (UK) s. 13; Defence Force Discipline Act 1982 (Cth) s. 29.

114 In some states, it might be possible to charge an associated civilian with conduct prejudicial to the discipline of, or bring discredit on, the armed forces. This provision captures disciplinary violations that other provisions cannot. It can also be used to prosecute conduct that has seriously violated local law. Civilians cannot be prosecuted for prejudicial conduct under UK or Australian law: Armed Forces Act 2006 (UK) s. 19; Defence Force Discipline Act 1982 (Cth) s. 60.

overseas,[115] although the host state may have more serious concerns with that possibility than with military courts. Second, even military courts are often prevented from sitting in zones of operations because of security concerns. Thus, several courts martial relating to the conduct of UK forces in Iraq have been held in the United Kingdom. Third, given the availability of audio-visual communication technology, the need to hold hearings overseas may not be as pressing as is sometimes suggested. Fourth, for more serious offences, in the time it takes for a case to reach the trial stage, the defendant may already be rotated back to the sending state. To then transfer him or her back overseas to stand trial may be unreasonable.

(d) The military justice system often contains a policing and investigative capacity that can be utilised for the purposes of trials before military courts. For example, the three countries I mentioned at the beginning have dedicated military investigation services that can be deployed on the same basis as the military courts.[116] They also have military police units to deal with preliminary matters such as pre-trial detention. That said, the internal investigative capacities may often lack the ability to conduct investigations into serious offences, which would necessitate the deployment of civilian law enforcement officials in any event.

In sum, there appear to be several reasons why states may wish to place associated civilians under the jurisdiction of military tribunals. While none of the difficulties appears to be insurmountable, they may, taken as together, lead to the conclusion that it is more efficient to try civilians alongside military personnel, and that this would also ensure a higher degree of accountability among associated civilians.

[115] See, for example, 'War Crimes Jury Relives History' *BBC News*, 16 February 1999 http://news.bbc.co.uk/2/hi/uk_news/280999.stm (British court visiting the alleged scene of WWII-era war crimes in Belarus); Rain Liivoja, 'Dish of the Day: *Justice sans frontiers à la finlandaise*' (2010) 1 *Helsinki Review of Global Governance*, p. 20 (a Finnish court holding hearings in a genocide trial in Rwanda).

[116] In the United States, every branch of the armed forces has its own investigative service, which is independent of the military police (and, at least as concerns the Navy, largely civilianised): Army Criminal Investigation Command (USACIDC or CID), Air Force Office of Special Investigations (AFOSI or OSI), Naval Criminal Investigative Service (NCIS), United States Marine Corps Criminal Investigation Division (CID), and Coast Guard Investigative Service (CGIS). In the UK, there is a Special Investigation Branch (SIB) in all three service police arms – the Royal Navy Police, the Royal Military Police and the Royal Air Force Police. In Australia, there is a uniform Australian Defence Force Investigative Service (ADFIS), whose commanding officer reports directly to the Chief of the Defence Force.

To return, once more, to the question of equality, a question arises as to *who* the associated civilians should be equal with. Indeed, it can be argued that the main reference point for equality should not be other civilians back home, but rather service members deployed on an operation abroad. In particular, given that private contractors increasingly perform tasks of a highly military character, which previously were undertaken by uniformed personnel, should they not be held accountable in a manner similar to the military personnel?[117] From this perspective, accompanying family members may be distinguishable from military contractors. Dependants often have little choice but to accompany a service member abroad – Mr Martin probably had no say in his father's deployment to Germany. Private contractors, on the other hand, willingly seek employment in the armed forces abroad. In some respects, they have become functionally (if not legally) equivalent to soldiers.

In her 2013 report, the UN Special Rapporteur on the independence of judges and lawyers, Ms Gabriela Knaul, carefully considered the broad question of the administration of justice through military courts and the trial of civilians in particular.[118] While the Special Rapporteur took the view that the jurisdiction of military courts should be restricted to the military offences of military personnel,[119] she conceded that more extensive jurisdiction 'may be required to prevent situations of de facto impunity arising in cases where civilians accompany the armed forces on extraterritorial deployments in States with weak or dysfunctional legal systems'.[120] Consequently, the Special Rapporteur made the following recommendation:

> The trial of civilians in military courts should be limited strictly to exceptional cases concerning civilians assimilated to military personnel by virtue of their function and/or geographical presence who have allegedly perpetrated an offence outside the territory of the State and where regular courts, whether local or those of the State of origin, are unable to undertake the trial.[121]

While this approach may not satisfy those looking for a straightforward ban on the military trials of civilians, the Special Rapporteur's recommendation appears to be far more consistent with the current human

[117] Ian Baldwin, 'Comrades in Arms: Using the Uniform Code of Military Justice and the Military Extraterritorial Jurisdiction Act to Prosecute Civilian-Contractor Misconduct' (2008) 94 *Iowa Law Review*, p. 287, at 312.

[118] Gabriela Knaul, Special Rapporteur, 'Independence of Judges and Lawyers' 68th Sess, UN Doc. A/68/285 (7 August 2013).

[119] Ibid., at [54], [100]. [120] Ibid., at [55]. [121] Ibid., at [102].

rights law standards than the rather absolute Principle 5 of the Draft Principles Governing the Administration of Justice.

VI Concluding remarks

As a general rule, international human rights law does not prohibit military trials of civilians, but places strict requirements of fairness on such trials, coupled with an obligation on states to justify the use of special courts. There may be good reasons for placing associated civilians deployed on overseas operations, particularly military contractors, under military law. Some of these factors may, in the light of the traditions of particular legal systems, create a strong preference for allowing military courts to try associated civilians and amount to sufficiently compelling reasons for human rights purposes. In recent years there have been serious difficulties in ensuring the accountability of military contractors. Therefore, it seems useful to explore what military justice has to offer. To mitigate some of the human rights concerns, it may be possible to make procedural adjustments: as noted, the United Kingdom now has court-martial panels made up entirely of civilians to try associated civilians under military law. In any event, a knee-jerk reaction to military justice in this context is not the answer.

6

The impact of military justice reforms on the law of armed conflict: how to avoid unintended consequences

VICTOR HANSEN

I Introduction

We are in the midst of a military justice revolution. That revolution is driven by the notion that 'traditional' military justice systems no longer work effectively and by a belief that they should conform to society's broader understanding of what constitutes a fair system of justice. Minor modifications are not enough. Many reformers, particularly those in common law countries, have called for fundamental changes to bring military justice into the modern age. If there is one overarching theme to these reforms, it is a clear trend towards 'civilianising military justice', that is, reforming military justice so that it mirrors the civilian justice system.

There are a number of influences driving this reform. The most important of these influences come from the human rights community and from those who argue that a division of institutional authority is essential to be considered fair. The human rights focus on military justice has largely been comparative. Reformers in this camp primarily examine the procedures and protections available in a given military justice system and compare them with civilian systems. To the extent that procedures in the military differ and seem to provide less protection, human rights advocates contend they should be overhauled. Many of these criticisms do not focus on individual cases or specific examples of injustice within the military justice system. Instead, they assume that, if these processes differ and seem less protective of individual rights than civilian systems,

Material from this chapter has previously been published in V Hansen, 'The Impact of Military Justice Reforms on the Law of Armed Conflict: How to Avoid Unintended Consequences' (2013) 21 *Michigan State International Law Review 229*.

military justice is inherently unfair and must be better aligned with civilian law.

Other reformers gauge the fairness of a military justice system by focusing on the way in which authority is divided. For example, are the key decisions on the disposition and adjudication of cases given to a single authority? I refer to those who focus on these questions as 'separation of power reformers'. They are critical of military justice systems that give a single office, typically the military commander, absolute authority to decide who to bring to trial, for what offences and the final disposition of the case. Separation of power reformers do not focus on proving injustices in specific cases, but instead argue that a system where so much power rests in one office is inherently unfair and must be changed.

The focus of this chapter is on the role of the military commander in the traditional military justice system. The chapter asks whether reforms reducing the role of the commander in military justice systems have adequately considered the commander's obligations under the law of armed conflict (LOAC). The last section of the chapter identifies those features of military justice where the commander's continued involvement is essential if the commander is to meet LOAC obligations and those areas where reforms can and should be made without diminishing the commander's essential functions.

II The role of the military commander and the law of armed conflict

Understanding the key role of the commander in military justice matters is important to an assessment of the merit of reforms to military justice. Certainly some rationale for placing the commander at the head of military justice derives from the fact that the commander needs to control all aspects of military operations to be effective. But if this is the only reason for the commander to remain at the apex of military justice, perhaps the reforms that have occurred in many countries are justified. This is because there are other offices and processes that can perform criminal justice functions as effectively as the military commander and in a way that provides greater protections for the accused service member. Efforts to better align military justice with civilian systems are only part of the equation. The critical issue of a military commander's responsibilities under the law of armed conflict is often unrecognised.

The law of armed conflict is a unique legal regime. It seeks to inject humanitarian regulation into the brutal endeavour of warfare. A person who has not experienced war can never truly understand the demands placed on warriors, officers and non-commissioned officers responsible for their leadership. Military training involves developing a genuine killer instinct – a willingness to take life on order and without hesitation. Professional warriors must also be able to essentially suspend that instinct at a moment's notice in order to exercise humanitarian constraint and preserve the crucial line between legitimate and illegitimate violence, the ultimate objective of LOAC.

The brutality, intensity and sheer terror of warfare therefore stress the ability of military leaders to ensure that their subordinates respect LOAC obligations. Commanders, staff officers and their legal advisors must understand these obligations and correctly apply the law during ongoing military operations. Beyond the commander's responsibility to know the law and harmonise operational decisions to the dictates of LOAC, commanders also bear the additional and critical responsibility to prepare their subordinates to respect these obligations and to establish a command culture that prioritises fidelity to the law.

The person responsible for moulding a group of individuals into an efficient and effective military unit is the commander. The commander holds a unique position in a military organisation. Primarily through the use of positive leadership and example, the commander sets the tone for the unit and ensures that soldiers are well trained and prepared to conduct military operations and achieve the unit's objectives. The commander is the focal point of military discipline and order within the unit and is thus responsible for maintaining command and control over subordinate forces. The commander stands on the line that separates a disciplined military unit from a lawless mob. Through the use of all available resources, including moral authority, law and collective purpose, the military commander ensures that forces under command effectively execute military operations – which often involve the decisive application of deadly combat power – in a manner that fully complies with LOAC. When military units fail to do so, it is largely attributable to the commander's failings.

A commander can fail this most vital responsibility in any number of ways. There are situations when the commander's actions are directly responsible for LOAC violations committed by his forces. For example, if a commander participates in the unlawful targeting and killing of civilians, there is direct criminal liability under LOAC for the resulting harm. Likewise, a commander who orders forces to attack a protected place is, as a result of ordering unlawful conduct, responsible for the subsequent LOAC violation. Similarly, a commander who encourages forces to kill or otherwise mistreat prisoners of war, or a commander who assists subordinates in covering up evidence of a past war crime, is criminally liable for those LOAC violations. In these examples, the commander's complicity with an LOAC violation is direct and punishable through the application of accomplice liability theory. Even if the commander's involvement is not direct, it is easy to see the way in which encouragement and assistance can contribute to LOAC violations, resulting in culpability.

There are numerous scenarios where a commander's action or inaction can have a close and direct nexus to the war crimes committed by subordinates. Even if a commander did not directly order forces under command to engage in conduct in violation of LOAC, the commander may have permitted or acquiesced in those violations. In such cases, the nexus between commander inaction and a subordinate's war crime exists because soldiers frequently and unquestionably interpret the commander's inaction and acquiescence as approval and permission.

One of the most important components of LOAC, therefore, is the mechanism that evolved to hold commanders accountable where their direct participation, encouragement, incitement, involvement, knowledge and/or acquiescence in LOAC violations is either direct, or where the nexus between the commander's actions and the crime is clear. Even if the commander's involvement were less direct, such as ordering forces to commit unlawful killings but not directly participating in those killings, the doctrine of accomplice liability would provide a solid basis for criminal accountability. If a commander ordered, encouraged or otherwise supported forces in committing war crimes, and shared in the criminal purpose or design of the perpetrators, and this action or failure to act aids, abets, counsels or commands the perpetrator to commit the offence, then the commander could be guilty as a principal.[1]

A *The command responsibility doctrine*

None of this is in any way remarkable. It is merely an application of traditional accomplice liability principles to cases where the offence is charged as a war crime or a violation of the Uniform Code of Military Justice (UCMJ) in the United States. LOAC relies so heavily on commanders executing their responsibilities that it is logical that legal mechanisms exist to hold commanders accountable when evidence establishes either that the commander is directly involved in LOAC

[1] Uniform Code of Military Justice, 10 USC § 877 (2010).

violations or that the commander has acceded as an accomplice or an accessory. Without such legal mechanisms, LOAC principles would be largely ineffective and unenforceable.

This legal structure would be incomplete, however, if these were the only mechanisms available to establish command responsibility for LOAC violations. Direct liability, accomplice liability and the liability of an accessory only address situations of commander complicity; where the evidence establishes that the commander has some independent or shared intent to commit war crimes or prevent their detection. Punishing commanders in these situations will certainly deter such complicity, but will not necessarily foster a command culture that emphasises LOAC compliance and condemns violations.

How does the law address situations where a commander's dereliction of duty contributes to subordinate LOAC violations? What about a commander who remains wilfully ignorant of battlefield reports indicating LOAC violations, or who upon receiving such reports fails to take appropriate remedial action? In these instances, it is the lack of action that contributes to subordinate violations, often without any intent to violate LOAC on the part of the commander. And yet, in such instances, the commander's failings may set the conditions for the commission of war crimes by the forces under command. As the individual in the critical position directly responsible for ensuring LOAC compliance within a military unit, should a commander bear responsibility when the risk becomes reality?

The answer is found in the doctrine of command responsibility, developed in customary international law.[2] Its purpose was to align the scope of a commander's criminal accountability for war crimes committed by subordinates with the full extent of the commander's obligation to ensure subordinate compliance with the law. The doctrine accounts for two situations: first, where responsibility for war crimes is established by traditional complicity principles; and second, where the commander was not complicit in the traditional sense but was derelict in the duty to ensure respect for the law by forces under command. If evidence establishes the commander's dereliction under this second prong of the doctrine, criminal responsibility may be imputed to the commander for the war crimes committed by soldiers. The commander is punished *as if he or she* had committed those crimes, not merely for

[2] Mirjan Damaska, 'The Shadow Side of Command Responsibility' (2001) 49 *American Journal of Comparative Law*, p. 455 at 455.

dereliction of duty as a commanding officer. Extending a commander's legal responsibility for subordinate misconduct beyond situations of traditional complicity ultimately provides a necessary incentive to train, monitor, supervise and correct subordinates, and in so doing, to establish a command culture of commitment to compliance with the law of armed conflict.

Command responsibility was firmly established as a legal doctrine in the war crimes tribunals following World War II but the idea of holding a commander responsible for subordinates' criminal and law of war violations had much earlier origins. One of the most frequently cited examples is the Ordinance of Orleans, issued in 1439 by Charles VII of France. The Lieber Code developed in the American Civil War is another example. Article 71 of the Lieber Code established that:

> Whosoever intentionally inflicts additional wounds on an enemy already wholly disabled, or kills such an enemy, or who orders or encourages soldiers to do so, shall suffer death, if duly convicted, whether he belongs to the Army of the United States, or is an enemy captured after having committed his misdeed.[3]

The Fourth Hague Convention of 1907 respecting the laws and customs of war on land was the first modern treaty to impose a form of command responsibility as a matter of express international legal obligation. Article 3 states, 'A belligerent party which violates the provisions of the said Regulations shall, if the case demands, be liable to pay compensation. It shall be responsible for all acts committed by persons forming part of its armed forces.'[4] The underlying premise of the modern command responsibility doctrine is also reflected in Chapter 1, Article 1 of the Hague Convention, which established what is recognised as a key characteristic of an army or other organised militia: the military organisation is 'commanded by a person responsible for his subordinates'.[5]

These historical antecedents to the contemporary command responsibility doctrine have several common themes. They all recognise the unique position a commander holds in a military organisation. They all reflect the axiom that command authority includes both the legal authority and the legal obligation to control subordinate conduct in order to

[3] Richard Shelly Hartigan, *Lieber's Code and the Law of War* (Chicago, IL, Precedent Publishing, 1983), p. 45.

[4] Hague Convention (IV) Respecting the Laws and Customs of War on Land, Annex to the Regulations Respecting the Laws and Customs of War on Land, The Hague, 18 October 1907, in force 26 January 1910, [1910] UKTS 9 (Hague Convention IV).

[5] Ibid., art. 1.

achieve military objectives while respecting the then existing humanitarian limits on the conduct of hostilities. All of these antecedents also implicitly recognise that imposing responsibility on the commander for the conduct of subordinates enhances the probability of such respect. These antecedents also recognise that a commander can be held accountable for subordinates' law of war violations if the commander was directly involved, or even in some cases where the involvement was less direct or obvious. From this foundation, the modern doctrine of command responsibility emerged at the end of World War II.

The most well known case of command responsibility was the trial of General Yamashita. At the end of World War II, General Yamashita was the Commanding General of the Fourteenth Army Group of the Imperial Japanese Army in the Philippine Islands. The Japanese government placed General Yamashita in command of these forces just ten days before the American forces landed in the Philippines. This was a desperate time for the Japanese forces, which turned Manila into a battlefield. The Japanese military was responsible for the death of an estimated 100,000 Filipino civilians and committed many other atrocities.

The prosecution argued that these violations were so flagrant and enormous that they must have been known to General Yamashita if he had made any effort to fulfil his responsibilities as a commander.[6] If General Yamashita did know of these offences, he was complicit by his failure to stop them. If he did not know of these acts, it was because he 'took affirmative action not to know'.[7] In either case, he bore individual criminal responsibility.

The military commission that tried General Yamashita rejected the assertion that because he took no part in the crimes committed by his troops, and because he did not know what was occurring under his command, he was not criminally liable. The commission found the 'crimes were so extensive and widespread, both as to time and area, that they must either have been willfully permitted by [Yamashita], or secretly ordered by [him]'.[8] The president of the commission stated:

> [W]here murder and rape and vicious, revengeful actions are widespread offences, and there is no effective attempt by a commander to discover and control the criminal acts, such a commander may be held responsible,

[6] See *Trial of General Tomoyuki Yamashita*, United States Military Commission, Manila (8 October–7 December 1945) and Supreme Court of the United States (judgment delivered on 4 February 1946), case extracted in UN War Crimes Commission, *Law Reports of Trials of War Criminals*, (1948) vol. 4, at 17 (*Yamashita*).

[7] Ibid. [8] Ibid., at 34.

> even criminally liable, for the lawless acts of his troops, depending upon their nature and the circumstances surrounding them.[9]

The key elements of the command responsibility doctrine emerged from this case. A commander's responsibility and liability is predicated on (1) a command relationship between the superior and subordinate; (2) information or knowledge that triggers the commander's duty to act; (3) if the duty to act is triggered, the commander must take some action regarding the ongoing or anticipated law of war violations by subordinates; and (4) a causal relationship between the commander's omission and the war crimes committed by the subordinates.

In 1977 Additional Protocol I to the 1949 Geneva Convention was promulgated and it included the first express treaty provision establishing individual criminal command responsibility.[10] The doctrine of command responsibility is central to the accountability framework in AP I. Articles 86 and 87 develop the command responsibility doctrine by articulating specific duties for a commander to ensure law of war compliance. The commander has the duty to prevent and repress breaches of AP I and the Geneva Conventions.[11] Commanders must also prevent violations, or take penal or disciplinary actions against violations of which they become aware.[12] Collectively, the commander's duties are to prevent future war crimes, suppress or stop ongoing crimes, and report and punish past crimes.

The International Criminal Tribunal for the former Yugoslavia (ICTY) and the International Criminal Tribunal for Rwanda (ICTR) initiated the contemporary evolution of the command responsibility doctrine. The command responsibility provision in the statutes for each tribunal, promulgated in 1993 and 1994, respectively, are virtually identical. Article 7(3) of the ICTY states:

> The fact that any of the acts referred to in articles 2 and 5 of the present Statute [Grave Breaches of the Geneva Conventions of 1949 and Crimes Against Humanity] was committed by a subordinate does not relieve his superior of criminal liability if he knew or had reason to know that the subordinate was about to commit such acts or had done so and the

[9] Ibid., at 35.

[10] Protocol Additional to the Geneva Conventions of 12 August 1949, and Relating to the Protection of Victims of International Armed Conflicts, 8 June 1977, in force 7 December 1978, 1125 UNTS 3 (AP I).

[11] AP I art. 86. [12] Ibid., art. 87 (1), (3).

superior failed to take the necessary and reasonable measures to prevent such acts or to punish the perpetrators thereof.[13]

The Rome Statute of the International Criminal Court[14] provides the most recent international codification of the command responsibility doctrine. The Rome Statute vests the International Criminal Court (ICC) with jurisdiction for cases involving genocide, crimes against humanity, war crimes and the crime of aggression. Article 28 of the Rome Statute is entitled 'Responsibility of Commanders and Other Superiors' and provides:

(a) A military commander or person effectively acting as a military commander shall be criminally responsible for crimes within the jurisdiction of the Court committed by forces under his or her effective command and control, or effective authority and control as the case may be, as a result of his or her failure to exercise control properly over such forces, where:
   (i) That military commander or person either knew or, owing to the circumstances at the time, should have known that the forces were committing or about to commit such crimes; and
   (ii) That military commander or person failed to take all necessary and reasonable measures within his or her power to prevent or repress their commission or to submit the matter to the competent authorities for investigation and prosecution.

(b) With respect to superior and subordinate relationships not described in paragraph (a), a superior shall be criminally responsible for crimes within the jurisdiction of the Court committed by subordinates under his or her effective authority and control, as a result of his or her failure to exercise control properly over such subordinates, where:
   (i) The superior either knew, or consciously disregarded information which clearly indicated, that the subordinates were committing or about to commit such crimes;
   (ii) The crimes concerned activities that were within the effective responsibility and control of the superior; and

[13] SC Res 808, UN SCOR, 48th sess, 3175th mtg, UN Doc S./RES/808 (3 May 1993) at 15. The equivalent provision of the Statute of the International Criminal Tribunal for Rwanda is located in SC Res 995, UN SCOR, 49th sess, 3453th mtg, UN Doc S./RES/955 (8 November 1994) art. 6(3).

[14] Rome Statute of the International Criminal Court, Rome, 17 July 1998, in force 1 July 2002, 2187 UNTS 3 (Rome Statute).

(iii) The superior failed to take all necessary and reasonable measures within his or her power to prevent or repress their commission or to submit the matter to the competent authorities for investigation and prosecution.[15]

The Rome Statute explicitly provides that a culpable commander 'shall be criminally responsible for crimes within the jurisdiction of the Court committed by forces under his or her effective command and control'.[16] This is a reflection of the traditional scope of command responsibility, holding the commander accountable not merely for a dereliction, but also for the offences caused by that dereliction. Since *Yamashita*, this concept has been a key component of the doctrine but the Rome Statute is the first specific codification of this imputed liability theory under international law.

B Command responsibility and the role of the commander in military justice

The doctrine of command responsibility, which is reflected in both customary law and various international treaties and statues, has important implications for the role of the commander with respect to military justice. Commanders are expected to control the forces under their command. They are expected to train their forces to comply with the laws of war, to assert positive leadership over their forces and to be fully engaged in combat operations. Most importantly, commanders must prevent, suppress and punish the forces under their command according to the law of war violations. Commanders who fail in any of these duties, whether due to negligence or to wilful blindness, may be held personally liable for the crimes committed by their subordinate forces.

If reforms and efforts to civilianise military justice systems reduce the commander's role in the system, what are the consequences for liability under the doctrine of command responsibility? If commanders lose a significant portion of the disciplinary authority, do they no longer occupy that critical position of responsibility over the forces under their command? Recent efforts to reform military justice based on human rights and separation of power principles have not focused on the way in which these reforms could impact on the commander's obligations with respect to the law of armed conflict and the doctrine of command responsibility.

[15] Ibid., art. 28. [16] Ibid.

III Reform efforts and the essence of command

In many jurisdictions, reforms to military justice have occurred in response to judicial decisions. The cases which have sparked these reforms are focused almost exclusively on comparing military justice systems to their civilian counterparts. This civilian focus can be seen most clearly in the reforms themselves. In Canada and the United Kingdom, for example, the commander has been essentially removed from the charging and convening process. These functions are now performed by offices independent from the commander. Similarly, calls for reform in the United States and Australia[17] seek to give military judges more authority and independence; the kind of authority and independence that judges in civilian courts enjoy. In addition, reformers in the United States want to abolish summary courts because of the control and influence the commander has over the process. These and other reforms appear designed to remove the commander from the military justice process because of concerns about command influence and the unfairness it might cause.

There is little indication, however, that courts and reformers gave much if any consideration to the impact of reforms on the commander's responsibilities under the law of armed conflict. The opinions in the European Court of Human Rights and in the Canadian Supreme Court make no mention of the doctrine of command responsibility or the obligations of commanders.[18] Nor do these cases consider how the military justice system and the commander's involvement in that system can aid the commander in meeting these obligations. The failure to directly consider the impact of reforms on command responsibility does not necessarily invalidate reforms to military justice but disregarding or ignoring the relationship between military justice and the commander's obligations under the law of armed conflict can have unintended consequences. Many questions relating to command responsibility are raised by reforms to military justice. Can prosecutors or judges be held criminally liable if they fail either to prosecute or to convene a court martial to try service members for law of war violations? Must these, or similarly situated, officials be consulted and involved in the training of service members and in the planning of military operations because they now have the responsibility for prosecuting and convening courts for law

[17] See Chapter 13.

[18] See, for example, *R* v. *Généreux* [1992] 1 SCR 259 at 286; *Findlay* v. *United Kingdom* (1997) 24 EHHR 221.

of war violations? Is the commander, who has lost some authority by losing the ability to maintain discipline through the military justice system, in a situation where he or she is given responsibility to maintain discipline and control without having sufficient authority to meet that obligation? Is the commander still likely to be held criminally liable for failings that are now beyond his or her control? Are the military forces less likely to respect and abide by the directions and commands of an officer who they know has little ability to punish them for their misconduct? What are the essential roles that a commander must perform in military justice? Under the law of armed conflict, what are the functions of the commander that cannot be delegated to others?

If the commander is accountable for taking all reasonable and necessary measures to prevent, suppress and punish war crimes committed by subordinate forces, and also has an affirmative duty to know what subordinate forces are doing during military operations, certain obligations are non-delegable. These include disciplining subordinates and understanding both the context of misconduct and its impact on order and discipline within the unit, establishing and modelling respect for the rule of law, specifically the obligations of the law of armed conflict, training subordinates on law of war compliance, and ensuring that operations are conducted in compliance with the law of armed conflict. These represent the core functions of command as it relates to compliance with the law of armed conflict. Each function will be examined separately.

A The commander as the source of discipline

As the commander is potentially responsible for the war crimes committed by subordinates, the commander must possess the ability to discipline those subordinates in order to prevent, suppress and punish law of war violations. Without this ability, any demands imposed by the commander to abide by the law will ring hollow. Subordinates who are not accountable to the commander have little incentive to comply with orders to conduct military operations in accordance with the law. Even in the best of times, it can be challenging for the commander to get subordinates to comply with all legal requirements through the tenets of positive leadership alone. For at least some members of the military unit, only the possibility of criminal and other disciplinary sanctions will provide the incentives for them to obey. These challenges are exacerbated during military operations, so it is essential that the commander has disciplinary authority which subordinates know can be enforced.

The commander is often also in the best position to understand the context in which alleged misconduct took place. There is certainly the real risk that commanders may seek to cover up misconduct out of fear that it will bring disrepute to the unit or subject the unit to additional investigations. That does not mean that commanders lack the ability and responsibility for putting potential misconduct in its proper context or applying the disciplinary tools that will best ensure good order and discipline. At times, for example, commanders may rightly employ severe disciplinary tools because they identify a danger that others in the unit will engage in similar misconduct. At other times, the commander may realise that a severe response is unwarranted due to mitigating factors that arise in combat.

The ability to assess the impact of a service member's alleged misconduct on unit cohesion is an essential part of what it means to be a commander. This responsibility cannot be delegated because the commander is in the unique position of ensuring good order and discipline within the ranks of his subordinate forces. The primary reason for the command responsibility doctrine is to identify the commander as the one person in the military unit who can best assure law of war compliance. If the disciplinary tools are taken away from the commander so this authority can no longer be exercised, the commander still has the responsibility for ensuring compliance but does not have the necessary authority to carry out those obligations.

B *Establishing and modelling respect for the rule of law*

In addition to disciplinary authority, commanders can best ensure law of war compliance through positive leadership, modelling appropriate respect for the rule of law in the commander's own conduct. This modelling occurs in several ways. The most obvious is in training and preparing forces to comply with the laws of war in the context of military operations. Perhaps the least effective way to accomplish this is to simply ask the unit's legal advisor to brief members of the command on the requirements of the law of war. Commanders who opt for this approach may meet the minimal requirements but will do little to help their unit understand the application of the law. Such commanders also send a message to the unit that they view these rules as obligations with which the military is forced to comply. Worse still are commanders who denigrate these obligations to subordinates. Telford Taylor, the US chief prosecutor at the Nuremberg tribunals, said of this kind of training,

'Of what use is an hour or two of lectures on the Geneva Conventions if the solider sent into combat sees them flouted on every side?'[19] On the other hand, commanders who understand both the legal obligations and the rationale behind them will seek to provide robust, contextualised and realistic training to subordinates. The commander will look for opportunities to raise LOAC compliance issues throughout the full spectrum of military operations and demonstrate the importance of following the law.

Regardless of the approach a particular commander takes, the point is simply that the commander holds a unique position within the unit and can do more than any other single official to either create an environment where compliance with the LOAC is a fundamental aspect of every military operation, or the commander can create an environment where compliance with the law of war is an external obligation that is seen to conflict with mission accomplishment. The responsibility for setting the tone on this issue cannot be delegated. The command responsibility doctrine recognises that essential aspect of command. If the military justice system does not support the commander's ability to set the appropriate tone for law of war compliance, there is a risk that subordinates will disregard their legal obligations.

C Ensuring that operations are conducted in compliance with the law of armed conflict

In addition to establishing and modelling respect for the rule of law, the commander is ultimately responsible for ensuring that all military operations comply with the laws of war. It will never be easy for commanders operating in a combat environment to place a high priority on law of war compliance, but they are expected to do precisely that. Among all of the competing demands placed on a commander, law of war compliance must be a top priority. That is the rationale behind the command responsibility doctrine. By holding the commander responsible and accountable for preventing, suppressing and punishing law of war violations, the doctrine encourages the commander to make law of war compliance a key component of any military operation. Military justice reforms must not unintentionally remove that incentive or dilute the applicability of the command responsibility doctrine. The primary responsibility of ensuring law of war compliance cannot be delegated to anyone else in the military unit. If law of war compliance is not a top

[19] Telford Taylor, 'Nuremberg in Son My' *New York Times*, 21 November 1970.

priority for the commander, it will not be a top priority for the military unit.

IV Essential areas of involvement

In light of the critical role that the commander must play in ensuring law of war compliance and the responsibilities that cannot be delegated to others, the critical question, and the one that has not yet been fully explored by most reformers, is: in what ways can a military justice system be reformed while preserving these essential aspects of command? This section explores this question by focusing on a number of proposed reforms to the military justice system in the United States. As noted earlier, some of these reforms have already been adopted by other countries. In those instances the question is whether some of these reforms should be reconsidered.

This section examines five areas that have been the focus of advocates for reform in the United States. These are: the commander's investigating authority; the commander's role in convening courts martial and exercising clemency; summary courts and the commander's ability to impose summary punishment; the role for military judges in the pre-referral phase of a court martial; and tenure for military judges. There are certainly other possible reforms but these particular functions are ones where the commander has the greatest involvement in the process and they serve as intersections between military justice reform and the commander's obligations under the law of armed conflict.

A The commander's investigating authority

In many military justice systems, the commander has the authority to initiate and conduct investigations into misconduct within the unit. US commanders typically appoint an investigating officer within the unit to investigate allegations of misconduct. Serious allegations of misconduct are usually investigated by military professionals trained in criminal investigations. These criminal investigations do not require the unit commander's approval before they are initiated. In either case, once the investigations are completed, reports are provided to the commander.

A system that relies so heavily on the commander's authorisation before investigations into misconduct can be initiated is subject to manipulation and potential cover-up by the initiating commander. There are modern examples – from the My Lai massacre in Vietnam to the killing of Iraqi civilians in Haditha during the Iraq war – where allegations of command cover-up and inaction surfaced. These and similar cases have led to calls for the removal of the commander from the investigative process. Under these proposed reforms the commander of the unit involved in the alleged misconduct would not be responsible for initiating or conducting investigations. This investigative function would be passed to another office outside the unit's command structure, such as a centralised office of military prosecutions.

Such reforms have the advantage of removing those who might have the most at stake personally and professionally from initiating and conducting investigations. This might lead to greater independence and reduce the risk that allegations of misconduct will go unreported and not investigated. However, completely removing the commander from the investigative process can conflict with the commander's command responsibility obligations to prevent, suppress and punish law of war violations. Having the authority to investigate allegations is critical to suppressing and punishing these violations. As commanders can be held criminally liable for failing to suppress and punish offences, they arguably have a greater incentive to ensure that credible allegations are investigated. A responsible commander is likely to be keener than one who has no command responsibility to initiate investigations and discover the relevant facts. Completely removing the commander from the investigative process violates a fundamental principle of the command responsibility doctrine and removes the incentive for the commander to meet relevant obligations under the law of armed conflict.

This is not to suggest that the commander must be the sole authority to initiate and conduct investigations. The risk of command cover-ups always exists, even if the commander could ultimately be held liable for the crimes because of the concealment. The best approach is to give commanders the authority and responsibility to conduct investigations, and also to vest investigative authority in offices outside the chain of command. This hybrid approach addresses the risk of command cover-up while still encouraging the commander to take personal responsibility to investigate allegations of misconduct. Investigative responsibilities could be either shared in any number of ways, or investigations could be conducted simultaneously.[20]

[20] Simultaneous investigations often occur in the US military, particularly in very serious cases. In the Abu Ghraib abuse cases for example, multiple investigations by the Congress, the Department of Defense, the Department of the Army and military criminal investigators took place at the same time. See, for example, James R. Schlesinger et al., *Final*

B The commander's role as the convening authority

1 The charging decision

Closely related to the removal of the commander from the investigative process are reforms that remove commanders from playing a role in the process of charging an alleged offender or in the process of convening a court martial to try the accused service member. These charging and convening authorities have been taken from the commander and given to other offices outside of the chain of command. Such reforms are said to provide the accused service member with a more independent tribunal free from undue influences of the military commander. This was at the heart of the reforms in both Canada[21] and the United Kingdom[22] and are high on the agenda for reform advocates in the United States.

The most significant responsibility a commander or convening authority possesses under the United States' Uniform Code of Military Justice is the convening authority's ultimate responsibility for deciding the disposition of a case.[23] It is the convening authority alone that decides if a service member should be tried and, if so, what level of court martial should be convened to try the alleged offender. Although the convening authority is required to make this decision only after consulting a legal advisor, the ultimate decision rests with the commander and it cannot be delegated to others within the chain of command.

If the commander is to continue to be the source of discipline within the unit, the authority to convene courts martial should not be given to some other office or authority. Removing the commander from this essential function risks undermining the commander's authority and violating the principles of command responsibility. It is critical for the commander to have final responsibility for imposing discipline within the unit and this requires that the commander convene courts martial. Simply having input into the convening determination or having the ability to refer cases to some other office is insufficient. Imagine that the commander believes alleged misconduct within the unit warrants a court

Report of the Independent Panel to Review DoD Detention Operations (2004), p. 10 www.defenselink.mil/news/Aug2004/d20040824finalreport.pdf; Anthony R. Jones, *AR 15-6 Investigation of the Abu Ghraib Prison and 205th Military Intelligence Brigade* (2004), p. 8, www.defenselink.mil/news/Aug2004/d20040825fay.pdf.

21 Jerry S.T. Pitzul and John C. Maguire, 'A Perspective on Canada's Code of Service Discipline' (2002) 52 *Air Force Law Review*, p. 1 at 9.

22 Simon P. Rowlinson, 'The British System of Military Justice' (2002) 52 *Air Force Law Review*, p. 17 at 18–19.

23 10 USC § 815 (2000).

martial but the office in charge of convening a court martial disagrees and elects to take no action. Such a scenario would seriously undermine the commander's authority. Members of the unit might in the future question or doubt whether the commander has the ability to punish them or initiate disciplinary proceedings against them. How can commanders prevent, suppress and punish law of war violations as required under the command responsibility doctrine if their subordinates doubt their disciplinary authority? The authority to convene courts martial is such a fundamental aspect of discipline and command authority that it cannot be taken away from the commander without undermining the command responsibility doctrine under the law of armed conflict.

While it is essential that the commander has the authority to convene courts martial, many of the convening authority's other functions can and should be given to other offices outside of the chain of command. In the US system, the convening authority has additional responsibilities, such as personally selecting the court members who will sit in judgment of the accused service member, deciding witness funding and availability issues, and the authority to approve court-martial findings imposing sentences and exercising clemency on behalf of a service member. I will address these additional responsibilities in turn.

2 Court member selection

The first, and by far the most controversial power that a convening authority has under the US military code is selecting those who will serve as the court members who sit in judgment of the accused service member. This power was contentious when it was codified in the UCMJ and that criticism has continued.[24] It is not surprising that reformers have focused on this issue. It is not difficult to imagine a convening

[24] See Fredric I. Lederer and Barbara S. Hundley, 'Needed: An Independent Military Judiciary – A Proposal to Amend the Uniform Code of Military Justice' (1994) 3 *William & Mary Bill Rights Journal*, p. 629 at 646. See also Major Guy P. Glazier, 'He Called for His Pipe, And He Called for His Bowl, And He Called for His Members Three – Selection of Military Juries by the Sovereign: Impediment to Military Justice' (1998) 157 *Military. Law Review*, p. 1 at 1; Michael I. Spak and Jonathon P. Tomes, 'Courts-Martial: Time to Play Taps?' (1999) 28 *Southwestern University Law Review*, p. 481 at 534–41 (calling for virtual abolition of the military justice system except in time of war or other overseas deployments); Matthew J. McCormack, 'Reforming Court-Martial Panel Selection: Why Change Makes Sense for Military Commanders and Military Justice' (1999) 7(4) *George Mason Law Review*, p. 1013 at 1049–51 (arguing that the military should remove the convening authority's power to handpick court-martial panel members); Lindsy Nicole Alleman, 'Who Is in Charge, and Who Should Be? The Disciplinary Role of the Commander in Military Justice Systems' (2006) 16 *Duke Journal of*

authority that could manipulate or unduly influence the outcome of a court martial by using the authority to choose those members who would be inclined to see the case in a similar way rather than deciding the case on its merits. While there are few reported cases of commanders overtly manipulating the process, the risk is real.

This provision of the UCMJ has long been a target for reformers but the military has been resistant to change. The military's arguments focus primarily on the logistical challenges of abandoning the current system for a system of random selection. There are undoubtedly some significant logistical and other challenges that would come with any reform but the important question is whether the commander's personal selection of the court members is such an essential aspect of command that its removal would undermine command responsibilities. It is difficult to see how choosing the members of a court martial facilitates the commander's responsibilities to prevent, suppress and punish service members for law of war violations. There does not appear to be a strong nexus between this power and command responsibilities. Accordingly, transferring this power from commanders to independent offices seems justified.

3 Witness funding

Convening authorities in the United States also enjoy considerable discretionary power over witness funding.[25] Before a service member's charges are referred to a court martial, the convening authority's decisions are not subject to review or appeal. Once the case is referred to trial, if the military judge determines that the convening authority's denial of witness funding is not justified, the military judge can abate the proceedings until the funds are made available. As with selecting court members, decisions regarding witness funding are administrative in nature. There is nothing in the nature of command that gives the commander any special insight into funding issues. These decisions do not go to the essence of command, and there is some risk that a commander could manipulate witness funding in order to inappropriately influence the

Comparative & International Law, p. 169 at 190–92 (suggesting a random selection method for choosing panel member that is tailored to meet needs of US military).

[25] *Manual for Courts-Martial*, Rules for Courts-Martial r 703(d) (2012). In some regards, the convening authority's power to fund and authorise witness employment and travel is limited by the military judge's ability to abate the proceedings if the convening authority refuses to fund a witness that the military judge has deemed essential to the case. Nevertheless, obtaining the convening authority's authorisation for witness funding is not a mere formality, and the convening authority's use of the power of the purse can certainly have an impact on the trial.

trial. Reforms that give this authority to someone other than commanders do not prevent commander from meeting their responsibility to prevent, suppress and punish war crimes.

4 Approval authority and clemency

After the conclusion of a court martial, no conviction or punishment is final until the findings and sentence are approved by the convening authority. Before the convening authority takes final action, it must first review the record of trial and obtain advice from a legal advisor on the factual and legal correctness of the findings and sentence.[26] The convening authority may dismiss any charge or specification by setting aside findings of guilt, change the findings of guilt to a lesser included offence, modify the sentence to any lesser sentence, or order a proceeding in revision or rehearing.[27] A finding of not guilty cannot be reconsidered. The convening authority can also grant clemency to the service member and has a broad discretion on the form of any clemency.[28]

Reform efforts that remove the commander from the charging and referral process also would take away the commander's authority to approve the court-martial findings or to exercise clemency on behalf of a convicted service member. This authority is more than an administrative function and, like the charging decision, goes to the essence of command. Commanders are in a position to place misconduct in the broader context of order and discipline within the unit. A commander is best suited to appreciate the overall tenor within a unit and understand how exercising clemency in a particular case will impact both the service member and the unit. Clemency decisions can have a direct relationship to how the commander will prevent, suppress and punish law of war violations. A commander who abuses this authority and fails to meaningfully punish violations can create an atmosphere of indiscipline within the unit and therefore increase the risk that subordinates will not take their obligations seriously enough to abide by the laws and customs of war. Similarly, commanders who are overly harsh can create resentment within the unit and a belief that they act arbitrarily and unfairly. This too can lead to a lack of discipline.

If such decisions are passed to someone other than the commander then they will be made by an official who does not have the key insights of the commander. It also undermines the commander's ability to exercise

[26] 10 USC §§ 860(c)(1)–(2) (2000). [27] 10 USC § 860(c)(3)(A) (2000).
[28] 10 USC § 860(e)(2)(A) (2000).

appropriate control over subordinates. Reforms that take away the commander's ability to exercise appropriate control are inconsistent with the principles of command responsibility and should be rejected.

5 Summary courts

A number of military systems contain summary courts martial or similar proceedings, which allow commanders to take swift disciplinary action.[29] In the United States, commanders at medium and high levels of command have the authority to convene summary courts. These courts are quite limited in the types of punishment that can be imposed.[30] Critics of the summary court system point to the minimal procedural protections and the risk of undue command influence.[31]

In some sense these summary courts are anachronistic and come from a bygone era, but summary proceedings can assist the commander in maintaining discipline. Some cases clearly warrant swift action. One is in a combat environment, where the commander may need to quickly address misconduct to prevent the spread of indiscipline. The time and resources may simply not be available for a more formal proceeding. In those instances, summary courts are an effective tool for the commander to maintain discipline. This tool can support and enhance the commander's ability to prevent, suppress and punish war crimes.

There should be appropriate limits on this authority to prevent the commander from abusing the power. If summary courts determine only relatively minor offences and impose limited punishments, their use could strike the right balance between supporting the commander's responsibilities while also protecting service members from the more serious consequences that might flow from unfair or arbitrary action. Reforms that completely remove the commander's authority to convene summary courts would go too far.

[29] See Chapter 17.

[30] See 10 USC § 820 (2000): 'Summary courts-martial may, under such limitations as the President may prescribe, adjudge any punishment not forbidden by this chapter except death, dismissal, dishonorable or bad-conduct discharge, confinement for more than one month, hard-labor without confinement for more than 45 days, restriction to specified limits for more than two months, or forfeiture of more than two-thirds of one month's pay.'

[31] See, for example, John S. Cooke, 'The Twenty-Sixth Annual Kenneth J. Hodson Lecture: Manual for Courts-Martial 20X' (1998) 156 *Military Law Review*, p. 1; The Cox Commission, *Report of the Commission on the 50th Anniversary of the Uniform Code of Military Justice* (May 2001), p. 2 www.nimj.org/documents/Cox_Comm_Report.pdf.

C The role for military judges in the pre-referral phase

Courts martial are *ad hoc* tribunals available in numerous military justice systems around the world. Civilian systems typically have permanent courts and sitting judges to whom an accused can petition throughout the pre-trial and trial phase of a case. In military systems, there is no such authority until a court is actually convened. In the United States, before a case is referred to a court martial the convening authority has the ultimate authority to decide and rule on all issues,[32] and such decisions are virtually absolute until the case is referred to trial and the issues can be brought before a military judge. This is particularly true for witness availability and pre-trial resource issues. This system can be problematic and unfair to service members. For example, service members who want assistance from an independent investigator to investigate or analyse evidence or interview witnesses before a case is referred to trial must request these resources from the convening authority.[33] In order to demonstrate the necessity for assistance, the defence must often reveal case strategy and other case-sensitive information to the convening authority and to the legal advisor. The convening authority has the sole responsibility for deciding these questions and typically does so after obtaining advice from a legal advisor, who is the same officer who supervises the prosecution of the case. Under this system, it can be difficult for the defence to obtain independent consideration of the issues. Waiting until the case is referred to trial so that the request can be made to the military judge might be leaving it too late, particularly when the issues involve investigatory resources.

Given the potential for unfairness, this area is ripe for reform. Such reform would not impact on the commander's essential responsibilities to maintain order and discipline over the forces. One logical reform is to expand the role of military judges, enabling them to decide these issues even before the case is actually referred to a court martial. Allowing military judges to decide such issues would ensure that someone with legal training, and intimate knowledge of both the rules and the legal precedents, decide important procedural decisions. Such changes would also streamline the trial process and prevent re-litigation of the issues once cases are referred to a court martial. The involvement of a decision-maker who was independent of the chain of command would also facilitate greater overall fairness within the system. Transferring this authority

[32] See, *Manual for Courts-Martial*, Rules for Courts-Martial rr 306, 401 (2012).
[33] Ibid., rr 703(d), (e) (2012).

from the commander to a military judge does not undermine the commander's responsibility or authority. The commander is not precluded from exercising disciplinary responsibilities but is instead relieved from the burden of deciding technical legal issues and can therefore focus attention on matters of command.

D Tenure for military judges

One final reform that has featured in both Canada and the United Kingdom is granting military judges a greater degree of independence from the chain of command and the executive.[34] There have also been calls for some type of tenure for US military judges, to give them the independence needed to decide issues and cases without fear of professional retribution by the command or the executive. Providing a more independent military judiciary would not adversely impact on the commander's ability to legitimately maintain order and discipline. Military justice must balance maintaining discipline and order with preserving fundamental fairness for the accused service member. If the commander can manipulate the system by sanctioning or adversely affecting a military judge's career, or be perceived to exercise that influence, there will be a chilling effect on judicial independence and an undermining of confidence in the system. The often stated rule of civilian legal systems, that justice must be done but also be seen to be done, has equal force in the military. Widespread distrust of military justice in a unit can undermine discipline in the same way as a lax command climate would. Commanders do not lose their legitimate authority when military judges are given meaningful independence and are free to decide issues and cases without undue influence from the commander.

V Conclusion

Over the past twenty years there has been a virtual revolution in military justice. One overarching theme of these changes is increasingly alignment of military justice to prevailing civilian standards. While the United States was at the forefront of military justice reform in the years following World War II, many reformers in the United States now look with envy

[34] See, for example, *R* v. *Leblanc* [2011] CMAC 2; *Findlay* v. *United Kingdom* (1997) 24 EHRR 221; Rowlinson, above n. 22, at 18–19.

to the civilianisation that has taken place elsewhere and advocate similar reforms.

In the push to modernise and civilianise military justice, the important reasons why military justice is separate from the civilian system should not be forgotten. A significant reason for a separate and different system is the obligations the law of armed conflict places on the military commander to ensure order and discipline within the military unit and to prevent, suppress and punish war crimes. Reforms to military justice should not undermine the commander's authority and responsibility to ensure law of war compliance. After all, no other office or official to take the place of the commander can meet these obligations. This chapter has looked at a number of proposed reforms. Many of these changes have already been implemented in other systems and are at the top of the list for reform advocates in the United States. Courts and legislative bodies must engage in careful analysis to ensure that changes do not have unintended consequences. This discussion and analysis has been generally absent in reform efforts, and proposals moving forward must embrace the concept of command responsibility before any significant structural changes are made to the current military justice system.

7

The impact of the 'civilianisation' of military administrative law on the 'command power'

ROB MCLAUGHLIN

I Introduction

Military administrative law encompasses those decisions concerning military personnel and operations which are amenable to merits or judicial review and which fall outside of the purely disciplinary law process. In Australia, military administrative law has long been 'civilianised' in the sense that it is interpreted in accordance with general administrative law principles and is amenable to judicial review. There are certain exceptions – for example, military justice proceedings pursuant to the Defence Force Discipline Act 1982 (Cth) (DFDA) (a type of administrative disciplinary procedure dressed, at the higher levels, in the paraphernalia of criminal law) are specifically exempted from the jurisdiction of the statutory framework for federal judicial review in Australia.[1] However, the concept of the 'command power' (perhaps generally definable as the power to require conduct or some other form of obedience, twinned with a power to impose or recommend a sanction for non-compliance) has long been viewed as a Rubicon for judicial review – the boundary beyond which judicial review could not, should not and would not tread in relation to military administrative decision-making.[2]

[1] Administrative Decisions (Judicial Review) Act 1977 (Cth), sch. 1, s. 3(o). Decisions under the Defence Force Discipline Act 1982 (Cth).

[2] For example, *X* v. *Commonwealth* (1999) 200 CLR 177, at 232–33 (Callinan J): 'The conditions and obligations of servicepeople today are governed largely by statute and regulation. However the historical obligations and special nature of military service . . . continue to find expression in the statutes and regulations governing military service today.' See generally Garth Nettheim, 'Do Members of the Armed Forces Have Any Rights in Their Employment?' (1972–1973) 5 *Federal Law Review*, p. 200; Mitchell Jones, 'Judicial Review of Administrative Action Against Members of the Australian Defence Force: Can a Warrior Win in Court?' (2005) 13 *Australian Journal of Administrative Law*, p. 8.

This chapter deals with the concept of 'the command power' as it relates to administrative law, with particular reference to the Australian context. It is my contention that many aspects of the command power have always been relatively 'civilianised'. In order to examine the command power, this chapter shall begin with a brief description of two key concepts that inform this issue: 'civilianisation' and 'military administrative law'. With these terms defined, the analysis will then turn to an examination of the nature of the command power, including a consideration of who can exercise the power and the forms that it takes. The analysis will conclude with some thoughts on the reviewability of exercises of the command power and its susceptibility to judicial review.

II Key background concepts

A 'Civilianisation'

The variety of ways in which military justice may be said to have been 'civilianised' has been distilled and explored by Matthew Groves.[3] At the macro level, 'civilianisation' has always been part of the Australian system of military law, given that:

> the boundaries of military law are set by the civilian government and those boundaries are ultimately policed by the government itself. The civilian courts assist in this 'policing' or 'border control' function . . . by exercise of their authority to declare and interpret the law.[4]

At the more discrete level of micro effects, civilianisation could be defined as 'the incorporation of the institutions and norms of the civilian legal system into military law'.[5] This development is attributable to a wide array of factors. First, as Timothy Edmunds and Anthony Forster highlight, 'civilianisation' is intimately related to a series of broader evolving 'challenges' to the relationship between military forces and their parent societies.[6] As they observe,

> there has been a change in the way that personnel relate to the institution that they work for, both in terms of what they expect it to do for them, and they for it. This includes a shift from seeing military service as a vocation to 'just a job'; a decline in deference, with service personnel more willing

[3] Matthew Groves, 'The Civilianisation of Australian Military Law' (2005) 28(2) *University of New South Wales Law Journal*, p. 264.

[4] Ibid., at 364. [5] Ibid., at 366–67.

[6] Timothy Edmunds and Anthony Forster, *Out of Step: The Case for Change in the British Armed Forces* (London, Demos, 2007), p. 17.

> to question and challenge the organisation they work within; and an erosion of the armed forces' traditionally claimed 'right to be different' in areas such as employment rights and social diversity legislation.[7]

Thus the core of this increasingly 'conditional attitude towards military service'[8] is underpinned by a civilianisation of expectations, as equally as a civilianisation of application and of implications.

A second element in this civilianisation of military justice, and indeed military law more generally, is very closely related to the decline in deference to military exceptionalism – both by military personnel to organisational superiors, and, arguably, by courts to military considerations more generally. This trend is detectable in the jurisprudence of the High and Federal Courts of Australia.[9] Such exceptionalism is often claimed and defined in such a manner as to exclude the authority, logic or justification of non-military review or challenge. What is important for any discussion of the command power, however, is not the existence of exceptionalism, but rather that it is claimed on grounds of variable persuasiveness. Courts are increasingly attuned to such claims, and have shown an escalating tendency to critically analyse them in detail when they are asserted as a justiciability or deference-generating discriminator.[10] As Edmunds and Forster note, where exceptionalism is explained by reference to 'tradition, custom and practice', it has become

7 Ibid., pp. 47–48. 8 Ibid., p. 53.

9 Kirby J was most eloquent on this trend. See, for example, *X* v. *Commonwealth* (1999) 200 CLR 177, at [166]–[167] (Kirby J): 'This appeal does not stand alone in the modern dialogue between the military and the courts. The military, including the ADF in Australia, have frequently enforced universal and discriminatory policies asserting that they are absolutely essential to the discharge of their mission. In many countries, there is nothing that those affected or the courts can do to question or disturb such policies. However, in other countries where the military is subject to civil power, constitutional norms or applicable principles of human rights enable and oblige the courts to scrutinise such decisions strictly and, when authorised by law, to decline to give them effect.' See also *Commonwealth* v. *Williams* [2002] FCAFC 435 (20 December 2000), at [29]–[34] (Hill, Heery, and Gyles JJ). One indicator of the willingness of courts to closely scrutinise arguments for deference based on claims of 'operational imperative' is evident in the distinctions drawn by Logan J in *Millar* v. *Bornholt* [2009] FCA 637 (15 June 2009), at [58] 'It is not difficult to see how, in the context of operational service in times of a large scale deployment of the Australian Army, the content of a procedural fairness obligation in respect of a redress complaint either as initially made or on referral may in some cases be very limited indeed. In the present case, though the occasion for the initiation of termination procedures arose from incidents on operational service, the decision making process occurred in more benign circumstances in Australia.'

10 See Chapter 4. For an Australian example, see the comments of Tamberlin J in *Hicks* v. *Ruddock* [2007] FCA 299 (8 March 2007).

increasingly difficult to insulate against broader civilian influences.[11] At the more serious end of the spectrum is the argument that exceptionalism is based in operational effectiveness. This issue is fundamental to the concept of the 'command power'.

B *'Military administrative law'*

The focus of my analysis is upon civilianisation within the realm of 'military administrative law'. In Australia, military administrative law is a broad concept, informed and underpinned by a diverse range of generally and specifically applicable statutes. These include statutes such as the Administrative Decisions (Judicial Review) Act 1977 (Cth), the Financial Management and Accountability Act 1997 (Cth) and the Defence Act 1903 (Cth) (Defence Act), regulations such as the Defence (Personnel) Regulations 2002 (Cth) and the Defence (Inquiry) Regulations 1985 (Cth), and a wide range of instructions, orders, standard operating procedures and other regulatory and managerial instruments (such as Defence Instructions, and Financial Management instructions). It is also arguable that military administrative law includes discipline law – a statutory code for particularised administrative review of acts and omissions in a military context.[12] As a long line of High Court of Australia authority notes, whilst military disciplinary tribunals act judicially (as must all administrative tribunals, as part of their obligation to provide procedurally fair decisions), in Australia they do not exercise the judicial power of the Commonwealth.[13] At least one judge of the High Court, Kirby J, has explicitly characterised military disciplinary proceedings as fundamentally administrative rather than criminal, and thus subject to the general principles and trends of administrative law.[14] This is not to say that military discipline law is precisely the same as general administrative law – clearly, it is not. Nevertheless, military

[11] Edmunds and Forster, above n. 7, p. 68.

[12] For example, *Hembury* v. *Chief of the General Staff* [1998] HCA 47, at [59] (Kirby J): referring to 'a non-judicial disciplinary body such as a court martial' and [72] 'a non-judicial administrative body with large powers to convict an accused person and to order that he or she be detained, fined and otherwise compulsorily dealt with'.

[13] See Chapter 13.

[14] For an example of Kirby J's views, see above n. 12. In *Re Tracey; Ex parte Ryan* (1989) 166 CLR 518, Mason CJ, Wilson and Dawson JJ, observed that the function of a court martial is not 'merely administrative' – an indication that it is, nevertheless at core, ultimately an administrative process, albeit one with additional overlays (such as the beyond reasonable doubt standard of proof) within a self-contained statutory code.

discipline law can be legitimately characterised as a specialist body of administrative law informed by criminal law and regulated via a self-contained 'statutory code' – the DFDA. However, as noted at the outset, this chapter will confine its scope to military administrative law as is generally understood, and will touch upon military discipline law only as necessary to distil the substance and exercise of the 'command power'.

III The nature of the 'command power'

A Some preliminary observations

The definition of 'command power' is of fundamental importance as it is vital for this analysis that a conceptual separation is maintained between 'the command power' on one hand, and the concept of 'command' on the other. That is, it is essential to separate expressions of the 'experience of command' from the legal power. There is no doubt that many – if not most – expressions, definitions or descriptions of command refer intuitively to aspects of the command power. This does not mean that they are the same thing. For example, LTGEN Peter Leahy, a former Chief of Army in Australia, described 'command' as follows:

> Command means something special to the military. It is about rights, responsibilities and obligations and extends beyond management and leadership. It is about efficiency, effectiveness, discipline and morale. Importantly it involves an exchange of trust between soldiers and commanders. These are very important words and we would do well to remind ourselves continuously that the primary purpose of the ADF [Australian Defence Force] is to engage in combat operations.[15]

Such definitions contain all of the core elements of the command power as a legal concept. But they also contain much more, and it is important to explore the 'much more' in order to distil the nub of the command power as a legal concept.

The second preliminary point is that there is no clear legal definition of the command power.[16] There are examples of its exercise, snippets as to what it might contain and ideas as to where it might originate. There are likewise indications that it is intimately linked with hierarchical status and authority, and reflects a – perhaps dwindling – interaction of

[15] LTGEN Peter Leahy AC (Retd), 'Perceptions of Military Justice' (Paper presented at Defence Watchdogs Seminar: The Administrative Oversight of Military Justice, 26 November 2008).

[16] Jones, above n. 2, at 15–20.

tradition, practice and formal rules.[17] But there is no consolidated single point of departure for developing a definition. This in itself may be problematic, given the centrality of the concept to military justice. It is arguable that the concept has enjoyed a long life of 'constructive ambiguity' precisely because it was thought best to leave its boundaries smudged, and because its insulation from judicial review has served to correspondingly insulate it from lawyers' predilection to compartmentalise, categorise and define.

B The role of the command power as both a substantive power and an instrumental power

The command power is a substantive power, but also an instrumental power. Nineteenth-century treatises on military law and martial law[18] suggest that the command power is a prerogative that draws shape, colour and content from three separate prerogatives. First, the command power is clearly a component of the prerogative for 'government, command, and disposition of the Army'.[19] Second, the command power can be described as a component of the general war prerogative. Third, the command power is a crucial element in the public emergency/internal security prerogative (expandable in certain situations to martial law). The command power draws both form and substance from these prerogatives, but is not the entirety of any of them. This is best illustrated through a brief analysis of some of the substantive prerogatives that shape and colour the command power.

1 Government, command and disposition of the forces

The prerogative concerned with government, command and disposition of the forces is a separate and distinct prerogative. This is clear from the writings of Charles M. Clode and W. F. Finlason in the context of nineteenth-century British military and martial law, and also from the very

[17] I am indebted to Professor Matthew Groves for this insight, noting, for example, the views of McHugh J in *Hembury* v. *Chief of the General Staff* [1998] HCA 47, at [27]: 'Status and authority may not have the influence in decision making that they once had. But no one can doubt, judges least of all, that status and authority remain influential factors in decision making.'

[18] The distinction is roughly as follows: military law is the law that governs the forces; martial law is an emergency measure whereby the normal law is displaced and military governance (and often law) is imposed over the civilian population.

[19] Charles M. Clode, *The Military Forces of the Crown: Their Administration and Government* (London, John Murray, 1869), vol. II, p. 316.

purpose of the prerogative. As will be discussed later, the war prerogative is targeted at defence of the realm against external threats, and the internal security prerogative at the more sensitive issue of suppression of riot and rebellion. The 'governance, command and disposition' prerogative, however, is squarely aimed at limiting and controlling the forces with a view to keeping them out of politics and firmly under civil control. This prerogative is based on the need to protect the realm from the existence of a potentially rampant and undisciplined armed force within its borders. In Clode's assessment, this prerogative is split between military and civil authorities. A military commander 'represents the inherent prerogative of the Crown in the command, as the Ministers represent the Constitutional power of the Crown in the Administration of the Army'. Each component of the general prerogative was, consequently, wielded by a different agent of the Crown – the military commander holding command power, the civil authority exercising administrative power.[20] Further, Clode expressly indicates the nature of those issues which fall within the 'administration' and 'disposition' elements of the general power devolved upon the civilian authorities (including the relevant minister, who at the time of Clode's writings was the Secretary of State for War): '1st, the number of the military forces to be maintained; 2ndly, the appointment of officers duly qualified; and 3rdly, the employment of the Army', with this latter power being characterised in the broad sense of directing the forces in terms of where they are stationed, when they are to be deployed and who they are to fight.[21] Additionally, Clode notes that these components of the 'governance, command and disposition' prerogative mandate that issues such as pay,[22] billeting,[23] and control and audit of military expenditure[24] are all governance and disposition matters which fall outside the command power and within the civil military administration power.

This raises an interesting issue as to what is encapsulated within the 'governance' component of the power. Clode describes an incident of the 'government of the Army' (indicating that it is different from the administration of the Army) as 'tribunals' – clearly evidencing a linkage between government as the ends, and discipline as the means.[25]

20 Ibid., vol. II, pp. 344–45. 21 Ibid., p. 316. 22 Ibid., p. 345.

23 Charles M. Clode, *The Military Forces of the Crown: Their Administration and Government* (London, John Murray, 1869) vol. I, Ch. XI.

24 Ibid., Ch. VII.

25 See, for example, Clode, *The Military Forces of the Crown*, vol. I, above n. 23, pp. 76 and 166.

Elsewhere, he again links governance with action 'against the status of Officers and Soldiers', whilst administration pertains, for example, to 'claims put forward against the public' and to 'report[ing] on circumstances' of incidents.[26] But, as is also clear, this governance of the force through discipline is a shared – or more appropriately, a split – prerogative. The wielders of the civil component of the 'governance' prerogative set the broad paradigm for the wielders of the command power element of the governance prerogative. Perhaps the key indicator of this bivalence was that although disciplinary tribunals were beholden to the military command power for their operation and their enforcement of the Articles of War against troops, it was a civil minister who routinely carried the Mutiny Act through Parliament.

This was significant because it was the Mutiny Act which placed limits upon the enforcement of the Articles of War by a commander. It also provided that 'no officer or soldier whatsoever should be exempted by that act from the ordinary process of the law'.[27] This arrangement required that such implementation, 'as far as possible . . . should proceed in accordance with the spirit and principles of ordinary law',[28] or 'within the known and prescribed limits of the common law of the realm'.[29] Additionally, as Clode observes, although the application of the Articles of War as a disciplining tool was a command prerogative vested in the military commander, the Articles themselves were 'drawn' by a civil officer (the Secretary of State for War) who then signed them 'on the King's authority'.[30]

An additional illustration of the complex division of powers within the 'governance' prerogative, between civil administration and control and military command, is evident in the different approach taken for disciplining the Militia as distinct from the regular army. As Clode notes, the 'governance' of the Militia (akin to a reserve force) was considered to be an entirely civil matter in that they were not ordinarily subject to the Articles of War, and discipline (beyond trivial consequences available to Militia officers under a corollary of the command power) was to be effected by a civil magistrate.[31]

[26] Charles M. Clode, *The Administration of Justice under Military and Martial Law* (London, John Murray, 1872), p. 173.

[27] Clode, *The Military Forces of the Crown*, vol. I, above n. 23, p. 206.

[28] W.F. Finlason, *Commentaries upon Martial Law, with Special Reference to Its Regulation and Restraint* (London, Stevens and Sons, 1867), pp. 244–45.

[29] Clode, *The Military Forces of the Crown*, vol. I, above n. 23, p. 76.

[30] Ibid., p. 144.

[31] Ibid., pp. 33–43.

2 War prerogative

The war or defence prerogative is primarily exercisable by civil ministers of the Crown and governs the most fundamental decisions relating to the defence of the realm from external threats. As Finlason noted in 1868 (quoting *Wood's Institutes of the Laws of England*), '[F]or time of war doth not only give privilege to those engaged in the war, but to all others within the kingdom'.[32] But the command power, operating through military agency, whilst drawing some of its substance and colour from the civil decision, is the means by which these prerogative authorisations are then implemented by the forces. It is, in many ways, essentially the 'jus in bello' component of the prerogative.

3 Public emergency/internal security prerogative

A similar analysis is available in relation to the internal security prerogative. It is clear, for example, that in the United Kingdom it was considered desirable that when faced with rebellion, it was a civil magistrate who would call on military assistance, and control the general deployment and employment of the force. However, it was equally clear that the civil magistrate could not give the order to open fire – this was the prerogative of the senior military commander present, and the troops were expected to follow the commander's orders, not those of the magistrate. The Admiralty issued explicit instructions in this regard:

> Instructions for the guidance of officers and party when the ordinary law prevails.
>
> . . .
>
> 7. If called upon to act for the suppression of riots and other disturbances when the ordinary law prevails, the following precautions are to be strictly observed: -
>
> The party is to be employed only at the requisition of the civil authority.
>
> The party is not to act without the presence of the civil authority, except for the purpose of self-defence, or the prevention of actual violence to the persons or property of Her Majesty's subjects.
>
> The party is to fire only by order of the officer in command.[33]

Although Clode notes elsewhere that 'there is no exact definition of what are the relative duties of the Civil and Military authorities when acting together in the suppression of Riot', he was nevertheless clear that

[32] W.F. Finlason, *A Review of the Authorities as to the Repression of Riot or Rebellion, with Special Reference to Criminal or Civil Liability* (London, Stevens and Sons, 1868), p. 77.

[33] Finlason, *Commentaries upon Martial Law*, above n. 28, p. 284.

the military commander, once called out, 'should act with his force and under his Code'.[34] Clode quoted, as indicative of the law, the findings in a report by Lords Eldon and Redesdale into an early nineteenth-century riot:

> [T]he Magistrate cannot require from the Military any assistance repugnant to the obligations of their military duty, such as to march from that part of the country in which they are stationed by their military orders, to another part of the country to which their military orders do not direct or authorise them; neither can they detach soldiers from their officers.[35]

Outside the United Kingdom – in the colonies – an almost identical distinction was drawn between the prerogative power of the Governor to give orders to the military commander to put down a rebellion, or indeed, to declare martial law, and the separate and distinct prerogative of the military commander to command the resultant operation:

> It has already been seen that the Crown will hold the Governor responsible for a general direction and control of the execution of martial law. But it is obvious that, as it is in its nature military power and military rule, probably exercised at considerable distance, and with great difficulties of communication, this control and direction can only be general, and that the immediate direction must be under the General in command of the district and the General Commanding-in-Chief. The Governor can only issue general directions or instructions to them.[36]

'Military measures', Finlason asserts, 'can only be taken by military force and under military authority' as a consequence of the fact that they are taken 'under military direction, and, as the military authority must be derived from the Commander-in-Chief of the colony [a military officer, regardless of any titular title in the Governor], the orders – more or less general – must emanate from him'. Thus a district military commander's refusal, during the Jamaica rebellion, to follow some of the Governor's directions in the absence of the Commander-in-Chief's orders, was correct – the Governor could give general directions 'by way of suggestion' to the Commander-in-Chief, who then decided how to give effect to such 'suggestions'.[37] Clode similarly records that under the Queen's Regulations of 1868, '[T]he Governor, though bearing the Queen's patent as Commander-in-Chief in the Colony, is restricted by the regulations of the service from interference with Imperial troops'.[38]

[34] Clode, *The Military Forces of the Crown*, vol. II, above n. 19, p. 153. [35] Ibid., p. 144.
[36] Finlason, *Commentaries upon Martial Law*, above n. 28, p. 262. [37] Ibid., pp. 190–91.
[38] Clode, *The Military Forces of the Crown*, vol. I, above n. 23, p. 15.

C Sources

As with most long-standing legal concepts in military law, the command power is a product of mixed legal provenance, being a creature of both statute and regulation, and of the prerogative. Clode refers to the *lex scripta* of 'orders' (including the Mutiny Act, the Articles of War, Regulations, Standing Orders') and the *lex non scripta* of orders (being 'those lawful orders which, viva voce or otherwise, the Commanding Officer may from time to time issue, bidding a subordinate to do or refrain from doing, as a Soldier, certain acts till then undisclosed to him').[39] This division is as to form of transmission, as opposed to source. The written orders he nominated were a mix of statute (such as those related to the Mutiny Act) as well as prerogative orders (such as the Regimental Colonel's command authority to establish standing orders). Verbal orders could similarly relate to a statutory purpose (for example, for a court martial under the Mutiny Act) or a more manifestly prerogative purpose (such as an order to advance upon the enemy during armed conflict). Form, consequently, offers no firm guide as to source. It is thus essential that we briefly examine each source in order to establish what aspects of the command power they may govern.

1 Statute/regulation

In Australia, the statutory and regulatory sources of authority focus upon the conferral, exercise and oversight of the command power. The Chief of Defence Force (CDF) and Service Chiefs exercise 'command', the CDF and the Secretary of the Department 'administer', and the Minister 'controls' and provides 'directions' to the CDF, the Secretary and the Service Chiefs.[40] Constitutionally, the Governor-General holds command-in-chief.[41] Yet, these statutory provisions 'do not provide the content of the power but merely specify who exercises it'.[42] But this is not straightforward as the 'administration' prerogative (as domesticated in Australia via the Constitution and the Defence Act) serves to indicate not only 'who' may exercise, but also the ambit of, the command power. However, as will become evident, there are other aspects of statute and

[39] Clode, *The Administration of Justice under Military and Martial Law*, above n. 26, pp. 13–17.

[40] Defence Act 1903 (Cth), ss. 8, 9, 9A.

[41] Constitution of the Commonwealth of Australia, s. 68.

[42] Cameron Moore, 'Militaries as Wielders of Executive Power' (2008) 8 *New Zealand Armed Forces Law Review*, p. 21, at 29.

regulation which clearly govern the content of the command power. Indeed, one of the two traditional components of the command power – the power to administer personnel – is almost completely reduced to statute and regulation.

2 Prerogative

The substance of the second aspect of the command power – operational decision-making – is traditionally found within the prerogative powers, as opposed to statute. Given that the matter of content is dealt with in greater detail later, it is pertinent to note at this stage that case law dealing directly with the 'command power' is sparse. Those judgments which do exist – such as the House of Lords decision in *Burmah Oil* v. *Lord Advocate*[43] – almost universally seek to attribute the residual of the command power, or an element of its content, to the prerogative. This appears to be the case regardless of whether the command power is an independent prerogative, or exists only as a series of subsets within the governance, administration and disposition prerogative, the war prerogative, and the public emergency/internal security prerogative. It thus suffices to say at this point that the command power is, ultimately, a creature of both statute and the prerogative, and thus it is only the residual substance of the power – that which has not been codified – that remains fundamentally prerogative in source.

D Who may exercise the command power?

An important distinguishing element of the command power in the Australian legal context is that it is exercisable only by military members. But it is not necessarily understood in this way in the United States, where the president is a substantive – as opposed to titular – commander-in-chief; nor, it would appear, in the United Kingdom since the creation of the Defence Council. In the UK, the Queen's Regulations for the Royal Navy provide that '[T]he government and command of each of the fighting Services is vested in Her Majesty the Queen, who has charged the Secretary of State with general responsibility for the defence of the

[43] [1965] AC 75. For example, Lord Pearce (with whom Lord Upjohn substantially agreed) noted that 'the prerogative in time of war has never been defined with precision' (at 145), but accepted that its substance at least included that the 'Crown [in its manifestation as a military officer in command of an operation] can by virtue of its prerogative in stress of war take that which it deems necessary, subject to the effect of any relevant legislation' (at 146–47).

Realm and established a Defence Council having command and administration over Her Armed Forces'.[44] However, it is evident that the various prerogatives from which the command power draws substance, or within which it operates as an instrument of implementation, have in general characterised the command power as within the military domain. This is not to say that the civil authority cannot exercise similarly substantive prerogative powers (indeed it is long practice that they do), but only to reinforce that the command power, properly understood, is available for use only within the military. The key element, to paraphrase Clode, appears to be that the service member has taken an oath of *military* obedience to the Crown and thus to the *military* commander the Crown places over him or her, which is enforceable under *military* law.[45]

The obvious flaw in this argument is that the command-in-chief of the Governor-General is a form of 'command power'. However, relying upon Sir Ninian Stephen's analysis of the legal nature of 'command-in-chief' in the Australasian colonies,[46] it is clear that the Governor-General's 'command-in-chief' power is fundamentally different to the command power exercised by military members. It is also clear, as is reflected in the Defence Act, that whilst the Secretary can 'administer', and the Minister can 'control' and even direct, the CDF and the Service Chiefs in their exercise of the command power, the command power is

[44] The Queen's Regulations for the Royal Navy (London, HMSO, 1967), p. v; see *The London Gazette*, No. 43277, 20 March 1964 www.london-gazette.co.uk/issues/43277/pages/2545. The membership of the Defence Council appointed at this time included the Defence portfolio Ministers, the Chief of Defence Staff (CDS) and three Service Chiefs, the Permanent Under-Secretary, and the Chief Scientific Adviser. The Vice-CDS was later added. See also the Letters Patent 16 February 2009, altering the membership of the Defence Council, but reaffirming that it was vested with authority 'to administer such matters pertaining to Our Naval Military and Air Forces as We shall through our Principal Secretary of State for Defence direct them to execute And to have command under Us of all Officers and Ratings Soldiers and Airmen of our Naval Military and Air Forces.' www.mod.uk/NR/rdonlyres/079FF8D3-E131-47D1-BFF0-AE8EE0C65591/0/20090713DCLettersPatentU.pdf. The *Levene Report* recommends that the only military officer who will in future sit on both the Defence Board and the Defence Council will be the CDS. See Defence Reform: An Independent Report into the Structure and Management of the Ministry of Defence (London, Ministry of Defence, 2007) www.mod.uk/NR/rdonlyres/B4BA14C0-0F2E-4B92-BCC7-8ABFCFE7E000/0/defence_reform_report_struct_mgt_mod_27june2011.pdf.

[45] Clode, *The Military Forces of the Crown*, vol. II, above n. 19, pp. 37–38.

[46] Sir Ninian Stephen, 'The Governor-General as Commander-In-Chief' (1983–1984) 14 *Melbourne University Law Review*, p. 563 at, for example, 566 (on the Revised Regulations for the Colonial Service specifying that appointment of a governor as 'commander-in-Chief' did not, without further appointment, carry with it actual operational command of the regular military forces stationed in the colony).

nevertheless not formally available to a civilian. This formulation appears to be entirely consistent with the complex division of sub-powers within the 'governance, command and disposition' prerogative as understood in the United Kingdom in the late nineteenth century (although not the United Kingdom today). It is possible, consequently, that on one view, the 'command power' in some jurisdictions is available to non-military executive agents – such as the civilian members of the UK Defence Council. But this is not a debate for the Australian context: statutorily, it is clear that the command power – regardless of its source as to content (statute or prerogative) – is exercisable by military members only. Its 'civilianised' analogies – be they 'administration', 'control' or 'direction' – whilst no less powerful, and available to cover the same scope of issues, cannot be characterised as exercises of the 'command power'.

E The form of the command power

The single most important point to make about the 'form' of the command power is that it is wider than just 'orders'. Certainly, traditional conceptions of the linkage between command power and discipline emphasise the purpose of 'instant obedience to lawful orders ... a person's willingness to carry out his or her assigned duties regardless of the danger, or lack of immediate supervision'.[47] However, not all exercises of the command power may be expressed in terms of an obligation with a disciplinary sanction attached to non-compliance.

1 Command power manifested as an order

Certainly, the command power most routinely manifests as an order, although the words 'order' and 'command' are used interchangeably in many disciplinary contexts. For example, in *Re Schneider's Appeal*[48] the Court Martial Appeal Tribunal (CMAT) noted that:

> We think that in any particular case words alleged to constitute a command must always be examined in the light of the circumstances in which they are used, and that this examination may show clearly enough that a set of words not otherwise supportable as a command was intended by the speaker to be a command, and was so understood by a person to whom they were spoken.[49]

[47] *Stewart* v. *R* (20 October 1993) CMAC-348, at 9 (DesRoches JA; Rutherford and Rouleau JA concurring).

[48] *Re Schneider's Appeal* (1958) 8 FLR 314.

[49] Ibid., at 324.

In *Re Manion's Appeal*,[50] the direction given by the Commanding Officer (CO) to Surgeon-Lieutenant Manion (to make the Ship's sickbay available as accommodation for a visiting civilian) was described interchangeably as an 'order' and as a 'command'.[51] Just as the CMAT noted that '[d]iscipline cannot depend on the mere nicety of words used', it is also the case that this form of the command power is understood in terms of its potential sanction; whether it is labelled 'order' or 'command' is of little consequence.

2 Command power manifested as a requirement to choose

However, not all forms of the command power are so binary in form or penal in consequence. The command power may also manifest as a requirement that a member make a choice between two options. This is the form of command power the New Zealand Court of Appeal, and the Privy Council, distilled from the facts in *R* v. *Attorney General for England and Wales (New Zealand)*.[52] This case concerned an NZ veteran of the UK SAS who had been captured and tortured during Gulf War I in 1991, and who – after leaving the service – sought to publish his version of the incident (as others had done). Whilst still in service, he (and all other UK Special Forces members) had been given an option to sign a very broad confidentiality agreement, or – if he refused – to be returned to his original unit. Although there was little doubt that the soldier's (R) appreciation of the situation was beholden to and informed by the command power, one of the issues the NZ Court of Appeal, and then the Privy Council, addressed was whether the signing had been as the result of an order. Lord Hoffman, delivering the majority judgment, was clear that even though the choice offered to R contained within it something R would characterise as a 'threat',[53] it was not an order.

> The judge's reasoning [in the High Court of NZ] was that R had signed the contract because he had been ordered to do so. The MOD could not give a serviceman an order which, as a matter of military law, he was obliged to obey after he had left the service and therefore it was an abuse of power for the MOD to try to extend the temporal reach of its orders by ordering the serviceman to sign a contract which could be enforced after he had left.
>
> If R had signed the contract because as a matter of military law he had been obliged to do so, their Lordships would see much force in this

[50] *Re Manion's Appeal* (1962) 9 FLR 91. [51] Ibid., at 94–95 (order) and 96 (command).
[52] *R* v. *Her Majesty's Attorney-General for England and Wales* [2003] UKPC 22, at [19]–[20].
[53] The threat was that he would be returned to his original unit, meaning he would cease being a serving member in the SAS.

> reasoning. But they agree with the Court of Appeal that this was not the case. There was no order in the sense of a command which created an obligation to obey under military law. Instead, R was faced with a choice.[54]

There was, however, no doubt that the command power extended to requiring R to make such a choice, even if the continuing reach of the consequence of that choice after separation from the Service was a matter of debate.

3 Command power manifested as instigating a process

It is clear that it is an exercise of the command power to instigate a process. The instigation of a Quick Assessment and the appointment of a Routine Inquiry Officer are, as ADF doctrine explains, exercises of the 'inherent power of command'.[55] This manifestation of the command power as a power to inquire, or to fact-find, is specifically analysed by Clode, who distinguishes commissions or courts of inquiry 'held by order of the Crown or a Commanding Officer under Prerogative, and without Statutory Authority' from 'Courts as are held . . . with such Authority given either by the Mutiny or some other Act, or by the Articles of War, or Regulations put forth under Statute by the Crown'.[56]

Clode's view of the evolution of non-statutory forms of inquiry, authorised under the command power, indicates that the purpose of such inquiries was primarily to enable a commander to 'report on [a] matter of fact'. The directions given by one Commanding General to the board appointed to report on an operational incident, as quoted by Clode, are indicative of this form of the command power.[57] Such inquiries, Clode notes, are connected to the administration of the force, not its governance (providing yet another indication that 'governance' pertains strictly to discipline). They have as their central purpose 'investigation

[54] *R* v. *Her Majesty's Attorney-General for England and Wales* [2003] UKPC 22, at [19]–[20] (Ld Hoffman). Lord Scott dissented on this point: see [41]. See also, Peter Twist, 'Limits to the Supreme Government, Command and Disposition of the Armed Forces: *Attorney-General for England and Wales v R*' [2002] *New Zealand Armed Forces Law Review*, p. 43.

[55] Australian Defence Force, *Administrative Inquiries Manual*, Executive Series, 2nd edn, ADFP 06.1.4 (Canberra, Australian Defence Force Publication, 2006), chs. 1–4 www.defence.gov.au/adfwc/Documents/DoctrineLibrary/ADFP/ADFP_06-1-4_Administrative_Inquiries_Manual_AL1.pdf; Australian Defence Force, *Guide to Administrative Decision Making*, Executive Series, 2nd edn, ADFP 06.1.3 (Canberra, Australian Defence Force Publication, 2010), at [2.43]–[2.45], [3.7] www.defence.gov.au/adfwc/Documents/DoctrineLibrary/ADFP/ADFP%2006.1.3.pdf.

[56] Clode, *The Administration of Justice under Military and Martial Law*, p. 170.

[57] Ibid., p. 172.

into subjects of most varied character under the authority of the General officer', as opposed to 'try[ing] a prisoner'.[58] Inquiries conducted under statutory authority – where the command power provides the means of implementing a statutory permission – included those authorised under the Articles of War in relation to wounded personnel and collection of Regimental debts from the estate of deceased members.[59] The modern ADF inquiry system, comprising command power-based and statutory mechanisms, is not so very different.

4 Command power manifested as a reviewable decision

The right to review of certain forms of command decision has both statutory and prerogative forms. The Redress of Grievance process, enabling a service member to seek review of certain command decisions, is fundamentally a regulatory (as opposed to prerogative-based) path to a remedy. It is only available to a military member who seeks to argue that the exercise of the command power created an 'injustice', or as Logan J more recently characterised its purpose, to 'temper the arbitrary, uncaring, ignorant or unjust exercise of authority within the Army'.[60] This right, as Clode described it, was:

> That no injustice may be done to a Soldier by his Captain without redress, the Articles of War provide that if he thinks himself wronged, he is to complain to the Colonel, who is bound to summon a Regimental Court of Enquiry for the purpose of determining whether such complaint be just.[61]

The right to seek such review is thus an internal check and balance to ensure that the command power is exercised in accordance with two primary criteria. The first principle is that it must be exercised for a valid military purpose.[62] The second principle is that it must be exercised in accordance with the general requirement for fairness and good faith which Parliament has long placed on the exercise of this prerogative. This is evident in Bentham's assessment that courts martial were 'courts of natural procedure . . . bound rather by the rules of natural good sense

58 Clode, *The Military Forces of the Crown*, vol. I, above n. 23, p. 188.
59 Clode, *The Administration of Justice under Military and Martial Law*, above n. 26, ch. IX.
60 *Millar* v. *Bornholt* [2009] FCA 637 (15 June 2009), at [25] (Logan J). Logan J provides a concise history of the redress right at [10]–[35].
61 Clode, *The Military Forces of the Crown*, vol. II, above n. 19, p. 58.
62 Clode (1872), pp. 15–16: 'orders must be plainly within the limits of the Officer's authority'; *The Military Forces of the Crown*, vol. I, above n. 23, pp. 155–64; *The Military Forces of the Crown*, vol. II, above n. 19, pp. 144–54: orders must be 'in bona fide discharge of their duty'.

and justice than by formal or artificial rules'.[63] It is also evident in the hard fought, and ultimately won, battle – played out through the Mutiny Act – to ensure that the obligation to obey, and the command power to command, are both bounded by the concept of lawfulness. As Clode records of the tumultuous history of the offence of disobedience, the Mutiny Act of 1717 required the subordinate 'to obey the military orders of his superior officer'. After great debate, this was amended in 1718 to 'any lawful command of his superior officer', and again in 1749 to create the offence of 'disobey[ing] any lawful command of his superior officer'.[64] This achievement reflected the view of Lord Hale that '[i]f the King command an unlawful thing to be done, the offence of the instrument is not thereby indemnified; for though the King is not under the coercive power of the law, yet in many cases his commands are under the directive power of the law, which consequently makes the act itself invalid if unlawful'.[65] In *A* v. *Hayden*, a High Court of Australia case that followed a poorly executed Australian Secret Intelligence Service (ASIS) training exercise in a busy hotel, Murphy J made a striking and powerful reference to 'death squads'.[66] The immediate issue in that case was the availability of remedies for members of the public affected by the conduct of the exercise. However, one defendant to the resulting civil claims had asserted that the executive could authorise the use of lethal force outside of situations of either self-defence or armed conflict. Murphy J was clearly mindful of the dangerous consequences of untrammelled executive power, and of the susceptibility and corruptibility of military or security forces who might rely on it. As is evident, the command power has long been considered subject to the overriding limitations of military purpose and lawfulness, with the latter concept arguably subsuming the former by 1718 as an element inherent within its definition.

The overriding requirement, therefore, was that the command power (as with all other public powers) should be exercised in line with the general conceptions of lawfulness and good faith in the common law. This was also made explicit in the preamble to the Mutiny Act, to the

63 Finlason, *Commentaries upon Martial Law*, above n. 28, pp. 238–39, discussing Bentham.

64 Clode, vol. I, at pp. 155–57; Clode (1872), at p. 58.

65 Quoted in Clode, *The Military Forces of the Crown*, vol. II, above n. 19, p. 147.

66 (1984) 156 CLR 532 (*ASIS Case*) – '[A]stonishingly one of the plaintiffs asserted through counsel that it followed from the nature of the executive government that it is not beyond the executive power, even in a situation other than war, to order one of its citizens to kill another person. Such a proposition is inconsistent with the rule of law. It is subversive of the Constitution and the laws. It is, in other countries, the justification for death squads' (Murphy J), at [3].

effect that not even a soldier should be exempted from the ordinary process of the law.[67] This principle holds two significant implications – one external, one internal. The external implication is that military actions in relation to the civil world must be governed by the 'ordinary' law: 'Nothing can be more terrible than that of detaching entirely the military from the civil part of our Constitution, and establishing in the former a blind obedience to the orders of their chief commander'.[68] The internal purpose achieved by this chapeau requirement, however, was to ensure that a superior's actions in relation to a subordinate *within* the military sphere were also expressly governed by reference back to the 'ordinary process of the law'. This protection apparently drew its rationale from the reportedly not uncommon proclivity of some commanders to arbitrarily pass capital sentences over very minor transgressions. The practice became so highly offensive to Parliament that it took the opportunity presented by the Mutiny Act to statutorily require some compatibility between the military and civil realms in relation to the imposition of capital sentences.

IV The content of the command power

The British *Manual of Military Law* (1907) declares that 'lawful command' means not only a command which is not contrary to the ordinary civil law, but one which is justified by military law; in other words, a lawful military command, whether to do or not to do, or to desist from doing, a particular act.[69]

The *Manual* lists the following examples of a proper military purpose: the maintenance of good order; the suppression of a disturbance; the execution of any military duty or regulation; and 'any purpose connected with the amusements and welfare of a regiment or other generally accepted details of military life'. As the Royal Navy's modern Queen's Regulations explains, the concept of 'command' is deconstructed into two components: conduct of military operations, and maintenance of good order and discipline.[70]

It thus seems evident that there is a long-standing coherence and consistency in 'definitions' of the content of the command power – regardless of where it is vested in the United Kingdom. The first, and

67 Clode, *The Military Forces of the Crown*, vol. I, above n. 23, p. 206.
68 Ibid., p. 165, quoting the Earl of Bath circa 1715.
69 War Office (Great Britain), *Manual of Military Law* (London, HMSO, 1907), p. 17, [10].
70 Above n. 44, at [0131].

primary, component of the command power is the power to do things in relation to operations – the primary purpose of the military. This aspect of substantive content, as should be evident from discussions earlier, is a reference to the two purposive prerogative powers of war and public emergency/internal security. Clode reflects this analysis in his assertion that the primary purpose of the military is defence of the realm, with the second purpose being 'aid to the civil power in the preservation of the public peace'.[71]

The second substantive element of the command power embodies those ancillary purposes which facilitate the primary purpose of conducting operations in terms of management and administration of military personnel. This is clear from the entirely personnel-focused component of 'governance' (disciplining), and in those elements of the power to administer the forces available for exercise by military personnel (welfare, health, morale, training, preparedness, but not, for example, pay, which is vested in the civil authority). For the purposes of analysis, I will call these two substantive limbs of the command power the 'command power to administer military personnel' and the 'command power to do things in relation to operations'.

It is important to explain why this characterisation and limitation on the substantive content of the command power is necessary. I argue that the command power to administer military personnel has been almost entirely subsumed by statute and instrument, such that there is little remaining of the prerogative in this area – that which remains is related to trivial or very low-level matters. It is also my argument that this aspect of the command power has long been subject to 'civilianisation'. This is due to the fact that whilst it is governed by a mix of general and context-specific rules, those rules which are distinctively 'military' are better viewed as military analogies to their more generally applicable legal equivalents, as opposed to departures from these rules. Thus, this component of the command power has long been reflective of, and sensitive to, the 'general' (non-military) law.

A *The command power to administer military personnel*

A military commander may still make a range of minor personnel-related decisions which are non-reviewable. Many such decisions remain fundamentally linked to the 'governance, command and disposition'

[71] Clode, *The Military Forces of the Crown*, vol. I, above n. 23, p. 1.

prerogative source of the command power, and have not been explicitly reduced to statute or regulation. This is not to say that guidance does not exist regarding the way in which such incidents of the command power may be exercised – clearly, procedures and other formalities have been promulgated as an aide to facilitating these types of command decision. But these incidents of the command power remain fundamentally uncodified and discretionary. An example is the command power to grant 'short absence' forms of leave to a military member under the decision-maker's command.[72]

In Australia, the 'governance' element of the 'governance, command and disposition' prerogative is now entirely subject to a statutory code – the DFDA. This Act governs the main components of the formal military disciplinary system (from summary level proceedings through to Courts Martial and Defence Force Magistrates), establishes a number of important roles within this system (such as the Director of Military Prosecutions and the Judge Advocate General), details disciplinary offences (such as endangering morale, insubordination and absence without leave), and prescribes a series of systemic accoutrements unique to the DFDA context (such as certain investigation, evidence and punishment provisions).

The 'personnel administration' element of the 'governance, command and disposition' prerogative concerns the multitude of non-trivial, but routine, personnel administrative decisions upon which the management of a modern military force is based. Such decisions include promotions, postings, access to certain training and advancement opportunities, readiness and competence, and (increasingly) suitability for deployment on operations. Most, if indeed not all, such personnel administrative decisions have now been almost entirely reduced to statute, regulation and instructions – Defence Force Regulations 1952 (Cth), Defence (Personnel) Regulations 2002 (Cth), Defence (Inquiry) Regulations 1985 (Cth) and Defence Instructions[73] providing the primary examples of such codifications. There remains some uncertainty as to the continuation of the unreviewable prerogative of the Crown to dismiss a member from service for any (or no) reason, although it is my view

[72] See, for example, Australian Defence Force, *Pay and Conditions Manual* ch. 5, pt. 1 [5.1.3] www.defence.gov.au/dpe/pac/V2_Ch5_Pt1.htm#bk35716PM513Leavetypes.

[73] See Defence Act 1903 (Cth), s. 3 (definition of 'defence instructions'): 'Defence Instructions means Defence Instructions (General), Defence Instructions (Navy), Defence Instructions (Army) or Defence Instructions (Air Force) issued under section 9A'.

that this power has also now been entirely reduced to statute and is regulated via the Defence (Personnel) Regulations 2002 (Cth).[74]

B The command power to do things in relation to operations

Operational decision-making – most notably those decisions that relate to the employment of forces on an assigned operational task or mission – still tends to be prerogative-based. The source for such authority is traceable to the 'defence/war' prerogative, and the 'internal security' prerogative. Of course, this does not mean that such exercises of command power-based operational decision-making are not reviewable at all – clearly, operational commands are reviewable on their merits by more senior commanders: the PTE Bewes Inquiry[75] is a recent example of an exercise of the command power to do something directly related to an operation being reviewed on its merits. In that inquiry, fundamentally operational command power-based decisions concerning the planning and conduct of the patrol in which PTE Bewes was participating when killed were subject to detailed merits review and assessment for, and on the order of, a more senior commander. But to what extent might an operational instance of the exercise of the command power also be subject to judicial review? More precisely, what criteria appear to govern the susceptibility of a command power-based operational decision to judicial review? The answer coalesces around three threshold questions.

1 Was it a lawful command?

This threshold question required little exegesis – courts will engage fully with this criterion, just as they have done in cases such as *A*

[74] As the Second Reading Speech for the Defence Legislation Amendment Act 1995 (Cth) made clear, the proposed (and ultimately adopted) amendments to the Defence Act and the Naval Defence Act were designed to 'replace the current blanket provisions [enshrining the Crown prerogative to dismiss] with provisions that specify the grounds on which an officer can be retired early or have an appointment terminated'. Commonwealth, *Parliamentary Debates*, House of Representatives, 31 May 1995, 808 (Mr Punch, Minister for Defence Science and Personnel). Recent jurisprudence on this particular prerogative as it applied in respect of the NSW Police Service (*Jarratt* v. *Commissioner of Police (NSW)* (2005) 224 CLR 44), along with the Parliament's 1995 expressed legislative intent, and the sweeping scope of the termination provisions in the Defence (Personnel) Regulations, provide ample grounds upon which to question the ongoing existence of this prerogative in its original and essentially unreviewable form.

[75] *Inquiry Officer's Report into the Death of Private Nathan John Bewes in Afghanistan on 9 July 2010* www.defence.gov.au/coi/reports/IO%20Report%20into%20the%20death%20of%20PTE%20Bewes_scanned%20for%20release.pdf at [47], [88].

v. *Hayden*.[76] As noted earlier, this seminal High Court case directly concerns the accountability of the Executive in relation to its obligation to abide by the law.

2 Was it for a purpose over which the command power may operate?

This threshold question relates to the two spheres of operation of the command power, as examined earlier. First, does the exercise of the command power relate to administering personnel or to doing things in relation to operations? A historical example which helps illuminate the sometimes diffuse borders of this categorisation (cited by Clode) is a case concerning an officer who refused to participate in a salute for a Catholic Saint Day celebration. Clode observed that the issue of whether the command to participate had been within the accepted purposes of the command power was subject to detailed judicial review. Similarly, as the *Manual of Military Law* notes, commands that have private ends or gains are not encompassed within the ambit of proper purposes as they do not relate to conducting operations or the morale, health, welfare and administration of troops.[77] Whilst a court will grant the commander a margin of appreciation – in nineteenth-century terms, interrogate the 'usages' – in assessing the military explanation of the nexus between the commanded act/decision and the two permissible purposes, this is subject to a reasonable level of review. The two *Shand* cases[78] offer a sound modern example of this approach, in that the court did not simply defer to the commander's assessment that persistent indebtedness and domestic problems were relevant factors in a decision to terminate a soldier's service – they examined the evidence and determined that issue for themselves. Indeed, as Burchett J specifically noted in the earlier case, 'it seems to me that the Army *was* entitled to regard a debt situation of the magnitude and persistence of that which was involved in the present case as properly its concern'.[79] Where they did allow a margin of command appreciation was in the linkage made by the commander between this situation and a valid military end state.

[76] (1984) 156 CLR 532.

[77] *Manual of Military Law*, above n. 69, p. 17: 'But a superior officer has no right to take advantage of his military rank to give a command which does not relate to military duty or usages, or which has for its sole object the attainment of some private end.'

[78] *Paul Anthony Shand* v. *Chief of the Army* [1998] FCA 265 (26 March 1998); *Private Paul Anthony Shand* v. *Chief of the Army* [1998] FCA 1507 (14 October 1998).

[79] *Paul Anthony Shand* v. *Chief of the Army* [1998] FCA 265 (26 March 1998).

3 Was it necessary to achieve that purpose?

It is apparent that a court will show much greater deference to the military explanation when assessing the element of necessity.[80] At this point, it is necessary to analyse the concept of a 'usage'. Finlason outlines a series of decisions which furnish examples of both the role of 'usage' in judicial review of the command power, and the effect that a requirement to defer to 'usage' has in increasing the deference shown for a decision in the context of operations:

> Thus, in *Barwise v Keppel* . . . where the question was as to the right of a commanding officer going beyond and in excess of the sentence of court-martial, it was found and stated as a matter of fact that it was in war and in presence of the enemy, and that it 'is generally and universally understood in the army' that he had such and such authority, and that by 'the constant custom and practice of the army' he had that power.[81]

Other cases Finlason reviews contained similar ratios – in operational situations, if the Mutiny Act and the Articles of War were silent, 'it was a matter of usage', 'usage is the test' and 'we are bound to look upon the usage of the subject, because that usage may assist us in forming a judgment'.[82] Operational command decisions, by their very nature, are and have long been considered to be informed to a significantly greater degree by 'usage of the service' than statutory authorisations. As a consequence, such decisions have long been treated by the courts differently to routine personnel decisions made distant from operational contexts. Thus *Commonwealth* v. *Human Rights and Equal Opportunities Commission*[83] (a case concerning non-acceptance for training and commissioning as an Army pilot on the basis of age) is entirely consistent with the court assessing the strength of the linkage between the command decision complained of, and the relatively select set of fundamental purposes for which it may be exercised. In that case, Wilcox J of the Federal Court of Australia affirmed the Human Rights and Equal Opportunity Commission (HREOC) finding that limiting the availability of Pilot Short Service Officer (SSO) Commissions to applicants under twenty-eight years of age at the time of appointment (Mr Bradley was at the relevant time thirty-seven years old, but an experienced helicopter

[80] Necessity is routinely referred to as a consideration when assessing the validity of an act's claim to authority under the command power: For a recent example, see Madgwick J's dissent in *Bromet* v. *Oddie* [2003] FCAFC 213 (29 August 2003), at [60].

[81] Finlason, *Commentaries upon Martial Law*, above n. 28, p. 145.

[82] Ibid., pp. 146–47.

[83] [1998] FCA 1295 (16 October 1998).

pilot), 'was not based on an inherent requirement of a job as an SSO pilot'.[84] The argument in that case concerned the ability of an older applicant to 'unlearn' certain elements of previous experience. But a command decision relating to age-based discrimination on an arduous deployment opportunity would most likely be treated very differently because of the more direct linkage to operational purposes.

V Concluding thoughts on the command power

In summary, I believe that the first category of command power content – the command power to administer military personnel – is (in its Australian manifestation) now almost entirely a creature of statute and regulation, and is thus routinely amenable to judicial review. These avenues include the review powers of the Defence Force Discipline Appeals Tribunal (a body which hears appeals from the decisions of Courts Martial and Defence Force Magistrates), and more generally those of the Federal Court and High Court of Australia. In respect of the command power to do things in relation to operations, however, I believe that a greater residue of the prerogative power remains available, although the trend has nevertheless been inexorably towards stronger external review. Four conclusions follow from this general assessment.

First, operational commands – incidents of the command power to do things related to operations – are more likely to be considered non-justiciable than personnel-related commands, although the category of non-justiciable decisions in general is rapidly shrinking. Second, where incidents of the command power to do things related to operations are justiciable, they are generally accorded a much greater degree of deference in the process of judicial review than incidents of the command power to administer personnel. This is because military claims of exceptionalism are increasingly harder to maintain in relation to personnel matters (particularly where these have become rule-bound and thus invite judicial scrutiny), but easier to justify in relation to operational matters (which are generally more urgent, fluid and 'abnormal' in terms of a court's judicial experience). This is, I believe, one way to understand and apply more recent Federal Court of Australia cases[85] on military

[84] *Commonwealth* v. *Human Rights and Equal Opportunities Commission* [1998] FCA 1295 (16 October 1998).

[85] For example *Millar* v. *Bornholt* [2009] FCA 637 (15 June 2009) (concerning, inter alia, removal from an operational theatre) and *Bromet* v. *Oddie* [2003] FCAFC 213 (29 August 2003) (concerning suspension and removal from flying training).

administrative law – that is, as markers along a coherent and consistent spectrum combining susceptibility to judicial review and deference. The more that an incident of the command power to administer military personnel tends towards a direct and easily recognisable linkage to the conduct of operations, the more deference a court will show. Thus a command decision related to leave without pay (LWOP) which is completely unrelated to operations (*Chief of Defence Force* v. *Clark*[86]), or concerning termination of service (*Stuart* v. *Sanderson*[87]) – where the influence of direct operational considerations is remote – will be more likely to be reviewed in detail than a command personnel decision that is closer to the actual conduct of operations. In this respect, one would place *Stuart, Clark* and similar routine personnel administration in 'peacetime' cases at the limited deference end of the spectrum, and a decision as to sending a Rifleman on a patrol in a combat context at the highly deferential, entirely non-justiciable, end of the command power spectrum. However, as the *Maya Evans Case* clearly attests, the more rule-bound an operational decision becomes – in this case, regarding transfers of detainees from UK forces to Afghan authorities – the more willing courts are to engage with the detail of these rules and procedures in order to see that they have indeed been followed.[88]

The third conclusion is that judicial review of incidents of the command power to do things related to operations often provides little scope for award of what the complainant would consider an effective remedy – particularly as many such decisions are time sensitive and the consequences cannot be easily reversed. This factor is in many ways analogous to – or perhaps a subset of – the more general jurisprudence related to urgency and impossibility. But importantly, the sphere of incidents of the command power to administer personnel, within which effective remedies – including reversal of the decision and restoration to a closely analogous position to that which existed prior to the command decision – are much more readily available. Finally, incidents of the command power to administer personnel are now almost completely encompassed within statutory and regulatory authorisations, with little scope for deference-generating 'usages' claims to operate. As Finlason notes (and

86 *Chief of Defence Force* v. *Clark* [2000] FCA 103 (10 February 2000); *Clark* v. *Chief of Defence Force* [1999] FCA 1252 (15 September 1999).

87 *Stuart* v. *Sanderson* [2000] FCA 870 (28 June 2000); *Stuart* v. *Chief of Army* [2003] FCA 1291 (13 November 2003).

88 *R (Maya Evans)* v. *Secretary of State for Defence* [2010] EWHC 1445 (Admin) (*Maya Evans Case*).

quotes) of a line of authority laid down by King's Bench, and summarised by Lord Tenterden in *Bradley* v. *Arthur*:

> The command of the army belongs entirely to the Sovereign, and it is matter for his discretion and his authority alone, except so far as this discretion and authority are regulated and controlled by the statute law. We must therefore look to the statute or the Articles of War, which are an emanation from the Crown under the statute law for any limitation of that authority. If the Mutiny Act, or the Articles of War (which have the same effect), had controlled the power of the commander-in-chief of the army, they would have been binding on him. But where they are silent on the subject we must look to usage.[89]

It is perhaps this variable degree of need for a court to look to 'the usages of the service' in any particular fact situation that offers the firmest indicator as to the likely susceptibility of an exercise of the command power to civilian judicial review against civilian administrative law concepts.

[89] Finlason, *A Review of the Authorities as to the Repression of Riot or Rebellion*, above n. 32, p. 79.

PART II

Comparative military justice

8

The new British system of courts martial

ANN LYON AND GEOFFREY FARMILOE

I Introduction

Periodically, a flurry of press indignation arises over the British court-martial system, complete with allegations of miscarriages of justice which would 'never happen' had the individual been tried by a civilian jury. The most recent example involves Sergeant Danny Nightingale of the SAS, who was sentenced to eighteen months' military detention on 7 November 2012 after pleading guilty to two charges under the Firearms Act 1968 (UK) involving unauthorised possession of a pistol and 338 rounds of ammunition.[1] There was a similar reaction in some quarters, although by no means all, when in November 2014 a court martial convicted Sergeant Alexander Blackman of murder and sentenced him to life imprisonment with a minimum term of ten years on the charge of killing a badly wounded Taliban insurgent during operations in Afghanistan.[2]

The court-martial systems of the Royal Navy and British Army evolved over a lengthy period in circumstances in which lawyers were simply not available (fleets at sea or garrisons abroad, at times when communications moved at the speeds of horse and sailing ship).[3] Although oversight

[1] The Court Martial Appeal Court quashed the original verdict on 12 March 2013 on the basis that Nightingale had been persuaded improperly to plead guilty by remarks made by the Judge Advocate to his counsel during pre-trial legal argument. See 'Former SAS Sniper Danny Nightingale "Elated" as Court Quashes Weapon Conviction' *The Daily Telegraph*, 13 March 2013. The original sentence had already been reduced by the Court Martial Appeal Court to twelve months' imprisonment, suspended for two years. On 10 July Nightingale was convicted of both offences following a retrial. On 25 July he was sentenced to two years' military detention, suspended for twelve months: 'Ex-SAS Sniper Sergeant Danny Nightingale Avoids Jail for Illegal Gun and Ammunition Possession' *The Telegraph*, 25 July 2013 www.telegraph.co.uk/news/uknews/defence/10201862/Ex-SAS-sniper-Sergeant-Danny-Nightingale-avoids-jail-for-illegal-gun-and-ammunition-possession.html.

[2] The Court Martial Appeal Court dismissed an appeal against conviction, but reduced the tariff to eight years: *R* v. *Blackman* [2014] EWCA Crim 1029.

[3] The Royal Air Force was formed on 1 April 1918, and its system follows that of the Army.

by a civilian Judge Advocate of the Fleet and Judge Advocate General existed from the early nineteenth century, the system operated largely without lawyers until the twentieth century. In the haphazard fashion traditional in Britain, a legally qualified Judge Advocate was appointed to advise each court martial on the law, although an unqualified president continued to conduct the trial. A specialist Army Legal Services branch emerged, along with specialist Naval Judge Advocates within the Royal Navy's Supply and Secretariat branch. Rather than relying solely on a 'Defending Officer' (normally unqualified), the defendant could engage a civilian lawyer, and legal aid became available for this purpose. Progressively, the balance of power within service justice moved towards the Judge Advocate conducting the court martial, replicating, in part, the Crown Court system.

Since the 1990s various aspects of the military justice system have been subject to legal challenges on the basis of breaches of art. 6 of the European Convention on Human Rights (ECHR). Article 6(1) requires that in the determination of a criminal charge 'everyone is entitled to a fair and public hearing within a reasonable time by an independent and impartial tribunal established by law'. In the same period, there have been radical changes to the system through the process of quinquennial review of the Armed Forces Acts 1996–2011. This chapter will examine these changes, and consider four areas of current controversy: the choice of forum in murder trials, the role of the court-martial president and members in sentencing, the president and members vis-à-vis the civilian jury, and the use of administrative discharge following acquittal.

II The jurisprudence of the European Court of Human Rights

Despite the judgment in *Findlay* v. *United Kingdom*,[4] the Ministry of Defence and the British Parliament were slow to deal with judicial criticism of the court-martial system. The criticisms in *Findlay* focused on matters of appearance rather than reality as by the date of the judgment, 1995, those responsible for decisions to prosecute and the administration of courts martial acted on the basis of legal advice. By way of contrast, in *Findlay* a non-legally-qualified Convening Officer (in Findlay's case the Major-General Commanding London District) had a role at every stage of the process and was formally responsible for all major decisions. The changes embodied in the Armed Forces Act 1996

[4] (1997) 24 EHRR 221 (*Findlay*).

(UK) (AFA 1996) were designed to achieve a formal separation between the chain of command and the prosecution, and to provide transparency and independence in the laying of charges, the convening of the court martial and its conduct. To this end, the Convening Officer was abolished and the roles divided between a new Army Prosecuting Authority, Court Martial Administration Officer and Reviewing Authority.[5] In addition, the confirmation of court-martial findings and sentence by the chain of command was abolished and replaced with a system of review by an independent Reviewing Authority, the Army Legal Services was split into three branches dealing respectively with prosecutions, legal advice and military legal aid, and the right of appeal against sentence alone was introduced.[6] Although the new Act received royal assent in July 1996, its implementation bore no signs of urgency. Instead, it was brought into force in 1997 by a series of Commencement Orders.[7] The services were content with a system of justice that had served them well for over forty years.[8] Neither the Ministry of Defence (MOD) nor the military were enthusiastic about change.

In a repetition of *Findlay*, the successive cases of *Coyne* v. *United Kingdom*[9] and *Hood* v. *United Kingdom*,[10] both involving courts martial heard before the 1996 Act came fully into force, followed the same route of judicial challenge via the European Court of Human Rights (ECtHR). Unsurprisingly, since the Convening Officer was still a part of the proceedings, it was inevitable that the Court would find a violation of art. 6(1). This represented an undeniable failure on behalf of the military to heed earlier warnings, both by the judiciary[11] and at common law. To await implementation of the AFA 1996 before giving effect to change was a flawed strategy as service justice was no longer wallowing in military obscurity and a procession of cases before the ECtHR and the now designated Supreme Court endorsed this fact.

5 Armed Forces Act 1996 (UK), sch. 1.

6 Ibid., ss. 15–17. Appeals from a court martial are dealt with by the Court Martial Appeal Court, which is the Criminal Division of the Court of Appeal under another title, in that the personnel are the same: Court Martial (Appeals) Act 1968 as amended by Armed Forces Act 1996 (UK), s. 17(2).

7 S.I. 1996/2474, S.I. 1997/304, and S.I. 1997/2164, subject to transitional provisions.

8 Since the enactment of the Army Act 1955 (UK), Air Force Act 1955 (UK) and the Naval Discipline Act 1957 (UK).

9 European Court of Human Rights, Chamber, Application No. 25942/94, 24 September 1997.

10 *Hood* v. *United Kingdom* (2000) 29 EHRR 365.

11 Jeff Blackett, *Rant on the Court Martial and Service Law*, 3rd edn (Oxford, Oxford University Press, 2009), p. 216, at [9.02].

The quinquennial review process (which was provided for by AFA 1996, s. 1), produced the Armed Forces Act 2001 (UK). That new Act had little of the overarching changes of its predecessor and instead merely 'fine-tuned' certain areas of practice. Key aspects included the provision of statutory powers for service police to stop and search personnel and search service accommodation (both barracks and married quarters). This brought their powers closer to those of their civilian counterparts under the Police and Criminal Evidence Act 1984 (UK).[12] A power enabling the Attorney General to refer unduly lenient sentences to the Court Martial Appeal Court was introduced, mirroring the system already in place in relation to civilian Crown Court sentences.[13] There was also an extension of the scope of Summary Dealing for offences allegedly committed by officers. Other changes included the restriction of judicial review of court-martial proceedings[14] and measures for the protection of children within Armed Forces families abroad.[15] The most significant changes enabled warrant officers to sit on courts martial involving personnel of ranks below warrant officer.[16] The inclusion of warrant officers[17] as members of a court martial reinstated a custom of the Royal Navy dating back to the eighteenth century, whereby judges of 'every rank' were empowered to try offences before a Ship's Court. The change was designed to deal with a frequent criticism of the system as 'officers' justice'.

The new Act also introduced powers for drug and alcohol testing to inform a Board of Inquiry in certain circumstances.[18] The introduction of drugs/alcohol testing created a limited power to obtain samples where an incident had occurred with life-threatening implications. However, the result of testing was only to be used to inform a service Board of

[12] Armed Forces Act 2001 (UK), ss. 2–10. [13] Ibid., s. 21. [14] Ibid., s. 23.

[15] Armed Forces Act 1991 (UK), s. 17, as amended by Armed Forces Act 2001 (UK), sch. 6, pt. 6, s. 57.

[16] Armed Forces Act 2001 (UK), sch. 2, s. 19. [17] Ibid., s. 19.

[18] Ibid., ss. 32–33. Boards of Inquiry are convened to investigate a range of incidents, including aircraft accidents and collisions between warships. Their purpose is not punitive, but to establish how the incident happened and to take steps to prevent similar incidents. To encourage witnesses to be entirely open when giving evidence, no evidence given to a Board of Inquiry may be used at subsequent disciplinary proceedings. The Armed Forces have a policy of random drug-testing via urine samples, but the results are not used for disciplinary purposes. Instead, a person failing a random drug test is administratively discharged, or, if an officer, required to resign his commission. Section 305 of the Armed Forces Act 2006 (UK) provides the current statutory authority for such drug testing, and makes it an offence to refuse to provide a urine sample when requested.

Inquiry and could not be used as evidence for any subsequent disciplinary proceedings.[19] This section fell considerably short of making provision to test for drugs/alcohol prior to any operational commitment and therefore had limited preventative capacity; certainly there would have been no impact in *R* v. *Donovan*, a case involving a charge of murder on board a submarine.[20]

By 2002 one might have expected the new military justice system to have become embedded and accepted. However, in *Morris* v. *United Kingdom*[21] a soldier in the Life Guards brought fresh proceedings under art. 6. During his initial riding course with the Household Cavalry Mounted Regiment, he was allegedly bullied and assaulted before going absent without leave for three years. Since the offence was purely military, Morris was not granted legal aid and declined to pay for independent legal representation. An officer from his regiment – Captain 'A', who had no legal training – was appointed to represent Morris as Defending Officer. The allegations of bullying were investigated internally, but no evidence was found to support them.

Morris appeared before a District Court Martial at Chelsea Barracks and pleaded guilty to being absent without leave. Captain 'A' presented to the court a letter that the applicant had written to his CO which stated, 'my inability to express sufficient enthusiasm during training sometimes resulted in physical abuse by certain NCOs [Non-Commissioned Officers]'. No other mention was made of bullying and no real defence was proffered by Captain 'A', who apparently believed that there was no possible defence on the facts. Morris was sentenced to dismissal from the Army and nine months, detention. Captain 'A' then gave him inaccurate advice in respect of the appeal process. Morris finally instructed a solicitor who petitioned the Defence Council (the relevant Reviewing Authority) and made an application for leave to appeal out of time to the Courts-Martial Appeal Court. Both were refused. Morris then appealed to the ECtHR, arguing that the general structure of the court-martial system was neither independent nor impartial and thus violated his right to a fair trial under art. 6.

[19] The use of samples in courts martial and other disciplinary proceedings is expressly prohibited: Armed Forces Act 2006 (UK), s. 32(6). Boards of Inquiry are convened to investigate a range of incidents, including aircraft accidents.

[20] *R* v. *Donovan* [2012] EWCA Crim 2749. In common with all first-instance decisions of the Crown Court, there is no published transcript of this case, and there has been no appeal to date. For a detailed discussion of this case and its issues, see sub-heading 'Current Issues' post.

[21] (2002) 34 EHRR 52 (*Morris*).

The ECtHR partially rejected this appeal, stating that 'the 1996 Act [had] gone a long way to meeting its concerns in the *Findlay* case',[22] and concluded that the separation between the prosecutor and the adjudicatory functions post *Findlay* did not of itself give rise to any violation of art. 6(1).[23] The Court did, however, conclude that there were insufficient safeguards in place in relation to two junior officers appointed to the Board and consequently the risk of outside pressure could not be excluded.[24] Moreover, the Reviewing Authority's power to alter the decision of a court martial was held to violate the principle of independence in art. 6(1).[25] Adjustments after *Morris* caused a temporary impasse in both the Army and RAF systems as all court-martial proceedings were suspended whilst a review was undertaken.[26] This review merely required administrative adjustment and the implementation of the *Morris Direction.*[27]

A succession of unsuccessful challenges followed *Morris*, including the case of *R* v. *Spear*[28] before the House of Lords. The first group of appellants raised concerns in relation to the presence of a Permanent President presiding over proceedings, while the second group argued that criminal offences committed in the United Kingdom should be heard before a civilian court. The House of Lords, having considered the judgment before the ECtHR in *Morris*, rejected the challenge based

[22] Ibid., at [1275]. [23] Ibid.

[24] This is an observation argued in *Cooper* v. *United Kingdom* (2004) 39 EHRR 8, at [189] alluding to the observations of Lord Rodger of Earlsferry, who in turn referred to both *Engel* and *Morris* in his judgment in *R* v. *Spear* [2002] UKHL 31. *Morris* demonstrates the ECtHR's differential treatment of courts martial and jury trials. In the former case, there is a perception that outside influence is likely and therefore positive safeguards need to be in place to prevent it. In the case of jury trials, there is no such assumption. The argument is that juries have no prior affiliation or association within their group and are therefore impartial. By contrast, steps have been taken within the court-martial system to exclude influence from within the chain of command and are more stringent than those in the civilian system: see A.E. Lyon, 'Two Swords and Two Standards' [2005] *Criminal Law Review* 850.

[25] *Morris* v. *United Kingdom* (2002) 34 EHRR 52, at [1278].

[26] HC. Written Answer 18 March 2002 Column 63W alluded to an assessment of the implications of the *Morris* judgment (Mr Ingram, Armed Forces Minister 2001–2007). www.publications.parliament.uk/pa/cm200102/cmhansrd/vo020301/text/20301w13.htm.

[27] The *Morris Direction* is an administrative direction from the Judge Advocate at the beginning of proceedings reminding Board members of their duties and obligations.

[28] *R* v. *Spear* [2002] UKHL 31.

on the role of the Permanent President[29] and dismissed their appeal. In relation to the second issue, Lord Rodger of Earlsferry stated that 'in principle, a military court can constitute an independent and impartial tribunal in terms of art. 6(1). What is required is that there should be sufficient safeguards of the independence and impartiality of its members.'[30] The judgment of the Courts-Martial Appeal Court was affirmed and the appellants' cases dismissed.

Based upon the preceding case law and the AFA 1996, the court-martial system had developed into a robust and transparent system. However, its fate was not yet sealed, with the further judgments of the ECtHR in *Cooper* v. *United Kingdom*[31] and *Grieves* v. *United Kingdom*[32] in 2003. The Court's findings were in complete contrast to one another, the RAF court martial in *Cooper* being found compliant with the ECHR, while in *Grieves* the naval court martial was found to violate the Convention. This result was due to the differing structures, functions and personalities in an RAF District Court-Martial as distinct from a naval court martial.

In *Cooper*, an RAF airman was convicted by a District Court-Martial of theft. The court martial included a Permanent President (Wing Commander), two officers of lower rank and a civilian Judge Advocate. The Reviewing Authority found no reason to vary finding or sentence and an appeal to the Courts-Martial Appeal Court was dismissed. The applicant then applied to the ECtHR on the basis of art. 6(1). Specifically, Cooper argued that service tribunals should have no role to play in the trial of criminal charges against service personnel or alternatively that the structure of the Prosecuting Authority (PA), Court Administration Officer (CAO), Permanent President of court martial (PPCM) and the ordinary members of the Board was neither independent nor impartial.[33]

29 Ibid., at [758]. The practice had developed in the Army and RAF systems of appointing a number of officers (Lieutenant-Colonels and Wing Commanders, respectively) as Permanent Presidents of District Courts Martial (those trying offences where the maximum sentence was two years' imprisonment or less). A DCM comprises the president, two officers of lesser rank (or one officer and one warrant officer where the accused is of a rank below warrant officer) and the Judge Advocate. A General Court-Martial has no limit on its sentencing powers except the maximum prescribed for the offence, and comprises the president, four other officers (or two officers and two warrant officers) and the Judge Advocate.

30 *R* v. *Spear* [2002] UKHL 31, at [766].

31 *Cooper* v. *United Kingdom* (2004) 39 EHRR 8 (*Cooper*).

32 *Grieves* v. *United Kingdom* (2004) 39 EHRR 2 (*Grieves*).

33 *Cooper* (2004) 39 EHRR 8, at [171].

The Grand Chamber reviewed the entire structure of the court-martial process and its earlier judgments before concluding that there was no such violation. The Chamber agreed with the finding in *Morris* that art. 6 did not preclude service tribunals hearing criminal charges against service personnel.[34] The ECtHR noted that the Prosecuting Authority was legally qualified and employed exclusively on prosecution duties, similar in nature to the Crown Prosecution Service (CPS).[35] The Prosecuting Authority, now the Service Prosecuting Authority (SPA), was answerable to the Attorney-General and not within the structure of command. Second, the CAO, although an RAF officer, was appointed by the Defence Council and operated independently of the chain of command and the Prosecuting Authority. The CAO's selection of Board members was laid down by procedure and gave little discretion to that officer in its selection, rebutting the applicant's claim of lack of transparency. The Court's opinion of the PPCM was that as a full-time senior ranking officer, at the conclusion of an RAF career with 'no effective fear of removal' from office, the applicant's suggestion of a lack of independence was unfounded.[36] Finally, it was noted that the Judge Advocate, a legally qualified civilian, was appointed to the Office of the Judge Advocate General OJAG by the Lord Chancellor and no grounds existed to question the independence of a Judge Advocate at an RAF court martial.[37] In conclusion, the Court found that the applicant's misgivings about the independence and impartiality of his court martial were not objectively justified and consequently the proceedings were not unfair.[38]

By contrast, in *Grieves* a naval rating (a non-commissioned sailor in the Navy) was convicted before a naval court martial of unlawfully and maliciously wounding with intent to cause grievous bodily harm. The court martial comprised a president (Captain RN), four naval officers and a Judge Advocate, who was a naval barrister and legal advisor to Fleet. As a Commander, the Judge Advocate's rank was lower than that of the president of the Board. Following advice from the Judge Advocate of the Fleet, the Navy Board, as the Reviewing Authority, upheld the verdict of

[34] In this respect, the Court noted its earlier judgments in *Engel* v. *Netherlands* (1979) 1 EHRR 647 and *Findlay. Cooper* (2004) 39 EHRR 8, at [204].

[35] *Cooper* (2004) 39 EHRR 8, at [113]. [36] Ibid., at [187].

[37] Ibid., at [117]. In practice, Judge Advocates are qualified to the same level as Circuit Judges, and most sit in the Crown Court as Recorders or Assistant Recorders.

[38] Ibid., at [134].

the court martial and a subsequent appeal to the Courts-Martial Appeal Court was unsuccessful.

As in previous cases, Grieves argued before the ECtHR that the court martial lacked independence and impartiality. The Court considered *Cooper* and contrasted the constitution of the naval court martial with that of an RAF District Court-Martial.[39] In the naval structure both the president and the Judge Advocate were serving naval officers. In the RAF system, the president was a permanent appointment, independent of the command structure and not subject to judicial reporting, and the Judge Advocate was a civilian holding office under the Judge Advocate General.

The Court examined the naval structure and found that there was insufficient independence in the system and accordingly a violation of art. 6(1).[40] Much of what has been considered in both these cases has now been addressed by the implementation of the AFA 2006 and a more independent and transparent system. In particular, concerns about the independence of naval Judge Advocates have been dealt with by extending the Army and RAF system to naval courts martial so that civilian Judge Advocates now sit on all courts martial.

One of the final successful challenges to the structure prior to the 2006 Act came in the case of *R* v. *Stow*,[41] involving a naval rating who pleaded guilty to two counts of drunkenness and using insubordinate language. He was sentenced to forty-two days, detention and dismissal from the service. He petitioned against his conviction to the Reviewing Authority and then to the Courts-Martial Appeal Court. Under the system at that time an Authorising Officer ordered a naval court martial and also appointed the Board and the Judge Advocate. This was a similar role to that performed by the Convening Officer within the Army in *Findlay*. However, in *Stow* the challenge was not to the institution of the Naval Prosecuting Authority but to the position and personality of the occupant, a matter not provided for in the legislation. Stow's argument was threefold; that the Prosecuting Authority was subject to the normal system of annual confidential reporting by superiors within the service,[42] that this was not a final posting, unlike Army and RAF counterparts, and that the rank (Captain RN) was significantly more junior than that of other service equivalents, both of whom were two-star postings.[43] Despite a robust argument proffered by the Crown, the appeal was allowed. Keene LJ stated that 'we are forced to

[39] *Grieves* (2004) 39 EHRR 2. [40] Ibid., at [91]. [41] [2005] EWCA Crim 1157.
[42] *R* v. *Stow* [2005] EWCA Crim 1157, at [13].
[43] That is, a Major-General and Air Vice-Marshal, respectively. *R* v. *Stow* [2005] EWCA Crim 1157, at [15].

conclude that the Naval Prosecuting Authority at the time of this court-martial did not enjoy necessary safeguards of his independence and impartiality'.[44] Since the AFA 2006 introduced a joint Service Prosecuting Authority under the stewardship of a Director of Service Prosecutions, the basis of the *Stow* appeal no longer exists.[45]

A *Legislative developments*

1 The Armed Forces Act 2006

The most radical reform to the service disciplinary system in modern times has occurred through the enactment of the Armed Forces Act 2006 (UK). This Act expunged the three separate service discipline Acts (Army Act 1955 (UK), Air Force Act 1955 (UK) and Naval Discipline Act 1957 (UK)) and replaced them with a single statute that now serves the Armed Forces homogeneously and wherever they operate in the world. This is in striking contrast to the previous legislation, which was procedurally diverse and contained disparate sentencing practices. The reasons for the rationalisation are obvious; with an integration of fighting ability in the twenty-first century, not only between the Armed Forces of the United Kingdom but on a global stage, it is necessary to provide an easily functioning and consistent disciplinary process. Further, there is obvious potential for cost-saving in a time of repeated cuts to the defence budget and major reductions in service manpower.

Whatever the nature of warfare and the diversity of geographical theatres of operation, the need for transparent equitable military justice remains. Certainly major consideration was given to the need to eradicate, or at least reduce, challenges to the ECtHR during the drafting process of the Act; indeed ECHR compliance has been an aspiration of all recent discipline Acts to a greater or lesser extent.

The Act also served to create a transparent and independent Service Prosecuting Authority. It was a far-reaching change to service law and centralised disciplinary review in the hands of the Director of Service Prosecutions, as opposed to the accused's Commanding Officer, who under the previous legislation decided whether to deal with the matter or to refer it to the appropriate Prosecuting Authority.[46] It also developed

[44] Ibid., at [39].

[45] Armed Forces Act 2006 (UK), s. 363 does not prohibit the appointment of a serving officer, but first and so far the only holder of the office is Mr Bruce Houlder QC.

[46] Although a service member subject to Summary Dealing was absolutely entitled to elect trial by court martial.

the role of an entirely neutral prosecutor, taken from any of the services, to work within the Service Prosecuting Authority and prosecute cases regardless of the rank or service of the defendant.

Given the process which led to the drafting of this Act, it would be expected that further successful challenges would be sparse. This was highlighted more recently in *R* v. *Twaite*.[47] The defendant, a Flight Lieutenant in the RAF, was charged with fraud by false representation and appeared before a court martial comprising five lay members and a Judge Advocate. He was convicted by a majority verdict. However, during the Board's deliberations on sentencing, the Judge Advocate became concerned about the basis upon which the Board had reached its decision. The issue was considered by the Judge Advocate General who in turn referred the matter to the Court Martial Appeal Court on several points of law, *inter alia*:

> 1. is a finding of guilt by a simple majority of a Board of five or more lay members in the court martial in a case where the defendant is in jeopardy of a significant sentence of imprisonment, as provided by the statute, inherently unsafe?
> 2. is a defendant deprived [of] his right to a fair trial under art.6 of the European Convention on Human Rights where he can be found guilty of a serious offence (within the ambit of Schedule 2 to the Armed Forces Act 2006 and any other offences where the maximum sentence is seven years' or more imprisonment) by a simple majority, thereby placing him in jeopardy of a significant sentence of imprisonment?
> 3. if the answer to (2) is in the affirmative, will the Courts-Martial Appeal Court make a declaration of incompatibility in relation to section 160(1) of the Armed Forces Act 2006, so far as it relates to the Armed Forces Act Schedule 2 offences and any other offences with a maximum sentence of seven years' or more imprisonment?

The Lord Chief Justice commented that no concerns had been expressed by either the House of Lords or the ECtHR regarding majority verdicts. Alluding to the speech of Lord Rodger in *Spear*, he noted that majority verdicts had been expressly highlighted in that case without adverse criticism.[48] The Lord Judge went on to say that 'there [was] no reason to conclude that a finding of guilt on the basis of a simple majority verdict is inherently unsafe' and that 'the trial process is intended to be fair and in this case is demonstrably fair'.[49] Although it was stated that a

[47] *R* v. *Twaite* [2010] EWCA Crim 2973. [48] Ibid., at [24]. [49] Ibid., at [29].

declaration of incompatibility was inappropriate, Twaite's conviction was quashed due to procedural irregularities.

Twaite presented a conundrum because it created a disparity between a trial by court martial and a trial in the Crown Court. In the former, a Board of three or five members may pass a finding of guilt by a simple majority with no need for a majority direction, whereas in the Crown Court the minimum majority required would be 10:2 if the judge so directs in circumstances where the jury cannot reach a unanimous verdict. One may note that juries in criminal trials in Scotland may convict on simple majority, though they number fifteen, not five. Further, in many continental jurisdictions, trial by jury is unknown and in some cases a judge will sit alone.

By contrast the military justice system of New Zealand, which initially corresponded closely to the British system, now requires that the finding of a court martial on a charge must be determined by the *unanimous* vote of the military members.[50]

One interpretation of the judgment in *Twaite* may be that the comprehensive drafting of the 2006 Act, which addressed previous ECHR challenges, together with the independence and impartiality of the current system, has resulted in a slowing down of judicial challenges to the ECtHR. However, *Twaite* was never argued before either the Supreme Court or the ECtHR and, therefore, its authority is still open to question.

2 The Armed Forces Act 2011

Following the most recent quinquennial review, the Armed Forces Act 2011 (UK) was enacted. It does not contain the broad ranging amendments found in the 2006 Act but was an adjustment exercise to further enhance the quality of military justice. The primary objectives of the Act were to provide for the statutory independence of service police forces and their oversight by Her Majesty's Inspectorate of Constabulary. It also enabled Judge Advocates to authorise the search of premises[51] in a similar way to their civilian counterparts. Other issues addressed included a broader range of drugs testing[52] and a provision for the Secretary of State to make an annual report to Parliament on the military covenant[53] (discussed later).

Following the far-reaching changes to the Service Prosecuting Authority under the 2006 Act, it is of no surprise that the service police should undergo the same scrutiny. Each of the services has its own service

[50] Court Martial Act 2007 (New Zealand), s. 55 [emphasis added].
[51] Armed Forces Act 2011 (UK), s. 7. [52] Ibid., s. 11. [53] Ibid., s. 2.

police force, the officers of which are called 'provost officers' and are commanded by a Provost Marshal.[54] The 2011 Act imposed a statutory duty[55] upon each Provost Marshal, who is directly answerable to the Defence Council, to ensure independence of investigations. This duty prevents the '*improper interference*' in investigations which is defined as '[including] any attempt by a person who is not a service policeman to direct an investigation which is being carried out by the force'.[56] This may appear to be an insignificant amendment but it clearly places the service police investigation outside the chain of command and outside the potential influence of the Commanding Officer of any relevant unit.

Oversight is now provided by Her Majesty's Inspectorate of Constabulary (HMIC), which inspects the relevant service police in a similar manner to the scrutiny exerted upon other Home Office police forces. HMIC must report to the Secretary of State on the 'independence and effectiveness of investigations carried out by each service police force'.[57] These provisions go some way to anticipating further judicial challenge(s) and have far-reaching implications in preventing the 'closing of ranks' apparent in previous investigations. The Deepcut Inquiry, which involved an investigation into the death of four soldiers, is a classic example of historical mismanagement.[58]

The provision for alcohol/drugs testing of both service personnel and civilian personnel (subject to service discipline) under the 2011 Act merely closes the omissions made under previous legislation. It now allows the evidence provided by screening to be used in criminal proceedings.

The final objective of the Act has been the Armed Forces Covenant, which until this point had no statutory recognition. Certainly during the Committee stage of the Bill,[59] a disproportionate amount of time was

54 Brigadier in the case of the Army, Group Captain for the RAF and Commander for the Royal Navy.

55 Armed Forces Act 2011 (UK), s. 3.

56 Ibid., s. 3 creating an additional section within the Armed Forces Act 2006 (UK), at 115A(1)–(3).

57 Armed Forces Act 2011 (UK), s. 4.

58 Nicholas Blake, *The Deepcut Review: A Review of the Circumstances Surrounding the Deaths of Four Soldiers at Princess Royal Barracks, Deepcut between 1995 and 2002* (London, The Stationery Office, 2006) www.official-documents.gov.uk/document/hc0506/hc07/0795/0795.pdf. Following an internal Special Investigation Branch investigation and three separate Home Office police investigations, it fell to Nicholas Blake QC in 2004 to oversee a further independent review. The perceived need for this final investigation provides some indication of the shortcomings of the earlier investigations.

59 Select Committee appointed on 17 January 2011 with a deadline to report to the House by 10 March 2011.

focused on deliberations regarding this one specific clause. Statutory recognition of the Covenant replaced the largely unwritten social and moral commitment between the nation, government and service personnel. The implication is that in return for the sacrifices made by service personnel, the state has an obligation to recognise their contribution and retain a long-term duty of care towards the Armed Forces and their families.[60]

The Covenant made provision for service personnel and their dependants to be supported in their unique environment, especially whilst personnel are deployed in operational theatre. Families of Armed Forces personnel have to adjust to the transient nature of service life and evidence exists that children and partners are often disadvantaged in comparison to their civilian counterparts in matters such as education and non-military housing.[61] This legislation addresses some of those disparities and makes provision for an annual report to be laid before Parliament. The process is accountable and transparent, and demonstrates the obligations placed upon government in their administration and oversight of the Armed Forces.

III Current issues

The drafters of the Armed Forces Act 2006 (UK) (AFA 2006) not only took into consideration the European Convention on Human Rights but also made a conscious effort to eradicate legislative anomalies. For example, until 2006 the most serious criminal offences, homicide and rape, if committed by a person subject to service law whilst in the United Kingdom, were solely the domain of Home Office police forces and the Crown Court. Pursuant to s. 42 of the AFA 2006 any offence subject to the law of England and Wales committed by a person subject to service law falls within the non-exclusive jurisdiction of a court martial.

The provision was relevant in a 2011 case involving a charge of murder on board the nuclear-powered submarine HMS *Astute* when moored in Southampton docks on a five-day goodwill visit. Able Seaman Ryan

60 Select Committee on the Armed Forces Bill 2011, *Special Report of Session 2010–11*, HC 779, at [7].

61 Both authors are the product of military families; each enduring repeated relocation during their formative years, attending six or seven different schools during their primary education. It may be noted that in recent years, service personnel are frequently being posted on unaccompanied operational tours, which impose their own brand of stress on their families.

Donovan was allocated to sentry duty and drew an SA80 rifle and ammunition from the weapons locker situated in an area linked to the control room by a narrow passageway. It was from this location that Donovan opened fire, discharging seven shots,[62] which fatally wounded Lt Cdr Ian Molyneux and caused serious injuries to Lt Cdr Christopher Hodge. Two senior ratings were also in the control room together with civilian dignitaries on a visit. Donovan was charged with murder and three counts of attempted murder.[63] He pleaded guilty to all counts before Winchester Crown Court and was sentenced to life imprisonment with a minimum recommendation of twenty-five years and 194 days before consideration of parole.

The incident is legally significant as it involved the first homicide by a member of the Armed Forces within the United Kingdom since the Armed Forces Act 2006 came into force. It was a homicide on a Royal Navy vessel, perpetrated by a naval rating, causing the death of a naval officer, on duty, whilst the vessel was moored in a British port. Clearly, this offence was triable within the court-martial system and possessed an overwhelmingly naval character. However, it was investigated by the Hampshire Constabulary and, following consideration by the Crown Prosecution Service, it was heard at Winchester Crown Court.[64] Consultation between the CPS and the SPA occurred but the decision was made by the CPS to retain primacy and allow the matter to be heard within the civilian jurisdiction. The prosecution team combined a civilian Queen's Counsel and a Captain RN. However, this in no way undermines the ability of the SPA to have taken this matter before court martial, subject to agreement. The current protocol[65] on criminal jurisdiction within England and Wales gives primacy to civilian jurisdiction but makes provision for either Director to consult the Attorney-General if necessary. This seems slightly surprising; if civilian jurisdiction is always to have primacy in cases taking place within England and Wales, there seems little practical point in giving courts martial

[62] Inquest of Lt Cdr Molyneux before HM Coroner K St J Wiseman, unpublished transcript provided by the coroner (on file with the author).

[63] Ryan Samuel Donovan was charged with one count of murder in respect of Lt Cdr Molyneux and three counts of attempted murder in respect of Lt Cdr Hodge, Chief Petty Officer McCoy and Petty Officer Brown.

[64] This case was not reported. The information contained in the text was obtained by the authors from Mr Nick Hawkins, Chief Crown Prosecutor, CPS Wessex region.

[65] 'Service Prosecutions Authority (SPA) concurrent criminal jurisdiction protocol'. This protocol on the exercise of Criminal Jurisdiction in England and Wales between the DSP, the DPP and the MOD was signed and ratified on 4 November 2011.

jurisdiction at all, except to cover the rare situation where the civilian authorities might decline to prosecute in a case of homicide or rape. Despite claims by the CPS that the offence took place in a civilian environment, given the presence of the civilian visitors, it is difficult to envisage a more military context for a murder than inside an operational submarine. The difficulty with such an emotive issue is public perception – the public is not familiar with seeing defendants tried in a military environment in the United Kingdom and is suspicious of the unknown. It will be necessary for the Act to 'bed in' and perhaps a greater understanding by all parties as to the intentions of Parliament when the Act was originally drafted to develop before it functions in a cohesive manner. Since the civilian police will always defer to the CPS in the decision-making process, it is necessary that senior CPS prosecutors consider the question of jurisdiction at an early stage and relinquish authority where appropriate. For this to be effective there should be a bilateral educational exchange between the SPA and the CPS.

It is also relevant to note that in the Donovan incident the defendant had abused alcohol excessively whilst ashore but was still issued with an SA80 rifle and ammunition to stand watch.[66] According to evidence given at the inquest into Lt Cdr Molyneux's death, naval personnel were at the time forbidden to drink alcohol in the ten hours before going on duty, and restricted to no more than ten units in the previous fourteen hours. Without powers of drink/drug testing, this was, however, difficult to enforce when personnel went ashore off duty, and it is reported that Donovan had consumed twenty pints of cider and lager, together with double vodkas and cocktails, in the forty-eight hours before drawing the weapon.[67] This fairly common occurrence of binge drinking was commented upon by HM Coroner[68] and is now the subject of recommendations under Rule 43 of the Coroner's Rules suggesting consideration of even more stringent drink/drugs testing amongst naval and military personnel.

A further area of concern which may in the future lead to litigation is the practice of the service in using discharge by administrative action as an alternative to disciplinary proceedings or, indeed, as an adjunct to

[66] Recorded from the narrative of the inquest verdict of HM Coroner K StJ Wiseman, p. 19, at [2]–[4].

[67] David Millward, 'Royal Navy Warship Crews Face Breath Tests under New Rules' *The Daily Telegraph*, 24 March 2013 www.telegraph.co.uk/news/uknews/9950986/Royal-Navy-warship-crews-face-breath-tests-under-new-rules.html.

[68] See above n. 64.

them. It has already been noted that a practice has been adopted by which personnel who fail random drugs tests are administratively discharged. This is equivalent to dismissal from employment in civilian life, and may have greater long-term effects through loss of significant pension rights, but unlike civilian counterparts, service members cannot seek redress via a claim for unfair dismissal in the Employment Tribunal.[69] Further, the services may discharge by administrative action after a person has been acquitted by court martial, again without any external source of redress. Lieutenant-Colonel Keith Pople, acquitted in 1998 on two charges arising from an affair with a more junior naval officer and its break-up, was subsequently required to resign his commission under provisions in Queen's Regulations. He then brought an action against the Ministry of Defence for sex discrimination on the basis that the female officer concerned had been equally culpable but had not been required to resign, but this failed when the Tribunal ruled that the Army and the Royal Navy were not the same employer, although both came under the authority of the Ministry of Defence.

Most recently Sergeant Nightingale is reported to have been recommended for discharge on medical grounds, while awaiting a retrial on charges of unlawful possession of a pistol and ammunition.[70] An attempt by his legal team to persuade a judge that a retrial would serve no purpose had already failed.[71] Nightingale's case appears to have become a *cause celebre* on the basis of a highly effective media campaign. That campaign focused on his position as an 'SAS hero' rather the factual background of the case.[72] Remarks made in the press by the prime minister at the time of the initial appeal also raise concerns about political interference in the judicial process and the decision to prosecute a second time. Given the likelihood of a medical discharge, triggered by the defence's claims at the initial court martial that Nightingale was suffering from memory loss caused by brain damage,[73] an acquittal at the retrial would have represented a pyrrhic victory in practical terms. In his sentencing remarks at the end of the retrial, the Judge Advocate General was highly critical not

[69] Provisions were included in the Employment Rights Act 1996 (UK) to extend the unfair dismissal jurisdiction to the Armed Forces, but these have never been brought into force.

[70] See *Nightingale* v. *R* [2013] EWCA Crim 405.

[71] 'Sgt Danny Nightingale Recommended for Medical Discharge' *The Telegraph*, 2 May 2013 www.telegraph.co.uk/news/uknews/defence/10034029/Sgt-Danny-Nightingale-recommended-for-medical-discharge.html.

[72] See *R* v. *Nightingale* [2012] EWCA Crim 2734, at [7] where the Court Martial Appeal Court stressed that publicity about the case has led to misunderstanding of its facts.

[73] See *R* v. *Nightingale* [2012] EWCA Crim 2734 for details of the medical evidence.

only of the 'spurious defence' put forward by Nightingale at the retrial (that the pistol and ammunition belonged to Nightingale's house mate), but also of the content of the media campaign, in particular the attempts made by some MPs and others to impugn the court-martial system.[74] The court-martial system is firmly in the spotlight once more and likely to remain so for the foreseeable future.

IV Conclusion

A number of further changes could be introduced to allay claims of continuing partiality within the court-martial system and to bolster public confidence in military justice.[75] First, the Judge Advocate should become solely responsible for sentencing, as in the Crown Court. Following a finding of guilty, a representative of the chain of command should be able to address the court on the military considerations to be applied in sentencing and provide a 'victim impact statement' where appropriate. Second, where the maximum sentence upon conviction is ten years or more, a court comprising a president and eleven members should be required, with a requirement for a minimum 10:2 majority. This change would align the size and voting requirements of military courts with those of civilian criminal trials in the Crown Court. Although the Armed Forces are currently severely stretched by operational commitments, this should not raise major logistical implications in practice, as such cases are likely to be rare. Third, Board members should be officers or senior non-commissioned officers to widen the pool of available personnel, with the caveat that Board members must be at least the military rank of the accused. Again precedent has been set in other military jurisdictions, in particular New Zealand. Fourth, in all cases where the maximum sentence is less

[74] Ben Farmer, 'Judge Criticises Former SAS Sniper Danny Nightingale's "Spurious Defence" as He Avoids Jail' *The Telegraph*, 25 July 2013 www.telegraph.co.uk/news/uknews/defence/10202288/Judge-criticises-former-SAS-sniper-Danny-Nightingales-spurious-defence-as-he-avoids-jail.html.

[75] See Joshua Rozenburg, 'Military Judge Raises Court Martial Concerns' *BBC News*, 25 June 2013 www.bbc.co.uk/news/uk-23003483, where Judge Blackett made these points in an interview on BBC Radio 4 *Law in Action*. It should be noted that Judge Blackett acted as Judge Advocate in the Nightingale retrial and required a unanimous verdict from the court. See Ben Farmer, 'SAS Sniper Freed after Public Campaign Found Guilty at Retrial for Possessing Pistol' *The Telegraph*, 10 July 2013 www.telegraph.co.uk/news/uknews/defence/10172542/SAS-sniper-freed-after-public-campaign-found-guilty-at-retrial-for-possessing-pistol.html.

than ten years, there should be unanimous verdicts, rather than the current simple majority. These recommendations would go some way to eradicating the concerns raised both within the judiciary and in the European Court of Human Rights, and popular misconceptions about the military justice system, without any detrimental effects on good order and discipline.

9

The reform of military justice in South Asia

U.C. JHA

I Introduction

South Asia encompasses Bangladesh, Bhutan, India, the Maldives, Nepal, Pakistan and Sri Lanka. Together, these countries account for almost a quarter of the world's population. Although the South Asian Association for Regional Cooperation (SAARC) – the only significant international institution in the region – binds these states loosely, they are bound intimately by a shared past. This chapter examines the key commonalities and differences amongst the military law systems of Bangladesh, India, Nepal, Pakistan and Sri Lanka with the aim of suggesting reforms to align these military justice systems more closely with those established in other parts of the world.[1]

In many democratic countries, the military organisation and its management have been the subject of wide-ranging reforms. Military legal systems across the world have also been challenged by higher courts, particularly final courts of appeal. Several of these challenges have been successful and resulted in substantial legal reforms based on the guarantees contained in international human rights law.[2] These guarantees include the greater independence of judges, the establishment of standing military courts, the increased right to elect trial instead of summary procedures and an increased right to legal representation. Furthermore, there has been a move to civilian, rather than military jurisdiction, particularly in peacetime, through a reduction in the competence of military courts, the abolition of such courts and the abolition of military

[1] For more details, see U.C. Jha, *The South Asian Military Law Systems* (New Delhi, KW Publishers Pvt. Ltd., 2010).

[2] For example, in Belgium, Canada, Chechnya, Finland, Ireland, Israel, Netherlands, New Zealand, South Africa, Switzerland, the United Kingdom and the United States. The influence of human rights law has been particularly strong in countries subject to the European Court of Human Rights, as explained in Chapters 2, 8 and 11.

prosecution. These trends are particularly visible in countries subject to the European Convention on Human Rights (ECHR).

While the five South Asian countries discussed in this chapter have modernised their military arsenals in the last twenty years, they have not reformed their military justice systems to take into account emerging human rights norms or the prevailing civilian criminal justice system despite calls for reform.[3] South Asian countries inherited their military justice systems from their colonial rulers. Some features of these colonial systems remain in place even though they are archaic in the modern world and appear to belong to an age when the army was a band of mercenaries. As South Asian military justice systems have been subjected to relatively little change in the last sixty years, much of the power within these systems remains within the control of the military commander, who exercises an almost unrestrained and unlimited power of discretion. The armed forces personnel in the South Asian countries are being deprived of the benefit of the developments which have occurred in many other nations in human rights, jurisprudential thought and judicial thinking. In light of these many failures, this chapter will highlight some key areas for the reform of military justice systems in the region.

II The legal basis of military justice

In a democratic country, the primary function of the armed forces is to fight and win wars.[4] In all five South Asian countries examined in this chapter, a written constitution provides the basis for the legitimacy of state institutions, including the armed forces, that protect the territorial integrity, the system of government and the maintenance of essential services. Military forces have assumed a direct role in the politics and governance of South Asian countries. Such a role may reflect the prevalence of military intervention in politics in the developing world more generally, but the nature and extent of that intervention varies

[3] On 30 June 2011, the Supreme Court of Nepal directed the Nepalese government to form a taskforce comprising legal experts, military officials, members of civil society and human rights defenders to review and recommend changes to the military justice system to make it compliant with the Interim Constitution and international human rights law. See *Bhuwan Prasad Niraula* v. *Constituent Assembly, Legislative Parliament & Ors*, WP No 0010-2065. In India, the Parliamentary Standing Committee on Defence (2005–2006) had recommended the establishment of an expert committee to thoroughly review the three service Acts to bring them in line with such Acts of other democratic countries.

[4] S.E. Finer, *The Man on Horseback: The Role of Military in Politics* (London, Pall Mall Press, 1962), p. 7.

considerably within South Asia. For example, Pakistan and Bangladesh have experienced many such military interventions as a result of the inability of the elected leaders to steer the state through a politically stable path in the initial years. The decline of democratic structures, such as political parties, pressure groups, parliament, judiciary and the executive, and the virtual death of political processes such as constitutionalism, have led to the strengthening of the military as an institution and force in public life, in Pakistan and Bangladesh. The governance of India since it gained independence provides a striking contrast. The democratic institutions of India are robust, which explains why the Indian defence forces have not intervened in domestic governance or expanded their role as has occurred in most other South Asian countries.

The British military justice system, conceived with the aim of 'disciplining' a mercenary force after the 1857 Indian Mutiny,[5] is the progenitor of the military legal systems of the South Asian countries. During their rule, the British trained and organised three separate defence forces. The army was the first to be raised on a regular basis under the statute of 1754,[6] followed by the navy in 1830 and the air force, which was the last to be established, in 1932. During World War II, these forces were highly organised and were governed pursuant to three separate but similar laws: the Indian Army Act, 1911, the Navy Discipline Act, 1934, and the Air Force Act, 1932. These laws were enacted relatively late in the colonial rule of India by Britain.

To preserve the continuity of the legal system, the Indian Independence Act 1947 (UK) provided that the existing laws of British India, including the services' laws, would continue to operate in the new countries until superseded by subsequent legislation.[7] In India, the laws with respect to the army and the air force were replaced by the Army Act, 1950, and the Air Force Act, 1950, respectively. The Indian Navy Act was passed in 1957.[8] In

[5] The Indian Mutiny was the single most violent and extensive revolt against British rule in Colonial India. The mutiny was led by local Indian soldiers. The total revision to colonial governance after this struggle included wide reforms to the military. See Ian Copland et al., *A History of State and Religion in South Asia* (London, Routledge, 2012), pp. 178–82.

[6] 27 George II, c. 9; An Act for punishing Mutiny and Desertion of Officers and Soldiers in the Service of the United Company of Merchants of England trading to the East Indies; and for the Punishment of Offences committed in the East Indies, or at the Island of Saint Helena.

[7] Similar arrangements operated in most other former British colonies.

[8] The Naval Discipline Act in existence at that time differed from the laws relating to the army and the air force in many respects. In the United Kingdom, a special committee was

essence, these laws were replicas of the British-Indian laws with only a few cosmetic changes. In Pakistan, the three services' laws continued to operate until they were repealed by the Pakistan Army Act, 1952, the Pakistan Navy Ordinance, 1961, and the Pakistan Air Force Act, 1953. In 2007 the Pakistan Army Act was amended to give powers to military courts to try civilians on charges of terrorism, anti-national activities, sedition, attacks on army personnel and attacks on the president. These laws, although greatly improved in language and form, are substantially similar to their predecessors. After Bangladesh gained independence in 1972, no significant changes were made to the Pakistan Army Act, 1952.[9] The Bangladesh army (Sena Bahini) is governed by the Act of 1952, the air force (Biman Bahini) by the Act of 1953 and the navy (Nou Bahini) by the Ordinance of 1961. Though the service laws have been amended on a few occasions, no substantial changes have been made. The Sri Lankan armed forces are governed by the Army Act, 1949, the Air Force Act, 1949, and the Navy Act, 1950. The democratic government in Nepal passed the Nepalese Army Act in 2006.[10] Thus, in essence, the military legal systems of the South Asian countries are substantially similar, if not identical. All remain heavily based on the legislative models that were introduced during colonial times and have not been significantly changed since each nation gained independence.

In general, the legal systems that regulate the armed forces of South Asian countries place certain restrictions on the fundamental rights of armed forces personnel. In India, article 33 of the Constitution suggests that Parliament can make a law abrogating or restricting the fundamental

established to examine the question of revision of the British Naval Codes, and the Government of India awaited the committee's report. The Navy Act, 1957, was finally passed by Parliament on 27 December 1957, and came into effect on 1 January 1958.

9 Adapted by the Bangladesh (Adaptation of Existing Laws) Order (1972).

10 The Nepalese Army Act, 2006, has been criticised because section 22 provides impunity to the armed forces. It states that no case can be filed against an army person who commits any act in good faith while discharging their duties, though it may result in the death of or loss to any person. Such provisions give statutory immunity. They are problematic and should be deleted. The International Commission of Jurists, a Geneva-based NGO, has urged for amendment of section 22, as it provides for amnesty for crimes under international law such as crimes against humanity, war crimes, and gross human rights violations in general such as extrajudicial killings, enforced disappearances and torture International Commission of Jurists, *Nepal: Recommendations for Amendments to the Draft Army Act* (2006) http://icj.wpengine.netdna-cdn.com/wp-content/uploads/2012/04/Nepal-amendments-draft-army-act-report-2006.pdf. In June 2011, the Supreme Court ordered the government to review the *Army Act* to ensure its compliance with Nepal's human rights obligations. The Army Act has not yet been revised.

rights of members of the armed forces, or the forces charged with the maintenance of public order only for two reasons: 'for ensuring the proper discharge of their duties' and 'for the maintenance of discipline among them'. Accordingly, s. 21 of the Indian Army Act, 1950 states that army personnel cannot (i) be associated in any way with any trade union, or any society, institution or association, or any class of societies, institutions or associations; (ii) attend or address any meeting or to take part in any demonstration organised by any body of persons for any political or other purposes; and (iii) communicate with the press or publish or cause to be published any book, letter or document.[11]

Similarly, article 8(3) of the Constitution of Pakistan expressly exempts laws relating to the armed forces from Part II (which deals with the Fundamental Rights and Principles of Policy). This exemption significantly curtails the enjoyment by military personnel of the basic rights constitutionally guaranteed to all other citizens. Article 45 of the Bangladesh Constitution declares that sections dealing with fundamental rights shall not apply to any provision of a disciplinary law relating to members of a disciplined force. The Constitution of Sri Lanka, in article 15(8), echoes the language of the article 33 of the Indian Constitution. The Constitution of Nepal (2015) makes no such restrictions on the fundamental rights of military personnel. However, s. 19 of the Nepal Army Act, 2006, imposes restrictions on the activities of persons subject to the Act which are very similar to those provided in Indian legislation.

The common thread between these constitutional articles, and the legislation adopted in some South Asian jurisdictions in consequence of those articles, is their acceptance that some of the constitutional rights enjoyed by civilians may be curtailed in their application to members of the armed forces. The most striking feature of the attenuated rights of members of the armed forces in South Asian countries is their constitutional basis. The analysis of the military justice systems of other nations in this chapter indicates that South Asian countries are unique in making express constitutional provision for the restriction of the rights of service personnel. This unique feature of South Asian constitutions has greatly influenced the structure and operation of military justice systems in South Asia.

[11] These restrictions are clearly valid even though the Constitution of India grants all citizens many civil rights, such as rights of association and free speech. The Indian Parliament is expressly empowered to enact legislation that limits the enjoyment of those rights by members of the armed forces: Constitution of India, Article 33.

III Jurisdiction over persons and offences

Persons subject to military law fall into two categories: those who are permanently subject to such law and those whose subjection is only temporary. The first category includes commissioned officers, junior commissioned officers (JCO), warrant officers and other ranks (below the rank of JCO). The second category comprises reservists, persons seconded (transferred) from the other services and civilians who become temporarily subject to military law under certain contingencies. The army and air force statutes of India, Bangladesh and Pakistan provide that persons[12] not otherwise subject to military law, on active service, become subject to military law.[13] These military services Acts remain applicable for three years after release or retirement from service and, during this period, the person may be taken into custody, tried and punished for offences as if he or she continues to be subject to the respective Act's provisions.[14] During martial law in Bangladesh and Pakistan, military courts were established for the trial of civilians, although the armed forces in other countries have no such powers. In January 2015, Pakistan amended its Constitution and the military Acts to allow military courts to try civilians for offences related to terrorism or who belong to "any terrorist group or organization using the name of religion or a sect".[15]

[12] Section 2(i) of the Indian Army Act, 1950 states: 'persons not otherwise subject to military law who, on active service, in camps, on the march, or at any frontier post specified by the Central Government by notification in this behalf, are employed by, or are in the service of, or are followers of, or accompany any portion of, the regular Army' shall be subject to the Army Act. Similar provisions exist in the Pakistan Army Act, 1952, and the Bangladesh Army Act, 1952.

[13] The Supreme Court of India has held that civilians become subject to the Army Act, Air Force Act or the Navy Act only when specified conditions of the respective Act become operative, and these persons are on active service, in camp. Although non-combatants, they are integral to the armed forces. The term 'active service' means the time during which the military or a part of it is 'engaged in operations against an enemy': *Cus Kutilingal Achudan Nair* v. *Union of India* AIR 1976 SC 1179.

[14] However, trial for the offence must commence within three years of the accused ceasing to be subject to the law, except where he or she is accused of desertion on active service, fraudulent enrolment or mutiny, for which there is no time limit. See the Indian Army Act, 1950 s. 122; the Pakistan Army Act, 1952 s. 91, the Bangladesh Army Act, 1952 s. 91; and the Sri Lankan Army Act, 1949 s. 56.

[15] The 21st Amendment to the Constitution inserts the military Acts and the Protection of Pakistan Act 2014 into the first schedule of the Constitution. Laws in the first schedule are exempt from the operation of Article 8(1) and (2) of the Constitution, which stipulate that the state shall not pass any law that violates fundamental rights, and that any law that violates the fundamental rights provisions of the Constitution shall be void.

The offences contained in the South Asian military Acts can be divided into the following categories:[16] (i) offences in relation to the enemy and punishable with death; (ii) offences in relation to the enemy and not punishable with death; (iii) offences punishable more severely on active service than at other times; (iv) mutiny, desertion and absence without leave; (v) striking or threatening superior officers, disobedience to superior officers, and insubordination and obstructions; (vi) fraudulent enrolment and false answers on enrolment; (vii) unbecoming conduct, certain forms of disgraceful conduct, ill-treating a subordinate and intoxication; (viii) permitting escape of a person in custody, irregularity in connection with arrest or confinement and escape from custody; (ix) offences in respect of property, extortion and corruption, making away with equipment and injury to property; (x) false accusations, falsifying official documents and false declaration, signing in blank and failure to report; (xi) offences relating to courts martial and false evidence; (xii) unlawful detention of pay; (xiii) offences in relation to aircraft and flying; (xiv) miscellaneous offences and violation of good order and discipline; (xv) attempt to commit any of the above offences and abetment of these offences; and (xvi) civil offences.[17]

In addition, the Sri Lankan Army Act deals with the issue of illegal gratification in connection with appointment or promotion.[18] In Sri Lanka, civil courts have absolute jurisdiction to try or punish any person subject to military law for any civil offence. However, if a person subject

[16] See the Indian Air Force Act, 1950 ss. 34–72 and the Indian Navy Act, 1957 ss. 34–77. Pakistan Army Act, 1952 ss. 24–59, Bangladesh Army Act, 1952 ss. 24–59, Sri Lankan Army Act, 1949 ss. 95–130. Nepalese Army Act, 2006 ss. 38–65.

[17] The term 'civil offence' has been defined as an offence that is triable by a criminal court. A person subject to military law, who commits any civil offence (defined in the Indian Penal Code, 1860), is deemed guilty of an offence under military law and can be tried by a court martial. However, for certain serious offences, i.e. an offence of murder against a person not subject to military law, or of culpable homicide not amounting to murder against such a person, or of rape in relation to such a person, a person subject to military law cannot be tried by a court martial. However, a person can be tried for these three offences by a court martial if committed (i) on active service, (ii) at a specified frontier post or (iii) at any place outside India. The Indian Army Act, 1950 ss. 69 and 70; the Pakistan Army Act, 1952 s. 59; the Nepalese Army Act, 2006 s. 66; the Sri Lankan Army Act, 1949 s. 47; and Bangladesh Army Act, 1952 s. 59.

[18] Section 130 of the Sri Lankan Army Act states: 'Every person subject to military law who gives or receives, or aids the giving or receiving of, any valuable consideration in respect of any appointment or promotion in or retirement from the army, or any employment therein, shall be guilty of a military offence and shall, on conviction by a court-martial, be liable to be dismissed from the army.' In other countries, such offences may be dealt with under 'violation of good order and discipline'.

to military law is convicted of an offence and sentenced to punishment by a court martial and is then tried, and convicted of, the same offence by a civil court, then the civil court must give due regard to such punishment imposed by the court martial.[19]

It is submitted that the jurisdiction of military courts should be limited to offences of a strictly internal military nature committed by military personnel, which largely means internal disciplinary measures. In contrast, serious crimes, including those that amount to human rights violations, committed by members of the armed forces while not on duty should be tried in ordinary civil courts, using established procedures in accordance with international standards. A limitation of military jurisdiction in such terms would align the scope and limits of the military justice systems of South Asia with those of most other nations. Such limits would also expand the control of civilian courts over serious offences committed by military personnel – such offences are now widely regarded as the province of civilian courts.

IV Punishments

In Bangladesh, India, Pakistan and Sri Lanka, the most severe penalty that can be imposed by a court martial is death.[20] Nepal has abolished the death penalty from its military and criminal justice systems.[21] Other punishments which may be inflicted in respect of offences committed by persons subject to the services Acts and convicted by courts martial, in descending order of severity, are: transportation for life or for any period not less than seven years; imprisonment, either rigorous or simple,[22] for any period not exceeding fourteen years; cashiering (disgraceful dismissal) in the case of officers; dismissal from the service; field punishment;[23] reduction to the ranks or to a lower rank or grade; forfeiture of seniority

[19] Sri Lankan Army Act, 1949 s. 77.

[20] Under section 60 (a) of the Pakistan Army Act, 1952, as amended in 1984, a court martial can award punishment of 'stoning to death'. There is no recorded example of such a sentence being passed.

[21] Nepalese Army Act, 2006 s. 101.

[22] Imprisonment is of two kinds: (i) rigorous and (ii) simple. In the case of rigorous imprisonment, the offender is put to hard labour such as grinding, digging earth, drawing water or cutting fire-wood. In the case of simple imprisonment, the offender is confined to jail and is not put to any kind of forced work. Imposition of hard labour on prisoners undergoing rigorous imprisonment has been held to be legal. See *State of Gujarat* v. *Hon'ble High Court of Gujarat* 1998 Cr LJ 4561: AIR 1998 SC 3164.

[23] Bangladesh, Nepal, Pakistan and Sri Lanka.

of rank; forfeiture of service for the purpose of increased pay, pension or any other prescribed purpose; reprimand; and forfeiture or stoppage of pay and allowances. Within the maximum punishment prescribed under a section of offence, the court martial has the discretion to apportion punishment according to the degree of guilt of the person convicted.[24] The Sri Lankan Army Act has additionally provided for award of specific punishments in the case of serious civil offences.[25] The Nepalese Army Act prescribes a peculiar punishment. A general court martial may impose a penalty of life imprisonment and the confiscation of the entire share of the ancestral property of a military accused if he is found guilty of offences relating to the enemy, mutiny and desertion on active service.[26] In case of the offence of disobedience to a superior officer, a court martial can award the punishment of confiscation of the entire share of ancestral property.[27]

The military statutes prescribe the death penalty for most offences relating to the enemy as well as mutiny, while for other offences the term of imprisonment ranges from seven to fourteen years. This prescription of harsh punishment needs to be rationalised, keeping in view the changes made in other democracies. Since a large number of South Asian military personnel participate in peacekeeping missions with the armies of other countries, there is a need to maintain parity among the military legal systems.

V Action against a military offender

In a military law system, a commander exercises discretion in deciding whether an offence should be charged and the punishment that should be prescribed. The commander has a number of options for the resolution of disciplinary problems, including choosing to take no action, initiating

[24] Indian Army Act, 1950 s. 71; Bangladesh Army Act, 1952 s. 60, the Pakistan Army Act, 1952 s. 60; and the Sri Lankan Army Act, 1949 s. 133.

[25] It provides: (1) where a person subject to military law is convicted by a court martial of the offence of treason, he shall be liable to suffer death; (2) where a person subject to military law is convicted by a court martial of the offence of murder, he shall be liable to suffer death; (3) where a person subject to military law is convicted by a court martial of the offence of culpable homicide not amounting to murder, he shall be liable to suffer simple or rigorous imprisonment for a term not exceeding 20 years; and (4) where a person subject to military law is convicted by a court martial of the offence of rape, he shall be liable to suffer simple or rigorous imprisonment for a term not exceeding 20 years: Sri Lankan Army Act, 1949 s. 131.

[26] Nepalese Army Act, 2006 ss. 38, 39, and 42(1)(a).

[27] Ibid., s. 101.

administrative action against a military offender, disposing of the offence summarily with a minor punishment or disposing of the case through a court martial.

A Summary punishment

The procedure for summary trial before the commanding officer is quite different from a trial in a magistrate's court.[28] The accused is not entitled to legal representation and does not plead to the charge, laws of evidence need not apply and the proceedings are not open to the public. Where a commanding officer, after hearing the case, considers that the accused is guilty, a penalty that involves loss of liberty, field punishment, or loss of pay or promotions may be imposed. The award of 'field-punishment' to personnel below the rank of Non-Commissioned Officer (NCO) – which is still followed in Bangladesh, Nepal, Pakistan and Sri Lanka – breaches human rights norms.[29] In India, an amendment to the military Acts in 1993 removed this practice.

In the case of trial of officers and JCOs, the commanding officer or superior officer may award one or more of the following punishments: (1) forfeiture of service or seniority not exceeding twelve months; (2) stoppages or forfeiture of pay and allowances to recover loss and damage; and (3) reprimand. In the case of the first punishment, which may affect the future service prospects of the accused, the accused is given the option to elect trial by court martial before the imposition of the punishment. However, this option is not available in the other cases.

There is no right of appeal against summary punishment. However, the proceedings may be reviewed by the superior authority, who is

28 Summary punishments do not apply to officers of the rank of Lt Col and above, who can be punished only by a court martial.

29 The Rules provide that during the punishment: 'He (the military accused) may be kept in irons, that is to say, in fetters or handcuffs or both fetters and handcuffs, and may be secured so as to prevent his escape. When in irons, he may be attached for a period or periods not exceeding two hours in any one day to a fixed object, but must not be so attached during more than three out of any four consecutive days, not during more than 21 days in all.' The explanations to the Rule further provide: 'The offender must be attached so as to be standing firmly on his feet which, if tied, must not be more than 12 inches apart, and it must be possible for him to move each foot at least three inches. If he is tied round the body there must be no restriction of his breathing. If his arms or wrists are tied, there must be six inches of play between them and the fixed object. His arms must hang either by the side of his body or behind his back.'

empowered to cancel, vary or remit an illegal, unjust or excessive punishment, if it is illegal, unjust or excessive in their opinion.[30]

The award of 'field punishment' is considered degrading and inhumane and should be abolished from the military statutes in Bangladesh, Nepal, Pakistan and Sri Lanka.

B Court martial

Courts martial are *ad hoc* military courts separately established for each trial. The Army Acts of India, Pakistan,[31] Bangladesh[32] and Nepal[33] provide for four kinds of courts martial: general court martial (GCM), district court martial (DCM), summary/field general court martial (SGCM or FGCM)[34] and summary court martial (SCM). The Sri Lankan Army Act provides for the GCM, DCM and FGCM, but not for the SCM.[35] The most senior officer appointed to a court martial acts as the presiding officer under the Nepalese Army Act,[36] the Indian Army Act[37] and the Indian Air Force Act,[38] whereas under the Bangladesh,[39] Pakistan[40] and Sri Lankan Army Acts[41] and the Indian Navy Act,[42] the presiding officer is appointed by the convening authority.

The Nepal Army Act provides for the constitution of a special court[43] with original jurisdiction in cases relating to corruption, theft, torture and disappearance. Cases relating to these offences are to be first investigated by a committee comprising the deputy attorney general, who acts as chairman, the chief of the legal section of the ministry of defence and a representative of the chief judge advocate not below the rank of lieutenant.[44] The special court has original jurisdiction to proceed and adjudicate the case further. An appeal against the decision of the special court may be preferred in the Supreme Court.[45]

30 Indian Army Act, 1950 s. 87 and Regulations for the Indian Army [442]; Nepalese Army Act, 2006 s. 118.
31 Pakistan Army Act, 1952 s. 80. 32 Bangladesh Army Act, 1952 s. 80.
33 Nepalese Army Act, 2006 s. 67.
34 Known as Field General Court-Martial (FGCM) in Bangladesh, Pakistan and Sri Lanka.
35 Sri Lankan Army Act, 1949 s. 45. 36 Nepalese Army Act, 2006 s. 80.
37 Indian Army Act, 1950 s. 128. 38 Indian Air Force Act, 1932 s. 127.
39 Bangladesh Army Act, 1952 s. 102. 40 *Pakistan* Army Act, 1952 s. 102.
41 Sri Lankan Army Act, 1949 ss. 46(4), 48(3) and 50(2).
42 Indian Navy Act, 1957 s. 97(12). 43 Nepalese Army Act, 2006 ss. 119(1) and (3).
44 Ibid., s. 62. 45 Ibid., s. 119(4).

The air forces of India, Bangladesh,[46] Pakistan[47] and Sri Lanka[48] have three kinds of courts martial – the GCM, DCM and S/FGCM. Under the Indian Navy Act and Sri Lankan Navy Act[49] there is one type of court martial, whereas the Bangladesh and Pakistan navies provide for GCM, DCM and SGCM. Under the Indian Navy Act, there is an additional disciplinary court that can be constituted during active service.[50] In India, a court martial convened under the services Acts is not a part of the judiciary and is not included among the courts that Parliament or the state legislature may ordain and establish under articles 246 or 247 of the Constitution. The same situation applies in the other countries.

C *Confirmation and revision of finding and sentence*

The finding or sentence of a GCM, DCM or SGCM is not valid unless confirmed.[51] The findings recorded by a court are in the nature of recommendations which may or may not be accepted by the authority empowered to confirm the findings and sentence. In the case of award of the death sentence, the finding and sentence of the court must be confirmed by the Central Government.[52]

If the confirming authority is dissatisfied with the findings of a GCM, DCM or SGCM, and a confirmation is required, the findings and sentence may be revised by order of the confirming authority. On such revision, the court, if so directed by the confirming authority, may take additional evidence. The court must consist of the same officers as were present when the original decision was passed.[53] When the finding is sent back for revision, the court reassembles in open court, the revision order is read and, if the court is directed to take fresh evidence, it will do so in open court. The court then deliberates on its finding in closed court. If it does not adhere to its earlier finding, it revokes the finding and sentence and records the new finding and, if necessary, passes a fresh sentence. When the sentence alone is sent for revision, the court cannot revise the finding. After revision, the proceedings are transmitted for confirmation.[54]

The power of revision can only be exercised once. If the second verdict by the court martial is the same, the confirming officer has no option but to

46 Bangladesh Army Act, 1952 s. 108.
47 Pakistan Army Act, 1952 s. 108.
48 Sri Lankan Air Force Act, 1949 s. 45.
49 Sri Lankan Navy Act, 1950 s. 33.
50 Indian Navy Act, 1957 s. 95. A disciplinary court may consist of not less than three and not more than five officers.
51 Indian Army Act, 1950 s. 153.
52 Regulations for the Indian Army, 1987 [472(a)].
53 Indian Army Act, 1950 s. 160.
54 Indian Army Rules, 1954 r. 68.

confirm the proceeding. The service Acts do not contemplate successive trials by a court martial until a verdict acceptable to the confirming authority is received. A second trial by a court martial for the same offence, whether any person subject to the Act has been convicted or acquitted, is prohibited.[55] It is generally believed that the confirming officers exercise 'command influence' over the court members while seeking the desired findings and sentences by making recourse to revision.[56]

D Summary forms of court martial

Two exceptional kinds of court martial are provided for under the military laws of the South Asian countries – the SGCM/FGCM and SCM – which have no parallel in Australian or US law. The FGCM existed in the British military system until 2006 but has rarely been convened in the last twenty-five years. It is merely a 'summary' form of the GCM and can be convened when it is not possible without serious detriment to the public interest for the offence to be tried by one of the other types of court martial. The FGCM consists of three officers with one year of service. It can try any person subject to the Act for any offence committed under the military Act and pass any sentence authorised thereby.[57] It can be convened during active service, as well as during peacetime. The FGCM is subject to exceptional rules under which the procedure is or can be of a more summary character than that of a GCM.[58] The court is not even required to frame a formal charge-sheet against the alleged accused.[59] The presiding officer and members of the FGCM as well as the prosecutor remain under command influence – the presence of a judge advocate is not necessary. The accused is not entitled to any defence counsel and thus the case may be determined by military members not trained in law.[60]

[55] Indian Army Act, 1950 s. 121.

[56] In Sri Lanka, the president, the minister of defence or any prescribed officer may revise any sentence passed by a court martial. While revising the sentence, the authority may (a) mitigate the punishment to a lesser amount of the same punishment; (b) remit the whole or a part of the punishment; or (c) commute the punishment to a different form lower in the scale of punishments authorised by the Army Act: Sri Lankan Army Act, 1949 s. 67.

[57] Pakistan Air Force Act, 1953 s. 117.

[58] Indian Army Rules, 1954, rr. 151–65.

[59] Rule 152 of the Indian Army Rules, 1954 states: 'Charge – The statement of an offence may be made briefly in any language sufficient to describe or disclose an offence under the Act.'

[60] Indian Army Rules, 1954 r. 96. The accused does not have a right to be represented by a counsel in the SGCM. Rule 159 provides that an accused may be allowed to have any person to assist during the trial.

An SCM is peculiar to the armies of the South Asian countries, except that of Sri Lanka. It may try any person below the rank of JCO under the command of the officer holding the court. It can award a punishment of dismissal with one-year imprisonment after a summary trial.[61] An SCM is legally authorised to take cognisance of all military offences committed by soldiers, however grave, provided the same are not subject to capital punishment or exclusively within the jurisdiction of a GCM.[62] Section 130 of the Indian Army Act, contains a provision that an accused can challenge his trial by the presiding officer/any member of the GCM, DCM or SGCM on the ground of bias or personal interest; however, no such right to challenge is available to an accused in an SCM. In India, the high courts and the Supreme Court have criticised trials held under the SCM,[63] as it is felt that the SCM awards excessive and harsh punishments and denies the procedural rights guaranteed under article 14 of the Constitution.

Trial by SCM in the South Asian armies does not meet recognised standards of justice. The accused is not entitled to the help of a counsel or defending officer. Similarly, the SGCM is empowered to award the death sentence in a summary trial in which the accused is invariably denied the right to a fair trial. Both these *ad hoc* systems of justice are not followed in other democratic countries and need to be abolished.

E Appeal

In the South Asian countries, until recently, there was no right of appeal against the finding or sentence of a court martial. In India, there has been a constitutional ban on appeals against the findings and sentences of courts martial. Article 136(2) of the Constitution provides that the

[61] Indian Army Act, 1950 s. 120.

[62] The Indian Army Act s. 120(2) dealing with the powers of SCM provides: 'When there is no grave reason for immediate action and reference can without detriment to discipline be made to the officer empowered to convene a district court-martial or on active service a summary general court-martial for the trial of the alleged offender, an officer holding a summary court-martial shall not try without such reference any offence punishable under any of the sections 34 (offences in relation to enemy and punishable with death), 37 (mutiny) and 69 (civil offences), or any offence against the officer holding the court.'

[63] *Capt. Paramjeet Singh* v. *Union of India* 1984 (3) SLR 675; *Ranjit Thakur* v. *Union of India* 1987 4 SCC 611, *Ex. Naik Sardar Singh* v. *Union of India* (1991) 3 SCC 213; *Lance Naik VP Singh* v. *Union of India*, WP (C) 2511/1992 decided by the Delhi High Court on 25 January 2008; *Ex. Gnr Krishan Kumar* v. *Union of India*, TA No. 312 of 2009 decided by the Armed Force Tribunal Principal Bench New Delhi on 19 October 2010.

Supreme Court[64] (article 227(4) in the case of a high court) cannot give special leave to appeal against any judgment, determination or sentence of a military court or tribunal. The military tribunals in India are not, however, exempt from the Supreme Court's writ jurisdiction under article 32 and the high court's writ jurisdiction under article 226 of the Constitution.

In India, the high courts and Supreme Court have entertained petitions from service personnel under their writ jurisdiction. In *Lt. Col. Prithi Pal Singh Bedi* v. *Union of India*,[65] the Supreme Court of India held that there was not a single right of appeal or review over the evidence, verdicts or sentences imposed by military tribunals. The Supreme Court urged the government to take steps to provide at least one avenue of judicial review in military service matters. The Court explained that the:

> Absence of even one appeal with power to review evidence, legal formulation, conclusion and adequacy or otherwise of punishment is a glaring lacuna in a country where a counterpart civilian convict can prefer appeal after appeal to hierarchy of courts . . . With the expanding horizons of fair play in action even in administrative decision, the Universal Declaration of Human Rights and retributive justice being relegated to the uncivilized days, a time has come when a step is required to be taken for at least one review and it must truly be a judicial review as and by way of appeal to a body composed of non-military personnel or civil personnel. And nothing revolutionary is being suggested. Our Army Act was more or less modelled on the UK Act. Three decades of its working with winds of change blowing over the world necessitate a second look so as to bring it in conformity with liberty oriented constitution and rule of law which is the uniting and integrating force in our political society. Even UK has taken a step of far reaching importance . . . enacted a Court Martial (Appeals) Act of 1951 and it has been extensively amended in Court Martial (Appeals) Act, 1968. The wind of change blowing over the country has not permeated the close and sacrosanct precincts of the Army.[66]

The decision of the Supreme Court led to the passage of the Armed Forces Tribunal Act in 2007, although the path of that reform was slow. The year after *Bedi* was decided, the combined military service headquarters were requested to consider the desirability of a court martial appeal court. However, the three services could not agree to a single appellate military court. In 1999 the army proposed the establishment of a separate armed forces appeal tribunal, to be staffed by serving military

[64] Constitution of India, article 227(4), debars the High Courts from entertaining appeals from the decisions of military tribunals.

[65] 1982 AIR 1413, 1983 SCR (1) 393 (*Bedi*).

[66] Ibid.

officers including the officers of the judge advocate general branch. The government rejected the suggestion that a separate appeal body should be created for only one part of the military, although support for a military appeal body remained strong. The Law Commission of India and several parliamentary committees also affirmed the need to establish an independent judicial tribunal with jurisdiction over military matters.[67] In 2005 the Ministry of Defence finally proposed the formation of an armed forces tribunal to adjudicate service matters and appeals from courts martial and the necessary Bill was introduced later that year.

The Armed Forces Tribunal and its Benches have been constituted under the Act of 2007 to hear appeals against the findings and sentences of a court martial.[68] Similarly, in Nepal, the Army Act, 2006, has created a Special Court to hear appeals from courts martial, and appeals can be taken to the Supreme Court. In India, a bench of the Tribunal has two members: a judicial officer and a retired senior service officer. The Special Court in Nepal consists of a judge of an appellate court, who functions as chairman, the Secretary, Ministry of Defence and the Chief Judge Advocate.[69] In Bangladesh and Pakistan, the Army Acts ban any appeal against the decision of a court martial.[70] The prohibition, however, is not absolute and the high courts in Pakistan have entertained collateral attacks on court-martial proceedings on limited jurisdictional grounds. On 12 January 2009, the Lahore High Court set aside a 1999 sentence of the FGCM against a lieutenant colonel it found guilty of filing fake income tax returns, including other instances of fraud. While not

67 Indian Law Commission, *Amendment of Army, Navy and Air Force Act* (Report No. 169, 1999). This report, like the decision of the Supreme Court in *Bedi*, was heavily influenced by the reforms to military justice in other countries.

68 There is a major lacuna in the Armed Forces Tribunal Act, 2007, in that it lacks the power of civil contempt. The Act does not contain any provision for the execution of the orders passed by the Tribunal. It has resulted in a situation where the government and military authorities have not taken any action on a large number of orders passed by the Tribunal. A proposal by the government to amend section 19 of the Act to provide the Tribunal with the power to punish for contempt has been vehemently opposed by the military. See Standing Committee on Defence (2012–2013) *The Armed Forces Tribunal (Amendment) Bill 2012, Eighteenth Report* http://164.100.47.134/lsscommittee/Defence/AFT%20Report.pdf.

69 Nepalese Army Act, 2006 s. 119.

70 Pakistan Army Act, 1952 s. 133 and the Bangladesh Army Act, 1952 s. 133 state that 'No remedy shall lie against any decision of a court-martial save as provided in this Act, and for the removal of doubt it is hereby declared that no appeal or application shall lie in respect of any proceeding or decision of a court martial to any court exercising any jurisdiction whatever.'

pronouncing on the other charges, the court ousted the jurisdiction of the FGCM in regard to the charges pertaining to income tax returns.[71]

Anyone convicted of a criminal offence has the right to a review of that decision by a higher judicial tribunal. The special court in Nepal and the Armed Forces Tribunal in India are not exclusive civilian appellate courts. An independent appellate forum consisting of judicial officers must be created in all South Asian democracies.

VI The role of military judiciary and higher authorities

In South Asian countries, the Judge Advocate General (JAG) is the superintendent of the administration of military justice.[72] The army, air force and navy have their own JAGs who head the judiciary of their respective services. The judicial department has a selected cadre of officers qualified in law. The JAG department is divided into two cells, known as the 'pre-trial section' and the 'post-trial section'. The JAG department renders pre-trial advice to the convening authorities, provides a judge advocate at GCMs and at important DCMs, and prepares reviews of all courts-martial proceedings. The JAG department's other functions include representing the government in cases at the higher civil courts and providing legal training to officers.

Unlike the military justice systems of other democracies like Australia, Canada, Israel, South Africa, the United Kingdom and the United States, the JAGs in the South Asian countries are organisationally and operationally subordinate to the convening authority, who controls their

[71] The Lahore High Court's Rawalpindi Bench has issued a judgment setting aside the conviction of a lieutenant colonel by the Field General Court Martial (FGCM). Lt-Col Munir Ahmed Gil had invoked the jurisdiction of the court in 2000 against his 1999 conviction by the FGCM on charges of concealing his property to claim financial benefit from the army. The petitioner was arrested in June 1997 by the special investigation branch on charges of receiving commission on the purchase of approximately 6,000 tons of sugar for military use. In 1999 he was convicted by the FGCM in Rawalpindi for receiving commission, concealing his property and filing false income tax returns. He was sentenced to one-year rigorous imprisonment and dismissal from service. Other charges against him were dropped. In August 1999, the Chief of the Army Staff (COAS) pardoned his prison term but upheld the other punishments. The petitioner pleaded to the Lahore High Court that FGCM had overstepped its jurisdiction while convicting him for filing false income tax returns as such charges can only be tried by a civilian court. The decision is considered important by analysts because it could open a flood of pleas to the civilian courts against the decisions of military courts. See Abdul Nishapuri, 'Lahore High Court makes history by setting aside sentence of the Field General Court Martial (FGCM)', Let Us Build Pakistan (LUBP) http://lubpak.com/archives/724.

[72] In Nepal, the department is led by the Chief Judge Advocate.

service career. Because of their position, the officers of JAG departments cannot be expected to give a fair and just opinion. They need to be insulated from the military chain of command.

The convening authority in South Asian military law systems is generally an officer above the rank of brigadier and holds an authoritative and influential position. The convening authority is responsible for: (i) making the decision to prosecute or not to prosecute; (ii) deciding the charges against the accused; (iii) appointing the military prosecutor; (iv) appointing members of the court according to his choice; (v) appointing a defending officer; (vi) detailing a judge advocate for trial – the judge advocate, the prosecutor and the court members come under his authority in the chain of command; (vii) reviewing the sentence awarded by the court martial and referring the proceedings back to the court for reconsideration (enhancing the punishment), even if an accused is acquitted by the court;[73] (viii) considering the pre-confirmation petition of the accused; (ix) confirming or not confirming the sentence awarded by the court martial; and (x) considering the post-confirmation petition of the convicted person.

The convening authority, by virtue of his position, has sweeping powers and virtually controls the entire judicial process. The power of convening authority needs to be rationalised and divided among independent authorities to meet international standards.

VII Conclusion

The South Asian countries that were subject to British rule inherited, on gaining independence, the military laws made for mercenaries. An outdated and obscure conception of military discipline still persists in the South Asian countries and this is not widely questioned by the courts, executive government or politicians. There is a need to redefine the rights and duties of military personnel in South Asia and this is not simply because the military forces of those nations should no longer hold the vestiges of colonial legal and administrative structures. The military justice systems of South Asia should be reformed so that commanders, service personnel and the wider societies that they serve should reflect the modernity to which these nations rightly aspire.

[73] Except in a court martial held under the Indian Navy Act, 1957.

10

Military justice in Latin America: a comparative analysis

IVETTE CASTAÑEDA GARCÍA

I The origins of military justice in Latin America

Military justice systems in Latin America predate the creation of most Latin American republics.[1] It is therefore not unusual to find members of the armed institutions of the region that refer to military justice as an institution in its own right. Such references to military justice highlight the fact that it is not seen simply as a separate legal instrument necessary for the armed forces but also as an important historical instance in nation building in Latin America.

Military officials typically believe that the main objective of military justice is to guarantee the obedience, discipline and order necessary for the operation of the armed forces. A separate military justice system fosters that objective by ensuring respect for the chain of command and decreasing the ability of individuals to challenge decisions taken by military forces or the wider legitimacy of military institutions.

From the social science perspective, military justice is a result of the 'total' institutional character of the armed forces.[2] The armed forces are frequently characterised in this manner because of their total nature,

[1] In most Latin American countries military justice is a legacy of Spanish domination. See in particular the provisions of the ordinances of Spanish King Carlos III in 1768, known as the 'Royal Ordinances for the Regime, Discipline, Subordination and Service of its Armies'. These were maintained with few significant changes until the mid-nineteenth century, and even part of the twentieth century, when the professionalisation of the military function and the reform of military education systems drove innovations in the regulation of military justice systems.

[2] The concept of total institution comes from Erving Goffman, *Asylums: Essays on the Social Situation of Mental Patients and Other Inmates* (Buenos Aires, Amorrortu, 1970). Goffman studied psychiatric hospitals and concluded that they comprised 'closed worlds', i.e. spaces where many people spent much or all of their lives and where they were cut off from society for a significant period of time and shared daily routines administered in a formal and thorough manner. This conception of the 'total' institution was also used in Michel Foucault, *Discipline and Punish – The Birth of the Prison* (London, Penguin, 1979).

developed from the early stages of military training. This training is intense and separated from the rest of society. It aims to reconstruct individuals by creating an intense bond between them as individuals and the institution in which they are trained. That bond is greatly strengthened during the four to five years in which the candidates for officers and non-commissioned officers are isolated in training bases while they receive military training and education. This process is established in a rigorous daily schedule, defined by internal rules and specific administrative bodies. It is complemented by the use of symbols, formalities and specific rituals among military trainees. Therefore, military training is crucial for the formation of a soldier,[3] and like military justice it serves an important role in the long-term maintenance of military forces.

The administration by a military force of its own justice system is an example of the wider habit of military forces in Latin America of creating autonomous versions of the institutions of civilian society. Other examples include centres and training institutes, health centres, military pension administration centres, recreational centres for military families and schools for the children of military officers. Military justice systems also affirm the autonomy of the armed forces from society, especially when faced with the ordinary judicial bodies that govern civilian society. Thus, military justice systems are both a functional tool for the service of the armed forces and a representation of the social and legal differences between military and civilian societies.

The recent history of Latin America confirms the idea of military justice as a prerogative and, above all, as an instrument which has been used in fields that go beyond the administrative or institutional areas. During the years of military dictatorships and internal conflicts in which the armed forces faced opposition groups and revolutionary movements, military justice systems performed many different political and institutional functions. Some examples of the extended use of military courts in the area can be found in Brazil, Peru and Uruguay.

During Brazilian military dictatorships of the second half of the twentieth century, military justice played three roles. The first was corporate justice, in which military justice tribunals judged military crimes, or what would traditionally be conceived as service disciplinary matters. The second was government justice, which was to carry out prosecutions against opponents of the regime and those accused of being a threat to

[3] Ivette Castañeda, *The Incorporation of Women in the Armed Forces of Latin America* (Undergraduate thesis, Pontificia Universidad Catolica del Peru, 2009).

national security. The third was as politic-corporate justice, which judged those framed for military crimes in cases with political motivations.[4]

In Peru during the 1980s and 1990s, military justice was used to protect military personnel implicated in corruption and human rights violations committed during their service in areas declared as a state of exception.[5] These were years in which states of exception were frequently used by the government as a part of its fight against terrorist groups such as the Shining Path (SL) and Tupac Amaru Revolutionary Movement (MRTA). Military courts also served as a means to prosecute individual members of the military who disagreed with government policies. Military courts were deployed against civilians, in trials preceded by 'faceless judges', who sentenced civilians accused of being members of MRTA and SL. A notable feature of this aspect of the Peruvian system was that the use of military justice as the armed forces' prerogative was made not by military dictatorships but by the existing civilian governments between 1980 and 2001.

In Uruguay, military justice was an instrument used to confront subversive movements as well as insurgents.[6] One of the charges commonly used was 'criminal association', defined as the involvement in an illegal association, which was prosecuted with up to six years of prison. According to Juan Rial, although there is no accurate information about the exact number of people prosecuted for such offences during those years, at least 4000 people were subject to such charges and most of them were sentenced to prison. Most cases were resolved in the first instance. Some cases were appealed to the Supreme Military Court and a few were also appealed to the Supreme Court of Justice.[7]

The widespread use of such charges in the second half of the twentieth century meant that military justice was often not simply a means for judging military members for military crimes. The military courts became an instrument for the military to prosecute other military involved in crimes beyond the occupational ones, such as human rights violations. They were also used to enable the military to prosecute

[4] Angela Moreira, *Dictatorship and Military Justice in Brazil: Operation of the Supreme Military Court (1964–1980)* (PhD thesis, Getulio Vargas Foundation, 2011).

[5] Rossy Salazar, 'Redefining Military Justice' in Legal Defense Institute (ed.), *The Defense Knots. Entanglements and Untangling for a Public Policy in Democracy* (Lima, IDL, 2005), p. 89.

[6] Insurgents used armed violence. Subversive movements preached non-violent action but opposed the prevailing system.

[7] Juan Rial (ed.), *Military Justice: Between Reform and Permanence* (Buenos Aires, Resdal, 2010), p. 24.

civilians accused of terrorism or actions that threatened national security.[8]

The return of democracy, the end of civil wars and the advance of instances encouraging defence and respect for human rights worldwide have caused important changes in Latin America. These changes have also led to widespread questioning of the role of military courts. The traditional model of military justice has become disputed in Latin America because it contradicts regional frameworks, such as the Inter-American Convention on Forced Disappearance of Persons.[9] It also contradicts many national legal frameworks and constitutional principles such as the separation of powers, the unity of the jurisdictional function and the independence and guarantee of impartiality of courts and tribunals in the administration of justice.

II Military justice in Latin America: a comparative analysis

A The structure of the military justice system

An overview of the models of military justice in Latin America reveals two important features: military justice systems in the region consist, on the one hand, of one or more codes[10] containing administrative, disciplinary, penal and procedural rules, all of which apply to personnel of the armed forces; and, on the other hand, of officers or specialised organs consisting of judges and clerks responsible for enforcing these codes. At the same time, military justice systems are typically divided into two sub-systems – the penal system and the disciplinary system. The penal sub-system has its main axis in the prosecution of military crimes, which are defined as actions under the military justice codes because they produce an effect on the military institution. On the other hand, the disciplinary sub-system works on disciplinary offences or actions defined as violations of military discipline.[11] While crimes are more serious and harmful to the institution because they involve actions that diminish the role of

[8] See Chapter 5.

[9] Inter-American Convention on Forced Disappearance of Persons, 9 June 1994, in force 28 March 1996, 33 ILM 1429, Art IX.

[10] In most countries, including Bolivia, Brazil, Chile, Ecuador, El Salvador, Nicaragua, Paraguay, Peru, Uruguay and Venezuela, there are two military codes – the first contains offences considered as crimes; the second contains military judicial procedures. In Mexico, one disciplinary code applies to each of the three forces.

[11] Dolores Bermeo, Ivette Castañeda and Gustavo Castro, 'The Military Justice System: Principles and Conceptual Approaches' in Rial (ed.), *Military Justice*, p. 34.

the military in providing national security, disciplinary offences are considered less serious since they relate to the most basic measures of discipline in military life. In the disciplinary sub-system, administrators of justice can be superior officers as well as discipline counsels, whereas in the case of crimes, the organs – such as courts or tribunals of military justice – are more complex and higher in the institutional hierarchy.

The analysis of the various military justice systems below will be based on the penal sub-system due to its potential incompatibility with the constitutional framework and the international regulation of human rights.

B The case studies

This chapter examines the military justice systems of Guatemala (Central America), Peru (Andean Region) and Argentina (Southern Cone). These systems provide useful examples because they display different levels of progress and raise varying issues about the role of military courts and military justice in the Latin American region. The case of Argentina highlights the broader transformation of military justice within that country, which has seen it opt for reforms that have almost entirely incorporated military justice within the ordinary justice system. In Peru, recent reforms to the military justice code and other regulations have motivated petitions to declare the changes unconstitutional. Finally, Guatemala maintains a military justice model that dates back more than 135 years and, in that time, has scarcely been reformed.

To facilitate the analysis of the three case studies, three key dimensions of military criminal justice operation are utilised:[12]

1. bodies responsible for administering military criminal justice (who judges?);
2. military criminal offences judged (what is judged?);
3. groups of people within the jurisdiction of military courts (who is judged?).

C The administrative bodies of military criminal justice

The definition or location of those who administer justice is a fundamental element of due process and the separation and allocation of

[12] These three variables were also used in the material in Bermeo, Castañeda and Castro, above n. 11.

powers within a society. Most Western nations have in recent years increasingly moved to both limit the scope of their military justice systems and increase the level of civilian involvement in and oversight of their military justice systems. Many of the military criminal justice systems in Latin America have not yet taken those steps. The Latin American systems are therefore frequently criticised for enabling military officials to administer justice to other members of their own institution.

The main criticism of this model centres upon its adverse effect on independence and impartiality in the administration of justice. It is argued that military justice is neither independent nor impartial, at least so long as military judges continue to be subject to a chain of military command. Judges who are subject to command from senior officers are naturally perceived as less able to discharge their judicial functions in an independent or impartial manner. Similarly, there are questions regarding the knowledge, training, payment and career paths open to members of these military criminal justice systems.

Those who criticise the relative lack of independence or impartiality in military justice generally favour the solution of incorporating jurisdiction over military offences into the ordinary criminal system. The predictable response from military officials, and also some politicians, relies upon the special features of the military. The typical institutional response is that no one other than military judges is suitably experienced and competent to understand and administer the military justice because only military judges know and understand the structure, processes and culture of the military forces. This argument emphasises the experience of military life and the knowledge of military organisations over other competing considerations, such as the independence of military judges. Such arguments also presume that civilian judges cannot acquire sufficient experience in military matters, just as they do with other novel areas of jurisdiction. As shown in Table 10.1, in the cases analysed in this study the military criminal justice models are diverse.

In Argentina the military criminal justice system no longer exists after reforms made in 2008. Law 26.394 has repealed the Military Justice Code, which dated from the middle of the last century.[13] Military members who commit crimes during peacetime are now judged in civilian jurisdictions.[14] Meanwhile, in both Guatemala and Peru, the administrative

[13] Código de Justicia Militar [Code of Military Justice] (Argentina) Law No. 14.029 of 6 August 1951.

[14] As a result of the new legislation, for criminal justice administration in times of war or in cases of other armed conflict, special courts martial will be created that include senior

Table 10.1 *Administrative bodies of the military criminal justice system*

Argentina	Guatemala	Peru
Ordinary criminal justice agencies – civil Judges	Ordinary War Councils, General Officers War Councils, Military areas Headquarters, Military Court and Court of Appeals – military Judges in all indicated instances, however, civilians participate as administrators of the justice in the final instance of appeal.	Police military courts, Superior Military courts and Supreme Military Police Court – Military Judges.

Source: Elaborated by the author, based upon the regulations of each country discussed. (Código de Justicia Militar [Code of Military Justice] (Argentina) Law No. 26.394 of 26 August 2008. Repeal the Military Justice Code and all the regulations, resolutions and provisions of an internal nature which regulate it and modify the Criminal Code and the Criminal Procedural Code of the Nation. Código Militar [Military Code] (Guatemala) Decree No. 214 of 15 September 1878, Last Amendment Decree No. 41–96 of 10 July 1996, art. 1. Ley No. 29.182 – de Organización y Funciones del Fuero Militar Policial [Law No. 29.182, Military and Police Justice Law Organization and Competencies] (Peru) Law No. 29.182 of 10 January 2008, Last Amendment Law No. 29.955 of 6 December 2012: Regarding Organization and Functions of the Military Police Jurisdiction.)

bodies of military justice remain largely autonomous and are embedded in the organisation of the armed forces. They have no real structural links to the civilian judiciary.

In Guatemala, the administration of military justice in the first instance is executed by military members within three bodies. The distribution of jurisdiction between these bodies is regulated by complex criteria that take into account the type of crime and the type of personnel accused of committing an offence. The first body comprises several Ordinary courts Martial and acts in relation to common or military offences committed by officers ranking from the common soldier to lieutenant or second

officers belonging to the justice echelons of the armed forces, or belonging to the Command corps, when they possess a law degree.

lieutenant. This body hears crimes of treason, espionage, sedition and rebellion committed by military personnel who are not officers. The second body comprises the General Officers War Council and hears charges of treason and espionage, sedition, rebellion, desertion crimes in times of war, and for acts against military service committed by retired or active officers. The third comprises the headquarters of military areas (the Military Zone), the authority of which extends to all armed forces' personnel who reside within the territory of this area. In the second instance, the Court Martial and the Court of Appeals serve as a forum for an appeal. The Court of Appeals hears cases on appeal from the Military Zones Headquarters, while the Court Martial hears cases on appeal heard by the other two bodies in the first instance, and only hears matters from the Military Zone Headquarters that relate purely to military offences.[15]

The administration of military justice in Peru is conducted by military members whether in the first instance (the jurisdiction exercised by the Military Police Courts), in the second instance (the jurisdiction exercised by Superior Military Police Courts) or in its ultimate instance (the jurisdiction of the Supreme Military Police Court). The jurisdiction of these bodies follows a territorial criterion. The Supreme Military Police Court is based in Lima and has a national jurisdiction. The Superior Military Police Courts and Military Police Courts have jurisdiction in different territorial areas of the location of the armed forces, as determined by the Supreme Court.[16] It is worth noting that, unlike the case of Guatemala, members of the ultimate or peak military body (the Supreme Military Police Court) are required to be qualified legal professionals.

D *Military crimes*

Military crimes are created by the military justice codes. In the codes of the military justice systems of the Latin American region, military penal crimes are defined as acts that affect the legal assets of the armed forces or are related to military service. Conduct affecting military discipline is perhaps the most common military offence in the region. A notable

[15] Código Militar [Military Code] (Guatemala) Decree No. 214 of 15 September 1878, Last Amendment Decree No. 41–96 of 10 June 1996, arts. 1, 23, 30, 252, 312, 359, 389, 467, 478.

[16] Ley No. 29.182 – de Organización y Funciones del Fuero Militar Policial [Law No. 29.182, Military and Police Justice Law Organization and Competencies] (Peru) Law No. 29.182 of 10 January 2008, Last Amendment Law No. 29.955 of 6 December 2012: Regarding Organization and Functions of the Military Police Jurisdiction art. 7.

example of such an offence in Guatemala is that of conduct against the morale of the armed forces.[17]

In general, the debate on the proper scope of military jurisdiction falls into two opposing arguments. On the one hand there are those who criticise the definition of a military crime, indicating that discipline is not a legal asset, but an institutional asset, for which there should be no courts or criminal proceedings. On the other hand, the sharpest criticisms are aimed at the inclusion of common crimes, as if they were crimes committed in the line of duty, in the military codes of several countries of the region.[18] Relevant principles from international law, international humanitarian law and constitutional doctrines indicate that military courts should only have jurisdiction to determine crimes committed in the line of duty. The military justice codes of many Latin American countries violate those principles by allowing military members who commit common crimes to be tried in military courts.

Table 10.2 presents the acts included as military crimes, or crimes that are aggravated when they occur in a military context, in accordance with the current regulations in each case study.

In Argentina, since 2008, many crimes previously included in the Code of Military Justice have been transferred to the Criminal Code. This change includes offences that incorporate the military character as an aggravating circumstance and crimes of proper *delicta*. It should be noted that the reform also added to the Criminal Code new forms of common crimes associated with damage to the institution or military function, as in the case of the violation of military instructions and public incitement to object to military service in times of armed conflict. The introduction of such offences into the civilian criminal code constitutes an important reform to military justice and the level of civilian control over the military because it allows civilian authorities and courts to prosecute members of the armed forces for unlawful conduct.

The position is different in both Peru and Guatemala because the jurisdiction of the military justice system of each of those countries is much wider. Both of these countries determine more of the crimes

[17] Código Militar [Military Code] (Guatemala) Decree No. 214 of 15 September 1878.

[18] Offences committed in the course of duty form the basis of the jurisdiction of military courts. Such offences must typically be committed by a member of the military and also involve conduct that in some way affects the military. In comparison, 'common crime' refers to violations of standards recognised by the legal framework that can be committed by any individual.

Table 10.2 *Military crimes*

Argentina	Guatemala	Peru
Crimes of proper delicta: Undermining of authority, resistance or disobedience, tumultuous request, usurpation of authority, authority abuse, dereliction of duty/control, abandonment of control functions, undertaking military operations without order, misuse of weapons, arbitrary subjection of the civilian population and ordering or exercising any type of unnecessary violence against any person, imprudent homicide, violation of military instruction in times of armed conflict, public incitement against the military service during times of armed conflict, disclosure of industrial and technological secrets. *Crimes where the military character is aggravated*: Homicide, treason, creating danger by hostile acts, violation of treaties concluded	*Crimes committed in the course of duty*: Crimes against national security (treason, sedition and espionage), crimes against internal security (ebellion), offences against military duty (desertion, insubordination, authority abuse and disobedience). *Common Crimes*: Crimes against property (theft, robbery), offences against public administration (embezzlement, forgery).	*Crimes committed in the course of duty*: Crimes against national security (treason, sedition, riot, negativity to avoid sedition or riot, conspiracy, collaboration with an illegal organisation, false alarm); crimes against unauthorised possession or dissemination of information related to national defence, crimes against the function of the security services (desertion, crimes committed by sentinel, sentry or responsible for security), crimes against institutional integrity (insubordination, disobedience, affront to a higher degree personnel), crimes related to the exercise of command involving excess against subordinate personnel; crimes against infringement of police military duty, crimes involving prohibited methods and means during hostilities.

Table 10.2 *(cont.)*

Argentina	Guatemala	Peru
with foreign nations, incitement to military service abduction, extortive kidnapping.		*Common Crimes*: Crimes against public administration (theft, robbery) are consigned as crimes affecting property totally or partially owned by the military or police institutions.

Note: These crimes reflect changes caused by a decision of the Constitutional Court on the constitutionality of several articles of the Código Penal Militar Policial [Military Police Criminal Code] (Peru) Legislative Decree No. 1094 of 31 August 2010.

A 'tumultuous request' refers to behaviour regarded as disorderly. An example of this offence occurred when security forces protested about their salaries, which breached a prohibition upon force members participating in collective protests. See http://noticias.terra.com.ar/politica/prefectos-y-gendarmes-vuelven-a-exigir-mejoras-salariales,1541c5fb6353d310VgnVCM20000099cceb0a RCRD.html.

Source: Elaborated by the author, based upon the regulations of each country discussed. (Código de Justicia Militar [Code of Military Justice] (Argentina) Law No. 26.394 of 26 August 2008. Repeal the Military Justice Code and all the regulations, resolutions and provisions of an internal nature which regulate it and modify the Criminal Code and the Criminal Procedural Code of the Nation. Código Militar [Military Code] (Guatemala) Decree No. 214 of 15 September 1878, Last Amendment Decree No. 41–96 of 10 July 1996, art. 1. Código Penal Militar Policial [Military Police Criminal Code] (Peru) Legislative Decree No. 1094 of 31 August 2010.)

committed by soldiers in trials before military courts. In addition, both the Peruvian Code of Military Police Justice and the Guatemalan Military Code incorporate common crimes that already exist in the criminal codes, such as offences against property and offences against public administration. In other words, each country allows for offences that could, and arguably should, be prosecuted under civilian authority in civilian courts to be determined in military courts. However, this extended scope of military jurisdiction may change, because, as is explained later in this chapter, this aspect of the Peruvian military justice system is in a state of flux. The Constitutional Court of Peru is currently

Table 10.3 *Subjects considered by military criminal jurisdiction*

Argentina	Guatemala	Peru
Active or retired armed forces personnel are judged in the ordinary criminal court and under the Criminal Code of the Nation.	Active military members, retired military members and public security forces.	Active and retired military or police members whose crimes were committed during service.

Source: Elaborated by the author, based upon the regulations of each country discussed. (Código de Justicia Militar [Code of Military Justice] (Argentina) Law No. 26.394 of 26 August 2008. Repeal the Military Justice Code and all the regulations, resolutions and provisions of an internal nature which regulate it and modify the Criminal Code and the Criminal Procedural Code of the Nation. Código Militar [Military Code] (Guatemala) Decree No. 214 of 15 September 1878, Last Amendment Decree No. 41–96 of 10 July 1996, art. 1. Código Penal Militar Policial [Military and Police Penal Code] (Peru), Legislative Decree No. 1094 of 31 August 2010, art. 7.)

considering questions about the proper scope of the military justice code and the validity of recent decrees issued by the executive, which have essentially ordered that many offences committed by members of the military in the maintenance of internal order, including human rights violations, be determined by military courts. This debate may dramatically change military justice and jurisdiction in Peru.

E The subjects considered by military criminal jurisdiction

The notion of military criminal jurisdiction refers to the power granted to military judges and courts to prosecute individuals accused of military crimes. Obviously, it is the current members of armed forces who would normally face military courts. However, some Latin American countries extend the jurisdiction of military tribunals to police personnel and sometimes even civilians in times of war. Table 10.3 describes the groups to which military justice jurisdiction is applied during peacetime.

As mentioned above, Argentinean military jurisdiction has been abolished. Accordingly, military personnel are tried by the ordinary courts of that country. The elimination of an autonomous military jurisdiction and the promotion of the principle that a soldier has the same rights as any other citizen[19] were key goals of the recent reforms. Accordingly, all Argentinean citizens, whether military members or not, face the same ordinary courts and are governed by the same Criminal Code.

In contrast, the Guatemalan and Peruvian military courts have a much wider jurisdiction. The Guatemalan Military Code and the Code of Military Police Justice of Peru are each applicable to both active and retired members of the military and of the police. In the case of Guatemala, until 1996 when the most recent modification to the Military Code occurred, all members of the armed forces were tried in the military courts, regardless of whether the crime was common or committed in the course of duty. However, the provision stating that the crimes and offences committed by members of the armed forces should be tried by military courts remains current in article 219 of the Guatemalan Constitution.[20] Since the 1996 reforms, this provision has been generally interpreted to mean that members of the armed forces should be tried in military courts only for military offences.

III Integration or autonomy? The debate on military justice models

The latest initiatives to reform military criminal justice and the state of the debate on the issues in the three case studies are presented in this section.

A Argentina: integration in the ordinary jurisdiction

The strikingly different approach taken by Argentina has been to integrate the military jurisdiction into the civilian courts. This approach is the result of an extensive process of broad institutional reforms that has taken place since the return of democracy to Argentina in 1983. In addition, a number of specific issues have mobilised a determination to reconfigure military justice.

Although there have been many initiatives since 1983 from different parts of government for the reform of the Argentine Military Justice Code,[21] this reform was one of several institutional changes which reordered and

[19] Note that the former Argentinean Military Justice Code was also criticised by military members because of its often harsh sanctions for military personnel for common and military crimes.

[20] Constitution (Guatemala, 31 May 1985).

[21] The initiatives even came from the armed forces themselves, who pointed out that the code was outdated as it restricted rights such as the right to choose defence counsel, and

clarified the civil–military relationship in Argentina. The overarching features of these changes were a strengthening of political power over the military through the Ministry of Defense, greater control and civilian leadership of the armed forces and the strengthening of the justice institutions in general. The latter was a key reform designed to banish the many unlawful and arbitrary practices which developed during the military dictatorship.[22] Another important objective of these changes was to clarify and reorder the administration of justice upon more democratic principles. Hence the reforms of the military code restricted the jurisdiction of military courts to try civilians, while also enabling the ordinary courts to prosecute members of the armed forces for violations of human rights.[23]

In 1996 the murder of a young conscript provided a crucial trigger for further debate about the role of military justice and highlighted the fact that the old model of military justice was an obstacle to ongoing efforts to strengthen democracy in Argentina. A criminal proceeding was instituted before the ordinary courts as a result of the murder. After Captain Rodolfo Correa Belisle, who conducted a search at the regiment of the conscript, explained to the jury how army intelligence tried to cover up the events in the case and stated that the Commander in Chief, General Martín Balza, had lied on his report about the events, Correa Belisle was arrested and found guilty of the military offence of 'disrespect' against a superior officer. The case, known as the *Correa Belisle* case, was taken to the Inter-American Court of Human Rights where it was argued that the procedures of the Argentinean military courts violated fundamental rights to due process.[24] The Inter-American Court concluded that the Argentinean State was responsible for the violation of arts. 7, 8, 13, 24, and 25 in conjunction with art. 1.1 of the American Convention on Human Rights.[25] Subsequently, the parties started a process of dialogue,

that its sanctions, including the death penalty, were too severe. Thus, there was an interest in a reformulation of military justice, both for civilians and military members.

22 Ruth Diamint, 'The Defense Policy of Argentina: Failures in 20 Years of Democracy' in Legal Defense Institute (ed.), *The Knots of Defense. Tangles and Disentanglements for Public Policy in Democracy* (Lima, IDL, 2005), p. 177.

23 Modificaciones al Código de Justicia Militar [Modifications to the Military Justice Code] (Argentina) Law No. 23.049 of 9 February 1984 – which included legal reforms that impose military courts and excludes natural judges – and Ley de Defensa de la Democracia [Defense of Democracy Law] Law No. 23.077 of 22 August 1984 – which reformed several articles of the Criminal Code – were implemented.

24 See Chapter 16 for further details regarding the case.

25 Inter-American Commission on Human Rights. *Admissibility Report No. 2/04* (24 February 2004) www.cidh.oas.org/annualrep/2004eng/Argentina.11758eng.htm.

which included the evaluation of different initiatives. They reached an agreement in which the Argentinean State committed to recognising its responsibility for the violation of the American Convention on Human Rights, including an apology to Rodolfo Correa Belisle, and to reformulating the military justice system in a comprehensive manner so that the military would be given the same guarantees of due process available to civilians.[26]

On the basis of the settlement in the *Correa Belisle* case, in 2006 the strengthened Ministry of Defense convened a commission composed of representatives of civil society organisations, academics, leading jurists and representatives of the armed forces to evaluate the military criminal justice system and consider whether it should be incorporated into the ordinary civilian justice system.[27] The subsequent report of the commission was subject to detailed negotiation with each of the three parts of the military forces. Finally, in 2008 Congress passed Law 26.394 to repeal the Military Justice Code and to establish an integrated system of the military criminal justice and disciplinary regime for the armed forces. Some of the most important changes made by Law 26.394 include the incorporation of crimes committed by military members into the Criminal Code and the Criminal Procedural Code of the Nation, the approval of the Military Penal Procedures in Time of War and Other Armed Conflicts, incorporation of instructions for the Civilian Population in Time of War, the adoption of the Discipline of the Armed Forces Code and the organisation of the Joint Justice Service of the Armed Forces.

This new legislation includes various remarkable innovations. An ordinary jury now hears crimes committed by military personnel in peacetime and also during war, as long as the process does not interfere with ongoing military operations and there are no insurmountable difficulties. Therefore, as far as possible, the procedure in peacetime is applied permanently. Additionally, homosexuality is no longer a military offence and crimes against military 'honour' have been removed from the new legislation. Also, sexual harassment in military institutions has been typified as a crime in the new legislation, in the context of the need to increase the participation of women in the Command Corps. These innovations strengthen egalitarian principles in the armed forces.

[26] Inter-American Court of Human Rights. *Report No. 15/10* (16 March 2010) www.cidh.oas.org/annualrep/2010eng/ARSA11758EN.doc-01/23/2012.

[27] Silvia Varela, Lucila Santos and Eva Muzzopapa, 'Defense and Human Rights Policies for the Armed Forces' in Center for Legal and Social Studies (CELS) (ed.), *Human Rights in Argentina: 2009 Report* (Buenos Aires, Twenty-First Century Publishers, 2009), p. 282.

Finally, as a consequence of the reform, the death penalty is no longer applicable in Argentina, making it possible for the country to ratify international conventions on that matter (the Second Protocol of the International Covenant on Civil and Political Rights and the Protocol to the American Convention on Human Rights to Abolish the Death Penalty).

B Peru: autonomy and struggle of powers

The current model of military justice in Peru has maintained its autonomy despite repeated calls for reform. The return to democracy did not bring any consensus about the nature of possible reforms to military justice. On the contrary, it reflected the strong legal and political debates during the last years concerning the structure and function of military institutions in Peruvian Society.

At the conceptual level, the debate has been focused on three aspects. The first is the question of whether military criminal jurisdiction should be autonomous. A key element of this issue concerns the nature of military offences: that is, what offences can properly be said to be military or what offences might fall within the course of military duty. Such questions revolve around the central question of whether military discipline needs an independent military jurisdiction. The second element of the debate around Peruvian military justice concerns the principle of independence in the selection of magistrates and judges. The third important issue concerns the trial of civilian (or 'common') crimes and crimes related to the violation of human rights by military courts.

In terms of regulation, the laws that have been subject to debate have been the Military Police Justice Code, the Law on Organization and Functions of the Military Police Criminal Code and the Law on the Use of the Force. These laws have been constantly refined and redefined in the past decade, as part of complex wider social and political forces that have shaped Peru, particularly the successive governments' fears of the resurgence of subversive groups and the increased number and intensity of domestic social conflicts.[28] Governments have invoked these problems to argue that the armed forces should again participate in the maintenance of internal order. The result is that the military justice system, long used

[28] The insurgency Peru experienced for many years has waned but Peruvian society remains deeply divided. More recently domestic social conflicts, especially those related to mining and extraction of natural resources in the rural areas of the country, have become critical for the government. See *Social Conflicts Reports 2004–2015* www.defensoria.gob.pe/conflictos-sociales/.

as an instrument to prosecute all types of crimes, including violations of human rights during the internal conflict, is now again being called upon to serve as an instrument to reinforce the military institutions themselves.

The reforms to military justice in Peru in recent years reveal the deep struggle surrounding the renewal of the Military Justice Code. That Code was enacted in 1980 and modified over the years during the course of wider social and political disputes that engulfed both the internal security of Peru and also its armed forces. In 2005 the Ombudsman commenced a case in the Constitutional Court, which led that Court to declare that several articles of the Military Justice Code and the Organic Law of Military Justice were unconstitutional. Congress did not enact new legislation to replace the impeached provisions. Instead it delegated this power to the Executive to create a new code. The Executive issued a new Code of Military Police Justice in 2006, but that was also declared unconstitutional. That same year, the Peruvian Congress decided to adopt an innovative model of military justice, which sought to link the administration of military justice to the judiciary and other agencies of government. Although this legislation maintained the election of judges and the majority of prosecutors from military personnel, this model would have increased the connections between the military and civilian justice systems and would almost certainly have increased civilian control over many military justice decisions. However, the Public Prosecutor Office strongly criticised this proposal and considered that it 'introduced a foreign external body in the judicial system, opening doors to undermine its unity and independence', violating the principles of exclusivity of the judiciary and the principle of autonomy of the Public Prosecutor Office.[29] The radical new model also faced strong opposition from the judiciary. There were even demands that the model should be declared invalid by the Constitutional Court.

In late 2007, Congress passed a new law governing the organisation and functions of Military Police Jurisdiction. This new model moved completely in the opposite direction to the previous reform proposal, emphasising the autonomous character of military justice, which depended on the Executive branch. This move provoked a further claim of unconstitutionality, declared by the Constitutional Court two

[29] Constitutional Court of Peru. Petition 0004-2006-PI/TC *Sentence of Plenary Jurisdiction of Constitutional Court* (Peru, 26 March 2006) www.tc.gob.pe/jurisprudencia/2006/00004-2006-AI.html.

years later. This time the Constitutional Court modified its traditional determinations on this matter and responded with a ruling that supported the new standard for the most part and only declared that some articles were unconstitutional. The Constitutional Court stated that the existence of a military justice system was constitutional. It also affirmed that since military justice is by its nature an exception to the exercise of the judicial function, it was unrelated to the principles governing the judiciary.[30]

In 2010, Congress declined again to exercise its legislative powers in matters of military justice and once again decided to delegate to the Executive the authority to legislate the military police code, the use of force, and procedural and prison standards related to prosecuted and convicted military and police. A month after this new delegation was made the Executive issued four Legislative Decrees: the Military Police Criminal Code, the Employment and Use of Force, the modification of the Law on the Organization and Functions of the Military Police Jurisdiction and the regulation of the application of procedural norms for offences involving the violation of human rights.[31] A constitutional challenge inevitably followed.[32] In 2012 the Constitutional Court of Peru upheld a complaint challenging the constitutionality of the law of Congress that delegated the legislative functions to the Executive.[33] The

[30] Constitutional Court of Peru. Petition 00001-2009-PI/TC *Sentence of Plenary Jurisdiction of Constitutional Court* (Peru, 4 December 2009) www.tc.gob.pe/jurisprudencia/2009/00001-2009-AI.html.

[31] Código Penal Militar Policial [Military and Police Penal Code] (Peru), Legislative Decree No. 1094 of 31 August 2010, Reglas de Empleo y Uso de la Fuerza por parte de las Fuerzas Armadas en el Territorio Nacional [Rules of employment and use of force by the armed forces in the country] Legislative Decree No. 1095 of 31 August 2010, Decreto Legislativo que modifica artículos de la Ley 29.182 de Organización y Funciones del Fuero Militar Policial [Legislative Decree amending the articles of the Law No. 29182, the Law on the Organization and Functions of the Military Police Court] Legislative Decree No. 1096 of 31 August 2010, and Decreto Legislativo que regula la aplicación de normas procesales por delitos que implican la violación de derechos humanos [Legislative Decree regulating the application of the procedural norms for offences involving the violation of human rights]. Legislative Decree No. 1097 of 31 August 2010.

[32] The process started a few days after the publication of the four legislative decrees, when some members of Congress demanded that the Constitutional Court declare unconstitutional Legislative Decree No. 1097, the fourth decree. However, before the Constitutional Court resolved the case (March 2011), and only fourteen days after its promulgation, Congress passed a law to revoke the decree: Ley No. 29572 que deroga el Decreto Legislativo No. 1097 [Law No. 29572 Repealing Legislative Decree No. 1097 of 14 December 2010].

[33] The Constitutional Court initially declared the claim not admissible, arguing formal considerations. Once the defendants corrected them, the Court admitted their petition.

claim also challenged the two Legislative Decrees that established the new Military Police Criminal Code and established a new regime governing the employment of military forces. The case has received considerable attention from the human rights community in Peru. The case also drew attention from the international human community, with one international body requesting a formal role in the proceeding.[34] The Peruvian Congress, the Ministry of Justice and the representative of the Military Police Justice submitted arguments in this proceeding. In 2015, the Constitutional Court issued the resolution on this case.[35]

The dramatic legislative events of recent years in Peru reflect a strong struggle over, and manipulation of, military justice by political groups who appear to want to protect the military as an institution. This struggle was not entirely settled by the recent decision of the Constitutional Court because its reasoning means that some crimes are no longer the province of military judges, but in other respects the Court reinforced the autonomy of military justice.

C *Guatemala: autonomy and continuity*

The current system of military justice in Guatemala is autonomous. There is very little public discussion about this model of military justice

Constitutional Court of Peru. Petition 00022-2011-PI/TC *Admissibility Resolution* (Peru, 7 April 2012) www.tc.gob.pe/jurisprudencia/2012/00022-2011-AI%20Admisibilidad1.html and (Peru, 3 May 2012) www.tc.gob.pe/jurisprudencia/2012/00022-2011-AI%20%20Admisibilidad2.pdf.

34 On 13 May 2013 Human Rights Watch presented a request to the Constitutional Court to intervene in the proceedings as amicus curiae. See www.hrw.org/es/news/2013/05/13/peru-proceso-de-inconstitucionalidad-contra-decreto-legislativo-n-1095.

35 The Court declared several parts of the DL N°1094 Police Military Code were unconstitutional, notably those related to the crimes committed in a state of emergency and against people protected by international humanitarian law. The Court also settled the interpretation of a key issue in dispute, which was the meaning of the term 'hostile group' in article 5.f of the DL N° 1095 Rules of Employment and Use of Force by the Armed Forces. The Constitutional Court has given the definition of 'hostile group' a more confined application than its original version. That phrase is taken now to refer to a plurality of individuals that are (i) minimally organised, (ii) have an ability and willingness to confront the state with firearms in a prolonged manner, (iii) participate or assist in such hostilities. This definitive new interpretation has greatly reduced possible confusion about hostile groups in the context of internal conflicts with social protests movements. Finally, the Constitutional Court reaffirmed central aspects of military justice, by declaring that important parts of the articles of the Military Police Code were constitutionally valid, notably those parts governing crime against internal security, crimes against prohibited methods and means in the treatment of hostilities and crimes against military duties.

in Guatemala. The Guatemalan code has proved impervious to reform initiatives, which arguably reflects the political influence of the armed forces. The Military Code of Guatemala has rarely been reformed since its inception in 1878. All reforms made to the Code are, with one exception, over fifty years old and predominantly address formal issues rather than substantive or structural matters.

The only and the most recent norm that addresses substantive content of the military justice model in democracy was Decree No. 41–96 of 1996.[36] That decree amended art. 2 of the Military Code, to remove the power of military officials to prosecute military members for crimes that exist in civilian law. This reform limits the scope of military justice to offences which are strictly military crimes. It should be noted, however, that this reform is somewhat incomplete because it has not included the necessary amendment to the Constitution. Art. 219 of the Constitution, which was adopted in 1985, in the midst of the armed conflict in Guatemala, states that all military members will be judged by military courts. The terms of the 1996 Peace Agreements, which ended thirty-six years of internal conflict, sought to reform this and other articles of the Constitution, but the constitutional reform process failed in the referendum of the same year. Accordingly, the only significant and recent reform has a limitation that contradicts the current Constitution.

The resistance to change of military jurisdiction in Guatemala reflects the political influence and interference of the military and the limitations that civilian society faces in attempts to rebuild the rule of law. A recent example of *de facto* power exercised by the armed forces, along with large economic groups, is the inability of civilian justice to condemn or prosecute those military members responsible for the violation of human rights during the internal conflict experienced in Guatemala. Notable officials who have not been brought to account include the former President and General Efrain Rios Montt.[37]

[36] Código Militar [Military Code] (Guatemala) Decree No. 214 of 15 September 1878, Last Amendment Decree No. 41–96 of 10 July 1996.

[37] Upon hearing of the sentence of eighty years for genocide against Rios Montt, the military Veterans Association of Guatemala (AVELMIGUA) threatened to mobilise up to 50,000 paramilitary of the Civilian Self Defense Patrols (PAC) and paralyse the country. Meanwhile, the Coordinating Committee of Commercial, Industrial and Financial Associations responded to the sentence with a statement rejecting the occurrence of genocide in Guatemala. See José Elías, 'Guatemala's Constitutional Voids the Conviction of Former Dictator Rios Montt', El País, May 2013 http://internacional.elpais.com/internacional/2013/05/21/actualidad/1369101633_290958.html. A subsequent ruling held that Montt should face trial although, due to his dementia, the trial

While it is arguable that Decree No. 41–96 signals some progress, the fact that the Decree does not actually operate confirms that the reform of military justice in Guatemala is still at an early stage. The current military code does not completely incorporate what was established in the Peace Agreements and the changes in national and international law since those Agreements were reached. The result is that much about military justice, including its content and relationship to the civilian justice system, contradicts basic constitutional principles because it does not ensure the independence of military judges. It also contradicts key elements of the criminal law and international regulations. The failure to reform the old military code arguably also stands in tension with the contemporary reality of the armed forces, whose organisation and operation have also advanced since 1878. Therefore, the military as an institution has advanced but its governing code has not.

IV Conclusion

Since its inception in Latin American countries, military law has operated as a specialised and autonomous law. Its original raison d'être was to provide armed forces guarantees for the performance of their duties but military justice has more recently been used for political and corporate ends during the years of military intervention in the political life of many Latin American countries. The restoration of democracy and the reconstruction of institutions of the law in those countries have sparked a necessary debate on the military justice system. There are two possible outcomes to this debate: either a total reform of military justice, including integration into ordinary civilian courts, or a partial reform, which reaffirms the autonomy of military justice and military courts but adapts them to ensure compliance with constitutional principles and international standards of human rights. The first alternative is radical in a legal sense but would also serve the important symbolic function of removing the military from the special status that it has long held in Latin American societies. The second reform option is the more cautious one and removes from military judges their power to prosecute crimes that can and should be determined in civilian courts.

should proceed in camera and without Montt present. See: Elisabeth Malkin, 'Genocide Retrial is Set for Guatemalan Former Dictator', *The New York Times* (25 August 2015), www.nytimes.com/2015/08/26/world/americas/genocide-retrial-is-set-for-guatemalan-former-dictator.html?_r=0.

The three case studies in the chapter show the different ways those issues have unfolded. Argentina has opted for a military justice model that is integrated into the ordinary civilian justice system. This reform is the result of a much wider reconstruction of state institutions in which civilian authorities have recovered political power in wider society. That control includes stronger civilian authority over the military. In Peru the armed forces retain considerable political power, which has led to an intense struggle between the institutions of the state itself, in a context where the armed forces retain a margin of control over political power. The debate about reform of the military in Guatemala also has a long way to go. After the return of democracy, Guatemala clings to a military code that is more than a century old. The striking differences in these three jurisdictions show the choices available to a society in deciding the appropriate model for military criminal justice. These different choices depend on the post-conflict political context, the scope of institutional reconstruction and the capacity for consensus in each nation. In other words, both military justice and its reform depend heavily on the political landscape of a nation.

But some more general regional trends are clear. Latin American governments have started to recognise that they have an outdated model of military justice. Some countries have begun considering which model is the most appropriate to their reality. This includes initiatives of different scope and type: legislatives initiatives (such as in Mexico and Chile), or institutional initiatives of the defence ministries (such as in Chile and Uruguay), and even constitutional reform (for example in Nicaragua and Bolivia). The changes in these other countries are similar to the case studies examined in this chapter because every process of reform is heavily influenced by internal political factors. Such factors include the control by civilians of the defence sector, the capacity of civilians to lead a technical debate, the level of power of the armed forces, and even the type of missions that currently are assigned to the armed forces (for example, those armed forces that are assigned public vigilance and internal order duties).

Until now, the predominant model of military justice in Latin American countries has been one that maintains the autonomy of the armed forces, with some reforms which bring those systems more in line with prevailing norms of international law. In many Latin American countries, however, this fundamental debate about the military and military justice has barely started. It is for this reason that the reforms in Argentina and Ecuador (the latter of which opted to integrate military jurisdiction into the civil justice system as part of the new constitution in 2008) set an important precedent in the region.

11

Military criminal justice in the Netherlands: the 'civil swing' of the military judicial order

BAS VAN HOEK

I Introduction

After World War II, the Dutch government faced a problem of apparent alienation between the armed forces and the organisation of military criminal justice.[1] The need to review military criminal law was apparent. To this end, in 1963 there was a partial and interim review of military criminal justice. The Ministers of Justice and Defence ordered a committee (the 'Doornbos Committee') to prepare a proposal aimed at the total revision of military criminal justice in the Netherlands. The report of that committee led the government to draft a note, which explored several alternatives. The favoured option, presented to parliament in 1966, proposed the wholesale modernisation of military criminal justice. The government's approach was to add elements of civilian criminal procedure to the criminal justice system, but to maintain a court martial. In 1972, however, some members of parliament submitted an amendment to abolish military criminal justice altogether.[2] Other parliamentarians responded by suggesting that military criminal justice should be aligned with civilian criminal justice as closely as possible, through the creation of military chambers in civilian courts. Such military chambers would be predominantly civilian in character and consist of specialised judges.[3] In 1972, parliament adopted this amendment to the government's

[1] Only minor adjustments in military criminal justice had been introduced since 1814. Developments in the *opinio iuris* regarding criminal procedures were more or less disregarded in the military justice system. As the administration of military criminal justice was based on the structure of the armed forces, the justice system had to be amended since the structure of the armed forces had changed dramatically since 1940 (Parliamentary Proceedings, Second Chamber, 1957–1958, 5169, No. 5, p. 1).

[2] Parliamentary Proceedings, Second Chamber, 1971–1972, 8706, No. 10.

[3] Parliamentary Proceedings, Second Chamber, 1971–1972, 8706, No. 24.

position[4] and in 1991, after an extensive legislative process, the current Military Criminal Procedure Code became effective.[5]

This 'civil swing' of military criminal justice is too broad and complex to discuss in its entirety in this chapter. Instead, this chapter will provide a historical review of the magistracy, the public prosecution service and the Royal Netherlands Marechaussee in military criminal justice by examining the discussions on which the current Dutch military criminal justice system is based. Before examining these elements, the broader issue surrounding the existence of the Dutch system of military justice, namely the jurisdiction of military judges, will be discussed.

II The military judges' competence: solely military offences?

The jurisdiction of military judges to deal with both military and civil offences has long been debated in the Netherlands. In 1864, van der Hoeven argued that the unique jurisdiction of courts martial was justified only by the special character of the armed forces. He reasoned that offences with no connection to the military status of a defendant should be dealt with by a civilian court.[6] Similar arguments emerged during the late nineteenth and early twentieth centuries from the Association for Dutch Jurists (Nederlandse Juristen-Vereeniging). In 1881, a small majority of the Association suggested that a separate military tribunal during peacetime would only be justified for strictly military offences. In 1900 a majority of the Association again asserted that maintaining a separate military judicial system during peacetime was not justified.[7] Debate about the jurisdiction of military judges again occurred several years later, during a parliamentary review of the Military Criminal Code and the Code of Military Discipline. Parliament proposed reforms in which only civil offences that related to military discipline would be tried

[4] Parliamentary Proceedings, Second Chamber, 1971–1972, 8706, No. 28.

[5] Regarding the establishment of the reviewed Military Criminal Procedure Code, van den Bosch states: 'I cannot think of any other elements of law that have been treated with equal ignorance, nonchalance and sluggishness.' T.W. van den Bosch, *Huidig en toekomstig militair strafprocesrecht* (Zwolle, Tjeenk Willink, 1983), p. 5.

[6] H. van der Hoeven, *Opmerkingen over de Nederlandse strafwetgeving voor het Krijgsvolk te Lande* (PhD Thesis, University of Leiden, 1864), pp. 128–96. Van der Hoeven was a prominent professor of criminal law at the University of Leiden and designer of the Military Criminal Code of 1903.

[7] G.F. Walgemoed, 'De bevoegdheid van de militaire strafrechter; het einde van't Gedrogt der ongelimiteerde militaire jurisdictie', in *Geleerde lessen, liber amicorum Simon Stolwijk* (Nijmegen, Wolf Legal Publishers, 2007), pp. 266–67.

before a military judge. The government rejected this proposal on the basis that it created undue discretion over the prosecution of members of the armed forces and might cause conflict between military and civilian agencies.[8]

The jurisdiction of military judges, particularly over offences that lacked any perceived military quality or connection, was again considered by the government in its 1966 note. The government position was that, within a just system of law, it was unacceptable that the military aspects of every offence had to be determined prior to any decision as to whether a case should be tried before a civil or a military judge. The government argued that this requirement caused many technical and procedural problems. It also rejected the more radical alternative, which was to have all civil offences tried by the civil judge. The government eventually decided that all civil offences committed by members of the armed forces should be tried before military judges, although it acknowledged that this alternative would remove civil judges from certain criminal cases.[9] The composition of the military chamber would be no different from the composition of a civil criminal chamber, except for the inclusion of a legally qualified military member. This apparent compromise should have removed the sting from the debate concerning the competence of military justice over civil offences.[10] However, in the 1980s parliament again posed the question whether a military judge should try civil offences committed by military personnel.[11] The Minister of Justice noted that the implications of many apparently civil offences could only be fully understood by the military context. The Minister also suggested that the creation of several courts or chambers to deal with the different permutations of offences committed by members of the armed forces would be overly complex.[12] The result was that by 1991, no distinction was drawn in the military criminal justice system between civil and military offences committed by members of the armed

[8] Ibid., p. 269.

[9] Also, criminal cases that lacked any military connection would be handled by a military judge. Parliamentary Proceedings, Second Chamber, 1965–1966, 8706, No. 3, p. 8. Some parliamentarians submitted an amendment in 1972 in order to limit the jurisdiction of the military court to military offences (see: Parliamentary Proceedings, Second Chamber, 1971–1972, 8706, No. 13). Parliamentary Proceedings, Second Chamber, 1971–1972, 8706, No. 28, p. 1. The government was prepared to make an exception regarding fiscal offences, social-economic offences and some traffic offences.

[10] Walgemoed, above n. 7, p. 270.

[11] Parliamentary Proceedings, Second Chamber, 1988–1989, 52–5123 (22 February 1989).

[12] Parliamentary Proceedings, Second Chamber, 1988–1989, 53–5179 (23 February 1989).

forces. The jurisdiction of the military chamber would be based on the military status of the accused and not on the type of offence charged.

III From court martial to military chamber

A Previous system

The government sought to integrate military criminal justice into the civil criminal procedural system and to align the standing of military judges to their civilian equivalent.[13] Prior to the 'civil swing' in 1991, military personnel stood trial, both at first instance (before a court martial) and in appeal cases (in the High Military Court), before a military judicial institution. Moreover, the majority of military court officials who tried such cases were military officers and did not necessarily have a legal education or legal qualifications.[14] Military justice was administered according to rules that did not conform to civil criminal procedure, according to which cases were tried by professional and independent judges. In the latter procedure, serious offences were tried by a three-member criminal chamber and less serious offences by a single judge. Until 1979, the Supreme Court was not competent to handle military cases.[15]

In the early 1960s the government took the view that the military justice system did not meet the same standard for the just and independent administration of the law as the civilian justice system.[16] The government concluded that a separate military criminal justice system was necessary in wartime.[17] However, the government was concerned whether the same was true in peacetime. In the end it answered that

[13] N. Jörg, *Recht voor militairen* (PhD Thesis, University of Utrecht, 1979), p. 31.

[14] In 1987 a committee of experts shared their criticism regarding the Bill with parliament. In their letter they remarked that almost all military members had a law degree (TW van den Bosch et al., *Herziening van het Militaire Straf- en Tuchtrecht (wetsontwerpen 16813 en 17804); brief aan de leden en plv. van de bijzondere commissie van de Tweede Kamer voor de herziening van het militair straf- en tuchtrecht*, 22 January 1987).

[15] Military Cassation Law of 22 February 1979, Gazette 1979, No. 69.

[16] Parliamentary Proceedings, 1965–1966, above n. 9, p. 4. A few years later it would appear that the European Court of Human Rights (ECtHR) and the European Commission for Human Rights could appreciate the way in which the trial of military personnel had taken shape; see *Engel* v. *The Netherlands* ECtHR (8 June 1976) (1976) 69 *Militair Rechtelijk Tijdschrift*, p. 385; A.D. Belinfante, 'Het arrest van het Europese Hof voor de Rechten van de Mens van 8 juni 1976' (1976) 69 *Militair Rechtelijk Tijdschrift*, p. 447. See also, *Donselaar* v. *The Netherlands* European Committee on Human Rights (application No. 11013/84) (4 March 1985) 78 *Militair Rechtelijk Tijdschrift*, p. 196.

[17] Parliamentary Proceedings, 1965–1966, above n. 9, pp. 4–5.

question in the affirmative and linked the justification for a military justice system during peacetime to the need for such a system in wartime, arguing that:

> The military judge's task during wartime demands extensive preparation. This demand can be best met by allowing the military judge to function in peacetime as well. In addition, the special character of the armed forces that is also reflected in military discipline, asks for the need of an expert judge possessing a certain level of empathy with military hierarchy and situations and to the coordination between criminal and disciplinary prosecution. A military judge who is also active during peacetime will be able to provide in such need.[18]

In the 1980s the government considered military criminal justice to be a specialisation of sufficient importance that it should be part of the civilian criminal court's composition.[19] At first, in 1966, the government proposed to maintain the court martial, but to amend its composition. It would comprise one professional civil judge (the chair of the court martial), one regular member who was appointed for life to the function of a military legal counsel and would act as an independent magistrate, and one officer who would be appointed for only a short period and would act as a flexible member.[20] This arrangement represented a clear move from the previous court-martial tribunal, which was composed of one professional judge, assisted by two officers who were not required to have legal training or expertise.[21] In the High Military Court two civilian judges and four military officers presided.[22] The addition of a flexible member to the new system was intended to contribute a level of military understanding.[23] When the final version of the Bill to enact these

[18] Ibid., p. 5.

[19] Parliamentary Proceedings, Second Chamber, 1982–1983, 17 804, No. 5, p. 7. The judicial system was familiar with specialisation. For instance, there had been chambers for the trial of economic crimes and experts had been added to the chambers in the past.

[20] Parliamentary Proceedings, 1965–1966, above n. 9, pp. 15–16.

[21] Administration of Army and Air Force, arts. 120 and 121; Article 122 and 124 Administration of Navy, arts. 122 and 124.

[22] Article 1 and 2 Provisional Instruction High Military Court, arts. 1 and 2.

[23] Parliamentary Proceedings 1965–1966, above n. 9, pp. 9 and 17. Initially, it was intended that the flexible member would be appointed for one year. The regular military member was deemed to resign in order to allow a new member to join. As the government remarked to this effect: 'it is not the intention for the regular member to remain seated until his 60th anniversary. It is in the best interest of military justice, such in the scope of the continuance of the integration of the actual military organization as well as for attracting new and fit candidates, that the regular member will be allowed after having served during a certain period of time, to continue his career elsewhere.' (See ibid., p. 16.)

arrangements was drafted in the early 1980s, the government introduced a clear shift towards the civil criminal justice system. The government proposed to replace the court martial by adding a military chamber in the civilian criminal court. Instead of one civilian judge and two military members, the chamber comprised two professional civil judges and one military member. The government sought to maintain a level of military expertise without compromising the legal expertise of this new court by requiring that military members should be legally trained.[24] The creation of a single court as the sole institution with military criminal jurisdiction was also intended to create a forum for the development of an appropriate level of specialisation in criminal justice and procedure.[25]

In the former system, military personnel always stood trial before a three-member court martial, whereas certain offences in the civil criminal justice system were heard before single-judge chambers (the police judge or magistrate). This magistrate presided over less complex or serious offences and could not impose sentences of imprisonment greater than a maximum of six months.[26] The government stated that a single member would be of practical use during times of conflict or in cases where units were stationed outside the Netherlands and therefore trial before a full court martial would be impractical.[27] Consequently, the government introduced a similar single-judge court, presided over by the police judge for military criminal justice, but concluded that the balance of expertise between military and civilian criminal justice issues could not be achieved in a court presided over by a single judge.[28] Eventually, the government considered that the required military expertise could be achieved in single-member courts if the police judge who heard a typical military criminal case, or one with a perceived military quality or military connection, could refer the case to a multiple chamber.[29]

As was the practice for cases in the civil criminal justice system, cases within the military criminal justice system were also subject to a pre-trial investigation. Investigations in the civil system were performed by a professional pre-trial examining judge, but in the military system that function was performed by a military officer appointed by the armed

[24] Parliamentary Proceedings, 1982–1983, above n. 19, p. 19. [25] Ibid., pp. 2 and 15.

[26] The authority of the police judge to impose sentences was expanded in 2002 to a sentence of up to twelve months of imprisonment. See *Wetboek van Strafvordering* [Criminal Procedure Code] (The Netherlands), art. 369.

[27] Parliamentary Proceedings 1965–1966, above n. 9, p. 18. [28] Ibid.

[29] Parliamentary Proceedings 1982–1983, above n. 19, p. 18.

forces for a limited period. As part of the move to integrate civil criminal procedure into the military justice system, the government decided that pre-trial investigations should be performed by a regular member of the criminal chamber. The government, however, accepted that the new arrangements should include some flexibility to enable the military member to participate in the pre-trial investigation in special cases, such as offences occurring partially or entirely overseas. In such cases, the greater mobility and particular expertise of military members might make them more suitable to conduct the preliminary investigation.[30] As military members were not formally a part of the judiciary, the government considered that they lacked the institutional authority to impose sentences that would deprive people of their freedom. The Council of State[31] advised the government to reconsider this limitation, but the government argued that, where independent judges were available, they should perform the function of imposing measures that would deprive defendants of their liberty.[32] The government drew support for its position from the decision of the European Court of Human Rights in *De Jong, Balget and Van Den Brink* v. *The Netherlands*.[33] The Court held that article 5 of the European Convention on Human Rights (ECHR) required that only a judge could deprive a person of their liberty for the relatively longer periods of detention that may be required during military pre-trial investigations. In that case the pre-trial detention of military personnel for periods of 6–10 days (authorised by a military officer) were held to breach the ECHR.[34]

B Present system

Under the current system, the military chamber of the Gelderland District Court and the Court of Appeal Arnhem-Leeuwarden are the only courts competent to deal with offences committed by military personnel.[35] The military chamber is granted jurisdiction over all

30 Ibid., p. 43.

31 The Council of State acts as an independent advisor regarding legislation and governance.

32 Parliamentary Proceedings, Second Chamber, 1982–1983, 17 804, A–C, p. 18.

33 Parliamentary Proceedings, Second Chamber, 1985–1986, 17 804, No. 10, p. 22.

34 The case *De Jong, Baljet and Van den Brink* (1984) *Militair Rechtelijk Tijdschrift*, p. 28. The ECHR, art. 5(3) requires that '[e]veryone arrested or detained . . . shall be brought promptly before a judge or other judicial officer authorised by law to exercise judicial power'.

35 Since 1 January 2013, as a result of a reorganisation of the justice administration, the names of both the district court and court of appeal in Arnhem have changed. The

criminal offences committed by Dutch soldiers. Dutch law also enables the military chamber of the District Court and the Court of Appeal to conduct sessions abroad.[36] Pursuant to this jurisdiction, the military chamber has held sessions in Germany on a regular basis while a Dutch brigade was stationed in Northern Germany.[37]

The military chamber of both courts consists of three members: two civilian professional judges, including the Court's President, and one military member, who is not part of the judicial system.[38] The District and Appeal Court assigns the judges to the military chamber.[39] As a general rule, the military member is drawn from the branch of the armed forces to which the suspect belongs.[40] The military members are appointed by Royal Decree, upon the recommendation of the Minister of Security and Justice and with the consent of the Minister of Defence. Military members are appointed for four years and are eligible for two reappointments. Those appointed as a military member must be a member of the military community but not the Royal Netherlands Marechaussee (Royal Military Police).[41] Those appointed to the military chamber of the Court of Appeal must be a qualified military lawyer of the rank of colonel, captain or group captain. Any military lawyer of the rank of (group) captain or colonel will be promoted, as a military member of the Court of Appeal, to the brevet rank of (air) commodore or brigadier.[42] Military members are granted the same legal status and protections as judges, so as to protect their independence.[43] Military members must also pledge or avow before the judicature and the oath is taken by the public prosecution service. Cassation at the Supreme Court is

Arnhem District Court is now called District Court Gelderland and the court of appeal respectively Court of Appeal Arnhem-Leeuwarden.

[36] *Wet Militaire Strafrechtspraak* [Military Criminal Procedure Code] (The Netherlands), arts. 3 and 8.

[37] R. van den Heuvel, *Militaire strafrechtspraak: de praktijk* ([Military Criminal Justice in Practice] MRT, 2008), p. 98.

[38] Act on Judicial Organization, arts. 55 and 68. Article 49 regulates the establishment of a single-judge military chamber (military police judge) at the Gelderland district court. This professional judge has a civilian status.

[39] Act on Judicial Organization, arts. 55 and 68. [40] Ibid.

[41] *Wet Militaire Strafrechtspraak* [Military Criminal Procedure Code] (The Netherlands), arts. 6 and 9.

[42] Ibid., art. 9. Contrary to the Court of Appeal, the law does not mention the rank of the military members of the District Court. In general, all members have the rank of colonel, captain or group captain.

[43] *Wet Militaire Strafrechtspraak* [Military Criminal Procedure Code] (The Netherlands), art. 6.

possible if there has been a violation of law or a breach of procedure. The Supreme Court does not comprise any military members.

With regard to pre-trial investigations, one of the judges in the military chamber will be appointed pre-trial examining judge. A military member can be appointed examining judge, but for the reasons described earlier military members cannot impose any measures of deprivation of liberty. Moreover, the military member may only be appointed an examining judge if the investigation takes place outside of the Netherlands either entirely or partially, or if the president of the military chamber considers it preferable to have the investigation performed by a military member.[44]

IV The public prosecutor, from advisor to *dominus litis*

A Previous system

Since the Criminal Procedure Code entered into force, the public prosecutor has held a monopoly over the prosecution of criminal offences committed by civilians.[45] Within the military criminal justice system, however, the position of *dominus litis* was held – within certain boundaries and under certain conditions – by the commanding officer (e.g. commander of a mechanised brigade) who decided whether or not the law would be enforced. The commanding general (e.g. Army Chief in Command) decided whether a suspect was to appear before a court martial, but that decision was required to be taken in consultation with the public prosecutor, who was a member of the public prosecution service, an autonomous organisation within the Ministry of Justice.[46] The civilian status of the prosecutor served as a guarantee that decisions regarding prosecutions would also include consideration of the law of criminal procedure. The public prosecutors were appointed by Royal Decree on the recommendation of both the Minister of Justice and the Minister of Defence.[47] The countersignature of the latter was a guarantee

[44] Ibid., art. 29.

[45] Wet op de rechterlijke organisatie [Act on Judicial Organization] (The Netherlands), art. 124 and Wetboek van Strafvordering [Criminal Procedure Code] (The Netherlands), art. 148.

[46] Both the commanding officer and commanding general were obliged to consult their military legal advisors. See R.M. Eiting, 'Een 'klok- en kleppel discussie op verschillende golflengten' (2004) *Carré*, p. 38.

[47] Rechtspleging bij de Land- en Luchtmacht [Administration of Army and Air Force] (The Netherlands), art. 126; Rechtspleging bij de Zeemacht [Administration of Navy] (The Netherlands), art. 131.

of the public prosecutor's experience regarding the military.[48] Where the commanding general decided, contrary to the prosecutor's advice, not to prosecute, the latter could file a complaint with the High Military Court.[49] After having decided to prosecute a suspect, the commanding general had to hand over the file to the public prosecutor as commanding officer was not authorised to present the case to the court martial. The military cases were handled by two separate public prosecutors' offices within the prosecution service.[50]

The government favoured full integration of military criminal justice into the civilian administration of criminal justice and therefore decided to charge the public prosecution service with military prosecutions. Since the trial of military criminal cases would be handled as a rule by the District Court in Arnhem, the prosecution of military offences was automatically allocated to the district public prosecutor in Arnhem.[51]

In the 1966 note, the government stated that knowledge of the military would not suffice and emphasised the importance of the public prosecutor having personal military experience.[52] During the legislative process, however, the government considered the requirement of military experience to be a matter of policy instead of law.[53] The government rejected parliament's suggestions that a separate military district office should be created or that a military element should be added on the basis that a separate district office was inconsistent with the idea of integration. It was also argued that the creation of a district court and a court of appeal to deal with two separate district public prosecutor offices was impractical.[54] Many members of parliament held the view that the public

[48] E.J. van den Boezem, Analyse van knelpunten door de Auditeur-militair n.a.v. de (concept) Memorie van Antwoord bij het ontwerp van et Militaire Strafrechtspraak c.a., 14 maart 1986, p. 20. According to Eiting, most public prosecutors did have a military background (Eiting, above n. 46, p. 38).

[49] Rechtspleging bij de Land- en Luchtmacht [Administration of Army and Air Force] (The Netherlands), art. 15; Rechtspleging bij de Zeemacht [Administration of Navy] (The Netherlands), art. 10. Van den Bosch, above n. 5, p. 54. The commanding general usually followed the prosecutor's advice, but was not bound to.

[50] One prosecutor's office focused on the Army and Air Force. The second office only handled criminal cases submitted by the Navy.

[51] Wetboek van Strafvordering [Criminal Procedure Code] (The Netherlands), art. 148.

[52] Parliamentary Proceedings, Second Chamber, 1965–1966, above n. 9, pp. 21 and 25; Parliamentary Proceedings, Second Chamber, 1970–1971, 8706, No. 5, p. 11; Parliamentary Proceedings, Second Chamber, 1971–1972, No. 28, p. 2.

[53] Parliamentary Proceedings, Second Chamber, 1982–1983, 17 804, No. 6, p. 6.

[54] Parliamentary Proceedings, Second Chamber, 1985–1986, 17 804, No. 10, p. 6. Parliamentary Proceedings, Second Chamber, 1987–1988, 17 804, No. 23, p. 7.

prosecution service needed to possess sufficient empathy with the military hierarchy and military situations, otherwise the armed forces would be concerned about the lack of expertise of public prosecutors in military matters. The government concluded that public prosecutors could gain the required expertise by practical experience.[55] The government also rejected calls for the appointment of military prosecutors upon the recommendation of two ministries because it contradicted the wider policy of integration.[56] The enactment of specific requirements of expertise or qualifications for the appointment of military prosecutors was rejected for similar reasons.[57] According to the government, this requirement could be realised through the prosecution service's general policy of appointment.[58] The military prosecution service, scholars and military legal practitioners at the court martial and the High Military Court were critical about the lack of attention shown by the government as regards the position of the public prosecution service.[59]

When the task of prosecution was handed over to the public prosecution service, it seemed logical that they should also be responsible for developing policy relevant to military criminal law. However, the government encouraged the public prosecution service to involve the Ministry of Defence and military commanders in this role. The overall implementation of the new legislation was managed by a centralised authority, although many issues at the operational level were divided between responsible authorities (as is the case for civilian criminal law, where deliberation occurs between the public prosecution service, the mayor and the police). The government stressed that effective collaboration between the public prosecution service, the appointed commanders and the Royal Netherlands Marechaussee was important to the new military justice system.[60] It also noted that incidental issues relevant to the military organisation could arise from particular criminal cases. The government encouraged both the public prosecution service and the Ministry of Defence to discuss such issues.[61] In view of the favoured collaboration, the commission charged with preparing the implementation of the new

[55] Parliamentary Proceedings 1987–1988, above n. 54, p. 8. [56] Ibid. [57] Ibid.

[58] Ibid., p. 8.

[59] Van den Boezem, above n. 48; van den Bosch, above n. 14. Basically, their view corresponded with the suggestions made by parliament.

[60] Parliamentary Proceedings 1985–1986, above n. 54, p. 6; Parliamentary Proceedings 1987–1988, above n. 54, p. 8.

[61] Parliamentary Proceedings 1985–1986, above n. 54, p. 19.

Military Criminal Procedure Code advised that a military liaison officer should be attached to the public prosecutor's office in Arnhem.[62]

B Present system

The district public prosecutor's office at the district court Gelderland in Arnhem is charged with supervising the investigation and prosecution of criminal offences committed by members of the Dutch armed forces. That task falls to the Division of Military Affairs, which currently consists of two public prosecutors, three clerks and two legal advisors of the Expertise Centre for Military Criminal Law.[63] The Military Affairs division also includes the Bureau Liaison Officer Armed Forces[64] and a liaison officer of the Royal Netherlands Marechaussee.[65] The public prosecutor may request legal advice from the Centre for Military Criminal Law. The Bureau Liaison officer is the liaison between the public prosecution service and the Ministry of Defence and facilitates the communication between both organisations.[66] The liaison officers of the armed forces assist the public prosecutor on matters of military organisation, operating procedures and the specific military rules and regulations that may be directly relevant to official actions to be taken by the public prosecutor.[67] In appeal cases, the prosecution is dealt with by the Advocate General (Advocaat-Generaal). Both the district public prosecutor and Advocate General handle cases involving offences committed by civilians alongside military cases.[68] In general, the clerks only handle military cases. Military experience is not a requirement for the position of public prosecutor or Advocate

62 J. Demmink, *Rapport van de begeleidingscommissie invoering wet militaire strafrechtspraak*, October 1990, p. 16.

63 This Centre was established in 2007 and is, *inter alia*, responsible for policy making and advising public prosecutors as regards enforcement of military criminal law during military operations. C.A. Hamers et al., 'Opsporing en vervolging in Afghanistan' (2009) 102 *Militair Rechtelijk Tijdschrift*, p. 261. For the position of head of this centre, experience as a military legal advisor is required.

64 The function of liaison officer is fulfilled alternatively by a military lawyer with the rank of lieutenant-colonel (commander or wing commander). The second position in the Bureau is, as a policy rule, fulfilled by an army captain. Both are seconded by the armed forces for a period of three years on average with the district public prosecutor's office in Arnhem. The liaison officer is appointed by the Director of Legal Affairs of the Ministry of Defence after consultation with the Chief Public Prosecutor in Arnhem.

65 This position is held by a captain of the Royal Netherlands Marechaussee.

66 H.C.J.L. Borghouts et al., *Evaluatie toepassing militair strafprocesrecht bij uitzendingen*, 31 August 2006, p. 56.

67 Parliamentary Proceedings, First Chamber, 2009–2010, 31 487, E, p. 2.

68 This is motivated by the small amount of military cases compared to regular cases.

General.[69] The public prosecutors build their expertise by daily practice, attending military legal courses and briefings military units and by visiting units during deployment.[70]

Policy deliberations about criminal procedure for the armed forces are conducted between the public prosecution service, the armed forces and the Royal Netherlands Marechaussee at both the national and regional level.[71] Similar deliberations take place at the start of a military mission abroad, during which the participants focus upon the acquaintance and exchange of information about policy and operating procedures for offences and other events that could occur during deployment.

V Royal Netherlands Marechaussee under different authority

A Past

Until the reforms of 1991, the commanding officer (for example, the commander of an air base or an army brigade) played an important role in criminal investigations. Any report of a criminal offence had to be filed through this commander, who had the ability to determine whether a criminal investigation should be initiated by the Royal Netherlands Marechaussee, a police organisation with military status.[72] A logical consequence of the government's policy that the new military criminal justice system should conform to the general law of civilian criminal procedure was the need to re-arrange the supervision of investigative officers of the Royal Netherlands Marechaussee, as well as the overall authority regarding those investigations. There appeared only one option available to the government: the authority was to be given to the public prosecution service.

When discussing the 1966 note, the government reasoned that the military commander needed some independent authority over criminal investigations and should, like the public prosecutor, be authorised to commence investigations.[73] The government concluded that in cases where proof of alleged criminal offences could be easily found within the military branch itself, the investigation could be performed by military personnel within the military branch concerned. The

[69] J.J.M. van Hoek, *Uitdagingen openbaar ministerie tijdens internationale operaties* (MRT, 2012), p. 137.

[70] Parliamentary Proceedings, Second Chamber, 2003–2004, 29 200 VI, No. 130, p. 2.

[71] Borghouts et al., above n. 66, p. 62; Parliamentary Proceedings, First Chamber, 2010–2011, 31 487, G, p. 31 (*Eindrapport evaluatie aanbevelingen Commissie Borghouts*).

[72] Van den Bosch, above n. 5, p. 51.

[73] Parliamentary Proceedings 1965–1966, above n. 9, p. 20.

government did not deem it necessary to use specialist military officers for such investigations.[74] At the same time as the military criminal justice system was reformed, the Military Criminal Code and the Military Discipline Code were fundamentally changed. One important change was the introduction of a strict separation between military criminal justice and military disciplinary procedure. The government and parliament agreed that commanding officers should not be authorised to handle disciplinary offences that also constituted a criminal offence. As a result, the commanding officers lost their specific responsibilities in military criminal justice.[75]

B Present

The Royal Netherlands Marechaussee was a part of the Royal Netherlands Army until 1998, when it became an autonomous branch of the armed forces. It now exists alongside the other three branches of the armed forces: that is, alongside the Royal Netherlands Army, the Royal Netherlands Air Force and the Royal Netherlands Navy. The Royal Netherlands Marechaussee has separate authority and administration. The Minister of Defence is responsible for the Marechaussee's administration and must ensure that the Marechaussee has all the required resources and expertise. In contrast to the civilian police system, the law provides an exhaustive list of tasks of the Royal Netherlands Marechaussee, one of which is the investigation of criminal offences committed by soldiers (the military police task).[76] Since 1991, the military police task is performed under the supervision of the public prosecution service.[77] Only the public prosecutor is authorised to give orders and instructions to the Royal Netherlands Marechaussee concerning criminal investigations.[78]

The Military Criminal Procedure Code provides that the Royal Netherlands Marechaussee is granted jurisdiction outside the

[74] Ibid., p. 18. This vision was strongly related to the then existing commander's authority to judge minor criminal offences in a disciplinary manner.

[75] Parliamentary Proceedings 1982–1983, above n. 24, p. 3. For a discussion of the role of the commanding officer in the US military justice system see Chapter 6.

[76] Politiewet 2012 [Police Act 2012] (The Netherlands), art. 4. The legislator has allocated eight tasks to the Royal Netherlands Marechaussee. Approximately 10 per cent of its time is spent on military policing.

[77] Politiewet 2012 [Police Act 2012] (The Netherlands), art. 14.

[78] Wetboek van Strafvordering [Criminal Procedure Code] (The Netherlands), art. 148.

Netherlands.[79] Where there are extensive military exercises and operations, a delegation of the Royal Netherlands Marechaussee, consisting of investigative officers and an assistant public prosecutor, supervise military justice in the field. During deployment, that delegation is housed administratively with the Dutch military contingency commando, whilst the legal authority of the public prosecution service remains unchanged.

VI Commentary on developments in military criminal justice

After World War II, there was a need to reorganise the military criminal justice system. The 1966 note initiated the procedure for review but it took twenty-five years for the new military criminal justice system to come into operation. After the new criminal justice system had taken effect, however, the world order changed dramatically. The end of the Cold War caused a substantial reorganisation and reduction in the Dutch armed forces. In addition, the compulsory tour of military duty was suspended in 1996 and the armed forces became a volunteer force. At the same time, their tasks changed. Until 1991, the armed forces were mainly focused on the defence of Dutch territory and the territory of its NATO partners. After 1991, the focus shifted to the execution of military operations outside those territories, particularly through crisis management operations. In the meantime, Dutch forces have been sent to several areas of conflict, including Bosnia-Herzegovina, Kosovo, Iraq, Afghanistan and Mali.

These developments have influenced the practice of military criminal justice. For instance, the number of military criminal cases and the nature of the cases to be tried have changed. The judicial decisions, published in the Dutch military law review, reveal that there has been a reduction in the number of military criminal cases in general, and cases concerning typical military offences in particular.[80] Most cases relate to offences

[79] Importantly, the jurisdiction to enforce is only valid if acknowledged by a valid basis in international law: Wet Militaire Strafrechtspraak [Military Criminal Procedure Code] (The Netherlands), art. 62.

[80] J.S. van Duurling, 'Delictgedrag van militairen – Ontwikkelingen en trends. Niet alles wat telt, is te tellen!' (2012) 105 *Militair Rechtelijk Tijdschrift*, p. 113. Van Duurling estimates that during the period 1999 to 2010, a total of 8000 felonies were tried by the court's military chamber. In 1991, around 850 cases were heard, whilst that number was a modest 561 cases in 2010. On average, 10 per cent of the cases are tried by the multiple-member military chamber and 60 per cent by a single-judge military chamber. The remainder of matters are minor offences. In 2005, there were 122 cases concerning typical military offences. Four years later, this number was merely 76. These numbers are indicative. Van den Heuvel (president of the military chamber at the Court of Appeal) argues that the

against civilian criminal law committed by service members while they are not on active duty and which lack any military quality or connection. These offences have little or no direct bearing on the armed forces.

Based on the foregoing, it could be argued that the appearance of the military member alongside the civilian judges has no added value. The rationale of the military chamber and the military member, however, has not been subject to detailed discussion in the last two decades, although questions about its existence and operation sometimes arise.[81]

However, there has been detailed discussion on the role and expertise of public prosecutors dealing with military cases. When reorganising military criminal justice, parliament noted that the public prosecutor's position was not mentioned in the Bill and was merely hinted at in the Bill's explanatory memorandum.[82] The parliament remarked that 'under

percentage of appeal cases is considerably lower than in civilian cases. He argues that in 2003, 34 cases were set down for a hearing. This number increased to 52 in the year 2004 and decreased to 28 cases in 2006 (van den Heuvel, above n. 37, p. 101).

81 The independence of the Military Chamber of the Court of Appeal was challenged at the ECtHR in *Jaloud* v. *The Netherlands* (ECtHR, Grand Chamber, Application No. 47708/08, 20 November 2014). The applicant argued that the independence of the Military Chamber of the Court of Appeal was tainted by the presence of a serving military officer in its midst. The ECtHR, however, was prepared to accept that the Military Chamber offers guarantees sufficient for the purposes of Article 2 of the ECHR. *Jaloud* v. *The Netherlands* (ECtHR, Grand Chamber, Application No. 47708/08, 20 November 2014) [195] and [196]. The applicant also challenged the independence of the Royal Netherlands Marechaussee because its investigators shared living quarters with army personnel. The ECtHR concluded that this in itself does not affect the independence of the Royal Netherlands Marechaussee unit to the point of impairing the quality of its investigations (see [189]). In October 2014 the Court of Appeal rejected a request to disqualify the military member of the Complaints Chamber in a case seeking criminal prosecution of the commander of the Dutch Battalion at Srebrenica in 1995 and two others (Court of Appeal 23 October 2014:ECLI:NL:GHARL:2014:8063). In 2011 a military member of the court saluted a military suspect in the session room. The suspect was decorated with the Military 'Willems-Orde', the oldest and highest military decoration in the Netherlands, for courage displayed in Afghanistan. One judge stated that the salute was inappropriate and suggested that such behaviour by military justice officials fostered public perceptions that a separate military chamber was no longer justified (H. Hermans, 'Een ongepast saluut' (2011) 5 *Trema*, p. 158). The administration board of the District Court Gelderland in Arnhem was also of the opinion that such a salute was not appropriate in the circumstances, but wider questions about the existence and operation of the military court were not considered (D.A. van Steenbeek, 'Een ongepast saluut: reactie' (2011) 6 *Trema*, p. 232). During an interview with the local press in March 2013, a professor in criminal law at the Radboud University in Nijmegen argued that the small amount of criminal cases concerning military offences justifies the abolition of the military chamber www.omroepgelderland.nl/web/nieuws/gelders-nieuws/2004666/sackers-militaire-rechtbank-is-overbodig.htm.

82 Parliamentary Proceedings 1983–1984, 17 804, No. 8, p. 3.

the new legislation, the prosecution service would play an important role, even more important than currently'.[83] The parliament stated that the authority to make prosecutorial decisions would no longer belong to the armed forces, but to the public prosecution service.[84] The public prosecution service also criticised the Bill as it lacked any safeguarding of military expertise within the prosecution service.[85] The same applies for a committee of experts in military criminal law.[86] Both advocated a separate district public prosecutor's office and involvement of the Ministry of Defence concerning the appointment of public prosecutors.

Concerns about the role of the public prosecutor have proved prophetic as the role of the public prosecutor in military criminal justice was fiercely discussed in 2004 after a marine non-commissioned officer on operations in Iraq was indicted for firing a warning shot in the direction of several people, allegedly killing an Iraqi civilian. The non-commissioned officer was acquitted at first instance and on appeal. The incident triggered debate about the expertise of the public prosecution service. The military chamber of the Court of Appeal remarked that:

> The court acknowledges that the willingness to cooperate has to come from both sides ('it takes two to tango'), but has to conclude to its regret, that in this case, the public prosecution service was apparently unprepared with regard to the question, how to handle a shooting incident like this. This has lead to, especially in the beginning, a far too grave assessment of the case, as mentioned before when the admissibility of the case was discussed. [. . .] In cases such as the one at hand, the result can be that the public prosecution service would deny a soldier the necessary legal backing during his work under difficult circumstances. The public prosecution service will have to develop the required 'situational awareness', just like the soldier sent on a mission to foreign conflict areas.[87]

Shortly after this incident, the parliament expressed concerns about the military expertise of the public prosecution service and connected these concerns to the integration of civil criminal procedure into military justice in 1991.[88] The Minister of Justice asserted that the public prosecution service had sufficient military expertise to handle military criminal cases.[89] Finally, parliament asked the Minister of Justice and the Minister of

[83] Ibid. [84] Ibid. [85] Van den Boezem, above n. 48, pp. 20 and 22.
[86] Van den Bosch, above n. 14, pp. 9–11.
[87] Diede-Jan Dieben and Thom Dieben, *When does War become Crime? Aspects of the Criminal Case against Eric O.* (Nijmegen, Wolf Legal Publishers, 2005), p. 38.
[88] Parliamentary Proceedings, Second Chamber, 2003–2004, 23 432, No. 152.
[89] Parliamentary Proceedings, Second Chamber, 2003–2004, 29 200 VI, No. 130, pp. 2–3.

Defence to evaluate whether the Military Criminal Procedure Code causes any complication when it has to be applied during a military mission or whether additional and/or special facilities were necessary.[90] The ministers created a committee of independent experts (the Borghouts Committee) to examine this issue.[91] The Committee concluded that a sufficient level of military knowledge and expertise was not always present within the public prosecution service. The report of the Borghouts Committee noted that a number of interviewees cited the 2004 Iraq case (discussed above) as an example of a lack of situational awareness within the public prosecution service.[92] The interviewees argued that the public prosecutors in military cases should be members of the military or at least have military experience.[93] The Committee was not in favour of these suggestions, on the basis that military knowledge was more important than military background. Furthermore, the Committee opined that the appointment of a service member on active duty as a public prosecutor would contravene the requirement of independence.[94] The Borghouts Committee reached a middle ground and stressed that the public prosecutor should possess sufficient knowledge of the military organisation and also the operational circumstances in which the armed forces are obliged to perform their duties during a mission abroad.[95] Two experts proposed that a team of specialists should be assigned – consisting of a public prosecutor, a pre-trial examining judge, specialised investigating judges and, if desired, one or more lawyers – to investigate incidents on location in the mission area (a Quick Reaction Team).[96] The Committee rejected this proposal as it would contravene the rules on criminal procedure. It also pointed to the measures taken by the public prosecution service and the Royal Netherlands Marechaussee in relation to obtaining expertise and considered that further measures were not required.[97]

Several years later, parliament again questioned the expertise of the public prosecution service in military operations.[98] This debate was not

[90] Parliamentary Proceedings, Second Chamber, 2004–2005, 29 800 X, No. 51.

[91] Decision to form a Committee for the assessment of the application of military criminal justice in cases concerning military missions, *Gazette* 23 December 2005, No. 250, p. 19.

[92] Borghouts et al., above n. 66, p. 54. [93] Ibid., p. 58. [94] Ibid., p. 59. [95] Ibid.

[96] Ibid., p. 57.

[97] Ibid. For instance, the public prosecution service had decided to establish a centre of expertise on military criminal law (ibid., p. 54). Among other things, the Royal Netherlands Marechaussee had formed a specialised unit for investigations abroad (ibid., p. 53).

[98] Parliamentary Proceedings, Second Chamber, 2008–2009, 31 487, No. 4, p. 4; Parliamentary Proceedings, First Chamber, 2009–2010, 31 487, B and D, pp. 1 and 2.

triggered by a particular case or the procedures of the prosecution service but instead by a Bill introduced by the government based on the Borghouts Committee's recommendation. The Bill was designed to adjust the existing ground for excluding criminal responsibility in the Military Criminal Code in cases of lawful use of force by soldiers and was based on the desire to maximise the soldier's legal certainty in court.[99] Government ministers again argued that the prosecution service had sufficient expertise to 'evaluate the justification of the use of force and violence by military personnel in an autonomic and trustworthy manner'.[100] The parliament recommended that the prosecutor consult a panel of military experts concerning a legal assessment of the use of force.[101] Based on the measures already taken by the public prosecution service and the Royal Netherlands Marechaussee and the fact that criminal procedure already allowed the prosecution service to involve military experts at any stage of the investigation, the government did not adopt this suggestion.[102] The same applies to a Quick Reaction Team, as discussed by the Borghouts Committee, when the parliament recalled the installation of such team during the parliamentary discussion on the aforementioned Bill.[103]

VII Conclusion

In 1991, after a twenty-five-year legislative process, the military judicial order underwent a 'civil swing'. Since that time the military elements in the civilian court have not been the subject of serious debate. The 'civil swing' regarding the prosecution of military cases, on the other hand, has received much attention after the public prosecution service had charged a marine non-commissioned officer for killing an Iraqi civilian. The prosecution service was blamed for a lack of empathy and expertise about military operations. Measures have been taken since and the government has stated on several occasions that these measures guarantee the required expertise of the public prosecution service. The

[99] The motion to amend the Military Criminal Code with regard to the addition of a ground for excluding criminal responsibility regarding justified use of force by military personnel (Parliamentary Proceedings with file number 31 487).

[100] Parliamentary Proceedings, Second Chamber, 2008–2009, 31 487, No. 5, p. 5; Parliamentary Proceedings, First Chamber, 2009–2010, 31 487, C and E, pp. 1–3.

[101] Parliamentary Proceedings, First Chamber, 2009–2010, 31 487, D, p. 1; G.J. Knoops, *Strafuitsluitend militair geweldgebruik binnen gewapende conflicten, nieuwe inzichten en spanningsvelden* (Nederlands Juristenblad, 2008), p. 2405.

[102] Parliamentary Proceedings, First Chamber, 2009–2010, 31 487, E, pp. 1–2.

[103] Parliamentary Proceedings, 2008–2009, above n. 98, p. 4.

association of military lawyers (Militaire Balie), however, remains unconvinced. In November 2011, during the twenty-year jubilee of the review of military criminal justice, those lawyers expressed their continued concerns about the apparent lack of direct affinity with the military organisation.[104]

The organisation of military criminal justice in the Netherlands is characterised by specialisation and expertise. Specialisation was codified when the government installed a military chamber within the civilian court and has gained force by charging one single court – the district and appeal court in Arnhem – with the trial of military criminal justice, to the exclusion of all other courts. In view of the link between the district court and the district public prosecutor, it may be concluded that the specialisation of the public prosecution service is also guaranteed. This specialisation has also been included in the investigation branch, since the parliament has specifically charged the Royal Netherlands Marechaussee with the military police task.

The military member in court will contribute the necessary military expertise. The legislator has reinforced this expertise by requiring that, where possible, the military member assisting in the military chamber must belong to the same branch of the armed services as the military suspect. The public prosecution service has also taken measures to guarantee military expertise, but these measures lack a legislative basis.

[104] P. Reitsma, 'Positie van de verdachte in het militair strafproces' (2012) 105 *Militair Rechtelijk Tijdschrift*, p. 135. The 'Militaire Balie' is a lawyer association specialising in military affairs. Most of the members, if not all, have a background as a soldier and/or a military lawyer.

12

The Israeli military justice system in the context of the Turkel Commission

MICHELLE LESH

I Introduction

The military justice system in Israel is the main body responsible for investigating alleged violations of the laws of war committed by members of the Israel Defense Forces (IDF). Israel's prolonged occupation of Palestinian territory and its recurring hostilities with the Palestinians and neighbouring Arab states contribute to the need for such an active army to be under the regulation of a well-functioning military justice system. In recent years public debate has ensued about the nature and scope of the duty to investigate military incidents by the IDF. This has been a result of international and domestic influences. The most notable international development was the *Goldstone Report*, which was born out of a UN Human Rights Council Fact-Finding Mission into 'Operation Cast Lead', the IDF operation in Gaza between December 2008 and January 2009. Among other things, the report criticised Israel's handling of investigations into that military operation.[1] Also significant are the follow-up UN reports to the *Goldstone Report* – the *Tomuschat Report* and the *McGowan Davis Report*.[2] Domestically, the Israeli military justice

I am grateful for the insightful comments of Roee Ariav, who read an earlier draft of this chapter, and for the helpful comments of the editors of this book, Alison Duxbury and Matthew Groves. The views expressed in this chapter are those of the author and do not reflect the views of any institution or body. All errors remain those of the author.

1 Report of the United Nations Fact-Finding Mission on the Gaza Conflict, *Human Rights in Palestine and Other Occupied Arab Territories*, 12th Sess, UN Doc A/HRC/12/48 (25 September 2009) (*Goldstone Report*). See also, B'Tselem, *Israel's Report to the UN Misstates the Truth* (2010) www.btselem.org/gaza_strip/20100204_israels_report_to_un.

2 *Report of the Committee of independent experts in international humanitarian and human rights law to monitor and assess any domestic, legal or other proceedings undertaken by both the Government of Israel and the Palestinian side, in light of General Assembly resolution 64/245, including the independence, effectiveness, genuineness of these investigations and their conformity with international standards*, 15 Sess, UN Doc A/HRC/15/50 (23 September 2010) (*Tomuschat Report*); *Report of the Committee of independent experts in*

system has come under the review of the Israeli Supreme Court and more significantly by a government-appointed commission of inquiry – the Turkel Commission.[3]

This chapter will review Israel's military justice system through the framework of the findings of the Turkel Commission. Section II will briefly set out the main structure and bodies within the military justice system. Section III will discuss the Turkel Commission and its significance in the context of the future of Israel's military justice system. In setting out Israel's international law obligations to investigate, the Commission provides recommendations on how the current system can better meet those obligations. Section IV will focus on two key findings of the Turkel Commission and their potential impact on the transitional state of military justice in Israel: one is the operational debriefing used in making a decision whether to open an investigation, the other is the responsibilities of the Military Advocate General (MAG) as the head of the military justice system, particularly the role's 'dual hat' in providing legal advice as well as acting as the prosecution. Section V will offer some concluding comments.

II The Israeli system

The legal institution responsible for deterring potential violations of the laws of war committed by the armed forces and for holding soldiers accountable is based almost entirely within the IDF.[4] The Israeli military

international humanitarian and human rights law established pursuant to Council resolution 13/9, 16 Sess, UN Doc A/HRC/16/24 (18 March 2011). It is important to note that in July 2014 the UN Human Rights Council established another commission of inquiry, eventually headed by Justice Mary McGowan Davis, to investigate alleged violations of international law that occurred during hostilities between the Israelis and Palestinians in Gaza in 2014. The work of the fact-finding mission was still ongoing at the time of writing this chapter. It is expected to submit its report to the Human Rights Council in March 2015. See *Ensuring respect for international law in the Occupied Palestinian Territory, including East Jerusalem*, UN Doc A/HRC/RES/S-21/1 (24 July 2014).

[3] See HCJ 9594/03 *B'Tselem and Association for Civil Rights in Israel* v. *Military Advocate General*, Judgment of 21 August 2011 (Hebrew); The Turkel Commission, *The Public Commission to Examine the Maritime Incident of 31 May 2010. Second Report: Israel's Mechanisms for Examining and Investigating Complaints and Claims of Violations of the Laws of Armed Conflict According to International Law* (February 2013) pp. 432–63 www.turkel-committee.gov.il/files/newDoc3/The%20Turkel%20Report%20for%20website.pdf (Turkel Commission Second Report).

[4] There is a certain level of civilian oversight from the Attorney General and the Supreme Court. See Section IV(b) for discussion of the oversight role of the Attorney General. The Supreme Court, sitting as the High Court of Justice, can hear petitions against governmental actions and those of its agencies. See Section 15 of the Basic Law: Judiciary. The Israeli doctrine of standing is very broad and covers individuals who can show that

justice system comprises three main bodies: the Military Advocates General Corps (MAG Corps), the Military Police Criminal Investigation Division (CID) and the courts martial,[5] each of which will be explained briefly.

A MAG Corps

The MAG serves as the commander of the MAG Corps. The Minister of Defence appoints the MAG based on the recommendation of the Chief of Staff and the Military Justice Law sets out the authority of this position.[6] The MAG is the legal advisor to the Chief of Staff and at the same time enforces law and order in the army, mainly through the Military Prosecution Service, with the aid of the CID.[7] The Chief Military Prosecutor (CMP) heads the prosecution arm of the MAG Corps. In 2007 the Military Advocacy for Operational Affairs (MAOA) was established as a prosecutorial unit specialising in cases concerning alleged violations of the laws of war. When the work of the MAOA indicates that a criminal investigation is required, the unit requests that the CID undertakes the necessary investigation.

B CID

The CID carries out criminal investigations.[8] Members of this unit are trained investigators.[9] The CID possesses authority to open investigations into offences committed in the military setting or by any person subject to the jurisdiction of the Military Justice Law.[10] In recent years the CID has dealt with incidents concerning some of Israel's military operations in

conduct by the executive branch denies their legally protected rights, as well as public petitioners, for example NGOs filing petitions on behalf of Palestinians.

5 Much of the debate concerning the military justice system in Israel concerns the investigative process prior to prosecution and therefore the prosecution stage of the investigation will not be explored in this chapter. In addition to courts martial, Israel also has a military courts system in the West Bank. See Sharon Weill, 'The Judicial Arm of the Occupation: Israeli Military Courts in the Occupied Territories' (2007) 29 *International Review of the Red Cross*, p. 395.

6 Military Justice Law 5715 (1955) arts. 178 and 317 (Hebrew).

7 *Position Paper of the Military Advocate General to Turkel Commission* at 1–2 www.turkel-committee.com/content-152-b.html.

8 CID's activity is regulated in the Military Justice Law; General Staff Order 33.0304; Order 5000 of the Chief Military Police Commissioner.

9 Criticism has been raised about the way the CID gathers evidence. The MAG has defended the conduct of the CID by pointing to the unique challenges the unit faces. See Yesh Din, *Alleged Investigation: The Failure of Investigations into Offenses Committed by IDF Soldiers Against Palestinians* (Tel Aviv, Yesh Din, August 2011), pp. 60, 74, 96; *Position Paper of the Military Advocate General to Turkel Commission*, above n. 7, p. 3.

10 Military Justice Law 5715 (1955) art. 256.

Gaza. For the purposes of this analysis, the two most recent operations deserve particular mention: Operation Pillar of Defense and Operation Protective Edge.[11] To date, no incidents arising out of Operation Pillar of Defense have reached the criminal investigation stage of the CID. Pillar of Defense was an operation launched on 14 November 2012 by the IDF in the Gaza Strip. It lasted eight days, until a ceasefire was reached between Israel and Hamas. According to the IDF, it attacked 1500 targets inside the Gaza Strip and Palestinian militant groups fired over 1500 rockets at Israel. Five Israeli civilians were killed from rocket fire.[12] Statistics compiled by B'Tselem (an Israeli human rights organisation) indicate that Israel killed 167 Palestinians, including at least 87 who did not take part in hostilities, 32 of whom were minors.[13] Based on publicly available information, thirteen incidents arising out of Operation Protective Edge reached the CID in the three months following the ceasefire.[14] Protective Edge was the fifty-day armed conflict in the Gaza Strip in the summer of 2014. It is estimated that approximately 2200 Palestinians were killed, at least 40 per cent of them civilians with a large proportion of those civilians being women and children, and thousands of houses were destroyed.[15] Seventy-three were killed on the Israeli side, 67 of whom were soldiers.[16]

[11] The CID also investigated incidents arising from Operation Cast Lead. According to the MAG, 52 investigations were opened, seven of which are still pending. See *Position Paper of the Military Advocate General to Turkel Commission*, above n. 7, Annex 1, pp. 95–101.

[12] *Operation Pillar of Defense: Summary of Events* (22 November 2012) Israel Defense Forces www.idfblog.com/2012/11/22/operation-pillar-of-defense-summary-of-events/.

[13] Shuli Schneiderman (ed.), B'Tselem, *Human Rights Violations during Operation Pillar of Defense: 14–21 November 2012* (May 2013) www.btselem.org/download/201305_pillar_of_defense_operation_eng.pdf.

[14] See Israel's Review by the UN Human Rights Committee, *Response of Colonel Noam Neuman, Head of the International Law Department, Military Advocate General Corps Israel Defense Forces* (20 October 2014) www.youtube.com/watch?v=R94noQ5rAMw; IDF MAG Corps, *Decisions of the IDF Military Advocate General Regarding Exceptional Incidents that Occurred during Operation 'Protective Edge' – Update No. 2* (7 December 2014) www.law.idf.il/163-6958-en/Patzar.aspx.

[15] As of November 2014, B'Tselem had not released final figures because it continues to conduct research into incidents that occurred during Operation Protective Edge. See, B'Tselem, *Initial Figures on Fatalities in Operation Protective Edge* (10 August 2014) www.btselem.org/gaza_strip/20140812_preliminary_data_on_fatalities. See also statement by Executive Director of B'Tselem: 'the harm caused to civilians in Operation Protective Edge was massive. B'Tselem's initial investigation indicates that some 40% of the Palestinians killed in the operation were minors, women, and men over the age of 60. In addition, thousands of homes were destroyed and hundreds of thousands of people were uprooted from their homes.'

[16] Israel Ministry of Foreign Affairs, *Operation Protective Edge: Israel under Fire, IDF Responds* (26 August 2014) http://mfa.gov.il/MFA/ForeignPolicy/Terrorism/Pages/Rise-in-rocket-fire-from-Gaza-3-Jul-2014.aspx.

1 Investigation policy

The MAG provides directives according to the circumstances in which a CID investigation is opened into operational activities in the West Bank and Gaza. These guidelines are known as 'the investigation policy'.[17] The policy has undergone a number of changes over the years in terms of the threshold (or grounds) for triggering an investigation. Until 2000, a CID investigation was opened into almost every case of a Palestinian death (and certain injuries) that occurred in the context of clashes with the IDF in the West Bank or Gaza. A change occurred in the policy with the outbreak of the intifada in September 2000. The MAG stated that because a situation of armed conflict existed, a CID investigation into the death of a Palestinian in the occupied territories was delayed until an 'operational debriefing' conducted by the unit involved in the incident was received by the MAG. The MAG opened an investigation only in circumstances where the information indicated a suspicion that an offence had been committed.[18]

In April 2011, the MAG changed the investigation policy again due to a shift in the nature of the IDF operational activity in the West Bank. According to the new policy the CID must open an investigation into every Palestinian death resulting from incidents involving the IDF, except in situations involving operations of a combat nature. In the latter cases the process of relying on operational debriefs remains in place. What the new policy seemed to be implying – from a legal perspective – is that the situation in the West Bank is generally akin to a law enforcement situation and therefore should be regulated accordingly, except in situations of combat operations where the rules regulating the conduct of hostilities are applicable.[19] The change in policy does not apply to the

[17] General Staff Order 33.0304; Turkel Commission Second Report, above n. 3, pp. 319–20.

[18] *Position Paper of the Military Advocate General to Turkel Commission*, above n. 7, pp. 13–14. For discussion of 'operational debrief', see pp. 9–11.

[19] What triggers the opening of an investigation differs under international humanitarian law (IHL) and international human rights law (IHRL). According to IHL, an investigation must be opened when there is a reasonable suspicion that a war crime has been committed. See Geneva Convention Relative to the Protection of Civilian Persons in Time of War of August 12, 1949, 12 August 1949, in force 21 October 1950, 75 UNTS 287, arts. 146–47; Protocol Additional to the Geneva Conventions of 12 August 1949, and Relating to the Protection of Victims of International Armed Conflicts, 8 June 1977, in force 7 December 1978, 1125 UNTS 3, arts. 86–87 (AP I). According to IHRL, every death and serious injury must be investigated. See International Covenant on Civil and Political Rights, 16 December 1966, in force 23 March 1976, 999 UNTS 171, art. 2. See Turkel Commission Second Report, above n. 3, pp. 52–150.

Gaza Strip, which Israel no longer considers occupied and where the IDF does not conduct law enforcement operations.[20]

It should be noted that the investigation policy as it existed between 2000 and 2011 was challenged in the Supreme Court by human rights organisations in 2003 on the basis that there is a legal obligation to investigate every civilian death, even in times of armed conflict.[21] While the case was still pending, the MAG announced the change in the grounds for opening an investigation. In its judgment, the Supreme Court endorsed the updated investigation policy.[22] According to the statistics of B'Tselem, since April 2011, CID investigations were indeed opened in fifteen of the sixteen cases involving the death of a Palestinian in the West Bank. However, as of August 2013, the MAG had reached a decision in only three of those fifteen cases.[23]

2 Reporting procedure

Incidents involving potential violations of the laws of war reach the MAG through various means. The aggrieved party can lodge a complaint or a human rights organisation can do it on their behalf. Armed forces are also required to report incidents. According to the IDF reporting procedure, an incident involving the death or injury of an uninvolved civilian must be reported within forty-eight hours and a 'preliminary report form' must be submitted to the MAG.[24] In addition, an operational debrief should be prepared by the commander of the unit and sent to the MAG within twenty-one days. The preliminary report is assessed by the MAOA and if it does not give rise to a suspicion that a crime has been committed, the decision to open an investigation is delayed until the debrief is received.[25]

[20] Israel Ministry of Foreign Affairs, *Special Update: Disengagement – August 2005* (15 August 2005) http://mfa.gov.il/MFA/AboutIsrael/History/Pages/Disengagement%20-%20August%202005.aspx. B'Tselem Petition for Order Nisi, available at www.btselem.org/download/hc9594_03_investigations_appeal.pdf.

[21] HCJ 9594/03 *B'Tselem and Association for Civil Rights in Israel* v. *Military Advocate General*, Judgment of 21 August 2011 (Hebrew); B'Tselem Petition for Order Nisi, above n. 20.

[22] HCJ 9594/03 HCJ 9594/03 *B'Tselem and Association for Civil Rights in Israel* v. *Military Advocate General*, Judgment of 21 August 2011 (Hebrew).

[23] B'Tselem, *B'Tselem Position Paper: Turkel Commission Report on Israel's Mechanisms for Investigating Complaints of Violations of International Humanitarian Law* (August 2013) at pp. 6–7, www.btselem.org/download/position_paper_on_turkel_report_eng.pdf.

[24] 'Reporting Procedure for Incidents in which Palestinian Civilians were Injured' in the Orders of the Operations Division in the Operations Department and of the Central Commander's Office (Hebrew).

[25] Turkel Commission Second Report, above n. 3, p. 340.

C *Conclusion*

The military justice system in Israel is structured within the IDF. The MAG, the CMP and CID investigators are all members of the IDF. Civilians are not involved in the investigative process except at an oversight level.

III Turkel Commission

The Turkel Commission – an Israeli government-appointed independent commission of inquiry chaired by retired Supreme Court Justice Jacob Turkel – issued its second and final report in February 2013.[26] The report addresses Israel's mechanisms for investigating violations of international law according to the laws of war.[27] The Commission reviewed Israeli military and civilian mechanisms for investigating behaviour by the IDF, the Israel Police, the Israel Security Agency (ISA), the Israel Prison Service and the civilian echelon, and the compatibility of those accountability structures with Israel's obligations under international law. It is beyond the scope of this chapter to cover the various mechanisms – the focus will be on the report's findings in relation to the IDF. The report is the first major study on the duty to investigate under international law and therefore, in addition to its potential significance for the future face of Israel's military justice system, it contributes to the direction of international legal debate on the scope on the international law obligation to investigate.

The Commission states that 'the examination and investigation mechanisms in Israel for complaints and claims of violations of international humanitarian law and the methods they practice, generally comply with the obligations of the state of Israel under the rules of international law'.[28] Yet, if they are implemented, the eighteen recommendations, set

[26] The other members of the Commission were Professor Shabtai Rosenne (until his death in September 2010), IDF General (Ret.) Amos Horev, Ambassador Reuven Merhav and Professor Miguel Deutch. There were also international observers: Lord David Trimble, Brigadier-General (Ret.) Kenneth Watkin (until May 2011) and Professor Tim McCormack (from June 2011).

[27] Resolution No. 1796 of the 32nd Government, Appointment of an Independent Public Commission, Chaired by Supreme Court Justice (ret.) Jacob Turkel, to Examine the Maritime Incident of 31 May 2010 (6 June 2010), at [5]. The Turkel Commission's first report was concerned with the maritime incident in which the IDF intercepted the Mavi Marmara, a flotilla sailing from Turkey for Gaza. See The Turkel Commission, *The Public Commission to Examine the Maritime Incident of 31 May 2010. Report: Part One* (January 2011) www.turkelcommittee.com/files/wordocs//8707200211english.pdf.

[28] Turkel Commission Second Report, above n. 3, p. 49.

out in the report, will create dramatic changes to the way in which investigations are conducted in the military justice system. It can therefore be inferred that the Commission took a generous approach to interpreting Israel's obligations under the international law.

A Legal obligation to investigate

In setting out Israel's obligations to investigate violations of the laws of war, the Commission found that 'the threshold required for an investigation is where a credible accusation is made or a reasonable suspicion arises that a war crime has been committed'.[29] Because Israel does not have comprehensive legislation addressing war crimes, the Commission recommended the value of incorporating international norms relating to war crimes into Israeli domestic legislation.[30] Significantly, it also emphasised that accountability for committing war crimes can extend up the chain of command to commanders and superiors who have a duty to prevent their subordinates from committing such violations.[31]

The Commission further developed the threshold for opening an investigation by explaining that the obligation to investigate the death of an individual will depend on the legal regime governing the specific activity, for example the laws of war or international human rights law. The death of an uninvolved civilian during armed conflict does not automatically give rise to an immediate duty to investigate because the principle of proportionality may permit collateral damage. However, in a situation of law enforcement the killing (or serious injury) of an individual by security forces requires an immediate duty to investigate because of the *prima facie* suspicion of criminality.[32] The report's approach to the threshold for opening an investigation is noteworthy when reflecting upon the MAG's investigation policy and the changes it has undergone. The Turkel Commission endorsed the investigation policy;[33] however, the subtext of the report (which can be derived from a combination of the recommendations it presented and its legal analysis) indicates that the Commission's position goes beyond the existing policy.[34]

[29] Ibid., p. 100. [30] Ibid., pp. 273–74; 362–66. [31] Ibid., pp. 366–69.
[32] Ibid., pp. 101–3. [33] Ibid., p. 377.
[34] For example, limiting the function of the debrief and emphasising that the investigative process is not only relevant in situations of active combat (Gaza) but also in situations of relative calm (West Bank).

B 'Effective investigation'

The Commission outlined the legal standards for the conduct of an investigation under the framework 'effective investigation'.[35] The general principles that have been accepted as comprising an 'effective investigation' are independence, impartiality, thoroughness and effectiveness, and promptness.[36] The Commission also identifies a fifth – transparency. The Commission's approach to the interaction of the normative frameworks is also reflected in its analysis of the general principles. The Commission sees 'no fundamental difference' between the four principles for conducting an effective investigation in a law enforcement context and an armed conflict context. It acknowledges, however, that the 'precise content' of the principles may differ in their application due to sensitivity to the surrounding context and circumstances.[37] The Commission drew on its legal analysis for an 'effective investigation' in many of its recommendations.

1 Recommendations

A credible investigation demands independence. The Commission found that a military justice system can be sufficiently independent to undertake an investigation. Nonetheless, it attempted to protect independence by addressing safeguards for the MAG's position, the head of this system.[38] It recommended that the MAG's professional subordination to the Attorney General should be institutionalised; the MAG should be appointed by the Minister of Defense based on the recommendation of a professional committee of which the Attorney General is a member or chair; and the MAG's tenure and rank should be fixed.[39]

Central to carrying out an investigation effectively is the reporting duty, including adequately documenting the scene of the incident.[40] The

[35] Turkel Commission Second Report, above n. 3, pp. 112–18; Judgment, *Halilović* (IT-01-48-T), Trial Chamber, 16 November 2005, at [97]–[98].

[36] See Basic Principles and Guidelines on the Right to a Remedy and Reparation for Victims of Gross Violations of International Human Rights Law and Serious Violations of International Humanitarian Law, 16th Sess, UN Doc A/RES/60/147 (21 March 2006); *Goldstone Report*, above n. 1, at [1814]; *Tomuschat Report*, above n. 2, at [30]; Michael N. Schmitt, 'Investigating Violations of International Law in Armed Conflict' (2011) 2 *Harvard National Security Journal*, p. 31, at 83; Amichai Cohen and Yuval Shany, 'Beyond the Grave Breaches Regime: The Duty to Investigate Alleged Violations of International Law Governing Armed Conflict' (2011) 14 *Yearbook of International Humanitarian Law*, p. 37, at 60.

[37] Turkel Commission Second Report, above n. 3, p. 115. [38] Ibid., pp. 123–25.

[39] Ibid., pp. 391–92. [40] Ibid., pp. 374–75.

Commission recommended that the reporting procedure be incorporated into Orders and adopted in all IDF units because in practice it is not being implemented.[41] Other recommendations which would improve the effectiveness of investigations include establishing a special department for the CID consisting of police officers trained in laws of war, including investigators fluent in Arabic and locating military bases in the areas where the incidents under investigation took place.[42]

The duration for processing an investigation must be prompt and efficient. IDF investigations have been criticised for being unjustifiably delayed at various stages of the investigative process.[43] The Commission was critical of the fact that often the decision to open an investigation is not immediate. It recommended that time frames be set for both the MAG's decision on whether to open an investigation and the duration of an investigation, in order to improve the investigative process.[44]

In relation to the Commission's position that transparency is an applicable principle for an 'effective investigation', it recommends a strict documentation procedure for the relevant files and that the law regulating the rights of victims to access information about a criminal proceeding apply to all investigative mechanisms covering law enforcement incidents.[45] The emphasis the Turkel Report places on transparency is in line with a number of UN reports submitted to the General Assembly only months after the Turkel Commission published its report.[46] In this context the UN

[41] Ibid., pp. 372–75. The [HCJ *Abu Rahma* case involved the investigation into the circumstances of the death of a Palestinian who was evacuated from a protest at Bil'in and died the following day at Ramallah hospital. Although the death occurred before the Turkel report was submitted (and before the change to the Investigation Policy in 2011), the Court noted the relevance of the report. It is therefore disappointing that it did not take the opportunity to emphasise, *inter alia*, the importance of the reporting procedures in the investigative process, as set out in the Turkel report, given that it was due to poor documentation of the incident that the circumstances surrounding Abu Rahma's death could not be ascertained. The Court accepted the Respondent's position that there was no reasonable suspicion of a criminal offence. See HCJ 6547/11 *Abu Rahma* v. *the MAG* (Hebrew).

[42] Turkel Commission Second Report, above n. 3, p. 397. See also Yesh Din, above n. 9, pp. 10, 20.

[43] B'Tselem, *B'Tselem Position Paper*, above n. 23, p. 6.

[44] Turkel Commission Second Report, above n. 3 pp. 385–86; 399.

[45] Ibid., pp. 399–400.

[46] *Promotion and Protection of Human Rights and Fundamental Freedoms while Countering Terrorism* (Interim Report), 68th Sess, UN Doc A/68/389 (18 September 2013) at 44–45 www.lawfareblog.com/wp-content/uploads/2013/10/Emmerson-Report.pdf; Christof Heyns, *Report of the Special Rapporteur on Extrajudicial, Summary or Arbitrary Executions*, 68th Sess, UN Doc A/68/382 (13 September 2013) at [97].

Special Rapporteur on extrajudicial, summary or arbitrary executions also noted the importance of victims' right to access information, but extended this right to continue in situations of armed conflict.[47]

C Conclusions on 'effective investigation'

The recommendations of the Turkel Commission promote ways in which an 'effective investigation' can be conducted. If Israel were to implement these recommendations it would involve significant changes to the way in which investigations are conducted within the military justice system. The Commission characterises the recommendations as 'best practice', and as recommending merely 'optimal improvements',[48] that would enable the current system to meet fully its obligations under international law. However, the potentially deep and far-reaching effect of these recommendations invites the question as to whether the current arrangements are more seriously deficient in meeting the international law obligations bestowed upon a state than such a characterisation would suggest.

The prime minister, Mr Benjamin Netanyahu, said he welcomed the Turkel report when it was presented to him in February 2013.[49] In January 2014 the government appointed an implementation team headed by Dr Joseph Ciechanover. At the time of writing this chapter, the implementation team continues its work and it is expected to submit its recommendations to the prime minister in early 2015.[50]

IV Two key findings of the Turkel Commission

Two findings of the Turkel Commission warrant particular attention. The first is the recommendation concerning the function of the

[47] Heyns, above n. 46, at [100]. [48] Turkel Commission Second Report, above n. 3, p. 50.

[49] Israel Ministry of Foreign Affairs, *PM Netanyahu Receives Second Half of Turkel Commission Report* (6 February 2013) http://mfa.gov.il/MFA/PressRoom/2013/Pages/PM-Netanyahu-Turkel-Commission-Report-6-Feb-2013.aspx.

[50] Decision number 1143 of the government (5 January 2014) www.pmo.gov.il/SECRETARY/GOVDECISIONS/pages/default.aspx?PN=1 (Hebrew). To date, of the eighteen recommendations, two of the most significant have been implemented (Recommendations 5 and 15). In June 2013, it was reported in the press that one of the harshest recommendations of the report (concerning the Israel Security Agency) was implemented. Barak Ravid 'Former Shin Bet Head: All investigations should be videotaped', Haaretz, (8 February 2013) www.haaretz.com/news/national/former-shin-bet-head-all-interrogations-should-be-videotaped.premium-1.502205; Turkel Commission Second Report, above n. 3, pp. 413–17. On the implementation of the Fact-Finding Assessment recommendation, see Section IV(a) and (a)(2) of this chapter.

operational debrief in conducting investigations. The second is the recommendation concerning the dual hat of the MAG.

A Limiting the operational debrief

An operational debriefing is a key 'organizational learning tool' of the IDF, which is aimed at improving the function of the military units.[51] Generally, a person in the chain of command of the unit involved in the operation conducts the debrief. The legal status of the debrief is regulated by the Military Justice Law and the rules are intended to effectively achieve its purpose of factually assessing the incident in order to draw operational lessons. The debrief is classified and the standard rules of evidence do not apply.[52] As noted earlier in the discussion of the investigation policy, for incidents that occur in the context of hostilities, it is one of the mechanisms relied on within the IDF when deciding whether to open a criminal investigation into alleged violations of the laws of war.

Critics of the way in which operational debriefs are utilised in investigations point out that the primary purpose of this operational tool is to learn lessons and it is therefore misguided to rely on it to determine individual criminal responsibility. This is because the debrief in itself hampers the possibility of conducting an investigation effectively. In practice there are long delays between the debrief and the investigation and this impacts on the quality of evidence.[53] The fundamental criticism is that the debrief is internal and it is not independent because it is conducted within the same chain of command as the suspects involved in the incident. The unit that is implicated in the alleged violation also reviews the violation.[54]

In his position paper to the Turkel Commission, the then MAG defended the function of the operational debrief in the investigative process. He claimed that, in part, the rules of the debrief contribute to its value for a criminal investigation:

[51] *Position Paper of the Military Advocate General to Turkel Commission*, above n. 7, pp. 15–16.

[52] Military Justice Law 5715 (1955) art. 539A.

[53] Turkel Commission Second Report, above n. 3, p. 339. See also Yesh Din, above n. 9, p. 9.

[54] Cohen and Shany, above n. 36, at 70–71. Yesh Din, above n. 9, p. 9. FIDH, 'Shielded from Accountability: Israel's Willingness to Investigate and Prosecute International Crimes' (2012), p. 9 www.fidh.org/en/north-africa-middle-east/israel-occupied-palestinian-territories/Shielded-from-accountability.

> the implementation of the rules [set out in the Military Justice Law] transforms the debriefing into a first rate tool for rapidly clarifying the facts and circumstances of operational incidents, and hence its vast importance for examining claims regarding legal violations that took place in their course.[55]

Using testimonies submitted to the Commission by human rights organisations, government and military representatives and academics, the Turkel Report outlined the debate over the use of the operational debriefing as a tool to decide whether to open an investigation.[56]

The Turkel Commission arrived at the conclusion that the operational debrief, in its current form, does not adhere to the principle of independence and should be limited to its operational function. It noted that in other countries surveyed in the Report, the operational debrief is not utilised in this manner.[57] The Commission recommended that a 'fact-finding assessment' be established in its place to ensure that the initial information about an alleged violation is gathered by a special team outside the chain of command rather than by the commander of the unit whose activity is under consideration.[58] The 'fact-finding' assessment is a mechanism created by the Commission for situations where more information is required to establish whether there is a reasonable suspicion of criminal activity within a specified time frame.

The government has implemented the proposal to limit the debrief – one of the most significant recommendations made by the Commission (Recommendation 5). A move away from reliance on the debrief by the MAG Corps became apparent in the investigative process into incidents that occurred during Operation Pillar of Defense. However, it was in the midst of the latest round of hostilities, Operation Protective Edge, that Israel officially announced that it had established a permanent fact-finding assessment mechanism in accordance with the Turkel Commission recommendation, whose function essentially replaces the operational debriefing. A brief overview of the use (or lack thereof) of the operational briefing in these two IDF operations in Gaza offers an insight into the development of the Israeli investigative system and the implementation of the Turkel Commission's Recommendation 5.

[55] *Position Paper of the Military Advocate General to Turkel Commission*, above n. 7, p. 16.

[56] Turkel Commission Second Report, above n. 3, pp. 380–82.

[57] Ibid., 152–264.

[58] Ibid., pp. 382–83.

1 Operation Pillar of Defense

The MAG Corps approach to investigations into incidents that occurred in Operation Pillar of Defense demonstrates that the IDF did not wait until the publication of the Turkel report to establish the relevant mechanisms to investigate the November 2012 operation. In April 2013, the MAG publicly issued an update on the investigative process. The document stated that in relation to the eighty-seven incidents that were cited as having occurred during Operation Pillar of Defense, it found no basis to open criminal investigations into approximately sixty-five incidents. Moreover, with respect to fifteen incidents, additional information was required in order to make a decision whether to open an investigation.[59] The document stated:

> The MAG Corps received and examined complaints alleging criminal offences. In addition, the IDF Chief of General Staff appointed a Special General Staff Commission, headed by Major-General Noam Tibon, and which included additional operations staff ('Commission'). The Commission collected command investigations that were relevant to the incidents examined, as well as raw intelligence and operational materials (including visual documentation of the airstrikes, to the degree that such existed), and also conducted supplemental inquiries. All of the materials and findings were transferred to the Military Prosecution, which reviewed them in order to check whether suspicions arose regarding the commission of criminal offenses in any of the incidents reviewed.[60]

It appears from this statement that the operational debrief was not relied on to make the decision to open an investigation. Rather some kind of 'preliminary examination' was carried out by 'a Special General Staff Commission'. This seems very much like the 'fact-finding assessment' and 'fact-finding assessment team' articulated by the Commission.

Nonetheless, the decision not to open an investigation into a single incident that occurred during Pillar of Defense (that is, the decision that the *threshold of reasonable suspicion of criminality* had not been met) was criticised by the UN Secretary General. He claimed that the MAG failed to provide sufficient reasons for why criminal investigations into incidents were not opened even though the UN's fieldwork led it to conclude that violations had occurred.[61] Presumably the IDF response to this

[59] IDF, *The Examination of Alleged Misconduct during Operation 'Pillar of Defense' – An Update*, www.law.idf.il/SIP_STORAGE/files/4/1364.pdf.

[60] Ibid.

[61] Report of the Secretary-General, *Israeli Practices Affecting the Human Rights of the Palestinian People in the Occupied Palestinian Territory, Including East Jerusalem*, 68th Sess, UN Doc A/68/502 (4 October 2013) at [31].

criticism relating to transparency would be that it would involve divulging classified information about the value of the target.[62] If the MAG investigative process into Pillar of Defense can be compared to the Turkel Commission's fact-finding assessment, then the principle of transparency would not in fact apply. The Commission briefly touches on how to conduct a fact-finding assessment effectively and references some of the general principles, but transparency is not included. It emphasises that a fact-finding assessment must be conducted according to its purpose, which is to collect relevant information about the alleged incident that facilitates rather than hinders a subsequent investigation.[63] It is worth noting that the UN Special Rapporteur on counter-terrorism and human rights welcomed the Turkel Commission's fact-finding assessment and expanded the Commission's approach to include the application of the principle of transparency to this preliminary investigation.[64]

The laws of war permit collateral damage in certain circumstances, and conducting investigations is timely and costly and should not be undertaken unnecessarily. Nonetheless, and irrespective of whether the MAG is required to provide public reasoning for why a decision was made not to open an investigation, there is reason to be uneasy about the fact that in those sixty-five cases not a single investigation was opened in an operation where civilian casualties occurred. The reason for unease is compounded by the growing intolerance amongst the public for civilian casualties in war and the increasing expectation that individual members of the military and also relevant members of the 'civilian echelon', such as the minister of defence and perhaps even the prime minister can, and sometimes should, be held accountable for acts committed during war.

Operation Pillar of Defense was largely an air operation involving pinpoint targeting strikes in the Gaza Strip, an area densely populated by civilians. The incidents under consideration in the MAG's update generally relate to whether there were violations of the principles of distinction and proportionality and whether adequate precautions in attack were taken.[65] For example, in a case involving the death of ten

[62] See *Position Paper of the Military Advocate General to Turkel Commission*, above n. 7, Annex I.

[63] Ibid., pp. 147–48, at [109]–[112].

[64] Emmerson, above n. 46, at [45]; *Promotion and Protection of Human Rights and Fundamental Freedoms while Countering Terrorism*, 25th Sess, UN Doc A/HRC/25/59 (10 March 2014) at 23.

[65] Protocol Additional to the Geneva Conventions of 12 August 1949, and Relating to the Protection of Victims of International Armed Conflicts, 8 June 1977, in force 7 December 1978, 1125 UNTS 3, art. 57 (1). See also art. 57(2).

members of the same family (the Al-Dalou family), the MAG concluded that the 'operations staff had not foreseen that as a result of the attack, collateral damage would be caused to the uninvolved civilians to the extent alleged'.[66] This is consistent with the legal test under the laws of war, involving the weighing of the expected damage caused against the anticipated military advantage gained. The principle of proportionality focuses on what the attacker knew before the attack in assessing the excessiveness of incidental death or injury to civilians expected.[67] The main conclusion that the MAG's update draws about the operation as a whole also relates to proportionality. It concludes that 'a considerable emphasis was put on minimizing collateral damage to uninvolved civilians and civilian property, beyond the requirements of the Law of Armed Conflict'.[68] It is worth noting that a 2013 report by the UN Special Rapporteur on counter-terrorism and human rights differentiated the Israeli practice of invoking the principle of proportionality to justify civilian casualties, from the practice of the United Kingdom and the United States. The latter countries do not authorise aerial strikes even if civilian casualties would be rendered proportionate because of high-value military targets.[69]

2 Operation protective edge

On 10 September 2014, shortly following Operation Protective Edge, the IDF officially announced that it had established a permanent Fact-Finding Assessment (FFA) mechanism as part of the process of implementing the Turkel report's recommendations.[70] There are six FFA teams headed by a senior officer with the rank of Major General. In accordance with the Turkel Commission's recommendation, the members of the teams are outside the chain of command and have relevant legal, operational and investigative expertise.[71]

The MAG Corps has explained that the task of the FFA teams is to collect information in order to determine the facts with respect to 'exceptional incidents' that occurred during Operation Protective Edge. Exceptional incidents are those incidents where the MAG has

[66] IDF above n. 59. [67] AP I, arts. 51(4), (5)(b). [68] Ibid.

[69] Emmerson, above n. 46, at [75].

[70] IDF MAG Corps, *Operation Protective Edge: Examinations and Investigations* (10 September 2014) www.mag.idf.il/261-6858-en/Patzar.aspx.

[71] Each team is headed by a senior IDF officer (in active service or in the IDF reserves), with a rank ranging from Colonel to Major General, with the teams being comprised primarily of high-ranking IDF reservist officers.

determined that additional information is required to determine whether there is a reasonable suspicion that a violation of the law has occurred, which would justify a criminal investigation. The aim is to provide the MAG with as much information as possible in order to decide whether to open a criminal investigation into the matter. It is also intended to provide information that would prevent or significantly reduce exceptional incidents in the future.

As of December 2014, more than one hundred exceptional incidents occurring during Protective Edge have been referred to the FFA mechanism for assessment. Such incidents include events allegedly resulting in significant and unanticipated civilian harm and military activities allegedly resulting in damage to declared UN facilities. In the three months following the ceasefire, the FFA mechanism had completed its work in relation to fifty incidents, all of which have been referred to the MAG for decision. The MAG closed nine of these incidents; returned over twenty incidents back to the FFA mechanism for further assessment; and ordered criminal investigations into five of the incidents. The remaining incidents are pending decision. Allegations where there was a *prima facie* suspicion of criminal responsibility were referred directly by the MAG for a criminal investigation and were not examined by the FFA mechanism. To date the MAG has ordered the immediate opening of criminal investigation into eight incidents.[72]

The establishment of the permanent FFA mechanism is a welcome development. The speed at which the teams are conducting their investigative work following Protective Edge indicates that the IDF is taking serious heed of the Turkel report's recommendations concerning the importance of promptness in carrying out investigations effectively. As noted in the above discussion of the investigative process into Pillar of Defense, transparency is not required by the Turkel Commission's FFA recommendation. In this regard, statements provided to the FFA teams and any materials that they may produce are privileged under the law. The MAG Corps has stated that, in order to ensure transparency, the MAG's decisions are publicised periodically and updates are found on the MAG's website (in English and Hebrew). To date updates have been published relating to nineteen incidents.[73] This is unlikely to satisfy the concerns of those who promote the need for full transparency in such

[72] See above n. 14; IDF MAG Corps, above n. 70; IDF MAG Corps, *Operation Protective Edge: Update re Individual Incidents*.

[73] IDF MAG Corps, above n. 14.

preliminary investigations, for example the Special Rapporteur on counter-terrorism and human rights.

There were dramatic changes to the investigative process into Protective Edge. The operational debrief has now been replaced by an FFA mechanism, demonstrating full implementation of the Turkel Commission recommendation on this matter. However, in order to provide a complete picture of the debate concerning accountability into Protective Edge, two significant factors require attention. The first is the response of two leading Israeli human rights organisations: B'Tselem and Yesh Din. They announced that they will stop cooperating with the IDF by providing material into the incidents that occurred during Protective Edge because past experience indicates that the IDF is not serious about accountability.[74] This is a serious move considering the strong reliance by the military on the information gathered by the human rights organisations into incidents that involve alleged violations. While there is merit to the claim that the NGOs should have given the IDF the benefit of time to see whether the changes in fact made a difference to accountability, one needs to consider the NGOs' decision in the context of the second relevant factor in the debate concerning accountability into Protective Edge. That second factor is the high number of civilian casualties and damage to civilian property.

The international community and the Israeli human rights community expressed indignation at the scale of Israel's response to rocket attacks. It is estimated that civilians amounted to at least 40 per cent of the Palestinian casualties during Operation Protective Edge.[75] B'Tselem claims that previous IDF inquiries after Operations Cast Lead and Pillar of Defense were systematically inadequate and that there is no reason to believe that the inquiry into Operation Protective Edge would be sufficiently different even if the Turkel recommendations were implemented. For that reason the human rights organisations decided that they would no longer be party to inquiries by an army that they felt was not seriously

74 B'Tselem, *Israeli Human Rights Organizations B'Tselem and Yesh Din: Israel is Unwilling to Investigate Harm Caused to Palestinians* (2 September 2014) www.btselem.org/press_releases/20140905_failure_to_investigate; B'Tselem, *Letter to Lt. Col. Ronen Hirsch* (4 September 2014) www.btselem.org/download/201400904_15390_letter_to_mag_corps_regarding_protective_edge_investiations_eng.pdf.

75 A number of human rights organisations are still conducting fieldwork and have not released final figures on the fatalities during Operation Protective Edge. According to B'Tselem, by 10 August 2014 at least 1767 Palestinians were killed, including 431 minors (one minor participated in hostilities), 200 women (under age 60), and 85 persons aged 60 and over. See B'Tselem, *Initial Figures*, above n. 15.

respecting its international law obligations and holding to account those responsible for this failure. The current number of thirteen criminal investigations that were opened into incidents where there was a reasonable suspicion that alleged violations occurred makes the investigative efforts seem less than impressive.[76]

Until the investigative process is complete, it is too early to make any judgment on whether that process was adequate in the light of obligations imposed by international law. However, based on figures alone, it appears that the FFA mechanism is replacing the function of criminal investigations.[77] This is not necessarily a problem if it achieves the level of accountability required by international law. When the number of civilians killed is compared to the number of incidents that the IDF found warranted a reasonable suspicion that there had been a violation of international law, the unease expressed in the earlier discussion concerning the figures for Pillar of Defense remains. Underlying this unease is the IDF's interpretation of the principle of proportionality, which ultimately guides their conception of accountability.

B Dual hat of the MAG

Applications of the principle of proportionality are controversial and there are arguments over whether there are intrinsic tensions that make such controversy inevitable. But in the case of the Israeli military justice system and the decisions of the MAG in terms of investigations into Operation Pillar of Defense, the difficulties inherent in the concept of proportionality are heightened because of the way in which the system is structured. The 'dual hat' of the MAG as head of the military prosecution system and legal advisor to the military authorities is especially problematic. The MAG's joint prosecutorial and advisory responsibilities have created the perception of partiality, as expressed, for example, in criticisms of investigations conducted by the IDF in the UN Tomuschat report. The follow-up report concluded that:

> [T]he dual role of the Military Advocate General to provide legal advice to IDF with respect to the planning and execution of 'Operation Cast Lead' and to conduct all prosecutions of alleged misconduct by IDF soldiers

[76] The number of thirteen investigations is based on publicly available information provided by the MAG Corps in December 2014, three months following the end of the Operation. It should be kept in mind that this is a figure from the beginning of the investigative process and the number of criminal investigations opened will likely increase.

[77] In Operation Cast Lead fifty-two criminal investigations were opened.

> during the operations in Gaza raises a conflict of interest, given the Fact-Finding Mission's allegation that those who designed, planned, ordered and oversaw the operation were complicit in IHL and IHRL violations. This bears on whether the military advocate general can be truly impartial – and, equally important, be seen to be truly impartial – in investigating these serious allegations.[78]

The MAG responded to this criticism directly in his submission to the Turkel Report and defended the dual hat of the MAG with respect to the investigations undertaken for Operation Cast Lead.[79] The MAG claimed that it created no conflict of interest and justified its legitimacy by comparing its situation to the position of the Attorney General, who similarly holds the dual functions of advice and prosecution.[80] It should be noted that the role of the Attorney General is different in Israel than in common law countries such as the United Kingdom or Australia, where the individual is an elected member of the Cabinet. In Israel the Attorney General is appointed independently by the government and combines prosecutorial and advisory functions. The Attorney General provides the main legal advice to the government and also represents the government and state authorities before the courts. The Turkel report accepted the MAG's position (and reasoning) and decided against disbanding the dual hat of the MAG, but instead recommended that safeguards be put in place, including a process of appeals of the MAG's decisions to the Attorney General.[81] In doing so, the Turkel Commission endorsed (and even strengthened) the Attorney General model because in addition to this specific recommendation, the Commission's main approach to addressing civilian oversight was to strengthen the position of the Attorney General.[82] This will not satisfy critics (of either the MAG or Attorney General). Such critics believe, first, that the dual hat function allows the (unelected) individual involved in the action to review that action and, second, that the effectiveness of these safeguards depends on a

78 *Tomuschat Report*, above n. 2, at [91].

79 *Position Paper of the Military Advocate General to Turkel Commission*, above n. 7, Annex I.

80 Ibid., pp. 74–76.

81 Ibid., pp. 392–96. It also recommended strengthening the status and independence of the Chief Prosecutor, which reduces the MAG's prosecutorial role.

82 See Commission's recommendations about the safeguards for the independence of the MAG discussed in Part III. Another way the Commission promoted civilian involvement was, for example, the recommendation to create an International Law Department in the Ministry of Justice, which will aid the Attorney General's oversight of the MAG's decisions. Turkel Commission Second Report, above n. 3, pp. 401–3, 408, 409.

political and civic culture that respects the independence of judicial processes, military and civilian. Doubt about both are strong amongst Israeli human rights organisations.

C *Conclusion on key recommendations*

The investigative process into Pillar of Defense points to a cautious approach by the IDF and the beginnings of their shift away from relying on the operational debrief. The initial stages of the investigative process into Protective Edge revealed a full implementation of the Turkel Commission recommendation on the FFA mechanism which replaced the operational debriefing. This is at least in part due to criticism of the IDF following Cast Lead as well as Israeli anxiety about potential prosecution before the International Criminal Court.[83] The Israeli justice system is attempting to improve its accountability mechanisms. The Turkel report has played a role in this effort. In the light of the rising number of civilian casualties in Israeli operations in Gaza, the low number of criminal investigations opened (Pillar of Defense: zero out of sixty-five cases; Protective Edge: thirteen out of one hundred cases) suggests that problems remain. Although these problems are in part due to the subjective nature of the principle of proportionality, they are in this case seriously compounded by the dual hat of the MAG.

V Concluding comments

The Israeli military justice system is in a state of transition because there is an expectation, both internationally and domestically, that the system is seriously contemplating, and is in the process of implementing, changes in response to scrutiny it has received in recent years. The Turkel Commission's report is the most substantial of those reviews. If all of its recommendations are implemented, dramatic improvements

[83] Israel is not a party to the Rome Statute. In January 2009, Palestine accepted the jurisdiction of the Court according to Article 12(3) of the Statute. In April 2012, the then Prosecutor stated that the Court only had jurisdiction over states. He pointed to determinations of the General Assembly as a guide to the existence of statehood. In November 2012, the General Assembly granted Palestine the status of non-member observer state within the UN framework (see *Status of Palestine in the United Nations*, 67th Sess, UN Doc A/Res/67/19 (4 December 2012)). Subsequent to the completion of this chapter, in January 2015, following the Government of Palestine's accession to the Rome Statute, the ICC Prosecutor opened a preliminary investigation into the situation in Palestine.

would be made to the way investigations are conducted. The recommendations do not, however, attempt to make any significant changes to the way in which the military justice system is structured. The system remains entrenched in the IDF and although civilian oversight would be slightly strengthened by the Turkel recommendations, no additional civilian mechanisms would be introduced to the system. The most fundamental aspect of the military justice system that will remain the same is the dual hat of the MAG. Therefore, the recommendations of the Turkel Commission are generally directed at operational rather than structural aspects of the investigative process.

One of the most important contributions of the Turkel report is its attempt to clarify the international law obligation to investigate. It makes clear that the standards for investigation are independence, impartiality, effectiveness and thoroughness, promptness, and transparency. Whether a state's military justice system is entirely within the military or entirely civilianised, it must adhere to these standards. The standards, however, lack meaning unless they are interpreted in good faith and with a preparedness to be held to account.

13

A threatened existence – the operation and adaptation of military discipline in Australia

PAUL CRONAN

I Introduction

The introduction of Australia's current military discipline system on 3 July 1985 ushered in a modern code of discipline common to the Navy, Army and Air Force.[1] The Defence Force Discipline Act 1982 (Cth) (DFDA) replaced three separate disciplinary systems peculiar to each service, which had been complex and archaic.[2] Yet, at various times since the commencement of the DFDA, the Australian Defence Force's (ADF) military discipline system has been subject to a number of constitutional challenges in Australia's highest court which threatened to drastically curtail its operation. In addition, modifications have been made to adapt its structures to anticipate emerging legal norms and satisfy domestic political and public expectations. This chapter outlines the operation of Australia's military discipline system and considers the basis and consequences of the many legal challenges made to its existence. It also considers the key adaptations, both successful and unsuccessful, made to its structures for the trial of serious service offences.

The views expressed in this article are those of the author alone and do not necessarily represent the views of the Australian Government, the Australian Defence Force or the Royal Australian Air Force. I would like to thank Colonel Jim Waddell for his assistance in researching the historical content of this chapter.

[1] Although the DFDA was passed in 1982, the operative parts commenced on 3 July 1985.

[2] For the Navy: the Naval Discipline Act 1957 (UK), the Queen's Regulations and Admiralty Instructions as in force on 6 November 1964, the Naval Defence Act 1910, the Defence Act 1903 (Cth) and the Naval Forces Regulations. For the Army: the Army Act 1881 (United Kingdom), Rules of Procedure 1947 (United Kingdom) as in force on 29 October 1956, the Defence Act 1903 (Cth) and Australian Military Regulations. For the Air Force: the Air Force Act (United Kingdom) as in force on 15 December 1939, Rules of Procedure 1933 (United Kingdom) as in force on 31 December 1956, the King's Regulations and Air Council Instructions for the Royal Air Force as in force on 18 July 1940, the Defence Act 1903 (Cth) and the Air Force Regulations (Cth).

II Operation of the military discipline system

The DFDA creates a range of service offences (in Part III), prescribes the legal principles that apply (in Part II), sets up a series of service tribunals (in Part VII), makes provision for the review of convictions and punishments (in Part VIIA), and addresses ancillary matters such as investigations (in Part VI). The combined effect of these different parts of the DFDA is aimed at creating a military discipline system that reflects an unusual hybrid of military and civilian influences. The civilian influences are reflected in the adoption of rules of evidence and criminal liability from civilian legislation but the military character of the system established by the DFDA is clearly reflected in the creation of specialist bodies to hear and review military disciplinary proceedings.

A Service offences and applicable legal principles

The DFDA changed the nature of military disciplinary offences in several important ways. It created service offences unique to the military for which there is no counterpart in civilian law.[3] Offences such as disobedience of a lawful command,[4] insubordinate conduct[5] and absence without leave[6] clearly belong in this category. The DFDA also created a number of service offences that are not unique to the military and for which there are clear parallels in civilian law, such as assault.[7] However, the effect on military discipline of such offences may be utterly unlike that in civilian life. Take the example of a soldier who strikes a superior officer. In civilian life, such an act would be a common assault. In the military, it would constitute a serious act challenging the hierarchy of authority on which the maintenance of discipline depends.[8] The wider military context of the offence means that such conduct assumes a different and far more serious character.

The Act also drew from civilian criminal law in a novel way. The DFDA contains a mechanism enabling service tribunals to try certain offences 'borrowed' from the criminal law although not specifically created by the DFDA[9] – 'a form of convenient legislative shorthand which removes the necessity to repeat, in the Act, all the provisions of an Australian criminal

[3] See DFDA, pt. III and *Re Tracey; ex parte Ryan* (1989) 166 CLR 518, 535 (Mason CJ, Wilson and Dawson JJ).

[4] DFDA, s. 27. [5] Ibid., s. 26. [6] Ibid., s. 24.

[7] Ibid., s. 33 with a maximum punishment of six months' imprisonment.

[8] Ibid., s. 25 with a maximum punishment of two years' imprisonment.

[9] Ibid., s. 61 which imports into the Act the offences of the criminal law of the Jervis Bay Territory. These offences are contained in the Crimes Act 1900 (ACT).

statute'.[10] For example, a service tribunal may try a charge of assault occasioning actual bodily harm under the Crimes Act 1900 of the Australian Capital Territory.[11]

The DFDA applies many basic principles of civilian criminal law and evidence law to military discipline. All service tribunals apply the criminal standard and onus of proof.[12] The accused is entitled to be represented without expenses.[13] The principles of criminal responsibility are generally those applicable under the Commonwealth Criminal Code,[14] and the rules of evidence – at least in the higher level service tribunals – are generally the rules of evidence under the Evidence Act 1995 (Cth).[15] Simplified rules of evidence apply in lower level service tribunals.[16]

B Service tribunals

Service tribunals exist at two broad levels. The first is a higher level consisting of courts martial[17] and Defence Force magistrates.[18] These are convened on an *ad hoc* basis in which experienced military legal officers are intimately involved. The other lower or summary level[19] is constituted in any given case by a single military officer without formal legal qualifications, but with limited powers of punishment.[20]

At the apex of the higher level service tribunals are general courts martial (GCM), which are convened as required for the trial of the most serious service offences.[21] A GCM consists of not less than five military officers, bound by the directions of a legally qualified judge advocate on any question of law.[22] It is tempting to think of the military officers comprising a GCM as a kind of jury, but they are not a jury.[23] They may

[10] *Re Colonel Aird; ex parte Alpert* (2004) 220 CLR 308, at 302 (Gleeson CJ).

[11] A criminal offence in the Jervis Bay Territory and therefore an offence under DFDA, ss. 61(1), (2) or (3) depending on the location of the alleged assault.

[12] DFDA, s. 11.

[13] See Summary Authority Rules 2009 r. 12 and DFDA, s. 137(2).

[14] DFDA, s. 10.

[15] Ibid., s. 146.

[16] Ibid., s. 146A and Summary Authority Rules *2009* pt. 9.

[17] DFDA, s. 114.

[18] Ibid., ss. 127, 129.

[19] Ibid., pt. VII div. 2.

[20] Contrast DFDA, sch. 2 – Punishments that may be imposed by a court martial or a Defence Force magistrate with sch. 3 – Punishments that may be imposed by a summary authority.

[21] Under DFDA, sch. 2 a General Court Martial has the greatest powers of punishment of any service tribunal.

[22] DFDA, ss. 114, 117, 134 and 196.

[23] The Australian Constitution s. 80 requires that there be a trial by jury for all offences upon indictment. The DFDA does not trigger that requirement because it does not categorise or label more serious offences as indictable. While it could be argued that the offences which are serious in character and carry substantial penalties could be regarded as indictable in a

not be junior in rank to the accused,[24] and there is no concept of a court martial being a trial by one's peers. Unlike a jury, any question for determination by a court martial is decided by a simple majority.[25] The most senior officer acts as president of the GCM and is formally responsible for the conduct of the trial.[26] In the event of a conviction, the military officers are solely responsible for determining all matters of punishment,[27] but are subject to the judge advocate's directions as to the legal principles involved.[28] In serious cases, punishments up to imprisonment for life may be imposed.[29] The officers of a GCM are required to take judicial notice of all matters within their general service knowledge.[30]

Another form of court martial, with powers of punishment not exceeding imprisonment for six months, is the restricted court martial (RCM) consisting of not less than three military officers,[31] again, bound by a legally qualified judge advocate's directions on any question of law.[32] Subject to these differences, an RCM operates in exactly the same manner as a GCM. The third form of higher level tribunal is trial by Defence Force magistrate (DFM).[33] These magistrates are legally qualified military officers who sit alone, which is standard practice for Australian magistrates in the civilian legal system.[34] They act judicially and have the same powers of punishment as an RCM.[35] They too are required to take judicial notice of all matters within their general service knowledge.[36] Unlike a court martial, conviction and punishment by a DFM are subject to a requirement to give reasons,[37] but a DFM lacks the collective authority of a court-martial panel.

At a trial by either form of court martial or by DFM, the prosecutor and the defending officer are almost always uniformed legal officers of the Navy, Army or Air Force.[38] Subject to the differences described, military trials are conducted on similar lines to a criminal trial.

substantive sense, and therefore subject to s. 80, that argument has never gained traction in the High Court.

[24] DFDA, s. 116. [25] Ibid., s. 133.

[26] Ibid., s. 114 and Court Martial and Defence Force Magistrates Rules r. 26.

[27] DFDA, s. 133 (6). [28] Ibid., s. 134. [29] Ibid., sch. 2. [30] Ibid., s. 147.

[31] Ibid., s. 114(3). [32] Ibid., ss. 117, 134 and 196. [33] Ibid., pt. VII, div. 4.

[34] Ibid., ss. 127 and 135. [35] Ibid., s. 135 and sch. 2. [36] Ibid., s. 147.

[37] Although a service tribunal does not exercise the judicial power of the Commonwealth of Australia, the powers of a service tribunal are 'to be exercised judicially': *Re Tracey; ex parte Ryan* (1989) 166 CLR 518, at 572 (Brennan and Toohey JJ, restated by Gleeson CJ in *White* v. *Director of Military Prosecutions* (2007) 231 CLR 570, at 586). This includes the giving of reasons, see *Wainohu* v. *New South Wales* (2011) 243 CLR 181, at 213–15 (French CJ and Kiefel J).

[38] I have been unable to locate any recorded case of a civilian legal practitioner or unrepresented individual appearing in a court martial or before a Defence Force magistrate since 1985.

Across the Defence Force, the number of charges tried by court martial or DFM is relatively small compared with the number of charges tried by summary authorities, that is, military officers without formal legal qualifications.[39] Summary authorities consist principally of 'commanding officers' who are inherently responsible for the operational effectiveness of the unit they command. They preside over the overwhelming majority of disciplinary trials in the Defence Force, and mostly determine relatively simple and usually minor infractions of discipline within their own, or sometimes a neighbouring, unit. These officers have no power of imprisonment, but may impose the punishment of military detention for up to twenty-eight days (forty-two days on active service), or a range of lesser punishments such as reduction in rank or restriction of privileges.[40] Although summary authorities are lay tribunals and although the prosecuting and defending officers are also usually non-lawyers, their proceedings are conducted on similar lines to a criminal trial.[41] While the subsequent discussion of constitutional challenges and structural adaptations to Australia's military discipline system relate directly to the operation of its higher level tribunals, that is, courts martial and DFMs, it is easy to forget that the discipline of the Defence Force is most commonly maintained and enforced from day to day at the lower or summary level.[42]

C Review

The DFDA contains a mandatory system of review for convictions. All proceedings resulting in conviction by a service tribunal are subject to automatic review by a reviewing authority, who may confirm, correct or quash the conviction, punishment or order of the tribunal.[43] Almost without exception, reviewing authorities are commanders without legal

39 See Judge Advocate General, Report for the Period 1 January to 31 December 2014 (Department of Defence, 2015) Commonwealth of Australia: Annexes E and N of that report state that in 2014 there were 1392 trials by summary authorities and 51 trials by courts martial or Defence Force magistrate.

40 DFDA, schs. 3 and 3A provide for the maximum punishments that may be imposed by summary authorities.

41 See Summary Authority Rules 2009, pt. 7.

42 Excluding matters dealt with by Discipline Officers, approximately 96 per cent of disciplinary matters are heard at the summary level. See: Annexes E and N of Judge Advocate General, Report for the Period 1 January to 31 December 2011 (Department of Defence, 2012) www.defence.gov.au/oscdf/jag/reports/JAG_AR_11.pdf.

43 DFDA, s. 158.

qualifications, but who act on legal advice.[44] Appeals on questions of law are heard by the Defence Force Discipline Appeal Tribunal, which is composed of civilian judges, usually from the Federal Court of Australia or the Supreme Court of a State or Territory.[45] Appeals on other grounds may be brought by leave.[46] A convicted member may also petition for further review by a different reviewing authority.[47] The supervision of disciplinary proceedings in this way by reviewing authorities is an inherent feature of a command-based discipline system that recognises an indissoluble connection between command and discipline.

III Rationale for existence of a military discipline system

Before discussing the constitutional challenges made to the operation of service tribunals in Australia, it is worth remembering the reason for the existence of a separate military discipline system. A separate military disciplinary system is commonly justified as recognising the unique function carried out by members of the Defence Force on behalf of the society from which they are drawn. Military personnel require a degree of training, discipline and unit cohesion that has no parallel in civilian life. They must develop in peacetime traits of character, patterns of behaviour and standards of performance which ensure the effective and controlled application of force on the battlefield. Operational service may be characterised by hazards and stresses utterly beyond the experience of civilian life in Australia, yet military duties must continue to be carried out efficiently despite confusion, danger, hardship, dispersion and isolation.

A military discipline system therefore seeks to achieve several objectives that civilian courts do not, or cannot, achieve. First, it promotes certain behaviours that are not required in civilian life, at least to the same level. Obedience to lawful orders is essential, because the actions of a single member at the tactical level can have strategic consequences for governments, threaten mission success and jeopardise lives. A military discipline system compels combatants, on pain of penalty, to do their utmost to resist the enemy. The behaviours required of members of the Defence Force include particular standards of performance, for example, for the operation of complex or dangerous weapon systems. And it is necessary to stamp out behaviours, for example, acts of theft, which

[44] Ibid., s. 154.

[45] The right of appeal is granted by the Defence Force Discipline Appeals Act 1955 (Cth), s. 20.

[46] Ibid., s. 20(1). [47] DFDA, s. 153.

threaten to undermine the mutual trust and morale on which the cohesion of small groups in the military depends.

Second, a military discipline system is attuned to the disciplinary needs of the Defence Force, which can only be achieved if discipline is administered by persons with service experience. A military discipline system is capable of being pressed into operation whenever it is required. Disciplinary imperatives do not have to compete with civilian caseloads or yield to civilian court listing priorities or resource constraints. Third, a military discipline system is completely portable and is the same regardless of regional or jurisdictional differences. That feature of the military discipline system proved increasingly important as the ADF participated in a growing number of peacekeeping and other such operations.

IV Constitutional challenges to operation of the discipline system

The constitutional validity of courts martial was raised in the High Court of Australia in two separate cases during World War II. Both cases held that military tribunals such as courts martial do not form part of the judicial system administering the law of the land.[48] Instead, they represented instances of Parliament's specific power to make laws for defence.[49] These tribunals exercised their functions judicially as a historic and practical exception to the principle that the Commonwealth's judicial power was exclusively exercisable by courts of justice, that is, by federal courts set up under Chapter III of the Constitution. This finding about the special status of military tribunals was important because it allowed them to exercise judicial power but did not require that they comply with the strict constitutional requirements governing the separation and exercise of judicial power.

From 1985 the DFDA provided a modern, Australian version of the British discipline systems that had been grafted on to Australia's federal system many years earlier; so the principles established in those wartime cases might have been expected to have a similar application to service tribunals, such as courts martial and Defence Force magistrates, established under the DFDA. Nonetheless, this has not prevented challenges being brought that question whether military discipline jurisdiction is wide enough to support the trial of service offences for which equivalents exist in

48 See *R* v. *Bevan; ex parte Elias and Gordon* (1942) 66 CLR 452, at 467 (Starke J); *R* v. *Cox; ex parte Smith* (1945) 71 CLR 1, at 13–14 (Latham CJ), at 23–24 (Dixon J) at 27 (Williams J).

49 *R* v. *Bevan; ex parte Elias and Gordon* (1942) 66 CLR 452, at 479 (McTiernan J), at 481 (Williams J).

civilian law, or whether it is legitimate to do so other than in a federal court established under Chapter III of the Constitution.[50] Throughout this succession of challenges the breadth of military discipline jurisdiction, and the validity of service tribunals established under Parliament's defence power, has been upheld; but the outcome has never been assured.

In 1989, in the first constitutional challenge to the DFDA, it was argued that a DFM was not competent to try a charge against a soldier of making a false entry in a service document[51] – essentially because the offence had a civil equivalent and should have been tried by a civil court. It was a challenge to the breadth of jurisdiction under the DFDA – in other words, to the extent to which Parliament could enact a disciplinary code standing outside Chapter III of the Constitution. While there was no clear majority on the High Court bench for any one of the three opinions expressed in the judgments,[52] the 'service connection' view espoused by Brennan and Toohey JJ has been described as the 'highest common factor' in the judgments.[53] Their answer was to hold that proceedings for such an offence (a military offence having a civil equivalent) were lawful if, but only if, they could reasonably be regarded as substantially serving the purpose of maintaining or enforcing service discipline.[54] This 'service connection' test, which aims to empower the maintenance of discipline without trespassing needlessly on civil jurisdiction, has been reflected in defence policy ever since.[55] Thus, where military and civilian jurisdiction exists in parallel, the High Court has resolved the overlap by applying a 'service connection' test in preference to the alternative 'service status' test which prevails in the United States.[56]

[50] For example, see *Re Nolan; ex parte Young* (1990) 172 CLR 460, *Re Tyler; ex parte Foley* (1994) 181 CLR 18 and *Re Colonel Aird; ex parte Alpert* (2004) 220 CLR 308.

[51] See *Re Tracey; ex parte Ryan* (1989) 166 CLR 518, at 519–20.

[52] The reasoning of Mason CJ, Wilson and Dawson JJ's joint judgment is significantly different to that in Brennan and Toohey JJ's joint judgment. Deane and Gaudron JJ also wrote separate judgments.

[53] R.A. Brown, 'Military Justice in Australia: W(h)ither Away? The Effects of Re Tracey; ex parte Ryan' (1989) 13 *Criminal Law Journal*, p. 263, at 270, quoted by Brennan and Toohey JJ in *Re Nolan; ex parte Young* (1990) 172 CLR 460.

[54] *Re Tracey; ex parte Ryan* (1989) 166 CLR 518, at 570 (Brennan and Toohey JJ).

[55] For example: *The Discipline Law Manual* (ADFP 06.1.1), 3rd edn, vol. 3, at [2.10] www.defence.gov.au/adfwc/Documents/DoctrineLibrary/ADFP/ADFP06.1.1-DisciplineLawManualVol3.pdf and Government Response to the Senate Foreign Affairs, Defence and Trade References Committee, Report on the Effectiveness of Australia's Military Justice System (Commonwealth of Australia, 2005), p. 14. www.defence.gov.au/mjs/docs/MJI_GOVERNMENT_RESPONSE_4oct052.pdf.

[56] *Re Colonel Aird; ex parte Alpert* (2004) 220 CLR 308, at 311–12 (McHugh J).

In *McWaters* v. *Day*[57] the High Court drew upon principles that had been discussed in *Tracey* in relation to service offences under the DFDA for which there existed an equivalent civil offence. The Court held that service offences of this kind were intended to create rights and duties that were *additional* or *supplementary* to those created under the ordinary criminal law, not to create rights and duties that would exclude the operation of the criminal law.[58] In that case, civil police had charged a soldier with driving under the influence of alcohol following an accident within an Army barracks. It would have been open for military authorities to charge him with an equivalent military offence. According to the High Court, parallel systems of military and criminal law were not mutually exclusive and were justified by the different purpose of proceedings before service tribunals and before civil courts.[59] Consequently, the civil court was entitled to try the soldier for the civil offence.

In *Re: Nolan; ex parte Young*[60] the High Court had an opportunity to clarify the effect of its judgment in *Tracey*. A soldier had been brought to trial before a DFM charged with a number of service offences connected with the falsification and use of pay lists for the purpose of increasing his own pay. Some of the offences charged were military offences which had civilian equivalents,[61] while the other offences were borrowed from the criminal law and charged as service offences.[62] It was argued on his behalf that offences which existed in the ordinary criminal law could not validly form part of a military discipline system, as such offences served no disciplinary or defence purpose. A narrow majority of the High Court rejected the argument, but again it was difficult to discern a *ratio decidendi* from the two majority opinions. Two of the majority judges, Mason CJ and Dawson J, pointed out that a rule of conduct required to be observed by the general community for the good of society was not for that reason any less necessary for the discipline of the Defence Force.[63] Brennan and Toohey JJ reiterated the service connection test they had advanced in *Tracey*, holding that the real issue was jurisdiction to try which varies with the circumstances.[64]

57 (1989) 168 CLR 289.

58 Ibid., at 299 (Mason CJ, Deane, Dawson, Toohey, Gaudron and McHugh JJ).

59 Ibid., 298. 60 *Re: Nolan; ex parte Young* (1991) 172 CLR 460.

61 Falsifying a service document (an offence under DFDA, s. 55(1)(a)) could be seen as analogous to forgery.

62 Using a false instrument, DFDA, s. 61(1), which imported, inter alia, s. 135C(2) of the Crimes Act 1900 (NSW) in its application to the Australian Capital Territory.

63 *Re Nolan; ex parte Young* (1991) 172 CLR 460, at 474 (Mason CJ and Dawson J).

64 Ibid., at [15] (Brennan and Toohey JJ).

The majority positions taken in *Tracey* and *Nolan* were maintained in *Re: Tyler; ex parte Foley*,[65] in which the High Court rejected a challenge to the court martial of an officer charged with the military offence of dishonestly appropriating a rental allowance. It had been argued that the court martial lacked jurisdiction to try the officer with a military offence when a similar civil offence could have been tried by jury in a civil court. On this occasion, five members of the High Court held that the court martial had the requisite jurisdiction.[66] Mason CJ and Dawson J maintained their view that it was within the power of Parliament to provide that any conduct that constitutes a civil offence shall constitute a service offence if committed by a member of the Defence Force.[67] Brennan and Toohey JJ considered that the court martial could reasonably be regarded as substantially serving the purpose of maintaining or enforcing service discipline.[68] McHugh J, who had been in the minority in *Nolan*, joined the majority in *Tyler* on the basis that Parliament and service authorities were entitled to regard the constitutional position as having been settled.[69] The Court also confirmed that trial by service tribunal did not attract the right to a jury trial for indictable offences in section 80 of the Australian Constitution.[70]

The three cases of *Tracey*, *Nolan* and *Tyler* represented a sustained constitutional challenge to the military discipline system introduced by the DFDA. While the system survived that challenge, none of the various doctrinal positions that emerged in these cases commanded universal support in the High Court. A decade passed before these issues were revisited in *Re Colonel Aird; ex parte Alpert*.[71] The case was brought on behalf of a soldier who was facing a court martial for the rape of a British tourist whom he had met in Thailand while on leave from his unit, which had been engaged in military training in Malaysia. The offence was a civil one borrowed from the criminal law and charged as a service offence.[72] The soldier contended that Parliament's defence power did not permit his trial for a service offence alleged to have been committed while on

[65] *Re Tyler; ex parte Foley* (1994) 181 CLR 18.

[66] The majority comprised Mason CJ, Brennan, Dawson, Toohey and McHugh JJ. Gaudron and Deane JJ dissented.

[67] *Re Tyler; ex parte Foley* (1994) 181 CLR 18, at 26.

[68] Ibid., at 31.

[69] Ibid., at 35–40.

[70] Ibid., at 26 (Mason CJ and Dawson J), at 29 (Brennan and Toohey JJ).

[71] (2004) 220 CLR 308.

[72] The soldier was charged under the DFDA, s. 61 which imports offences punishable under the Crimes Act of the Australian Capital Territory in its application to the Jervis Bay Territory. Rape was one such offence.

leave from his unit in another country where, for all intents and purposes, he was an ordinary tourist far removed from any military service. A majority of the High Court rejected the argument.[73] There was strong support for the service connection test espoused in earlier cases,[74] even by dissenting judges who disagreed on the facts by which it had been satisfied.[75] The factors which were said to satisfy the service connection test included the representational role of soldiers overseas, the link between Private Alpert's military service in Malaysia and his recreation leave in Thailand, and the detrimental effect on discipline of the conduct charged.[76]

Finally, undeterred by the High Court's previous pronouncements on the matter, another challenge was brought in *White* v. *Director of Military Prosecutions*,[77] on behalf of a sailor charged with committing acts of indecency without consent upon subordinates – offences borrowed from the criminal law and charged as service offences.[78] White's challenge sought to reopen the issue of whether service tribunals exercised the judicial power of the Commonwealth in a manner precluded by Chapter III of the Constitution. All but one member of the High Court rejected her argument.[79] The Court confirmed Parliament's capacity to provide for service tribunals in exercise of its defence power,[80] and that the jurisdiction of service tribunals could not be limited to offences of an exclusively disciplinary nature.[81] Disciplinary imperatives existed as much in the overlap between service offences and civil offences as in the range of offences unique to the military.

So the constitutional issues surrounding the operation and jurisdiction of service tribunals as presently established appear to have been settled. If the minority views expressed in the early High Court judgments had gained ascendancy, it is likely that Australia's military discipline system would have operated within a much narrower compass than it does today.

[73] The majority being Gleeson CJ, McHugh, Gummow and Hayne JJ. Kirby, Callinan and Heydon JJ dissented.

[74] (2004) 220 CLR 308, at 312 (McHugh J), at 304 (Gleeson CJ agreeing), at 345 (Hayne J agreeing). Although Gummow J's reasoning at 318–20 appeared to be an application of the service connection test, he expressly declined to settle that issue: 316.

[75] Ibid., at 345 (Callinan and Heydon JJ). Kirby J rejected the test: 326–27.

[76] Ibid., at 314 (McHugh J), at 319–20 (Gummow J). [77] (2007) 231 CLR 570.

[78] The sailor faced one charge of assault under the DFDA, s. 33(a) and six charges under the DFDA, s. 61(3) in conjunction with Crimes Act 1900 (ACT), s. 60.

[79] Kirby J dissented.

[80] (2007) 231 CLR 570, at 586 (Gleeson CJ), at 598 (Gummow, Hayne and Crennan JJ). Callinan J's analysis and rebuttal of the plaintiff's argument (at 646–48), which with minor qualification was adopted by Heydon J, is founded on this proposition.

[81] Ibid., at 586 (Gleeson CJ), at 602 (Gummow, Hayne and Crennan JJ).

V Key adaptations to military discipline system

This chapter will now consider the key adaptations made to Australia's military discipline system since 1985 in an endeavour to anticipate and respond to emerging legal norms and to domestic political and public expectations. These adaptations have been implemented to enhance the discipline system, as well as to avoid the threat of successful constitutional challenge. The primary drivers of change have been the application of human rights law overseas where traditional court-martial structures had been held not to provide a fair and impartial trial,[82] combined with concern that these developments had not received much attention in the High Court.[83]

Many more adaptations of a minor nature have been made for the specific purpose of keeping up with the changing needs of the Defence Force. A careful survey of amendments to the DFDA over the last twenty-eight years would traverse the introduction of many useful innovations. These include the introduction of the discipline officer scheme to deal administratively, and without trial, with minor infringements admitted by junior members of the Defence Force.[84] They would include the introduction of new offences, such as specific offences relating to the negligent or unauthorised discharge of weapons,[85] and certain provisions enhancing the rights of persons under investigation or on trial.[86] Such a survey would also note the harmonisation of DFDA offence-creating provisions with the Commonwealth Criminal Code in 2001,[87] when the elements of each offence were redefined to clarify the physical and fault elements required to be proven in any prosecution.

A The role of convening authorities

This first adaptation concerned the role of 'convening authorities'. For many years after 1985, senior officers in the Defence Force held secondary

[82] For example, *Findlay* v. *United Kingdom* (1997) 24 EHRR 221 and *R* v. *Généreux* [1992] 1 SCR 259.

[83] However, see comments by Kirby J in *Re Colonel Aird; ex parte Alpert* (2004) 220 CLR 308, at 337–39 and *White* v. *Director of Military Prosecutions* (2007) 231 CLR 570, at 619.

[84] See DFDA, Part IXA. [85] DFDA, ss. 36A and 36B, respectively.

[86] The Defence Legislation Amendment Act 1995 (Cth) amended aspects of Part VI of the DFDA with regard to the making of recordings of service police interviews and the cautioning of suspects prior to questioning and inserted s. 101JA providing conditions for the admissibility of oral confessions.

[87] By the amendments contained in the Defence Legislation Amendment (Application of Criminal Code) Act 2001 (Cth).

appointments as convening authorities, by which they were the sole arbiters of whether subordinates accused of serious service offences would face trial by court martial or DFM. These officers were not legally qualified but decided many important legal questions, such as what, if any, charges would be prosecuted against an accused. They also signed the charge sheet, appointed the prosecutor, selected and appointed the members of the court martial (who were usually from the ranks of officers under their command), and appointed the judge advocate or the DFM. In the event of conviction, the convening authority typically changed hats and acted as reviewing authority, confirming or correcting the tribunal's findings and punishments.

Although such a concentration of functions and power is unthinkable in civilian life, few seriously questioned the centralisation in military discipline of these multiple roles in a single commander because it was long accepted that discipline was a key aspect of command. While it is not an approach readily understood outside of the Services, commanders regarded themselves as being concurrently responsible for the maintenance of discipline, including the decision to bring charges; and for the welfare of the accused, including the obligation to ensure that he or she was treated fairly. These responsibilities were not mutually exclusive; they were regarded as complementary. Of course, convening authorities and reviewing authorities acted on legal advice; but in any event, their function was connected with the administration of discipline, not the administration of justice. Few seriously suggested that the requirements of independence and impartiality in the administration of justice applied with equal rigour to the administration of discipline.

By the late 1990s a body of jurisprudence from the European Court of Human Rights (in relation to the United Kingdom)[88] and Canada[89] highlighted the tension between a command-based discipline system and the importance of structural independence and impartiality in the notion of a 'fair trial'. The court-martial structures of these countries had previously shared similar characteristics with the Australian system. While this overseas jurisprudence had developed in the context of human rights instruments[90] which had no direct parallel in Australia, it pointed to trends likely to enjoy increasing prominence in Australia.

[88] See, for example, *Findlay* v. *United Kingdom* (1997) 24 EHRR 221.

[89] See, for example, *R* v. *Généreux* [1992] 1 SCR 259.

[90] Such as the Convention for the Protection of Human Rights and Fundamental Freedoms, Rome, 4 November 1950, in force 3 December 1953, 213 UNTS 222 and Canada Act 1982 (UK) c. 11, sch. B pt. I (*Canadian Charter of Rights and Freedoms*). See Chapter 8 for discussion of cases involving the UK before the European Court of Human Rights.

In Australia, the role of the convening authority came under increasing criticism in a series of defence and parliamentary reviews of the military discipline system, commencing in 1997 with a report by Brigadier the Honourable Justice Alan Abadee, a Deputy Judge Advocate General.[91] Abadee was commissioned to examine the Canadian and United Kingdom jurisprudence and assess its relevance to the Australian system. He noted that the Canadian and European human rights provisions were generally based on the International Covenant on Civil and Political Rights (ICCPR) which Australia had ratified but not incorporated into municipal law.[92] Abadee accepted that the human rights instruments which had forced many of the changes to English and Canadian law had no counterpart in Australia, although he also recognised that the ICCPR was playing an increasing role in Australia.[93]

Abadee recommended changes to separate the role of the convening authority for trials by courts martial and DFMs from the role of the reviewing authority.[94] He recommended the establishment of an independent Director of Military Prosecutions (DMP) in place of convening authorities.[95] He also recommended interim policy changes to remove from the convening authority the role of selecting the judge advocate and court-martial members and to place Judge Advocates and Defence Force magistrates under the command of the Judge Advocate General.[96] In time, Abadee's recommendations would be implemented via legislation.[97]

[91] In 1995 the then Chief of the Defence Force commissioned Brigadier the Honourable Justice Alan Abadee RFD to conduct 'A study into the Judicial System under the Defence Force Discipline Act'. Abadee reported his study to the Chief of the Defence Force in August of 1997. It was subsequently published as Study into the Judicial System under the Defence Force Discipline Act (DFDA) (Department of Defence, 1997).

[92] Ibid., at [2.26].

[93] That assessment seemed timely because two years earlier in *Minister of State for Immigration and Ethnic Affairs* v. *Teoh* (1995) 183 CLR 273 the High Court of Australia held that although the United Nations Convention on the Rights of the Child formed no part of Australian municipal law, Australia's ratification of the Convention created a legitimate expectation that government decisions would be made in accordance with the terms of the Convention. The *Teoh* case was later strongly doubted, but not overruled, in *Minister for Immigration and Multicultural and Indigenous Affairs; ex parte Lam* (2003) 214 CLR 1.

[94] Abadee, above n. 91, at [1.26.2]. [95] Ibid., at [126.4]. [96] Ibid., at [1.26.6–7].

[97] Notably the establishment of the statutory offices of the Director of Military Prosecutions and the Registrar of Military Justice to replace the convening authority's roles in the decision to prosecute and the organisation of the trial by the Defence Legislation Amendment Act (No. 2) 2005 (Cth).

Abadee's recommendation to consider establishing an independent DMP was echoed by the Joint Standing Committee report on Military Justice Procedures in 1999.[98] However, while those recommendations were still under consideration, the ADF's military discipline system again came under the spotlight when the Joint Standing Committee on Foreign Affairs, Defence and Trade investigated allegations of indiscipline which had emerged from the 3rd Battalion, the Royal Australian Regiment (3RAR).[99] The Committee's findings were limited to 3RAR, so the Chief of the Defence Force decided to appoint Mr James Burchett QC, a former Federal Court judge, to inquire into how widespread and pervasive in the Defence Force was the culture of indiscipline identified in 3RAR.[100] While Burchett concluded that the culture of indiscipline was not widespread,[101] he made a number of useful recommendations to enhance military discipline, including the appointment of an independent DMP and a Registrar of Courts Martial.[102] Burchett's recommendations resolved the indecision that had followed previous reviews and a DMP was established on an interim, non-statutory basis in 2003.[103]

The role of the DMP was enshrined in legislation in 2006, at which time convening authorities were finally abolished and their functions divided between the DMP and a newly created Registrar of Military Justice.[104] From that time onwards, the DMP would decide whether or not serious service offences would be prosecuted, and if so would appoint the prosecutor.[105] The Registrar would convene the trial.[106] The establishment of an independent authority to decide whether offences should be prosecuted and to manage those prosecutions aligned broadly with the independent prosecution structures that had long existed in Australian civilian law.

[98] Joint Standing Committee on Foreign Affairs, Defence and Trade, *Military Justice in the Australia Defence Force*, Report No. 89 (1999).

[99] The Joint Standing Committee on Foreign Affairs, Defence and Trade, *Rough Justice? An Investigation into Allegations of Brutality in the Army's Parachute Battalion*, Report No. 99 (22 May 2001).

[100] Mr James Burchett QC was appointed as an Investigating Officer by the Chief of the Defence Force on 15 December 2000 and reported his investigation on 12 July 2001. The inquiry was conducted under the Defence (Inquiry) Regulations 1985 and was subsequently published as *Report of an Inquiry into Military Justice in the Australian Defence Force, Department of Defence* (2001) (Burchett Report).

[101] Ibid., pp. 5–8. [102] Ibid., 29–41.

[103] See the Judge Advocate General, Report for the Period 1 January to 31 December 2003 (Department of Defence, 2004), p. 14.

[104] Both changes were made by amendments to the Defence Force Discipline Act 1982 (Cth) by the Defence Legislation Amendment Act (No. 2) 2005 (Cth).

[105] DFDA, s. 188GA. [106] Ibid., s. 188FA.

B A permanent military court?

In October 2003 the Senate's Foreign Affairs Defence and Trade References Committee began an inquiry into the military justice system. The inquiry was broad-ranging and clearly sought to overcome a history of piecemeal change. The Committee explained:

> A decade of rolling inquiries has not met with the broad-based change required to protect the rights of Service personnel. The committee considers that major change is required to ensure independence and impartiality in the military justice system and believes it is time to consider another approach to military justice.[107]

The Committee made a number of far-reaching recommendations to that effect in its report of June 2005, although not all were supported by the government of the day.[108] For present purposes, the principal recommendation was the abolition of the *ad hoc* system of courts martial and DFMs and the establishment of a permanent military court under Chapter III of the Australian Constitution.[109] The Committee was aware of the jurisprudence in Canada and Europe which had found that command-based systems of discipline lacked independence and impartiality. Further, it was concerned that previous High Court decisions had left open the possibility of a future challenge to the Australian system on the basis of its ability to provide a fair and impartial trial.[110]

The Committee's recommendation that a permanent or standing military court should be established was a radical one because it contemplated a complete severance of the disciplinary function from command at the higher levels. It was made all the more radical because the constitutional prohibitions on the appointment of serving military officers meant that judges of the new court could only be civilians. On the creation of the court, these civilian judges would, for the first time, have dispensed discipline from outside the Defence Force.

107 *The Effectiveness of Australia's Military Justice System* (Canberra, Commonwealth of Australia, 2005), p. xxi.

108 See Government Response to the Senate Foreign Affairs, Defence and Trade References Committee, Report on the Effectiveness of Australia's Military Justice System (Department of Defence, 2005).

109 *The Effectiveness of Australia's Military Justice System*, pp. liii–liv (recommendations 18–19).

110 Ibid., p. xxii.

It should be noted, however, that no change to the structure of the military discipline system was proposed at the lower or summary level where disciplinary charges were tried in the greatest numbers. As the Judge Advocate General put it in his submission to the Committee,[111] it was not possible to imbue summary authorities, such as commanding officers, with the guarantees of independence appropriate to the higher level tribunals.

The Government supported the idea of a permanent court, but preferred to establish such a court within the Defence Force as an exercise of Parliament's power to make laws for defence, rather than as part of the federal court structure.[112] This became the short-lived Australian Military Court (AMC), which commenced operation on 1 October 2007.[113]

There was much to be said in favour of a standing court: independence, case management, expertise, status (in terms of its judgments and rulings) and its place in the judicial firmament. The judges of the AMC were experienced military legal officers,[114] and it incorporated interesting features such as military juries.[115] Importantly, the AMC was a tribunal of final decision.[116] Its decisions, punishments and orders were not subject to review by the chain of command.[117] The AMC represented a

[111] Maj Gen Justice Roberts-Smith, Submission 27 to the Senate Foreign Affairs, Defence and Trade References Committee, *Effectiveness of Australia's Military Justice System*, 16 February 2004.

[112] See Government Response to the Senate Foreign Affairs, Defence and Trade References Committee, Report on the Effectiveness of Australia's Military Justice System, p. 4.

[113] The Australian Military Court came into existence on 1 October 2007 although its first sitting was not until 12 November 2007, see Chief Military Judge, Report for the Period 1 October to 31 December 2007 (Department of Defence, 2008).

[114] The Chief Military Judge was Regular Army legal officer Brigadier Westwood AM. The other two military judges appointed were experienced Reserve Army legal officers Colonel Morrison RFD and Lieutenant Colonel Woodward.

[115] The implementation of which was not without initial problems and the AMC did not commence a jury trial until 23 June 2008. See Chief Military Judge, Report for the Period 1 October to 31 December 2007, pp. 13–14, and Chief Military Judge, Report for the Period 1 January to 31 December 2008 (Department of Defence, 2009) pp. 9–11.

[116] Unlike the decisions, punishments and orders of the previous system of courts martial and Defence Force magistrates, all decisions, punishments and orders of the AMC were effective immediately without the necessity for a superior military authority's approval.

[117] Prior to the amendments to the DFDA creating the AMC, the decisions, punishments and orders of a court martial or Defence Force magistrate were subject to review by a reviewing authority appointed by the Chief of the Defence Force or a Service Chief: DFDA, s. 150. That review included a legal report on the proceeding (s. 154), and certain punishments (primarily the more serious such as dismissal and imprisonment) and orders (for restitution or reparation) did not take effect until approved by the reviewing authority (s. 172).

clear break with the command-based discipline system whose higher levels it had replaced.

Within these parameters, the AMC operated effectively for about twenty-two months until its sudden demise as a result of the High Court's unanimous decision in *Lane* v. *Morrison*.[118] In this case, a sailor had been charged with an act of indecency without consent and with assaulting a superior officer.[119] He sought orders prohibiting his trial on the basis that the AMC was a body exercising the judicial power of the Commonwealth which had been constituted other than in accordance with Chapter III of the Constitution. The High Court unanimously agreed.[120] Legislative attempts to establish the AMC as a service tribunal established under the defence power, while purporting to give it many of the attributes of a court, had failed.

The High Court concluded that the absence of review by the chain of command of the decisions, punishments and orders of the AMC showed, above all else, that the provisions establishing the AMC had strayed beyond a valid exercise of the defence power.[121] By operating as a tribunal of final decision, the AMC was functioning as a court, not as a service tribunal.[122] In other words, legislative attempts to introduce independence in military adjudications were the undoing of the AMC. That reasoning came as a surprise to those who had believed that breaking with a command-based discipline system would insulate the AMC from legal challenge.

Legislation was rushed through Parliament restoring the previous *ad hoc* system of trial by court martial or Defence Force magistrate on an interim basis,[123] and that interim system continues to operate today. That legislation survived challenge in *Haskins* v. *Commonwealth*,[124] where the High Court placed considerable reliance on the availability of review within the chain of command of punishments imposed by the former

[118] (2009) 239 CLR 230.

[119] The offences were respectively charged under DFDA, ss. 60(2), 61(3), s. 25.

[120] *Lane* v. *Morrison* (2009) 239 CLR 230, at 250–51 (French CJ and Gummow J), at 267–68 (Hayne, Heydon, Crennan, Kiefel and Bell JJ).

[121] Ibid., at 250 (French CJ and Gummow J), at 266 (Hayne, Heydon, Crennan, Kiefel and Bell JJ).

[122] Ibid., at 251 (French CJ and Gummow J), at 261, 265 (Hayne, Heydon, Crennan, Kiefel and Bell JJ).

[123] The *Military Justice (Interim Measures) Act (No 1) 2009* (Cth) and *Military Justice (Interim Measures) Act (No 2) 2009* (Cth) each took effect on 22 September 2009. Both were introduced as Bills only thirteen days earlier.

[124] (2011) 244 CLR 22.

AMC.[125] The restoration of this system was clearly intended to be a temporary measure. Within hours of the High Court's decision in *Lane v. Morrison*, the Minister for Defence indicated publicly that the Government's longer-term approach was to move towards a Chapter III solution – in other words, to replace the interim system of trial by courts martial or DFM with a court established as part of the federal court structure, outside the Defence Force.[126]

On 24 May 2010 the Government formally announced its plan to establish a Military Court of Australia under Chapter III, and a Bill was introduced to Parliament in June 2010.[127] The Bill lapsed when Parliament was prorogued for the 2010 Federal Election.[128] On 21 June 2012 the Government introduced two Bills for the establishment of the Military Court of Australia and the transition to its operation.[129] The Bills were referred to the Senate Legal and Constitutional Affairs Legislation Committee for inquiry and report. The Committee reported on 9 October 2012. The report comprised a majority report, a dissenting Liberal Party Senators' report and an additional comment by an Australian Greens Senator.[130] The majority report recommended passage of the Bills.[131] The dissenting Liberal Party Senators' recommended amending the Bills to: provide for trial by jury for service offences with a maximum punishment of more than twelve months imprisonment;[132] and allow Australian Defence Force Reservists to be eligible for appointment as judicial officers to the Military Court, to the extent allowed by the Constitution.[133] The Australian Greens Senator on the Committee made an additional comment recommending amendment to allow for the right

125 Ibid., at 33, 36–37 (French CJ, Gummow, Hayne, Crennan, Kiefel and Bell JJ).

126 See Senator the Hon John Faulkner, Minister for Defence, *Press Release* (Australian Government Department of Defence, 26 August 2009) www.defence.gov.au/minister/90tpl.cfm?CurrentId=9411.

127 The Military Court of Australia Bill 2010 (Cth) was introduced into Parliament on 24 June 2010.

128 On 19 July 2010.

129 The Military Court of Australia Bill 2012 (Cth) and the Military Court of Australia (Transitional Provisions and Consequential Amendments) Bill 2012 (Cth).

130 The terms of reference, the submissions, the transcript of the hearing and the report are available at www.aph.gov.au/Parliamentary_Business/Committees/Senate_Committees?url=legcon_ctte/completed_inquiries/2010-13/military_court_2012/index.htm.

131 Senate Legal and Constitutional Affairs Legislation Committee, Report of inquiry into Military Court of Australia Bill 2012 and Military Court of Australia (Transitional Provisions and Consequential Amendments) Bill 2012 (Senate Publishing Unit, 2012), p. 51.

132 Ibid., p. 57. 133 Ibid.

to trial by jury for 'the most serious offences' (which were not further defined).[134] Like their predecessor Bill, these Bills lapsed when the 43rd Parliament was prorogued for the 2013 Federal Election.[135]

At the time of writing, the new coalition Government has not indicated its intention regarding reintroduction of the Military Court Bills.[136] If the new Government proceeds to establish a Military Court of Australia, that Court will try serious service offences and other service offences in relation to which the accused has elected to be tried by the Court instead of by a summary authority[137] or which have been referred to the Court by a summary authority.[138] The Court will have a lower Division staffed by full-time judicial officers with status equivalent to judges of the Federal Circuit Court of Australia,[139] and an upper Division staffed by a Chief Justice and other judges of Federal Court status.[140] Service offences will be tried by the Court without a jury, because they will not be classified as indictable offences.[141]

If a Chapter III court for the trial of serious service offences is established, it would represent the most significant change to Australia's military discipline system since Federation. For the first time in Australia's history, military discipline would be dispensed from outside the Defence Force. Importantly, however, these changes would not fundamentally affect the operation of the lower or summary level of the system, where the majority of disciplinary work occurs. It is, however, proposed that members who are charged even with minor service offences at the summary level would have the option to elect to be tried by the Military Court of Australia instead of by a summary authority.[142]

134 Ibid., p. 60. 135 On 5 August 2013.

136 This chapter reflects the position as on 15 November 2015.

137 See Military Court of Australia (Transitional Provisions and Consequential Amendments) Bill 2012 (Cth) sch. 1, arts. 73 and 83.

138 The effect of the amendments to the Defence Force Discipline Act 1982 (Cth) in the Military Court of Australia (Transitional Provisions and Consequential Amendments) Bill 2012 (Cth) sch. 1, arts. 73 and 83 will mean that a reference of a charge by a summary authority to the Director of Military Prosecutions may result in the charge being prosecuted in the Military Court of Australia.

139 Division 3 of the Military Court of Australia Bill 2012 refers to Federal Magistrates however, since the Bill's introduction into Parliament, Parliament has passed legislation renaming the Federal Magistrates Court of Australia as the Federal Circuit Court of Australia and retitled 'Federal Magistrates' as 'Judges'.

140 See Military Court of Australia Bill 2012 (Cth) div 3. 141 Ibid., cls. 62, 74 and 75.

142 See Military Court of Australia (Transitional Provisions and Consequential Amendments) Bill 2012 (Cth) sch. 1, art. 73.

If the proposed Chapter III court is not established, it is possible that a future plaintiff will challenge the existing command-based structures on the basis of the human rights norms at the heart of Canadian and European jurisprudence, that is, the right to 'a fair and public hearing by a competent, independent and impartial tribunal' recognised by Article 14 of the ICCPR. The application of international human rights law to Australia's military discipline system was raised in the dissenting opinion of Justice Kirby in *Ex parte Alpert*.[143] Nevertheless, the ICCPR has not been implemented in Australia's municipal law and it is by no means clear that human rights norms applicable to the determination of criminal charges and the adjustment of civil rights and obligations would be held to apply to the military discipline system, whose *raison d'être* is different.

VI Conclusion

Since the commencement of the DFDA, military discipline in Australia has been characterised by challenges to the constitutional status and jurisdiction of service tribunals. The same period has also been characterised by a series of defence and parliamentary reviews which recommended structural adaptations to accommodate emerging legal norms.

The abolition of convening authorities and the division of their functions between an independent DMP and Registrar has done much to allay concerns about command influence in the conduct of a 'fair trial'. The High Court's decision in *Lane* v. *Morrison* which brought about the demise of the AMC represents a watershed in our understanding of the hallmarks of a discipline system based on Parliament's defence power, on the one hand, and of a court exercising federal judicial power, on the other. Despite criticism of command-based discipline systems in overseas jurisprudence and by the Senate Foreign Affairs, Defence and Trade References Committee in its 2005 report, the acceptance of the validity of the previous system by the High Court in *Haskins* v. *The Commonwealth* can arguably be interpreted as an endorsement of the command-based discipline system. Today, the higher level of Australia's military discipline system is at a crossroads. The next steps by Government will determine the kind of system that will service the needs of the Defence Force in the future.

143 Ibid., 337–39.

14

Human rights and Australia's military justice system

JOHN TARRANT

I Introduction

Human rights have gained significant importance in many jurisdictions in recent decades. This chapter examines the impact of human rights norms in the context of Australia's military justice system. The primary focus is on the fair trial provisions, and the requirement of equality before the law, located in the International Covenant on Civil and Political Rights.[1] Such an analysis is timely in the Australian context because the Australian military justice system is at an important crossroads. At the same time that the Australian government is showing an increased interest in international human rights compliance, it has also been considering the creation of a new military justice system that will include a Military Court established under Chapter III of the Australian Constitution. These two events mean that human rights considerations are now of greater relevance to Australia's military justice system. The creation of a Chapter III court for the military might overcome constitutional problems identified with the demise of the Australian Military Court in 2009[2] because such a court would contain the institutional features required for the valid exercise of judicial power. But the creation of such a court for the military could have some unintended human rights consequences as it would move military justice outside of the jurisdiction of the military for the first time and, in that context, different human rights considerations may apply.

It is important to appreciate that when examining human rights in the Australian context that, at the Federal level, there is no Bill of

[1] International Covenant on Civil and Political Rights, 16 December 1966, in force 23 March 1976, 999 UNTS 171 (ICCPR).

[2] See *Lane* v. *Morrison* (2009) 239 CLR 230.

Rights or comprehensive human rights legislation. Although some individual human rights are contained in specific legislative contexts,[3] the full range of human rights, such as those found in the ICCPR, are not comprehensively enacted in Australian domestic law.[4] In a practical sense this means that other legal frameworks, such as the common law and the Australian Constitution, can be more relevant in the Australian human rights context, although the ICCPR, and other international human rights instruments, may be relevant to the interpretation and application of Australian domestic law. Accordingly, although the ICCPR is relevant from an international law perspective, its relevance in the Australian context is likely to be more indirect.

This chapter is divided into two sections. Section II examines recent developments in relation to the implementation of human rights in Australia and how such developments are impacting on the introduction of a new military justice system in Australia. Section III examines the application of the ICCPR to the military justice system in Australia. Despite the increased focus on human rights in Australia it is argued that there are a number of reasons why, in the Australian context, Australia's military justice system will not be directly impacted in the immediate future by international human rights norms. These include the fact that Australia has rejected the introduction of a general human rights Act for the protection of human rights in favour of a parliamentary model limited to the scrutiny of new legislation; many international human rights norms are not found in Australian domestic law; there are very limited human rights protections in the Australian Constitution; and the courts have accepted that there is justification for some flexibility in the application of human rights in the military justice system given the objective of the maintenance of discipline.

3 For example, Privacy Act 1988 (Cth), Sex Discrimination Act 1984 (Cth), Disability Discrimination Act 1992 (Cth), Age Discrimination Act 2004 (Cth) and Racial Discrimination Act 1975 (Cth).

4 Exceptions are the Human Rights Act 2004 (ACT) and the Charter of Human Rights and Responsibilities 2006 (Vic). These two statutes enshrine some, but not all, of the rights adopted in the ICCPR respectively for the Australian Capital Territory and the State of Victoria. The Australian military is regulated by the federal government and federal legislation and is therefore unaffected by these human rights statutes.

II Recent developments in Australia

A Increased concern with human rights

Australia has long been labelled as a nation reluctant to embrace rights in any systematic or substantive sense,[5] but there have been recent signs of change. The Australian Federal Government has taken a more proactive role in recent years to the implementation of human rights norms in Australia. In December 2008 the government established the National Human Rights Consultation Committee (Committee) which was tasked with seeking a range of views from across Australia concerning the protection and promotion of human rights. The Consultation was run by an independent committee who were supported by a Secretariat in the Attorney-General's Department. The Committee reported to the government on 30 September 2009 on the issues raised from its consultation and the options identified for the government to consider for the purpose of enhancing the protection and promotion of human rights.[6]

The Committee recommended the enactment of a national human rights Act similar to the United Kingdom Human Rights Act 1998. However, the Federal Government did not adopt that option. The Committee also recommended that the Federal Government conduct an audit of all federal legislation, policies and practices to determine their compliance with Australia's international human rights obligations.[7] In addition, the Committee recommended that a statement of compatibility be required for all Bills introduced into the Federal Parliament, all Bills before the third reading (so as to allow scrutiny of amendments), and legislative instruments as defined by the Legislative Instruments Act 2003 (Cth). The Committee recommended that a compatibility statement should assess the proposed law's compatibility with Australia's international human rights obligations. The Committee also recommended that a Joint Committee on Human Rights be established to review all Bills and relevant legislative instruments for compliance with Australia's human rights obligations.[8]

These recommendations of the Committee reflect the fact that there are many ways in which human rights norms can be protected. Santow

[5] Hilary Charlesworth, 'The Australian Reluctance about Rights' in Philip Alston (ed.), *Towards an Australian Bill of Rights* (Canberra, Centre for International and Public Law, Australian National University, 1994), p. 21.

[6] National Human Rights Consultation, *National Human Rights Consultation Report* (Barton ACT, Commonwealth of Australia, 2009).

[7] Ibid., p. 356. [8] Ibid., p. 357.

has noted that a common form of legislation to protect human rights in Australia is statutes that protect a single human right, such as the right to privacy or freedom from racial discrimination.[9] Such statutes deal 'with a broad variety of situations, but only in relation to one particular right' whereas other legislation will focus on protecting rights with reference to an activity such as employment laws that 'often protect against conduct that would breach multiple human rights'.[10] Santow notes that both 'of these legislative forms are common in Australia and elsewhere, and are now almost entirely without controversy'.[11] It is the third method of statutory protection of human rights that is more controversial, particularly in Australia, and that method is a general human rights statute that seeks to protect human rights more broadly. Santow notes that these statutes are generally referred to 'as a "Bill of Rights", "Human Rights Act" or "Charter of Human Rights"'.[12] The main recommendation of the Committee was the adoption of a Human Rights Act model widely known as a dialogue model.[13] Santow explains that the 'word "dialogue" denotes that each of the three arms of government has a role to play in relation to human rights protection, and that to some extent at least their roles should be integrated'.[14] A feature of the dialogue model 'is its requirement for other laws to be interpreted consistently with protected rights'.[15] But the recommendation of such a model by the Committee was not adopted by the government.

Instead the government adopted a model based solely on a role for the parliament. On 2 June 2010 the Commonwealth Attorney-General introduced the Human Rights (Parliamentary Scrutiny) Bill 2010 (Cth) (Scrutiny Bill) into the House of Representatives. The Attorney-General also issued Australia's Human Rights Framework in April 2010,[16] which outlined the intention to introduce the Scrutiny Bill. The Scrutiny Bill was passed by Parliament and became the Human Rights (Parliamentary Scrutiny) Act 2011 (Cth) (Scrutiny Act) and reflects the recommendations of the National Human Rights Consultation

[9] Edward Santow, 'The Act That Dares Not Speak Its Name: The National Human Rights Consultation Report's Parallel Roads to Human Rights Reform' (2010) 33 *University of New South Wales Law Journal*, p. 8 at 12.

[10] Ibid. [11] Ibid. [12] Ibid.

[13] That description, which is not without controversy, was coined in Peter Hogg and Allison Bushell, 'The Charter Dialogue between Courts and Legislatures' (1997) 35 *Osgoode Hall Law Journal*, p. 75.

[14] Santow, above n. 9 at 12. [15] Ibid., 21.

[16] Hon Robert McClelland, *Australia's Human Rights Framework* (Canberra, Commonwealth of Australia, 2010).

Committee in relation to scrutiny of new legislation. The substantive provisions of the Scrutiny Act came into force with effect from 4 January 2012. The Scrutiny Act established a Parliamentary Joint Committee on Human Rights (the PJCHR) to examine Bills for Acts that come before either House of Parliament for compatibility with human rights and to examine Acts for compatibility with human rights. The PJCHR established by the Scrutiny Act is based on a committee of the United Kingdom parliament of the same name.[17]

Human rights are defined by s. 3(1) of the Scrutiny Act to include rights and freedoms recognised or declared by a number of international instruments including the ICCPR. Section 8 of the Scrutiny Act requires that a member of Parliament who proposes to introduce a Bill for an Act into a House of Parliament must cause a statement of compatibility (SOC) to be prepared in respect of that Bill. A statement of compatibility must include an assessment of whether the Bill is compatible with human rights. A similar requirement is contained in the two Australian jurisdictions that have enacted a wide ranging statutory charter of rights.[18]

Williams and Burton have noted the system adopted by the Australian parliament 'is unique in democratic nations in that it provides no role for the courts'.[19] They go on to say that this '"exclusive parliamentary model" of rights protection requires Parliament to self-regulate because there is no threat of judicial challenge or review'.[20] Williams and Burton also note that the 'Parliamentary Scrutiny Act does not specify the length or level of detail which an SOC should contain'.[21] Importantly they note that there 'is no requirement to explain the reasons for finding a bill compatible or incompatible'.[22] They conclude that 'most SOCs are brief and many display a disturbing lack of analytical rigour'.[23] It is also important to note that a SOC has limited legal effect because the Scrutiny Act provides that a SOC 'is not binding on any court or tribunal' and that the validity of legislation is not affected by a failure to comply with any provision of the Scrutiny Act.[24]

The most important aspect of the Scrutiny Act is that it adopts 'an "exclusive parliamentary model" that places sole responsibility for the recognition and protection of human rights on Parliament and creates no

[17] Santow, above n. 9 at 25.

[18] Human Rights Act 2004 (ACT) s. 37; Charter of Human Rights and Responsibilities 2006 (Vic) s. 28.

[19] George Williams and Lisa Burton, 'Australia's Exclusive Parliamentary Model of Rights Protection' (2013) 34 *Statute Law Review*, p. 58 at 59.

[20] Ibid. [21] Ibid., at 75. [22] Ibid. [23] Ibid., at 81. [24] Scrutiny Act, ss. 8(4) and 8(5).

scope for judicial supervision'.[25] This structure means that the 'model is entirely self-regulating' and there 'is no legal sanction for a failure to comply'.[26] Williams and Burton conclude that the 'absence of judicial scrutiny greatly diminishes the incentive for parliamentarians to comply with the scrutiny regime'.[27]

Despite the limitations of the model adopted by the Scrutiny Act it is possible that over time the PJCHR will develop expertise in human rights and also some expertise in how human rights impact on the Australian military. This may not happen immediately but it may develop over time. The experience of other jurisdictions suggests that continuous parliamentary oversight of the military can become more effective over time. In their analysis of parliamentary scrutiny of defence in the United Kingdom House of Commons Defence Committee (HCDC), George and Morgan noted that during the early period of the HCDC '[l]ittle use was made of outside advice and the committee sometimes appeared overawed by government ministers and defence chiefs'.[28] But they also found that the HCDC eventually 'developed its expertise and increased its effectiveness'.[29] There is a very good chance that the PJCHR will also develop similar expertise in human rights and their impact on the military. The PJCHR will be examining every Bill for its impact on human rights, which will provide significant continuity in the performance of its role. In relation to military matters many members of the Federal Parliament have expertise in relation to the military arising from the Senate Legal and Constitutional Affairs Legislation Committee, the Senate Foreign Affairs, Defence and Trade Legislation Committee (FADTC) and the Joint Standing Committee on Treaties (JSCOT). Parliamentary expertise in military matters has also been informed by a large number of parliamentary inquiries into Australia's military justice system.[30] Accordingly, there is reason to believe that the PJCHR will quickly develop the general expertise required to perform its role

25 Williams and Burton, above n. 19 at 89. This argument presumes the validity of the section in the Scrutiny Act which provides that any failure to comply with requirements of the Act does not affect the validity of legislation.

26 Ibid., at 90. 27 Ibid., at 92.

28 Bruce George and David Morgan, 'Parliamentary Scrutiny of Defence' (1999) 5 *The Journal of Legislative Studies*, p. 1 at 4.

29 Ibid., at 5.

30 For example, the Joint Committee on Foreign Affairs, Defence and Trade report, *Military Justice in the Australian Defence Force*, 21 June 1999 and the Senate Foreign Affairs, Defence and Trade References Committee report, *The Effectiveness of Australia's Military Justice System*, 16 June 2005.

effectively and the specific knowledge necessary to critically examine human rights claims affecting the military.

B Proposed military court of Australia

The Military Court of Australia Bill 2012 (Cth) (MCA Bill) seeks to establish a new court, the Military Court of Australia, under Chapter III of the Australian Constitution. The requirement for a new court arose after the Australian Military Court was declared to be constitutionally invalid in 2009.[31] The MCA Bill was scrutinised by the Senate Legal and Constitutional Affairs Legislation Committee (Senate LCALC).[32] The Senate LCALC received submissions including comments on the human rights impact of the MCA Bill. Appleby and Williams[33] submitted that the proposed move to a Chapter III court 'brings Australia into line with many of its international obligations, most particularly the right to a trial before an independent and impartial tribunal'.[34] They added that 'internationally, and particularly in Europe, courts-martial have been seen as lacking the requisite independence from the Executive, the possibility of partiality because of influence, conscious or not, from the military chain of command, and the review of decisions by a non-independent body'.[35] The submission of Duxbury, Liivoja and Groves made similar comments on the human rights aspects of the MCA Bill and noted that the 'European Court of Human Rights views the presence of civilians as contributing to the independence and impartiality of a military justice system.'[36] They also pointed out that under the provisions of

[31] See *Lane* v. *Morrison* (2009) 239 CLR 230 and discussion in Chapter 13.

[32] The Senate Legal and Constitutional Affairs Legislation Committee, Report, Military Court of Australia Bill 2012 and Military Court of Australia (Transitional Provisions and Consequential Amendments) Bill 2012, October 2012.

[33] Gabrielle Appleby and John Williams, 'Submission: Inquiry into the Military Court of Australia Bill 2012 and Military Court of Australia (Transitional Provisions and Consequential Amendments) Bill 2012', 12 July 2012 www.aph.gov.au/parliamentary_business/committees/senate_committees?url=legcon_ctte/completed_inquiries/2010-13/military_court_2012/submissions.htm.

[34] Ibid., 5.

[35] Ibid. Appleby and Williams cited *Van de Hurk* v. *The Netherlands* (1994) 18 EHRR 481 (ECHR); *Findlay* v. *United Kingdom* (1996) 21 EHRR 221 (ECHR); *R* v. *Boyd* [2002] UKHL 31; *Brumarescu* v. *Romania* (2001) 33 EHRR 35 (ECHR); *Morris* v. *United Kingdom* (2002) EHRR 1253 (ECHR); *Cooper* v. *United Kingdom* (2004) 39 EHRR 171 (ECHR), 172; and *Grieves* v. *United Kingdom* (2004) 39 EHRR 51 (ECHR).

[36] Alison Duxbury, Rain Liivoja and Matthew Groves, 'Submission to the Senate Standing Committee on Legal and Constitutional Affairs: Inquiry into the Military Court of Australia Bill 2012 and Military Court of Australia (Transitional Provisions and

the MCA Bill 'judges will be civilians and will also have the requirements of tenure recognised by international human rights law, and most importantly, the *Commonwealth Constitution*'.[37]

Although these features of the MCA Bill would clearly enhance the protection of human rights, the Senate Committee remained concerned about the absence of trial by jury. Clause 64 of the MCA Bill provides that all charges of service offences are to be dealt with otherwise than on indictment. Such a provision would effectively circumvent the protection in s. 80 of the Constitution for trial by jury for indictable offences. The Senate LCALC noted a submission by McLure[38] that a number of serious offences punishable by life imprisonment could be tried by a single judge of the MCA without a jury.[39] These offences include aiding the enemy and mutiny under the Defence Force Discipline Act 1982 (Cth) (DFDA), and murder and other serious civilian offences incorporated into the DFDA by s. 61 of the DFDA.[40] The majority report of the Senate LCACA accepted that it was appropriate in the military justice context that members of the Australian Defence Force (ADF) be tried without a jury. The majority report stated that 'defence personnel do not cease to have the rights and protections of Australian citizens, however, they do give up some rights by voluntarily enlisting in armed service and becoming subject to military discipline, including the service offences listed in the Defence Force Discipline Act'.[41] It also noted that 'no right to trial by jury existed previously for those charged with serious service offences tried before courts martial or defence force magistrates'.[42] The majority also suggested that 'the legal framework and the practical requirements of the military justice system complicate the introduction of trial by jury for serious service offences'.[43] Specifically in relation to s. 80 of the Constitution they said that 'the literal interpretation of section 80 has been affirmed in a consistent series of High Court decisions. The current

Consequential Amendments) Bill 2012', 13 July 2012 www.aph.gov.au/parliamentary_business/committees/senate_committees?url=legcon_ctte/completed_inquiries/2010-13/military_court_2012/submissions.htm at p. 2 (citing *Grieves* v. *United Kingdom* (2004) 39 EHRR 2, [78]).

[37] Ibid., at 2–3.

[38] David McLure, 'Submission: Inquiry into the Military Court of Australia Bill 2012 and Military Court of Australia (Transitional Provisions and Consequential Amendments) Bill 2012', 8 August 2012, www.aph.gov.au/parliamentary_business/committees/senate_committees?url=legcon_ctte/completed_inquiries/2010-13/military_court_2012/submissions.htm.

[39] The Senate Legal and Constitutional Affairs Legislation Committee, above n. 32, p. 39.

[40] Ibid. [41] Ibid., p. 49. [42] Ibid. [43] Ibid., p. 50.

legal position is that it is for the parliament to determine which offences will proceed on indictment'.[44]

The five Liberal party members of the Senate LCALC issued a dissenting report in which they said:

> While the argument was made that service offences are not criminal offences ... this distinction is blurred. Many service offences, such as theft or assault, have civilian criminal law equivalents. Further, section 61 of the Defence Force Discipline Act imports the civilian criminal law of the Jervis Bay Territory to apply to defence personnel in Australia and overseas. These include civilian criminal offences which are indictable and are tried with a jury in a civilian context.[45]

The dissenting Senators concluded that:

> all members of the ADF are entitled to the same rights and protections as other Australian citizens before a Chapter III court. This is in keeping with Australia's international obligations, including Article 14 of the International Covenant on Civil and Political Rights which provides that all persons shall be equal before courts and tribunals. Accordingly, Liberal Senators recommend that the bills be amended to incorporate a right to trial by jury before the Military Court for all service offences which would otherwise be on indictment in a civilian context.[46]

The Australian Greens member of the Senate LCALC expressed similar concerns that the Bill could abrogate the rights of service members to a trial by jury.[47] These concerns have not been resolved. The MCA Bill was not enacted and lapsed when a federal election was held in September 2013.

But the human rights implications of the MCA Bill were at least publicly examined. The enactment of the Scrutiny Act meant that the introduction of the MCA Bill required the government to prepare, and table in parliament, a Statement of Compatibility with Human Rights for the MCA Bill. Such a statement was included in the Explanatory Memorandum to the Bill. The Explanatory Memorandum emphasised that 'the trials of service offences are not criminal proceedings as such'[48] and that the DFDA 'complements, and does not replace, Australian criminal law'.[49] The Explanatory Memorandum stated that article 14(1) of the ICCPR, which provides for the right to a fair and public hearing by a competent, independent and impartial tribunal in the determination of

[44] Ibid. [45] Ibid., p. 53. [46] Ibid., p. 55. [47] Ibid., p. 60.
[48] Explanatory Memorandum, Military Court of Australia Bill 2012 (Cth), at [24].
[49] Ibid., at [26].

any criminal charge against a person, or of a person's rights and obligations in a suit at law, 'is engaged because serious service offences will be an offence against the law of the Commonwealth and conviction may attract punishments including fines, imprisonment or military detention'.[50] Accordingly, it is clear that the MCA Bill did impact on human rights. Any further scrutiny of the issue depends upon whether a revised Bill is introduced into the new parliament.

The MCA Bill was not the only Bill concerning military justice that was considered by the Parliament in 2012 and 2013. Some of the interim arrangements for Australia's military justice system put in place in 2009 by the Military Justice (Interim Measures) Act (No 1) 2009 were due to expire in September 2013. To extend the interim arrangements the Military Justice (Interim Measures) Amendment Act 2013 (2013 Interim Measures Act) was passed in June 2013 and received royal assent on 1 July 2013. The 2013 Interim Measures Act extended the tenure of a number of statutory office holders for a further two-year period until September 2015. The Explanatory Memorandum stated that the then proposed legislation, the Military Justice (Interim Measures) Amendment Bill 2013 (2013 Interim Measures Bill), 'does not have an impact on human rights'.[51] The PJCHR thought otherwise and reported that it had written to the Minister for Defence seeking clarification as to whether or not the interim arrangements 'are consistent with the criteria of an independent and impartial tribunal as required by article 14(1) of the ICCPR'.[52] The PJCHR noted that under the current interim arrangements the appointment of the Chief Judge Advocate and the current full-time judge advocate was for a fixed term but with the ability of the Minister of Defence to terminate an appointment prior to the expiry of the fixed term.[53] The PJCHR expressly referred to the United Nations Human Rights Committee's General Comment No 32 when it stated 'the fact that the term of appointment of a member of a court or tribunal is terminable at the discretion of a member of the executive, raises concerns about the independence of the tribunal'.[54] After the Minister of Defence responded to these

[50] Ibid.

[51] Explanatory Memorandum, Military Justice (Interim Measures) Amendment Bill 2013 at [9].

[52] Australian Parliament, Parliamentary Joint Committee on Human Rights, Sixth Report of 2013 (May 2013) at [1.157].

[53] Ibid., at [1.150]. [54] Ibid., at [1.154].

concerns,[55] the PJCHR concluded that no further scrutiny of the 2013 Interim Measures Bill was required.[56]

The concerns of the PJCHR with the proposed 2013 Interim Measures Act demonstrate that the new human rights scrutiny regime clearly extends to legislation concerning Australia's military justice system. It is too early to determine what, if any, impact this scrutiny will ultimately have on the military justice system in Australia. It also remains to be seen what concerns the PJCHR may have if the MCA Bill reintroduced into the parliament.

III Application of the ICCPR to Australia's military justice system

The ICCPR prima facie applies to all offences under the DFDA. However, the extent of its application to specific articles of the ICCPR will depend on the scope of each individual article and the extent to which Australian law is influenced by the ICCPR, given that the ICCPR has not been enacted in Australian domestic law. Some articles of the ICCPR only apply in specified circumstances, such as article 14 of the ICCPR dealing with fair trial rights, while others are of more general application, such as article 26 concerning equality before the law. Article 14 is of particular importance to all trials including military trials. The essence of a military justice system is to provide for military discipline and such an objective will only be achieved where fair trial rights are provided by the system.

A Application of article 14 of the ICCPR to military tribunals

Because the ICCPR has not been directly incorporated into Australian domestic law it is necessary to examine Australian law more generally to determine how the provisions of the ICCPR will indirectly apply to military tribunals in Australia. The right to a fair trial in Australia is primarily a common law right, supplemented by some legislation. As Bagaric, Alexander and Ebejer note, accused persons throughout Australia 'have a statutory right to be informed of the charge against them, the right to an interpreter, the right to the provision of legal aid,

[55] Australian Parliament, Parliamentary Joint Committee on Human Rights, Tenth Report of 2013 (June 2013).

[56] Ibid., p. 125.

and the right to silence'.[57] Those authors argue that the right to a fair trial in Australia is illusory because it 'is simply a right to a hearing which is as fair as a court can make it given the matters over which a court has control'.[58]

Some have argued that limited fair trial rights might be derived from the Australian Constitution. Section 80 of the Constitution provides for the right to a trial by a jury but only in trials of indictable offences. In relation to impartiality, which primarily arises under Australian common law, it has been suggested that the impartiality requirement has a constitutional dimension. In *Ebner* v. *Official Trustee in Bankruptcy*,[59] Gaudron J said that 'in my view, Ch III of the Constitution operates to guarantee impartiality and the appearance of impartiality through the Australia court system'.[60]

Accordingly, in Australia the notion of the right to a fair trial will primarily be derived from the common law and from statute, and perhaps in a limited way from the Constitution. The common law can be developed in accordance with international law and in this respect the fair trial provisions in international law become relevant in the Australian context. Article 14 of the ICCPR provides that all persons shall be equal before the courts and tribunals and that everyone shall be entitled to a fair and public hearing by a competent, independent and impartial tribunal established by law. Article 14 also provides that in the determination of any criminal charge everyone shall be entitled to the following minimum guarantees: to be informed of the relevant charges; to be tried without undue delay; to be tried in his or her presence; to be legally represented by a person of their own choosing; and to be able to examine witnesses.

In relation to the right to a fair trial it is important to note that military members in Australia voluntarily join the ADF and it can be inferred that such members by joining the ADF are acknowledging, at least in general terms, that the military justice system is acceptable to them. As Rowe notes, 'where the armed forces consist of volunteers only it is reasonable to infer that the disciplinary system is acceptable to them, otherwise they would not have joined'.[61] Rowe states that they 'may be presumed to have agreed, by joining, to subject themselves to a disciplinary system more

[57] Mirko Bagaric, Theo Alexander and Marlene Ebejer, 'The Illusion That Is the Right to a Fair Trial in Australia' (2011) 17(2) *Australian Journal of Human Rights*, p. 59 at 64.

[58] Ibid., at 60. [59] (2000) 205 CLR 337. [60] Ibid., at 363.

[61] Peter Rowe, *The Impact of Human Rights Law on Armed Forces* (Cambridge, Cambridge University Press, 2005), p. 66.

stringent than any other operating within the civilian sphere'.[62] Importantly Rowe also makes the point that to 'argue that by accepting this type of employment members of the armed forces have also accepted the risks of being treated unfairly under it, or that they can be dealt with in any way that their superior officers consider appropriate, is to misunderstand the nature of their voluntary acceptance of military service'.[63] Clearly an agreement to be bound by a different system of justice within the military context is not an agreement to be treated unfairly. As Rowe argues, an 'army which declared that it would ignore the human rights of its soldiers during its disciplinary procedures may find it difficult to recruit and retain them where it depends upon voluntary enlistment'.[64]

At an international level it is well established that article 14 applies to military justice. On 23 August 2007 the United Nations Human Rights Committee issued General Comment No 32[65] which deals expressly with article 14 of the ICCPR. General Comment No 32 noted that the 'provisions of article 14 apply to all courts and tribunals within the scope of that article whether ordinary or specialized, civilian or military'. In the view of the Committee, article 14 'contains guarantees that States parties must respect, regardless of their legal traditions and their domestic law'.[66] The first sentence of article 14 provides that 'all persons shall be equal before the courts and tribunals'. The Committee expressed the view that this guarantee must 'be respected whenever domestic law entrusts a judicial body with a judicial task'.[67] The Committee stressed that equality before the courts and tribunals 'requires that similar cases are dealt with in similar proceedings'.[68] It has also made clear that the notion of a tribunal under article 14 'designates a body, regardless of its denomination, that is established by law, is independent of the executive and legislative branches of government or enjoys in specific cases judicial independence in deciding legal matters in proceedings that are judicial in nature'.[69]

Although the right to a fair trial applies to military tribunals the case law from Europe suggests that the courts in Europe will provide a degree of flexibility for the military justice systems of States. In *Morris* v. *United Kingdom*[70] the European Court of Human Rights held that 'the practice of using courts staffed in whole or in part by the military to try members of the armed forces is deeply entrenched in the legal systems of many

[62] Ibid. [63] Ibid. [64] Ibid., p. 68.
[65] Human Rights Committee, *General Comment No 32 Right to Equality before Courts and Tribunals and to a Fair Trial (Article 14)* UN Doc CCPR/C/GC/32 (23 August 2007).
[66] Ibid., at [4]. [67] Ibid., at [7]. [68] Ibid., at [14]. [69] Ibid., at [18].
[70] (2002) 34 EHRR 52.

member states.'[71] The Court accepted that a military court could, in principle, constitute an independent and impartial tribunal and explained that 'the Convention will only tolerate such courts as long as sufficient safeguards are in place to guarantee their independence and impartiality.'[72] In *R* v. *Spear*[73] Lord Rodger conceded that in *Morris* v. *United Kingdom*, while 'it is perhaps possible to detect some lack of enthusiasm in the use of the term "tolerate", the passage shows clearly that, in principle, a military court can constitute an independent and impartial tribunal in terms of article 6(1)'.[74] Lord Rodger went on to say that what 'is required is that there should be sufficient safeguards of the independence and impartiality of its members'.[75] These cases suggest that sufficient safeguards will be required in the military context, but that some degree of flexibility will be provided by the courts.

In the Australian context offences under the DFDA may be classified for some purposes of the ICCPR as disciplinary offences or as criminal offences or as both disciplinary and criminal. That is, some minor offences under the DFDA may not be criminal offences but rather purely disciplinary in nature. The classification is significant in relation to the fair trial provisions in article 14 of the ICCPR because the fair trial guarantees only apply to the determination of a 'criminal charge' and a 'suit at law'. However, the European cases discussed above suggest that the focus should be on the substance of the penalty imposed rather than on the labelling of offences as criminal or disciplinary.

In *Engel* v. *The Netherlands*[76] the European Court of Human Rights considered, in the context of military discipline law applicable in the Netherlands, provisions in the European Convention on Human Rights[77] that are similar to those in article 14 of the ICCPR. The Court noted that the ECHR 'applies in principle to members of the armed forces'.[78] The Court held that any classification made by a state between discipline law and criminal law is not of itself decisive. Instead what is required to determine whether or not an offence involves a criminal charge is to look at three factors. The three factors considered by the Court in *Engel* are: the categorisation of the allegation in domestic law; whether the offence

[71] Ibid., at [59]. [72] Ibid. [73] [2003] 1 AC 734. [74] Ibid., at 766. [75] Ibid.

[76] (1979) 1 EHRR 647.

[77] Convention for the Protection of Human Rights and Fundamental Freedoms, 4 November 1950, in force 3 September 1953, as amended by Protocol 14 to the Convention for the Protection of Human Rights and Fundamental Freedoms, 13 May 2004, CETS no 194, in force 1 June 2010, 213 UNTS 221 (ECHR).

[78] Ibid., at [54].

applies to a specific group or is of a generally binding character; and the severity of the penalty attached to it.[79] This will means that offences such as drug trafficking and fraud are clearly criminal and article 14 will therefore apply. In England the courts have largely focused on the severity of the penalty to determine whether a particular proceeding involves a criminal charge.[80] If the penalty includes a period of imprisonment, for the purposes of article 14[81] the offence will be classified as criminal.[82]

In *Engel* the Court accepted that a criminal charge was involved. But the Court did accept that when interpreting the ECHR 'the Court must bear in mind the particular characteristics of military life and its effects on the situation of individual members of the armed forces'.[83] The Court went on to say that each State 'is competent to organise its own system of military discipline and enjoys in the matter a certain *margin of appreciation*'.[84]

In the Australian context the absence of domestic law incorporating the provisions of the ICCPR remains a significant difference between Australia and Europe. The indications are that courts and tribunals in Australia may not place much weight on the provisions of the ICCPR because the ICCPR is not part of Australian domestic law. In *Stuart* v. *Chief of Army*[85] the Defence Force Discipline Appeal Tribunal (DFDAT) considered an argument that the Australian military justice system was infected by inherent bias and accordingly that the system was in breach of article 14 of the ICCPR. Heerey, Underwood and Mildren JJ noted that the DFDAT 'is not bound by decisions of the European Court of Human Rights' and that the ICCPR 'is not part of Australian domestic law and, therefore, has only a limited role to play in this country'.[86] Such reasoning is also consistent with the parliamentary model adopted by the Scrutiny Act. As discussed earlier the parliamentary model provides that it is parliament's role to determine what human rights will be incorporated into legislation. The model adopted in the Scrutiny Act can be contrasted with the dialogue model reflected in a Bill of Rights approach that has not been adopted in Australia. A dialogue model has a role for the judiciary but the decision in *Stuart* provides support for the proposition that there is currently a very limited role for courts and tribunals in relation to

79 Richard Clayton and Hugh Tomlinson (eds.), *Fair Trial Rights*, Volume 1 (Oxford, Oxford University Press, 2008), p. 840.
80 Ibid., p. 716. 81 ECHR, art. 6. 82 Clayton and Tomlinson, above n. 79, p. 716.
83 *Engel* at [54]. 84 Ibid., at [59] (emphasis added). 85 [2003] ADFDAT 3.
86 Ibid., at [37].

human rights treaties in circumstances where treaties such as the ICCPR are not part of Australian domestic law and Australia does not have a general human rights statute such as a Bill of Rights.

In addition to military hearings that are similar to the determination of a criminal charge it is important to consider a 'suit at law'. As noted above, article 14 guarantees a fair trial in a 'suit at law'. If dismissal of a member from the ADF was undertaken as a separate administrative procedure from a disciplinary hearing, then the provisions of article 14 would not be applicable. This is because such a procedure would not be a criminal proceeding and nor would it be a suit at law. In General Comment No 32 the Human Rights Committee said that 'there is no determination of rights and obligations in a suit at law where the persons concerned are confronted with measures taken against them in their capacity as persons subordinated to a high degree of administrative control, such as disciplinary measures not amounting to penal sanctions being taken against a civil servant, a member of the armed forces, or a prisoner'.[87] This suggests that if dismissal action was taken as an administrative decision, rather than a punishment under the DFDA, the provisions of article 14 would not apply to such an administrative decision.

In Australia, in the context of detention of non-citizens, the Courts have drawn a similar distinction between criminal punishments and non-punitive administrative actions. In *Al-Kateb* v. *Godwin*[88] the High Court of Australia drew a distinction between detention as a criminal punishment and detention as a valid exercise of administrative power. The appellant had been detained under provisions of the Migration Act 1958 (Cth). He unsuccessfully applied to the Federal Court of Australia for a declaration that he had been detained illegally and for an order that he be released. He then appealed to the High Court of Australia. In the High Court Gleeson CJ said that administrative detention 'is not a form of extra-judicial punishment'.[89] His Honour went on to say that the administrative power to detain a person 'is not punitive in nature, and does not involve an invalid attempt to confer on the Executive a power to punish people who, being in Australia, are subject to, and entitled to the

[87] Human Rights Committee, *General Comment No 32 Right to Equality before Courts and Tribunals and to a Fair Trial (Article 14)* at [17].

[88] (2004) 219 CLR 562. See also *Plaintiff M47/2012* v. *Director-General* (2012) 292 ALR 243; and Ben Saul, 'Dark Justice: Australia's Indefinite Detention of Refugees on Security Grounds under International Human Rights Law' (2012) 13 *Melbourne Journal of International Law*, p. 1.

[89] (2004) 219 CLR 562 at 571.

protection of, the law'.[90] McHugh J said that as 'long as the purpose of the detention is to make the alien available for deportation or to prevent the alien from entering Australia or the Australian community, the detention is non-punitive'.[91] Hayne J agreed and said that 'the continued exclusion of such persons from the Australian community in accordance with the regime established by the Migration Act does not impinge upon the separation of powers required by the Constitution'.[92] Callinan J also agreed, holding that 'detention of aliens, certainly for the purposes of deportation, clearly falls within the exception traditionally and rightly recognised as being detention otherwise than of a punitive kind'.[93]

The distinction between detention as a criminal punishment and detention as a lawful administrative act provides a useful parallel to the criminal/administrative distinction drawn in General Comment No 32. It is also possible that the absence of a general human rights statute in Australia may partly explain the tolerance of Australian courts to administrative detention.

B The right to an impartial hearing before a military tribunal

Even without the incorporation of the ICCPR into Australian domestic law it is widely accepted that those appearing before a military tribunal are entitled to an impartial hearing as set out in article 14. There are two aspects to this right. The first is a system that is characterised by institutional independence and impartiality, and the second is a hearing free from bias, including both actual and apprehended bias. For a person to receive a fair hearing, as required by article 14, both of these requirements must be met.

The requirement that article 14 requires a system that is characterised by institutional independence and impartiality arose in the military context in *R* v. *Spear*,[94] which involved two groups of appeals. In the first group, three defendants were convicted by courts martial. They appealed against their convictions on the basis that the court that convicted them was presided over by a permanent president and that they had not been afforded a fair hearing by an independent and impartial tribunal as required by the ECHR. In the second group, nine defendants were convicted or pleaded guilty at various courts martial. They contended that a trial by a court martial of an offence against the ordinary

90 Ibid., at 573. 91 Ibid., at 584. 92 Ibid., at 651. 93 Ibid., at 659.
94 [2003] 1 AC 734.

criminal law was incompatible with the Convention. The Courts-Martial Appeal Court dismissed all the appeals. Further appeals were made to the House of Lords. In relation to the permanent presidents of Air Force courts martial, Lord Rodger noted that such officers were subject to annual reports reviewing their performance.[95] Lord Rodger said that such reports were 'undesirable' and 'unnecessary'.[96] But importantly Lord Rodger concluded that the reports themselves did not give the 'slightest reason' for considering that the president of the court martial's independence or impartiality was compromised.[97] Lord Rodger also considered the issue of sentencing in relation to the issue of courts martial dealing with offences under the civil law. His Lordship said that the sentences which a court martial imposes may 'not coincide exactly with the sentences which a civil judge would pass on the same facts'.[98] In Lord Rodger's view that did not call the decisions of the courts martial into question.[99] Lord Rodger concluded that no 'fair-minded and informed observer' would conclude 'that there was a real possibility that the courts-martial in these cases lacked independence or impartiality'.[100] The appeals were dismissed.[101]

The disqualification for bias principle applies to military tribunals[102] and prisoners of war are also entitled to be tried by an independent and impartial court.[103] A number of cases have considered the requirement of an impartial tribunal in the military context. In the Australian context in *Hogan* v. *Chief of Army*[104] Gallop, Underwood and Mildren JJ held that the bias rule applied to military tribunals.[105] In *R* v. *Wayne Lawrence (No 2)*,[106] the New Zealand Courts Martial Appeal Court similarly held that the bias rule applied to military tribunals.

Although the disqualification principle applies to military tribunals some relaxation of the rules will be allowed in certain circumstances. In *R* v. *Taare*[107] the appellant was convicted by a field court martial in Korea.

95 Ibid., at 773. 96 Ibid. 97 Ibid., at 774. 98 Ibid., at 781. 99 Ibid.

100 Ibid., at 783.

101 Lord Bingham agreed with Lord Rodger: 752. Lords Steyn and Hutton both agreed with Lord Bingham and Lord Rodger (at 752), as did Lord Scott (at 753).

102 For an examination of recusal in the military in the United States, see B.T. Quann, *Recusal in the Military*, A thesis presented to the Judge Advocate General's School, United States Army, 1 April 1974. For an examination of the disqualification for bias principle, see John Tarrant, *Disqualification for Bias* (Annandale, NSW, Federation Press, 2012).

103 See article 84 of the Geneva Convention III Relative to the Treatment of Prisoners of War (1949) and article 75(4) of Additional Protocol I to the Geneva Conventions Relating to the Protection of Victims of International Armed Conflicts (1977).

104 [1999] ADFDAT 1. 105 Ibid., at [72]. 106 [2001] 1 NZCMAR 414.

107 [1955] 1 NZCMAR 1.

The appellant challenged his conviction on a number of grounds including that the judge advocate was the legal staff officer who had drawn up the charge sheet. Hutchison J, delivering the judgment of the New Zealand Courts Martial Appeal Court that included L.M. Inglis and Sir Howard Kippenberger, stated that it was 'undesirable as a general rule that an officer should be appointed judge advocate when he has himself prepared the charges against the accused' but that this might be unavoidable in small formations.[108]

A limited relaxation of the bias rule might be justified in the circumstances that arose in *R* v. *Taare* but a more general relaxation of the bias rule is not appropriate in the military. The context needs to be carefully considered. The courts have emphasised that the bias rule must be understood in context and this means that in the civilian judicial context it will be relevant that the decision-maker is a trained judicial officer. As Lord Hope said recently in *O'Neill (No 2)* v. *Her Majesty's Advocate*,[109] in relation to disqualification for bias, the 'obvious starting point is the context'.[110] Lord Hope went on to say that in cases where the relevant decision-maker was a judicial officer the 'fair-minded and informed observer would appreciate that he was a professional judge who had taken the judicial oath and had years of relevant training and experience'.[111] But in the military context it is important to appreciate that the context is a system that has a hierarchical structure and is in many ways closed to the public. Summary proceedings are conducted with less formality than a civilian court and an accused person is usually defended by a non-lawyer. The presiding officer will often be a commanding officer with little or no legal training. These characteristics of the military justice system reinforce the requirements for a strict application of the bias rule in the military context with only limited flexibility to accommodate proceedings occurring during military operations.

The limited decisions in the military context do not support a general relaxation of the bias rule to accommodate the military. With an increased focus on human rights, and the possible move to a Chapter III military court, it is probably now less likely that a general relaxation of the bias rule would be permitted by the courts and there is arguably no justification for any general relaxation of the bias rule for military tribunals.

[108] Ibid., at 6. [109] [2013] 1 WLR 1992. [110] Ibid., at [53]. [111] Ibid.

C Application of article 26 of the ICCPR

Equality before the law is also an important principle in the military context. Article 26 of the ICCPR provides that:

> All persons are equal before the law and are entitled without any discrimination to the equal protection of the law. In this respect, the law shall prohibit any discrimination and guarantee to all persons equal and effective protection against discrimination on any ground such as race, colour, sex, language, religion, political or other opinion, national or social origin, property, birth or other status.

In *Engel* v. *The Netherlands*[112] the European Court of Human Rights held that inequality of treatment between persons of different ranks did not breach the requirement of equal treatment before the law. The Court was considering the enjoyment of rights pursuant to article 14 of the ECHR, which is in similar terms to the right to equal treatment under article 26 of the ICCPR. In *Engel* the complainants pointed to the inequality of treatment between ranks in terms of punishments. The Court accepted that the 'hierarchical structure inherent in armies entails differentiation according to rank'.[113] The differing responsibilities of various ranks 'justify certain inequalities of treatment in the disciplinary sphere'.[114] Accordingly, 'the European Convention allows the competent national authorities a considerable margin of appreciation'.[115] But it is critical to note that the Court was focused on the disciplinary sphere and not on the criminal sphere. Disciplinary and criminal offences may be based upon similar or even identical conduct but give rise to different penalties because only criminal offences attract the protection of article 14 of the ICCPR.

In *Engel* the Court held that some of the charges were disciplinary in nature but others were criminal in nature because of the potentially severe punishments they could attract. Their 'aim was the imposition of serious punishments involving deprivation of liberty'.[116] The Court held that it is the potential punishment available for an offence that is relevant, not the actual punishment given to a person.[117]

The issue of inequality in the military context was considered by the Supreme Court of Canada in *MacKay* v. *The Queen.*[118] At issue was whether a member of the army could be tried by a military tribunal for a civilian drug trafficking offence incorporated into the National Defence

112 (1979) 1 EHRR 647. 113 Ibid., at [72]. 114 Ibid. 115 Ibid. 116 Ibid., at [85]. 117 Ibid. 118 [1980] 2 SCR 370.

Act 1970 because of a requirement of equality before the law in s. 1 of the Canadian Bill of Rights which provided at the time that:

> It is hereby recognized and declared that in Canada there have existed and shall continue to exist without discrimination by reason of race, national origin, colour, religion or sex, the following human rights and fundamental freedoms, namely, (*a*) the right of the individual to life, liberty, security of the person and enjoyment of property, and the right not to be deprived thereof except by due process of law; (*b*) the right of the individual to equality before the law and the protection of the law.

This reasoning is similar to the requirements of article 26 of the ICCPR. In Canada this equality before the law had been held not to be infringed if legislation is enacted for the purpose of achieving a valid federal objective. Accordingly, a majority in *MacKay* held that a lack of equality arising from a civilian criminal offence being tried by a military tribunal did not offend the requirements of s. 1 of the Bill of Rights.[119] Laskin CJC and Estey J dissented and said that the relevant law was inoperative because it treated people differently.[120]

It is also important to appreciate that *Engel* was decided in 1976 and *MacKay* in 1980. Subsequently in November 1989 the Human Rights Committee issued General Comment No 18 on the ICCPR dealing with the issue of non-discrimination under article 26. The General Comment notes that article 26 of the ICCPR 'entitles all persons to equality before the law'.[121] Although there is a right to derogate from certain obligations under the ICCPR this is only available in times of emergency.[122] The General Comment states that the term 'discrimination' as used in the ICCPR 'should be understood to imply any distinction . . . which is based on any ground such as . . . status, and which has the purpose or effect of nullifying or impairing the recognition, enjoyment or exercise by all persons, on an equal footing, of all rights and freedoms'.[123]

Article 2(1) of the ICCPR provides that all persons are entitled to their rights under the ICCPR to be respected without distinction of any kind. Importantly the General Comment makes it clear that the right to be protected against discrimination provided for in article 26 is not limited to rights arising under the ICCPR.[124] The General Comment explains that 'article 26 provides that all persons are equal before the law'.[125] The Committee's view is that 'article 26 does not merely duplicate the

[119] Ibid., 391–98 (Martland, Ritchie, Pigeon, Beetz and Chouinard JJ), 406 (McIntyre J).
[120] Ibid., 380–86. [121] Ibid., [1]. [122] ICCPR, art. 4(1).
[123] General Comment No 18, at [7]. [124] Ibid., [12]. [125] Ibid.

guarantee already provided for in article 2 but provides in itself an autonomous right'.[126] It 'prohibits discrimination in law or in fact in any field regulated and protected by public authorities'.[127] Thus, 'when legislation is adopted by a State party, it must comply with the requirement of article 26 that its content should not be discriminatory'.[128] But discrimination might be possible in some very limited circumstances. General Comment No 18 concludes that 'the Committee observes that not every differentiation of treatment will constitute discrimination, if the criteria for such differentiation are reasonable and objective and if the aim is to achieve a purpose which is legitimate under the Covenant'.[129]

It therefore remains to be seen what forms of difference in treatment will contravene the requirement that all persons be treated equally under the law. The difficulty of examining this issue in the context of military justice is that a system of military justice often operates as a separate and distinct system of justice from the civilian criminal system rather than part of a single overall system of justice.

D *Inequality in the context of Australia's military justice system*

There is a right under the First Optional Protocol to the ICCPR, to which Australia is a party,[130] for individuals whose rights enumerated in the Convention have been violated, and who have exhausted all available domestic remedies, to submit a written communication to the Human Rights Committee.[131]

One domestic remedy that may be available is a constitutional challenge to the DFDA on the basis that there is an implication in the Australian Constitution that people must be treated equally under the law based on Chapter III of the Constitution. A member of the ADF, if tried and punished in a military tribunal, could be punished under s. 68(1)(c) of the DFDA with dismissal from the ADF. Such a punishment could not be imposed if an ADF member was tried for a similar offence in the civilian criminal justice system. It could be argued that this effectively discriminates between civilians and non-civilians for offences that can be committed under either the civilian system or the DFDA. The question is whether or not the different potential punishments are constitutionally

[126] Ibid. [127] Ibid. [128] Ibid. [129] Ibid., [13].

[130] Australia signed the Optional Protocol to the ICCPR on 25 September 1991.

[131] Optional Protocol to the International Covenant on Civil and Political Rights, 16 December 1966, in force 23 March 1976, 999 UNTS 302, art. 2.

valid and this in part depends upon whether or not the offences should be seen as the same offences or different offences.

The issue of equality under the Australian Constitution arose in a non-military context, but was not completely resolved, in *Leeth* v. *Commonwealth*[132] which involved different non-parole periods for federal offenders serving their sentences in state prisons. Although a majority of the High Court of Australia held that the legislation was valid there were indications that different maximum penalties for the same offence might offend a doctrine of equality implied in Chapter III of the Australian Constitution. It must be noted here that it may be permissible to apply a different sentence in different parts of the country for some legitimate reason but this should be seen as part of a sentencing discretion. But this is a different issue to the issue of a statute, or a number of statutes, setting a different maximum sentence for the same offence. However, it must be recognised that an offence under the general criminal law that is incorporated into the DFDA under s. 61 is strictly speaking a different offence from its civilian counterpart. A member of the ADF who is alleged to have committed an offence that is incorporated into the DFDA is charged with committing an offence under s. 61 and reference is then made to the relevant civilian offence that is incorporated into the DFDA. In essence the civilian offences are read as if they formed part of the DFDA. In practical terms this means that the relevant ADF member is charged with committing an offence under the DFDA. The incorporation of the offences into the DFDA through s. 61 is simply a mechanism that removes the need to enact within the DFDA itself each and every offence within the civilian criminal statutes. It also removes the need to amend the DFDA every time a civilian criminal offence is amended or enacted.

Although DFDA offences based on the civilian criminal system are strictly speaking different offences when charged under the DFDA it is still possible for an accused person to argue that the offences in all relevant respects are identical. If such an argument were to be accepted by the courts, any constitutional right of equality before the law could more readily be raised. This issue is of more relevance to any new military justice system that might incorporate a Chapter III court as part of the system than it is to the current military justice system which is entirely outside of Chapter III. In *Leeth* Brennan J said that it would be offensive to the constitutional unity of the Australian people 'to expose offenders

132 (1992) 174 CLR 455.

against the same law of the Commonwealth to different maximum penalties dependent on the locality of the court by which the offender is convicted and sentenced'.[133] His Honour said that it follows 'that the maximum penalty prescribed for a breach of the law must be the same irrespective of the locality of the court before which the offender is tried and sentenced'.[134] In their joint judgment, in dissent, Deane and Toohey JJ referred to the 'underlying or inherent theoretical equality of all persons under the law and before the courts'.[135] Their Honours described this equality as 'a fundamentally and generally beneficial doctrine of the common law and a basic prescript of the administration of justice under our system of government'.[136] Importantly their Honours were concerned with the conceptual basis of the Constitution, which their Honours described as 'the free agreement of "the people" – all the people – of the federating colonies to unite in the Commonwealth under the Constitution'.[137] Their Honours went on to say that '[i]mplicit in that free agreement was the notion of the inherent equality of the people as the parties to the compact'.[138] But their Honours did not suggest that there would be equality in all circumstances. They suggested that, in relation to a court's obligation to act judicially, courts have a duty 'to extend to the parties . . . equal justice, that is to say, to treat them fairly and impartially as equals before the law and to refrain from discrimination on irrelevant or irrational grounds'.[139]

Gaudron J said that all 'are equal before the law. And the concept of equal justice – a concept which requires the like treatment of persons in like circumstances, but also requires that genuine differences be treated as such – is fundamental to the judicial process.'[140] In *Kable* v. *DPP (NSW)*[141] Gaudron J repeated the view that equal justice was an essential feature of the judicial process. In *Wong* v. *R*[142] Gaudron, Gummow and Hayne JJ stated, in a case not concerning Chapter III, that equal justice 'requires identity of outcome in cases that are *relevantly* identical. It requires *different* outcomes in cases that are different in some relevant aspect.'[143] In *Cameron* v. *R*[144] McHugh J suggested that if 'there is one principle that lies at the heart of the judicial power of the Commonwealth, it is that courts, exercising federal jurisdiction, cannot act in a way that is relevantly discriminatory. To deny that proposition is to deny that equal justice under the law is one of the central concerns of

[133] Ibid., at 475. [134] Ibid. [135] Ibid., at 485. [136] Ibid., at 486. [137] Ibid.
[138] Ibid. [139] Ibid., at 487. [140] Ibid., at 502. [141] (1996) 189 CLR 51, at 107.
[142] (2001) 207 CLR 584. [143] Ibid., at 608. [144] (2002) 209 CLR 339.

the judicial power of the Commonwealth.'[145] His Honour went on to say that where 'the facts and circumstances of crimes and the subjective factors of those who commit them are the same, arguably equal justice requires that there be an identity of, and not different, outcomes in the punishments that they receive'.[146]

Stellios has concluded on the basis of these decisions that 'a narrow requirement of equal justice, derived from Ch III, seems to have substantial support'.[147] The precise content of any constitutional requirement of equality is less clear. Stellios suggests that what 'may prove to be difficult in this respect, is not establishing that the principle exists, but in determining when there has been impermissible discrimination to warrant a finding that the principle has been breached'.[148]

The relatively few cases on the concept of a constitutional principle of equality before the law provide only a very limited development of the principle and none of the cases discussed above was concerned with the military context. The development of the concept of a constitutional principle of equality before the law has not sufficiently developed in Australia to provide any confidence that the courts would accept such a principle in relation to military offences. Nevertheless, the principle that all persons should be treated equally before the law, regardless of whether the context is military or not, is at least arguable. But if an argument based on equality before the law under the Constitution was accepted by the courts as a general principle, it is possible to argue that the military justice system operates as an exception to that general principle.

An exception to such a general principle, that would allow a different treatment within the military context, can be justified because the military justice system is important to maintain discipline within the ADF and the potential punishment of dismissal from the ADF is essential for maintaining discipline. It is important to note that some conduct will be an offence under the DFDA but the same conduct engaged in by a civilian outside the military context would not be an offence under the civilian criminal system. An example is the offence of creating a disturbance on service land contrary to s. 33(b) of the DFDA. In the recent case of *Li* v. *Chief of Army*[149] the appellant was an officer in the ADF who caused a confrontation with an employee of the Department of Defence, during which he spoke in an aggressive manner and also refused to leave the

[145] Ibid., at 352. [146] Ibid., at 353.

[147] J. Stellios, *The Federal Judicature: Chapter III of the Constitution* (Chatswood, NSW, LexisNexis Butterworths, 2010), p. 305.

[148] Ibid. [149] (2013) 210 FCR 299.

employee's office when requested to do so. He was convicted under s. 33 (b) of the DFDA on the basis that the confrontation amounted to the creation of a disturbance. His conviction was upheld by the Defence Force Discipline Appeal Tribunal.[150] The appellant appealed to the Full Court of the Federal Court of Australia. One of the grounds of appeal was that causing a confrontation was not an offence known to the law. Keane CJ, Jagot and Yates JJ dismissed the appeal, holding that 's 33(b) encompasses, as a matter of ordinary language, conduct whereby defence personnel and those with whom they work on service land are disrupted in, or distracted from, the performance of their duties by other members of the defence force'.[151] Their Honours went on to say that having 'regard to both the immediate and the broader context in which s 33(b) appears, it is not a leap to conclude that it is not limited to "tumults" or "riots" or breaches of the peace, but is, as a matter of ordinary parlance, apt to proscribe the disruption of the orderly conduct of defence personnel in and around defence facilities'.[152] Their Honours concluded that on 'that footing, one may say that s 33(b) of the Act is transgressed, and free speech has passed its limits, when loud argument disrupts the orderly performance by others of their duties' and accordingly 'conduct which disrupts the orderly performance of their duties by those subject to, or witnessing it, is conduct which creates a disturbance'.[153] Logan J dissented on the issue of what amounted to a disturbance for the purposes of s. 33(b) of the DFDA. His Honour said that 'as used in s 33(b) of the DFDA, "disturbance" means a breach of the peace'.[154] Logan J went on to say that 'a breach of the peace is some form of actual harm done to a person or his or her property in that person's presence or some other form of violent disorder'.[155]

Major Li appealed to the High Court of Australia. In *Li* v. *Chief of Army*[156] the High Court comprising French CJ, Crennan, Kiefel, Bell and Gageler JJ allowed the appeal on the basis that the judge advocate had misdirected the court martial on the physical elements of the offence. On the scope of s. 33(b) of the Act their Honours favoured the approach taken by the majority in the Full Court of the Federal Court of Australia. French CJ, Crennan, Kiefel, Bell and Gageler JJ emphasised the military context of the offence when they said that the 'legislative history suggests that the mischief to which s 33 of the DFDA is addressed is appropriately

[150] *Li* v. *Chief of General Army* (2012) 261 FLR 266. [151] (2013) 210 FCR 299, at [63].
[152] Ibid., at [69]. [153] Ibid. [154] Ibid., at [169]. [155] Ibid., at [190].
[156] (2013) 250 CLR 328.

identified broadly as the maintenance of order and discipline rather than narrowly as the elimination of violence'.[157]

The approach adopted by the majority of the Full Court of the Federal Court of Australia, and all five judges in the High Court of Australia, emphasises that there are offences within the military that have no direct civilian counterpart. In both *Li* v. *Chief of Army*[158] in the Federal Court and *Li* v. *Chief of Army*[159] in the High Court the meaning of disturbance for the purposes of s. 33(b) of the DFDA was held to be different from the broader meaning of disturbance as used in civilian offences concerned with a breach of the peace. As a consequence the same conduct will be treated differently when subjected to the military discipline system. This difference can be justified on the basis that service discipline requires that certain conduct is not tolerated in the military context. The absence of equality between the military justice system and the civilian criminal justice system can be justified on the basis that the two systems have two very different objectives.

It remains to be seen if different treatment of members of the military, for military offences that are essentially the same as civilian criminal offences, will be challenged in the future. That issue could very well arise for consideration in the future if the Australian parliament enacts legislation to create a Military Court of Australia that conforms to the requirements of Chapter III of the Australian Constitution.

The potential for the inequality argument to be raised at all arises because of the significant overlap between the civilian criminal justice system and the military justice system. This overlap could be removed, or at least reduced, if a narrow conception of the military justice power was adopted. Crowe and Ratnapala argue that the jurisdiction exercised by a military tribunal in Australia should be seen as an exercise of the judicial power of the Commonwealth.[160] They also argue that such judicial power can be validly exercised by a tribunal not falling within the definition of a Ch III court because it is 'a limited exception to the rule confining the judicial power of the Commonwealth to courts established in accordance with Chapter III'.[161] Importantly Crowe and Ratnapala argue that military tribunals should not be granted jurisdiction over any offence but only those that are directly related to military discipline and can be justified as falling within a limited exception to Chapter III.[162] They go

157 Ibid., at 337. 158 (2013) 210 FCR 299. 159 (2013) 250 CLR 328.

160 Jonathan Crowe and Suri Ratnapala, 'Military Justice and Chapter III: The Constitutional Basis of Courts Martial' (2012) 40 *Federal Law Review*, p. 161, at 176.

161 Ibid. 162 Ibid., at 177.

on to argue that a narrow scope of the military judicial power coupled with a service connection requirement 'offers a logical way of dealing with service and civil offences constituted by the same actions'.[163] If such a narrow scope of the military judicial power was adopted, much of the overlap between the civilian criminal and military justice systems would be removed. Any potential argument based on inequality between the two systems would necessarily become more difficult to argue.

IV Conclusion

The enactment of the Scrutiny Act means Australia's military justice system will be subject to additional human rights scrutiny. The Scrutiny Act has effectively brought the international human rights norms included in the ICCPR into the Australian Parliament for direct consideration when new laws are proposed. This is not a direct enactment of human rights but creates a process that will inform all future law making at the federal level in Australia. It is too early to determine the full implications of this process for Australia's military justice system.

Despite the increased focus on human rights in Australia there are a number of reasons why Australia's military justice system will not be directly impacted by international human rights norms. Australia has rejected a dialogue model for the protection of human rights in favour of a limited parliamentary model. Many international human rights norms are not legislated at all in Australian domestic law. There are very limited human rights protections in the Australian Constitution. There is also some justification for a flexible application of human rights in the military justice system where the objective of the system is the maintenance of discipline, though the extent of that flexibility remains deeply contested.

However, it must be accepted that changes to the implementation of human rights norms can have unintended consequences and these may not always become apparent until challenges to legislation or procedures are challenged in the courts. There is a history in Australia of challenges to Australia's military justice system and it is possible that in the future a challenge based on the application of human rights could have some unintended, and unpredictable, consequences.

[163] Ibid., at 178.

PART III

International law and military justice

15

The influence of human rights law on the reform of military justice

PANAGIOTIS KREMMYDIOTIS

I Introduction

At the end of World War II, the effectiveness of military justice needed to be reassessed. Initially, most countries established separate military justice institutions, but later, and particularly in the two last decades of the twentieth century, there was a tendency to place jurisdiction over military justice in the civilian court system. Consequently, the civilian influence on military-legal matters has grown in importance.[1] During the last decade, the fundamental basis for the existence of military justice has been reconsidered, particularly in light of the need to ensure that military justice complies with the internationally applicable human rights law.[2] The Universal Declaration of Human Rights (UDHR), the European

[1] Π. Κρεμμυδιώτη, Η Τάση Ενσωματώσεως του Αντικειμένου της Στρατιωτικής Δικαιοσύνης στην Κοινή Δικαιοσύνη, Ποιν. Χρον. ΜΘ, 888 επ. (Panagiotis Kremmydiotis, 'The Tendency for the Jurisdiction of Military Courts to Be Embodied within That of Civil Courts' (1999) *Penal Chronicles* at 888 et seq.).

[2] With the exception of the Declaration on the Protection of All Persons from Enforced Disappearance, 92nd plen mtg, UN Doc A/Res/47/133 (18 December 1992) and the Inter-American Convention on Forced Disappearance of Persons, 9 June 1994, in force 28 March 1996, 33 ILM 1429, there are no specific norms of either a treaty-based or declaratory nature, within the international human rights law relating to military offences, military jurisdiction or 'military justice'. Eugene R. Fidell, 'A Worldwide Perspective on Change in Military Justice' in Eugene R. Fidell and Dwight H. Sullivan (eds.), *Evolving Military Justice* (Annapolis, MD, Naval Institute Press, 2002), pp. 209 et seq.; Federico Andreu-Guzmán, *Military Jurisdiction and International Law: Military Courts and Gross Human Rights Violations*, vol. 1 (Geneva, International Commission of Jurists, 2004), pp. 17 and 110 et seq.; Peter Rowe, *The Impact of Human Rights Law on Armed Forces* (Cambridge, Cambridge University Press, 2006), pp. 68 et seq.; Robert Husbands, 'Human Rights Applicable to Military Justice, and in Particular the Potential Role of the Draft Principles on the Administration of Justice by Military Tribunals' in Stanislas Horvat, Ilja Van Hespen and Veerle Van Gijsegem (eds.), *International Conference on Military Jurisdiction* (Brussels, International Society for Military Law and the Law of War, 2013), pp. 465 et seq.

Convention on Human Rights and Fundamental Freedoms (ECHR), the International Covenant on Civil and Political Rights (ICCPR) and also the jurisprudence of the European Court of Human Rights[3] (dealing with arrest, detention and fair trial)[4] have been significant in achieving this aim. Some countries (including New Zealand)[5] have adopted a new military justice system to respond to the need to respect both human rights and international humanitarian law. However, other countries have yet to enact such changes. Although the fundamental importance of guaranteeing the right to a fair and public hearing by an independent and impartial tribunal has been recognised by states, a number of members of the Council of Europe have placed reservations on arts. 5 or 6 of the ECHR (dealing with liberty and security of the person and the right to a fair and public hearing respectively) in relation to military justice. Such

[3] Eugene R. Fidell, Elizabeth L. Hillman and Dwight H. Sullivan, *Military Justice Cases and Materials: 2010–2011 Supplement* (LexisNexis, 2012), pp. 117 et seq.; National Institute of Military Justice, Continuity and Change in Military Justice, London Conference, 12 December 1998, p. 3; Peter Kempees (ed.), *A Systematic Guide to the Case Law of the European Court of Human Rights, 1960–1994*, vol. I (The Hague; London, Brill, Martinus Nijhoff, 1996); Andreu-Guzmán, above n. 2, pp. 61 et seq; *Draft Principles Governing the Administration of Justice Through Military Tribunals*, UN ECOSOCOR, 66th Sess, Supp No. 11(d), UN Doc E/CN.4/2006/58 (2006); Dan E Stigall, 'An Unnecessary Convenience: The Assertion of the Uniform Code of Military Justice (UMCJ) over Civilians and the Implications of International Human Rights Law' (2009) 17 *Cardozo Journal of International and Comparative Law*, p. 5; Π. Κρεμμυδιώτη, Η Προβληματική της Αναγκαιότητας και Αποτελεσματικότητας του Θεσμού των Στρατοδικών στη Χώρα μας, Ποιν. Χρον. ΝΕ, σελ. 778 επ. (Panagiotis Kremmydiotis, 'The Issue of the Necessity and the Effectiveness of Military Jury in our Country' (2005) *Penal Chronicles*, pp. 777 et seq.; Σ. Κύρκου, Η Επίδραση της Νομολογίας του Ευρωπαϊκού Δικαστηρίου Ανθρωπίνων Δικαιωμάτων στον Εκσυγχρονισμό του Θεσμικού Πλαισίου της Ποινικής Διαδικασίας Ενώπιον των Στρατιωτικών Δικαστηρίων: Κατακτήσεις και Προοπτικές (Sotirios Kyrkos, 'The Impact of the Jurisprudence of the ECHR on the Reform of the Legal Frame of the Penal Procedure in Military Courts – Achievements and Prospects' (Paper presented at 4th International Seminar on International Law, Panteion University, 1–4 May 2008)) www.militaryjustice.gr/athra/epidrasi%20nomologias%20tou%20edda.pdf.

[4] Convention for the Protection of Human Rights and Fundamental Freedoms, 4 November 1950, in force 3 September 1953, 213 UNTS 222, arts. 5 and 6 (European Convention on Human Rights); Mark W. Janis, Richard S. Kay and Anthony Wilfred Bradley, *European Human Rights Law: Text and Materials* (Oxford, Oxford University Press, 2008), pp. 718 et seq.; Rowe, above n. 2, pp. 192 et seq.; *Draft Principles Governing the Administration of Justice Through Military Tribunals*, above n. 3, at 19 et seq. As regards the human rights of the armed forces personnel, see Alexander Arabadjiev, Council of Europe Parliamentary Assembly, doc 10861, *Human Rights of Members of the Armed Forces* (24 March 2006), at 16 et seq.

[5] 'New Zealand: National Report' in Horvat, Van Hespen and Van Gijsegem, *International Conference on Military Jurisdiction*, above n. 2, p. 366.

countries include the Czech Republic, France, Lithuania, Moldova, Portugal, Russia, Slovakia, Spain, Turkey and Ukraine.[6]

This chapter analyses the diversity in the reform of military justice systems across the world and the way in which international standards have influenced the reform of military justice. Rather than examining all aspects of military justice, it will focus on three main areas: the status of military judges and prosecutors, the structure of military courts and the right to appeal, and summary (disciplinary) courts. These are not the only areas where human rights law has impacted on reform,[7] but, by concentrating on the institutional design of military justice, it is possible to see both the influence of international human rights law on recent reform efforts, as well as the diversity of responses to calls for reform. Before examining these core changes in military justice, a brief reference will be made to the role and institutions of military justice.

II The role of military justice

The role of military justice depends on the characteristics of each country, its legal system and the requirements of the armed forces. Military tribunals have a special jurisdiction, which stems from the existence of the armed forces. Military judges, like civilian judges, are responsible for guaranteeing the administration of justice, constitutional order and human rights, but their functions cannot always be directly equated with those of civilian judges. Initially, the main purpose of military justice was the enforcement of discipline – the administration of justice was a secondary consideration. Currently, the challenge faced by military justice systems is to determine the way in which disciplinary obligations should be enforced consistently with the rights to a fair trial and due process.[8] Accused persons before a military court must be tried in a way that is compatible with their human rights and ensures the impartiality not only of military courts, but also of military judges.[9] However, military judges must not only remain focused on the fair trial principle, as located

[6] Hans Born and Ian Leigh, *Handbook on Human Rights and Fundamental Freedoms of Armed Forces Personnel* (Warsaw, OSCE Office for Democratic Institutions and Human Rights, 2008), pp. 31 et seq. and 222.

[7] For example, the capacity of military justice systems to try civilians has also been examined from the perspective of human rights law: see Chapters 5 and 16.

[8] Volker Schleiff, *The Right to a Fair Trial – Requirements of Impartiality and Independence under Articles 14(1) ICCPR, 8(1) IACHR and 6(1) ECHR in Relation to Military Courts* (Master's Thesis, University of Bern, 2008), pp. 7 et seq.

[9] Fidell, Hillman and Sullivan, above n. 3, pp. 120 et seq.

in both domestic law and international law, but must also take into account the good order of the armed forces in exercising their functions.[10]

The need for a separate military justice system is based on a number of different considerations. The requirement of consistent obedience, not only in war but also in peacetime, from members of the military constitutes the legal basis for preserving an independent, if not totally distinct, system. This is based, in part, on international humanitarian law, which presupposes the existence of a disciplinary system which 'shall enforce compliance with the rules of international law applicable in armed conflict'.[11] However, separate military justice systems have been criticised by the European Court of Human Rights for their lack of independence and the failure to accord equality of treatment between defendants brought before a military court and those brought before a civilian criminal court.[12]

Many, if not most, changes to military justice systems can be viewed as a result of the influence of international human rights standards. However, it should be recognised that human rights law is not the only influence on recent reforms to military justice. Other reforms relevant to the armed forces have impacted on military justice, including the increasing number of civilians employed in military institutions at home and abroad, the participation of the military in peacekeeping operations, as well as the engagement of troops in non-declared wars and in protecting against terrorist attacks. These changes require a flexible system for

[10] Peter Rowe, 'The European Convention on Human Rights and the Armed Forces' in Bernard S. Jackson and Dominic McGoldrick (eds.), *Legal Visions of the New Europe: Essays Celebrating the Centenary of the Faculty of Law, University of Liverpool* (London; Boston, MA, Graham & Trotman, 1993), pp. 249 et seq.; Ann B. Ching, 'Who Questions the Questioners? Reforming the Voir Dire Process in Courts-Martial' (2010) 204 *Military Law Review*, p. 182 at 221 et seq.; *Askeri Yargitay 'In 95' Inci Kurulus Yildonumu Sempozyumu (6–7 Nissan 2009) Symposium for the 95th Anniversary of the Military High Court of Appeals (6–7 April 2009)* (Ankara, Genelkurmay Basimevi, 2009), p. 215.

[11] Protocol Additional to the Geneva Conventions of 12 August 1949, and Relating to the Protection of Victims of International Armed Conflicts, 8 June 1977, in force 7 December 1978, 1125 UNTS 3, art. 43.1. See also Hague Convention (IV) Respecting the Laws and Customs of War on Land, Annex to the Convention, Regulations Respecting the Laws and Customs of War on Land, art. 1.

[12] Α. Παπαδαμάκη, Οι Προσανατολισμοί του Στρατιωτικού Ποινικού Δικαίου κατά την Ιστορική του Διαδρομή και η Ανάγκη Μεταρρύθμισής του, Υπεράσπιση 1992, σελ. 709 (A. Papadamakis, 'Military Penal Law through the Years and the Need for Its Reform' (1992) 12 *Defence Law Review*, p. 709. Born and Leigh, above n. 6, pp. 219 et seq.; *Symposium for the 95th Anniversary of the Military High Court of Appeals*, above n. 10, pp. 155 et seq. and 216.

controlling discipline and administering military justice, which has to be fully embodied in the broader judicial framework of a country.[13] In some states, the law has proven slow to adapt to the changing factual circumstances of these new military missions.[14]

III The status of military judges and prosecutors

The status of military judges as officers of the armed forces or as civilian judges, who are granted functional and personal independence, is one of the main characteristics of a military justice system. Of course, the concept of the independence of a judge cannot be disassociated from the organisation of the prosecutors and the investigators, as an effective military justice system requires institutional independence at all levels. The gradual renunciation of the model of the officer-military judge in favour of the civilian model first occurred after World War II and is now becoming increasingly common. In particular, the subordination of military justice as a whole, irrespective of the status of military judges, to a state's Ministry of Defence is a crucial element. For example, military judges in Russia, although uniformed, are not officers and are totally independent of the Ministry of Defence. In Turkey, although military judges are uniformed military personnel belonging to the 'Military Judge Branch', which is directly subordinate to the Ministry of Defence, they enjoy the same privileges and immunities as civilian judges. In Tunisia, military judges in peacetime are appointed by the President of the Republic after a recommendation from the Minister of Defence. Furthermore, in Tunisia, criminal military jurisdiction is dependent on the Minister of Defence and under the control of the military justice administration.

Leaving aside these countries, there is a wide diversity of practices amongst countries when appointing military judges. There are still a number of countries where military judges maintain the status of an officer of the armed forces. For example, in Africa, military judges are members of the armed forces in the Congo and Rwanda.[15] Among the

13 For the interrelationship between international humanitarian law and human rights law, see Constantine Antonopoulos, 'The Relationship between International Humanitarian Law and Human Rights Law' (2010) 63 *Revue Hellenique de Droit International*, p. 599.

14 National Institute of Military Justice, Continuity and Change in Military Justice, above n. 3, p. 4, *Symposium for the 95th Anniversary of the Military High Court of Appeals*, above n. 10, p. 157.

15 In the Congo, this status remained intact after the 2005 enactment of the new constitution. In Rwanda the relevant law determining the organisation, functioning and jurisdiction of the courts came into force in 2004. *The Democratic Republic of Congo: Military*

countries of the American continent, this is also the case in the United States of America,[16] Chile, Ecuador, Uruguay, Paraguay, Peru, Argentina, Venezuela and Brazil. In Asia and the Pacific, this regime exists in Nepal, Kyrgyzstan, Iran, China and Australia. In Europe, military judges are officers of the armed forces in Belarus, Croatia, Slovakia, Switzerland, Ukraine and Romania. In Ireland, although military judges are members of the armed forces, since 2007 they have been granted the same functional and personal independence as non-uniformed colleagues and are appointed by the Judge Advocate General.[17] In the majority of examples, the officer status of a military judge entails his or her subordination to the Ministry of Defence, which, subsequently, has the authority to intervene not only in the process of appointment, but also in promotion.

However, it is also true that the number of countries in which military judges do not belong to the armed forces is gradually increasing. In these cases military justice systems are usually staffed by law graduates who have previous experience as lawyers or legal advisers. In some countries

Justice and Human Rights – An Urgent Need to Complete Reforms (Johannesburg, Open Society Institute for Southern Africa, 2009), p. 2.

16 *Manual for Courts-Martial*, United States (2012), rr. 501–4.

17 Born and Leigh, above n. 6, p. 227; *Symposium for the 95th Anniversary of the Military High Court of Appeals*, above n. 10, pp. 179, 207; Horvat, Van Hespen and Van Gijsegem, *International Conference on Military Jurisdiction*, above n. 2, pp. 152, 174, 248, 260, 284, 298, 307, 311, 362, 374, 396, 473. Π. Κρεμμυδιώτη, Η Τάση Ενσωματώσεως του Αντικειμένου της Στρατιωτικής Δικαιοσύνης στην Κοινή Δικαιοσύνη, ό.π., σελ. 891 επ. (Kremmydiotis, above n. 1, p. 891 et seq.); Jamie Fellner, Wendy Gimbel and Diego García Sayán, *Human Rights in Ecuador* (New York, Americas Watch Committee; Lima, Andean Commission of Jurists, 1988), p. 81; Fuero Militar Political, *What Is the Military and Police Jurisdiction* www.fmp.gob.pe/FMP/Html/2009-08-26/what_is_the_military_and_police_jurisdiction.html; Ana Gabriela Veroti Farah, *Overview of the Legal System in Brazil* http://thebrazilbusiness.com/article/overview-of-the-legal-system-in-brazil; Council of Europe, Parliamentary Assembly, Documents – Working Papers, 2005 Ordinary Session (Fourth Part) 3–7 October 2005, vol. VII, Documents 10671–10714 (Council of Europe Publishing), pp. 76 et seq.; Jon Tracy, *Nepal Supreme Court Orders Reform of Military Justice*, National Institute of Military Justice, 1 July 2011 www.nimjblog.org/2011/07/nepal-supreme-court-orders-reform-of.html; Susan Finder, *The Chinese Military Legal Framework Must Be Improved*, Global Military Justice Reform, 20 May 2014 http://globalmjreform.blogspot.gr/2014/05/the-chinese-military-legal-framework.html; Gabrielle Appleby, *Reforming Military Justice*, Public Law Blog, 18 October 2012 http://blogs.adelaide.edu.au/public-law-rc/2012/10/18/reforming-military-justice; Arne Willy Dahl, International Trends in Military Justice, Presentation at the Global Military Appellate Seminar at Yale Law School, 1–2 April 2011 www.law.yale.edu/2011-04_International_trends.pdf; Courts and Tribunals Judiciary, 'Military' www.judiciary.gov.uk/about-the-judiciary/the-justice-system/jurisdictions/military-jurisdiction; Judicial System of the Republic of Azerbaijan, http://courts.gov.az/judicial_power/?lng=en.

they wear a uniform as an insignia of their duties but not their status as officers. For example, following reforms in Russia in 1999, military judges resigned from the armed forces and thus became independent of the Ministry of Defence, but kept their position as judges, subordinate to the Department of the Supreme Court. Similarly in Denmark and Bulgaria, military judges, although civilians, wear a uniform to work and a robe when members of a court.[18] In the United Kingdom, with the exception of the members of summary courts, military courts are solely composed of civilian judges, typically appointed by the Crown, but in practice by the Justice Department. Civilian judges in military courts can also be found in Azerbaijan, Singapore, Latvia and Greece, whereas military chambers in civil courts composed of civilian judges can be found in Hungary, Tunisia, Estonia, the Netherlands, New Zealand, Lithuania, Czech Republic, Norway and North Korea. In France, judges sitting on military courts are appointed by the Ministry of Defence and include both civilians and military personnel. Civilian and military personnel also serve on military courts in Luxemburg and Canada. Finally, in Germany, civilian judges with the ability to hear military cases in Disciplinary Courts are appointed by the Federal Ministry of Defence, unlike those who serve in the Federal Administrative Court (appellate court), who are nominated by the Federal Ministry of Justice.[19]

There are also variations in the appointment of military prosecutors. In Hungary, although military prosecutors wear a uniform, they are not part of the armed forces. Instead, their superior is the Chief Military Prosecutor, who is responsible to Parliament, but not subordinate to the Ministry of Defence. In Turkey, military prosecutors have a constitutional obligation to act independently, whereas in Estonia, Singapore and the Netherlands they are civilians. Since June 2000, in Tunisia the

[18] Horvat, Van Hespen and Van Gijsegem, *International Conference on Military Jurisdiction*, above n. 2, p. 181.

[19] *Symposium for the 95th Anniversary of the Military High Court of Appeals*, above n. 10, pp. 134, 139 et seq., 147 et seq., 156, 184, 193; Born and Leigh, above n. 6, pp. 227–28; Andreu-Guzmán, above n. 2, pp. 295 et seq.; Georg Nolte, *European Military Law Systems* (Berlin, De Gruyter, 2003), p. 161; Horvat, Van Hespen and Van Gijsegem, *International Conference on Military Jurisdiction*, above n. 2, pp. 236, 343, 353, 366, 389, Π. Κρεμμυδιώτη, ό.π., σελ. 891 επ., (Kremmydiotis, above n. 1, p. 891 et seq.); Chris Madsen, *Another Kind of Justice: Canadian Military Law from Confederation to Somalia* (Vancouver, University of British Columbia Press, 1999), p. 3; Ercan Yavuz, 'Military Officers Tried by Civilian Courts around the World, Parliamentary Report Reveals' *Today's Zaman*, 11 October 2009 www.todayszaman.com/news-189537-military-officers-tried-by-civilian-courts-around-the-world-parliamentary-report-reveals.html.

General Military Prosecutor, although appointed by the president of the Republic, works under the supervision of the Ministry of Defence. In Chile, Ecuador, Peru, Paraguay, Argentina, Venezuela and Iran, military prosecutors have the status of an officer. Finally, in Russia, since 1992, military prosecutors exercise their authority independently of the federal bodies of the state.[20] The aim behind all of these reform efforts is to ensure the independence and impartiality of military judges and prosecutors in accordance with the requirements of human rights law. As demonstrated by the above examples, states have adopted a diverse range of approaches when faced with the need to update their military justice to conform to such standards.

IV The structure of military courts and the right to appeal

Concerns about equal treatment focus on the extent to which members of the armed forces enjoy the same rights to due process as do civilians when appearing before military justice institutions.[21] The way in which military courts are structured, including the possibility of an appeal to a higher (civilian) court, has an important role to play in ensuring due process rights.[22] In some states, including Turkey, Iran and Syria, the first instance courts are composed of a single judge, whereas in others, including Rwanda, Republic of Korea, Greece, Canada and Nepal, the first instance military courts are composed of at least three members.[23]

[20] Born and Leigh, above n. 6, p. 228, Horvat, Van Hespen and Van Gijsegem, *International Conference on Military Jurisdiction*, above n. 2, pp. 176, 213, 261, 298, 312, 376, 390.

[21] See also *Engel* v. *Netherlands* (European Court of Human Rights, Plenary, Application No. 5100/71, 8 June 1976); *Hood* v. *United Kingdom* (European Court of Human Rights, Grand Chamber, Application No. 27267/95, 18 February 1999); *Cable* v. *United Kingdom* (European Court of Human Rights, Grand Chamber, Application No. 24436/94, 18 February 1999); *Coyne* v. *United Kingdom* (European Court of Human Rights, Chamber, Application No. 25942/94, 24 September 1997); *Mills* v. *United Kingdom* (European Court of Human Rights, Third Section, Application No. 35685/97 5 June 2001); *Martin* v. *United Kingdom* (European Court of Human Rights, Third Section, Application No. 63608/00, 19 February 2004).

[22] For the difficulties in classifying military courts, see Andreu-Guzmán, above n. 2, pp. 154 et seq.

[23] Π. Κρεμμυδιώτη, ό.π., σελ. 890 (Kremmydiotis, above n. 1, p. 890); Horvat, Van Hespen and Van Gijsegem, *International Conference on Military Jurisdiction*, above n. 2, pp. 199, 270, 286; Hon. Gilles Létourneau, 'Status of the Military Nexus Doctrine in Canada' (Paper presented at Global Military Appellate Seminar, Yale Law School, 1–2 April 2011) www.law.yale.edu/The_Status_of_the_Military_Nexus_Doctrine_in_Canada.pdf; Judge Sotirios Kyrkos, 'Military Justice in Greece' (Paper presented at Global Military Appellate Seminar, Yale Law School, 1–2 April 2011) www.law.yale.edu/

The first instance military court of the Chinese People's Liberation Army can be grouped into three levels. The first level comprises the 'grassroots' military courts, which are established within naval fleets, regional air force units, provincial military commands and some Armed Police Provincial contingents. The second level military courts are established within the top units of the Navy, the Air Force and the People's Armed Police, while the aforementioned courts of the Army belong to the third level. Moreover, the courts of the third level consist of a criminal, a civil and a supervisory section.[24]

In the United States the Uniform Code of Military Justice also provides for three levels of trial before military courts martial: the Summary, the Special and the General Courts Martial. The distinguishing characteristics of the different types of courts martial are the level of command authorised to convene the court, the personnel required to conduct the court and the amount of punishment that the court can impose. The Summary Court Martial is convened by a Battalion-level commander to adjudicate minor offences. The Special Court Martial is composed of a Military Judge and is convened by a Brigade-level commander to adjudicate more serious offences. Finally, the General Court Martial is convened by a Division-level or higher commander to adjudicate the most serious cases. It is composed of a judge, a prosecutor and a defence counsel, who are all military lawyers, together with at least five non-lawyer court members.[25]

In Russia the military courts system consists of 119 Station Military Courts of first instance and twelve District Military Courts of first, cassational and supervisory instances. The Military Collegium, which is

Military_Justice_in_Greece.pdf; Brigadier General Seok Ko, 'Military Justice in the Republic of Korea' (Paper presented at Global Military Appellate Seminar, Yale Law School, 1–2 April 2011) www.law.yale.edu/Military_Justice_in_ROK.ppt; M.J. Shah, 'Constitutional Jurisprudence of Military Justice in the Context of Nepal' (2012) *The Judge Advocate Journal* at 102; Republic of Rwanda Military of Defence, *Military Justice System* www.mod.gov.rw/?MILITARY-JUSTICE-SYSTEM; Ismail Aksel, *Turkish Judicial System* (Ankara, The Ministry of Justice of Turkey, The Department for Strategy Development, 2013), pp. 67 et seq.; Michal Shammas, *Restructuring Judicial System in Future Syria* (London, Strategic Research and Communication Centre, 2012), pp. 9 et seq.; Tom Lansford, *Political Handbook of the World 2013* (CQ Press, 2013), pp. 1404 et seq.

24 *Symposium for the 95th Anniversary of the Military High Court of Appeals*, above n. 10, pp. 176 et seq.

25 Criminal Expo 1997, *3rd International Military Criminal Law Conference, The Criminal Law Aspects of the Misbehaviour of the Soldiers (4–6 June 1997)* (Budapest, Office of the Prosecutor General, 1997), pp. 89 et seq.

part of the Supreme Court of the Russian Federation, operates as the court of a higher instance for district (naval) military courts. Therefore, not only does it adjudicate offences at first instance, but it also has a cassational and supervisory authority. In Turkey, the president of a military court can be an officer, instead of a military judge, if the officer is at a senior level. However, the hearing of a case is always presided over by the senior Military Judge. Finally, in Azerbaijan it was proposed that the state prosecutor who participated in a first instance hearing of a case should be involved in the appeal court proceedings, as the prosecutor has knowledge of the particular case.[26] These disparate examples show there are differing approaches to the level of involvement of military officials in more than one stage of a military justice hearing.

The right of appeal against conviction is recognised by major human rights treaties,[27] although such treaties do not stipulate the particular type of appeal court. The appeal from a military court to a civilian court is an important safeguard; it helps to ensure that the lower court is correctly applying the law and is also a method of correcting possible errors, including any that might arise from command influence. Thus, the integration of military courts into the civilian legal system can correct miscarriages of justice and help increase public confidence in the military legal system. Since less serious disciplinary matters are punished by a superior officer, an appeal may be the first opportunity for a formal hearing with procedural safeguards.

In practice, states provide for appeals in a variety of ways. In some countries an appeal lies only to a higher military court, whereas others provide for a final appeal to the state's supreme court (although sometimes on restricted grounds). Some countries, such as the United States and Canada, provide an intermediate appeal to a military court as well.[28]

[26] Fidell, Hillman and Sullivan, above n. 3, pp. 463 et seq., *Symposium for the 95th Anniversary of the Military High Court of Appeals*, above n. 10, pp. 134, 166 and 207.

[27] International Covenant on Civil and Political Rights, 16 December 1966, in force 23 March 1976, 999 UNTS 171, art. 14(5); American Convention on Human Rights, San José, 22 November 1969, in force 18 July 1978, 1144 UNTS 123, art. 8(2)(h); African Charter on Human and People's Rights, 27 June 1981, in force 21 October 1986, 1520 UNTS 217, art. 7(1)(a).

[28] The US military justice system's appellate courts have generally followed civilian 8th amendment to the Bill of Rights case law, while recognising that 'there may be circumstances under which the rules governing capital punishment of service members will differ from those applicable to civilians'. *United States v Matthews* in Fidell, Hillman and Sullivan, above n. 3, p. 277; Lawrence J. Morris, *Military Justice: A Guide to the Issues* (Santa Barbara, CA, Praeger, 2010), p. 90; *Manual for Courts-Martial*, United States (2012), rr. 1201–10.

In the United Kingdom, where there is no military appeals system, the convicted have the right to appeal to the civilian Court of Appeals only for matters of law (a right similar to cassation), and the facts of a case cannot be re-examined. The states that provide three types of court (lower, appellate and cassation) include Azerbaijan, Germany, Bulgaria, Greece, Russia, Kyrgyzstan, Turkey and Uruguay. After the constitutional reform of 2002 in the Congo, the decisions of military courts have been subject to review by civilian high courts.[29]

There are some countries where the right to appeal is final, so there is no third instance court jurisdiction offering a right to cassation. In Pakistan the right to appeal exists within the military court system, with no civilian court having the right to question their judgment.[30] In El Salvador, article 216 of the Constitution provides that military jurisdiction exists in special tribunals to try military felonies and misdemeanours on first and second instance. Moreover, civilian felonies committed by members of the armed forces have to be prosecuted within the common penal system. However, the lack of cooperation between the military and the common penal system has rendered military personnel essentially immune from prosecution in the civil courts. This last example demonstrates that even where a system of military justice enables individual prosecutions, they may not occur due to other circumstances.

V Summary (disciplinary) courts

Summary courts are first instance courts competent to try disciplinary offences. The enforcement and maintenance of discipline is a task closely linked to the chain of command. Most armed forces provide for minor disciplinary matters to be dealt with speedily and relatively informally by a superior officer.[31] However, concern for military

[29] *Symposium for the 95th Anniversary of the Military High Court of Appeals*, above n. 10, pp. 141, 179, 183; *The Democratic Republic of Congo: Military Justice and Human Rights – An Urgent Need to Complete Reforms*, above n. 15, p. 2; Andreu-Guzmán, above n. 2, p. 363; Aksel, above n. 23, pp. 44 et seq. In 2011, the Uruguayan Executive sent a Bill reforming the Military Penal Code to Parliament, in order for members of the armed forces who commit military offences to be tried in civilian courts. However, the effort never prospered. See Eugene R. Fiddell, 'Military Justice Caseload Statistics (and nonreform) in Uruguay', Global Military Justice Reform, 14 July 2014 http://globalmjreform.blogspot.gr/2014/07/military-justice-caseload-statistics.html.

[30] Peter R. Blood (ed.), *Pakistan: A Country Study* (Washington, DC, Department of the Army, 1995).

[31] Nolte, above n. 19, pp. 144 et seq.

readiness, efficiency, discipline and morale has in some countries given rise to military summary courts, which are distinct from military courts.[32] Under normal circumstances summary courts try breaches of discipline and not offences provided in the military penal code or the common penal code.

Essentially, the matter of disciplinary punishment can be approached in two different ways. The most common method is to treat disciplinary matters and criminal offences separately. The advantage of this approach is that, in criminal matters, the same procedure applicable to civilians may be used for members of the military. Of course, practical problems may arise in determining the type of the court in which the trial should take place. The disadvantage, however, is that the accused may suffer successive penalties for the same action, which, in some cases, may be disproportionate to the offence, particularly when compared with the treatment of a civilian in comparable circumstances.[33] The other approach (of which the United Kingdom is a clear example) is to permit military courts to deal with criminal charges and disciplinary offences by incorporating all criminal offences into the armed forces legislation together with disciplinary offences.[34] Pursuant to this approach, the potential problem of double punishment is eliminated, although the discrepancies in the procedure of the courts, when compared to those of civilian criminal courts, may be highlighted.

Summary courts exist in a number of countries, including the United States, Germany, Nepal, Ireland, Spain, Belgium, Argentina, Singapore, Netherlands, New Zealand, Turkey, Norway, Pakistan, Nepal, Syria, India, Ecuador and Canada.[35] In Syria the court is composed of a single judge, while in Nepal, Turkey and Ecuador such cases are decided by three judges. Usually, summary courts are located in large units, although the number of countries where these courts can be summoned by the commander on an *ad hoc* basis is increasing.[36]

[32] For a thorough examination of the law on disciplinary measures and disciplinary procedure and its compliance with the European Convention on Human Rights, see Nolte, above n. 19, p. 141 et seq.

[33] Convention for the Protection of Human Rights and Fundamental Freedoms, 4 November 1950, in force 3 September 1953, 213 UNTS 222, art. 14[7]. Nolte, above n. 19, p. 142.

[34] Armed Forces Act 2006 (UK).

[35] *Manual for Courts-Martial*, United States (2012), rr. 1301–5. *Rassegna della Giustizia Militare [Review of Military Justice]* (1998), pp. 211 et seq. Horvat, Van Hespen and Van Gijsegem, *International Conference on Military Jurisdiction*, above n. 2, pp. 179 and 390.

[36] J.W. Rant, 'The British Court-Martial System – It Ain't Broken but It Needs Fixing' (1996) 152 *Military Law Review* 179, at 185; Fidell, Hillman and Sullivan, above n. 3, pp. 69 et seq.; Serge Lazareff, *Status of Military Forces Under Current International Law* (Leiden,

The question of whether summary courts are necessary is directly related to the extent of the criminalisation of disciplinary matters. In the majority of states the armed forces consist of professional personnel. Given that the majority of the crimes included in military penal codes are based on the protected value of discipline,[37] it is necessary to question the purpose of providing penal sanctions, as such acts do not require a broader social protection beyond maintaining discipline in the armed forces. The question also arises: what type of punishment would be more effective in maintaining discipline? The need for summary courts depends on the circumstances existing in each country. One of the problems faced by summary courts is the need to fulfil the requirements set by international human rights law.[38] According to the jurisprudence of the European Court of Human Rights, the fact that the superior officer of the defendant in a military trial appoints the judges to try the case and the prosecuting or defending counsel, as well as prepares the evidence, is incompatible with the right to a fair trial by an independent and impartial court.[39] In addition, the Court has concluded that, although art. 6 of the ECHR refers to a 'criminal charge', it is clear that this concept may include disciplinary measures in some cases, based on the nature of the punishment.[40] Therefore, irrespective of whether states decide to maintain or establish military summary courts, their proceedings must comply with the obligations derived from international human rights treaties and the general principles of international law.

VI Conclusion

The increased role of the military in peacekeeping and anti-terrorism operations in recent years means that military justice systems may apply to a wider

Sijthoff, 1971), pp. 220 et seq., Criminal Expo 1997, *3rd International Military Criminal Law Conference*, above n. 25, p. 89, Born and Leigh, above n. 6, p. 220, *Symposium for the 95th Anniversary of the Military High Court of Appeals*, above n. 10, pp. 156 and 209; Nolte, above n. 19, p. 143; Horvat, Van Hespen and Van Gijsegem, *International Conference on Military Jurisdiction*, above n. 2, pp. 27, 359, 372, 437.

37 For example, desertion, disobedience and insubordination. 38 See Chapter 17.

39 See *Öcalan* v. *Turkey* (2005) 41 EHRR 955; *Findlay* v. *United Kingdom* (1997) 24 EHRR 221; *Çiraklar* v. *Turkey* (European Court of Human Rights, Chamber, Application No. 70/1997/854/1061, 28 October 1998); *Sahiner* v. *Turkey* (European Court of Human Rights, First Section, Application No. 29279/95, 25 September 2001) and *Tsaridi et Bellou* v. *Greece* (European Court of Human Rights, Application No. 74927/01, 18 March 2004).

40 Ι. Σαρμά, Η Νομολογία του Ευρωπαϊκού Δικαστηρίου Δικαιωμάτων του Ανθρώπου και της Επιτροπής, 1998, σελ. 205 επ. (Ioannis Sarmas, *The Jurisprudence of the ECHR* (1998), pp. 205 et seq.).

and very complex range of circumstances. These circumstances give rise to the question whether military courts must adopt more of the features and procedures of civilian courts in order to meet those challenges. It is of utmost importance to ensure that military judges and military courts can function in a similar way to that of the civilian courts. For this purpose, it is necessary to ensure that accused persons under military jurisdiction enjoy comparable rights to civilians. Although it is difficult to establish commonly accepted criteria worldwide, there are some factors that can be considered prerequisites in ensuring the compatibility of military justice institutions with internationally accepted requirements.[41] According to the Committee on Human Rights of the Council of Europe, there are two general parameters used to evaluate a military justice system: impartiality and independence.[42] These two requirements refer to the independence of military judges from the chain of command, the associated independence of military prosecutors and investigators, the non-subordination of military courts to the Ministry of Defence, the right to appeal to a civilian court, and a constitutional guarantee for the functional and personal independence of military judges.

Given the need for rapid and on-the-spot administration of justice in order to maintain discipline, particularly when the military is deployed overseas, the recent tendency of states to abolish military courts should be re-evaluated. Recent reforms in military justice in countries such as New Zealand and Ireland, where civilian influence within the existing military justice system not only responds to the rapidly changing environment, but also respects human rights and humanitarian law, demonstrate that the abolition of military courts is neither an obligatory nor a necessary means of providing the equivalent protection according to international human rights standards. Despite the diversity of responses, the adoption of international human rights requirements concerning the structure of military justice institutions is now a common characteristic of all reforms.

[41] See the seven basic recommendations made by the Cox Commission to advance principles of justice, equity and fairness in American military justice in Fidell, Hillman and Sullivan, above n. 3, pp. 313 et seq.; Eugene R. Fidell, 'Recent Revisions of Military Justice Systems' in Horvat, Van Hespen and Van Gijsegem, above n. 2, pp. 450 et seq; Mindia Vashakmadge, *Understanding Military Justice* (Geneva, DCAF, 2010), pp. 15 et seq.

[42] The ICCPR does not contain any specific provisions on the subject of military courts. However, art. 2(3) establishes the right to an effective remedy of a judicial nature. In addition, art. 14 recognises the right to a hearing by an independent and impartial tribunal and the right to the judicial guarantees that are necessary for a fair trial. Andreu-Guzmán, above n. 2, pp. 16 et seq.; Alexander Poretschkin, 'Military Justice – A Breach of the Separation of Powers?' in Horvat, Van Hespen and Van Gijsegem, above n. 2, pp. 477 et seq.

16

The inter-American system and military justice

CHRISTINA M. CERNA

Obedezco pero no cumplo.[1]

I Introduction

In 1959, when the Inter-American Commission on Human Rights (Commission) was created, much of Latin America was governed by right-wing dictators supported by the military. In Cuba, a left-wing revolutionary had seized power and promised or threatened, depending on your political inclinations, to bring revolutionary change to the rest of Latin America. From the mid-1960s to the mid-1980s, the Americas were convulsed by internal armed conflicts and resultant massive human rights violations, such as extrajudicial executions, forced disappearances and torture. Marxist guerrillas took up arms and employed weapons of terrorism, committing abuses not only against the perceived illegitimate state but also against the civilian population in order to seize power. Similarly, the state employed its own form of terrorism. As a result of their military campaigns 'to eradicate' Marxist guerrillas, thousands of persons were 'disappeared'. International humanitarian law, applicable during situations of armed conflict, provides for the prosecution of either side to the conflict, whichever party or parties commit grave breaches of their obligations under the Geneva Conventions.[2] International human rights law also applies during armed conflicts and provides for the investigation, prosecution and punishment of state actions that violate international human rights norms.

[1] The phrase 'I obey but do not comply' characterised Spanish America's attitude towards the Spanish crown during colonial times.

[2] On the Commission and Court's failure to apply international humanitarian law to situations dealing with armed conflict see Christina M. Cerna, 'The History of the Inter-American System's Jurisprudence as Regards Situations of Armed Conflict' (2011) 2 *Journal of International Humanitarian Legal Studies*, p. 3.

Consequently, most countries in Latin America have laws for the prosecution of members of the military for military crimes and for violations of human rights. Despite the existing laws, and in some cases even despite the constitution, the practice in some countries has been to try military personnel only in military courts. The fair trial guarantee in the American Convention on Human Rights provides that everyone has the right to a hearing before an 'independent, and impartial tribunal'.[3] A tribunal comprising military officials in the chain of command has been held not to comply with the American Convention's requirements of independence and impartiality. The jurisprudence of the inter-American system for the protection of human rights in cases involving violations by members of the military restricts military jurisdiction to disciplinary offences committed by military personnel and absolutely prohibits the application of military jurisdiction to civilians.

In order to understand the way in which this tension between military jurisdiction and international human rights law plays out in the inter-American system, it is useful first to provide an overview of the inter-American system for the protection of human rights.

II Overview of the inter-American human rights system

The Inter-American Commission on Human Rights, a principal and autonomous organ of the Organization of American States (OAS), is located in Washington, DC.[4] The Commission comprises seven members of 'high moral character and recognized competence in the field of human rights' who are elected by all the member states of the OAS to

[3] American Convention on Human Rights, 22 November 1969, in force 18 July 1978, 1144 UNTS 123 art. 8 (American Convention).

[4] Article 53 of the Charter of the Organization of American States, in force 13 December 1951, 119 UNTS 2; amended by Protocol of Amendment to the Charter of the Organization of American States Buenos Aires (B-31), Buenos Aires, 27 February 1967, in force 27 February 1970, 721 UNTS 324 (Protocol of Buenos Aires); Protocol of Amendment to the Charter of the Organization of American States Buenos Aires (A-50), Cartagena de Indias, 5 December 1985, in force 16 November 1988, 25 ILM 527 (Protocol of Cartagena de Indias); Protocol of Amendment to the Charter of the Organization of American States Buenos Aires (A-56), Washington DC, 14 December 1992, in force 25 September 1997, 33 ILM 1005 (Protocol of Washington); Protocol of Amendment to the Charter of the Organization of American States Buenos Aires (A-58), Managua, 10 June 1993, in force 29 January 1996, 33 ILM 1009 (Protocol of Managua).

serve a four-year term.[5] Commissioners represent all member states of the OAS, not the countries of which they are nationals or that elected them. The American Declaration of the Rights and Duties of Man (American Declaration), the first human rights instrument of the inter-American system, was adopted by the OAS on 2 May 1948, in Bogota, Colombia, during the Ninth International Conference of American States, which adopted the OAS Charter and established the OAS.[6] The American Declaration antedates by seven months the UN's adoption of the Universal Declaration of Human Rights[7] on 10 December 1948.

The inter-American system for the promotion and protection of human rights was modelled on the European human rights system but the two systems are quite different. One similarity, however, is that the inter-American system, like the former European system, comprises both a human rights commission and a court. The OAS created the Commission in 1959 by a Resolution of the Fifth Meeting of Consultation of Ministers of Foreign Affairs.[8] During the first eleven years of its existence, the only human rights instrument available to the Commission was the American Declaration, which, like the Universal Declaration, was not designed to be legally binding. Nevertheless, the Court has intimated that the Declaration is a source of legally binding obligations on OAS member states, without specifying exactly what that means.[9]

The Commission holds at least two regular sessions per year and as many special sessions as deemed necessary.[10] The primary functions of the Commission are the processing of petitions, which must be decided by the Commission before they can be sent to the Court; the litigation of

5 Statute of the Inter-American Commission on Human Rights, art. 2. Reprinted in Basic Documents Pertaining to Human Rights in the Inter-American System (Updated to June 2010), OEA/Ser.L/V/1.4 rev.13, 30 June 2010, p. 171.

6 American Declaration of the Rights and Duties of Man, OAS Res. XXX, adopted by the Ninth International Conference of American States (1948), reprinted in Basic Documents Pertaining to Human Rights in the Inter-American System, above n. 5, pp. 13–18.

7 Universal Declaration of Human Rights, GA Res 217A (III), UN GAOR, 3rd sess, 183rd plen mtg, UN Doc A/810 (10 December 1948) (Universal Declaration).

8 The Fifth Meeting of Consultation of Ministers of Foreign Affairs took place in Santiago, Chile from 12 to 18 August 1959. Final Act. OEA/Ser.C/II.5, pp. 4–6.

9 Interpretation of the American Declaration of the Rights and Duties of Man within the Framework of Article 64 of the American Convention on Human Rights, Inter-Am Court HR, Advisory Opinion OC-10/89, 14 July 1989.

10 New Rules of Procedure of the Inter-American Commission on Human Rights, art. 14. Reprinted in Basic Documents Pertaining to Human Rights in the Inter-American System, above n. 5. The Rules of Procedure were amended with effect from 1 August 2013. The amendments may be found on the Commission's web site www.cidh.oas.org.

cases before the Court; on-site visits by thematic or country Rapporteurs, or sometimes by the Commission as a whole; the issuance of precautionary measures and requesting provisional measures from the Court; and promotional activities, such as presentations or the organisation of conferences and seminars in order to raise awareness of human rights and the inter-American system in the Americas.[11] Individuals have the right to petition the Commission for violations of their human rights as set forth in the American Declaration or the American Convention. The respondent member states of the OAS are obliged to make reparations for the rights found by the Commission and/or the Court to have been violated.

The OAS Inter-American Specialized Conference on Human Rights, which met in San Jose, Costa Rica, adopted the American Convention on Human Rights.[12] The treaty entered into force on 18 July 1979, and today twenty-three of the thirty-five OAS member states are states parties.[13] Member states accept one of three levels of obligations under this system. The highest level is becoming a party to the American Convention and accepting the compulsory jurisdiction of the Court. Of the twenty-three state parties listed below, all except Dominica, Grenada and Jamaica have accepted the Court's compulsory jurisdiction, and those three countries comprise the second level of obligation (i.e. states parties to the American

11 The Commission receives approximately 2000 petitions per year, and it transmits approximately 25 per cent or 400 to the respondent governments for their observations. It issues approximately twenty merits decisions per year under the American Convention on cases that may be transmitted to the Court. Since 2001, its Rules of Procedure require the Commission to transmit every case to the Court in which the state has not complied with its recommendations.

12 American Convention on Human Rights, San José, 22 November 1969, in force 18 July 1978, 1144 UNTS 123 (American Convention).

13 The twenty-three states parties to the American Convention are: Argentina, Barbados, Bolivia, Brazil, Chile, Colombia, Costa Rica, Dominica, Dominican Republic, Ecuador, El Salvador, Grenada, Guatemala, Haiti, Honduras, Jamaica, Mexico, Nicaragua, Panama, Paraguay, Peru, Suriname, and Uruguay. The twelve countries that are not states parties to the American Convention and to which the Commission applies the American Declaration are: Antigua and Barbuda, Bahamas, Belize, Canada, Cuba, Guyana, Saint Kitts and Nevis, Saint Lucia, Saint Vincent and the Grenadines, Trinidad and Tobago, the United States and Venezuaela. Trinidad and Tobago acceded to the American Convention on 28 May 1991. On 26 May 1998, Trinidad and Tobago became the first country to notify its intention to denounce the American Convention, pursuant to art 78 (1). Venezuela was the second state to denounce the American Convention, effective 10 September 2013. Cuba, the 35th member state of the OAS, does not participate in its activities. On Cuba's status, see Christina M. Cerna, 'Introductory Note to Recent OAS Documents on Cuba and Honduras: Democracy and the Inter-American Democratic Charter' (2009) 48 *International Legal Materials*, p. 1242.

Convention that have not accepted the Court's compulsory jurisdiction). Once a state party accepts the compulsory jurisdiction of the Court, it cannot descend a level and cancel its acceptance of that jurisdiction while remaining a state party to the American Convention.[14] The only remedy available is for a state to denounce the American Convention, as Trinidad and Tobago and Venezuela have done, which then places the state in the third or lowest level. The third level is comprised currently only of English-speaking states that are subject to the Commission's jurisdiction under the American Declaration. They constitute almost one-third of the OAS membership, and include the United States, Canada and a number of small island countries in the Caribbean.[15] These states have not become parties to the American Convention. The absence of the majority of English-speaking states has led some to characterise the system as Latin American rather than inter-American. The patent inequality created by these three very distinct levels of obligations gave rise to a 'reform' process, initiated by OAS member states in 2011, which was intended to level the playing field. However, internal disagreements have left the process uncompleted.[16]

With the entry into force of the American Convention in 1978, the Court was created and established in 1979 in San José, Costa Rica. The Court consists of seven judges, nationals of the OAS member states, but not necessarily of the states parties to the American Convention.[17] They are elected 'in an individual capacity from among jurists of the highest moral authority and of recognized competence in the field of human rights, who possess the qualifications required for the exercise of the highest judicial functions under the law of the State of which they are nationals or of the State that proposes them as candidates'.[18] Unlike the members of the Commission, the judges are not elected by all the member states of the OAS but only by the states parties to the American Convention.

The American Convention requires that the procedure before the Commission be completed before a case can be brought to the

[14] Peru attempted to do this in July 1999 with no success. (See *Ivcher Bronstein* v. *Peru* [1999] Inter-Am Court HR (ser. C) No. 54 at [32]–[55].

[15] See above n. 13. Pursuant to article 78(1) of the American Convention, Venezuela's denunciation entered into force one year after the notification was made.

[16] See [2] AG/RES.1 (XLIV-E/13) 'Results of the Process of Reflection on the Workings of the Inter-American Commission on Human Rights with a view to Strengthening the Inter-American Human Rights System', 24 March 2013 (to instruct the Permanent Council to continue the dialogue on the core aspects for strengthening the IAHRS).

[17] Statute of the Inter-American Commission on Human Rights, art. 4. Reprinted in Basic Documents Pertaining to Human Rights in the Inter-American System, above n. 5, p. 205.

[18] Ibid.

Court.[19] Only the Commission or a state party to the American Convention can submit a case to the Court.[20] The American Convention further requires that the Commission appear in all cases before the Court.[21]

Article 44 of the American Convention provides that '[A]ny person or group of persons, or any nongovernmental entity legally recognized in one or more member states of the Organization may lodge petitions' with the Commission against a member state of the OAS for a violation of human rights under the American Declaration or the American Convention. The admissibility requirements for a petition are that the:

1. petition be filed on behalf of a victim who is a human being (Article 1(2) American Convention) who is under the jurisdiction of a member state of the OAS (*ratione personae*);
2. petition be filed within a period of six months from the date on which the party alleging a violation of his or her rights was notified of the final judgment of the highest domestic court (*ratione temporis*) or within a 'reasonable time'[22];
3. alleged violation occurred in a territory of a member state or under the effective control of a member state (*ratione loci*);
4. petition allege a violation of a human right protected by the American Declaration, the American Convention, or one of the instruments set forth in Article 23 of the Commission's Rules of Procedure (*ratione materiae*).[23]

III Review of the inter-American system's case law on military jurisdiction

A Characteristics of the jurisprudence

To date the Inter-American Court has issued judgments under the American Convention in approximately 200 cases. These judgments,

[19] American Convention, arts. 44–51. See also, *In the Matter of Viviana Gallardo* [1981] Inter-Am Court HR (ser. A) No G101/81.

[20] American Convention, art. 61. [21] Ibid., art. 57.

[22] Embedded in this requirement is the most important requirement of all, namely, that domestic remedies be exhausted before the petitioner may come before the international instance.

[23] There are, of course, denial of justice exceptions to these admissibility requirements, set forth in art. 46(2) of the ACHR: (1) the domestic legislation does not afford due process; (2) the alleged victim has been denied access to remedies under domestic law or has been prevented from exhausting them; (3) there has been unwarranted delay in rendering a final judgment.

pursuant to article 68(1) of the American Convention, are legally binding only on the parties to the litigation.[24] The Court's 'control of conventionality' doctrine, however, requires that all national judges determine whether their domestic law is in conformity with the judgments and interpretations of the judgments of the Inter-American Court and not only in those cases in which the state is a party.[25]

In 1991 the OAS celebrated the fact that all the governments of the member states, except Cuba, were the product of democratic elections.[26] Given the history of military dictatorships in the region, this was an important milestone. This democratisation of the Americas led to voluntary armed forces *in lieu* of forced conscription and a restriction on the scope of military jurisdiction. The tension between the *de facto* expanded scope of military jurisdiction in the region and the requirements of international human rights law has impacted on the jurisprudence of the inter-American system throughout the 1990s and 2000s. In 1992, in two decisions involving Argentina and Uruguay, the Commission broached the issue of *de jure* impunity for the first time and declared the amnesty laws in these respective countries to be incompatible with the state's obligations under the American Convention.[27] These decisions were ignored at the time by Argentina and Uruguay but they opened the door to a gradual hammering away at the self-granted amnesty laws and the unwillingness or inability of military courts to actually prosecute military officials.

The very existence of a separate administration of justice based on status, parallel to the ordinary judicial system, contradicts the notion that international human rights standards are universally applicable. As the Commission noted in an early case before the Court involving the exercise of military jurisdiction over the military personnel accused of the crime of arbitrarily killing a young civilian:

[24] Article 68(1) of the American Convention provides that states parties to the Convention 'undertake to comply with the judgment of the Court in any case to which they are parties'.

[25] See concurring opinion of Judge Ad Hoc Eduardo Ferrer Mac-Gregor Poisot in regard to the *Cabrera García and Montiel Flores* v. *Mexico* [2010] Inter-Am Court HR, Case 735/01, Report No. 11/04, at [51].

[26] Since Fidel Castro announced he was a Marxist-Leninist, Cuba was deemed to have voluntarily separated itself from the principles and purposes of the OAS Charter. From 1962 to 2009, Cuba was suspended from participation in OAS activities although it continued to be considered a member state of the organisation. In order to participate again, it must request to do so and be willing to engage in a dialogue with the OAS.

[27] *Herrera* v. *Argentina* [1993] Inter-Am Ct HR, Case 10.147, Report No. 28/92 and *Mendoza* v. *Uruguay* [1992] Inter-Am Ct HR, Case 10.029, Report No. 29/92.

> Decrees 591 and 600 created conditions conducive to the violation of the right to a fair trial, to due process and to equal treatment by granting broad margins of discretion and leaving it to the Army's High Commanders to sanction those 'involved' or to let them go unpunished, and by placing '*the soldiers of the Sandinista Popular Army on a different level to the rest of Nicaraguan society, with adverse effects on the rights enshrined in the American Convention.*'[28]

International human rights law guarantees certain rights that are not found in the codes of military justice of countries in the hemisphere. The American Convention, in Article 8(1), for example, provides that:

> Every person has the right to a hearing, with due guarantees and within a reasonable time, by a competent, independent, and impartial tribunal, previously established by law, in the substantiation of any accusation of a criminal nature made against him or for the determination of his rights and obligations of a civil, labor, fiscal, or any other nature.

This provision applies to all persons who fall under the jurisdiction of the state party to the treaty. No exception is made for members of a distinct social class, such as members of the military or of the clergy. Article 8 also provides minimum guarantees for a person accused of a criminal offence, including the right to be presumed innocent, the right to be assisted by legal counsel of one's own choosing, and the right to appeal the judgment to a higher court.

How do the requirements of a military justice system sit with the requirements of international human rights law? The military criminal justice system cannot be considered a real judicial system, as it is not part of the judiciary. The military criminal justice system is part of the executive branch of government, since the president is the Commander-in-Chief of the Armed Forces in most democratic countries. Judges in military justice systems are generally active-duty members of the military, which means that they are in the chain of command. This connection renders illusory the due process requirement of impartiality, since members of the Armed Forces have a natural inclination to protect those who fight alongside them.

The Inter-American Commission and Court have developed significant jurisprudence on the issue of military jurisdiction given the historically high profile of the military and military jurisdiction in the hemisphere. Most cases have involved one of three situations. First,

[28] *Genie-Lacayo* v. *Nicaragua* [1997] Inter-Am Court HR (ser. C) No. 21 at [15(f)] [emphasis added].

questions relating to the treatment of civilians by military courts. Second, military court proceedings, or the lack thereof, against military officials charged with violations of human rights. Third, questions as to whether military jurisdiction, when applied within the restricted scope for which it was created, violates international human rights standards because it establishes an alternative (i.e. inferior) system of justice outside the ordinary judicial system. In some countries this alternative system of justice is perceived as a source of privileges for the military, a separate class in society. Yet, it has also been perceived as providing a reduced set of guarantees, inferior to those applicable to the rest of the population. Consequently, members of the military have also petitioned the Commission for recognition of their human rights under the American Convention.

The codes of military justice of many countries in the hemisphere establish that criminal offences will be judged by civilian courts, and offences pertaining exclusively to military service, or 'service-related offences' committed by military personnel, are to be heard by military courts. Military courts also frequently have jurisdiction over common crimes, when committed by military personnel in service-related acts when the injured persons and accused are members of the military. Some countries transfer members of the armed services to military courts regardless of whether the offence is a military one or is service-related, or simply because of the status of the accused as a member of the military. When military jurisdiction is extended to cover any act committed by a member of the military, even when such jurisdiction contradicts express constitutional provisions to the contrary, impunity is the result.

Impunity is a serious problem in the administration of justice in the hemisphere, particularly when human rights violations are committed by state agents. The Inter-American Court has defined impunity as the total lack of investigation, prosecution, capture, trial and conviction of those responsible for violations of the rights protected by the American Convention. A state has the obligation to fight it by all means at its disposal since impunity fosters the chronic repetition of human rights violations and renders the victims and their families defenceless. The failure of military courts to investigate military personnel for human rights violations has resulted in *de facto* impunity in many countries, in addition to the *de jure* impunity that has been conferred by amnesty laws. The inter-American human rights system has declared amnesty laws to be in violation of a state's obligation to investigate human rights abuses and the obligation to provide the victim with effective judicial recourse.[29] International law requires that every violation of an international obligation, which results in harm, creates a duty to make adequate reparation and that the state has the obligation to investigate, prosecute and punish those responsible for the violation.

B *Summary of relevant cases*

The following is a short summary of the type of cases that have come before the inter-American system concerning military jurisdiction.

1 Cases involving the treatment of civilians by military courts

(a) The Peruvian 'treason' and 'terrorism' cases: military judges are prohibited from trying civilians The first group of cases dealt with the treatment of civilians by military courts. These cases involved Peruvian civilians and foreign nationals from Chile and the United States who were charged by the state with crimes of 'treason' (despite the fact that foreigners owe no allegiance to the Peruvian state) or 'terrorism' and summarily tried and convicted by 'faceless' military tribunals.[30] These military court proceedings were subsequently annulled for failure to afford the guarantees of due process and a fair trial. In most of these cases the civilians were retried by 'faceless' civilian courts years later. The civilian trials were similarly flawed because the judges generally relied on the evidence used in the earlier military trials.

In *Castillo Petruzzi* v. *Peru*, a case in which four Chileans were tried in Peru for the crime of 'treason', the Inter-American Court reiterated its doctrine that military courts did not meet the requirements of independence and impartiality in Article 8(1) of the American Convention. It underscored that civilians must be tried in ordinary civilian courts, not in military courts, since civilians have no military functions or duties:

[29] See, for example, *Barrios Altos* v. *Peru* [2001] Inter-Am Court HR (ser. C) No. 75; *Barrios Altos* v. *Peru* [2001] Inter-Am Court HR (ser. C) No. 82, *Almonacid-Arellano* v. *Chile* [2006] Inter-Am Court HR (ser. C) No. 154; *Gomes-Lund et al.* (*Guerrilha do Araguaia*) v. *Brazil* [2010] Inter-Am Court HR (ser. C) No. 219; *Gelman* v. *Uruguay* [2011] Inter-Am Court HR (ser. C) No. 221. See also, Catherine A. Sunshine (ed.), *Victims Unsilenced: The Inter-American Human Rights System and Transitional Justice in Latin America* (Washington, DC, Due Process of Law Foundation, 2007).

[30] See, for example, *Loayza Tamayo* v. *Peru* [1997] Inter-Am Court HR (ser. C) No. 33; *Castillo Petruzzi* v. *Peru* [1999] Inter-Am Court HR (ser. C) No. 52; *Cantoral Benavides* v. *Peru* [2000] Inter-Am Court HR (ser. C) No. 69; *De la Cruz Flores* v. *Peru* [2004] Inter-Am Court HR (ser. C) No. 115; and *Lori Berenson Mejía* v. *Peru* [2004] Inter-Am Court HR (ser. C) No. 119.

> This Court notes that several pieces of legislation give the military courts jurisdiction for the purpose of maintaining order and discipline within the ranks of the armed forces. Application of this functional jurisdiction is confined to military personnel who have committed some crime or were derelict in performing their duties, and then only under certain circumstances. This was the definition in Peru's own law (Article 282 of the 1979 Constitution). Transferring jurisdiction from civilian courts to military courts, thus allowing military courts to try civilians accused of treason, means that the competent, independent and impartial tribunal previously established by law is precluded from hearing these cases. In effect, military tribunals are not the tribunals previously established by law for civilians. Having no military functions or duties, civilians cannot engage in behaviors that violate military duties. When a military court takes jurisdiction over a matter that regular courts should hear, the individual's right to a hearing by a competent, independent and impartial tribunal previously established by law and, *a fortiori*, his rights to due process are violated. That right to due process, in turn, is intimately linked to the very right of access to the courts.[31]

In this case the Commission ordered that 'the persons in question be guaranteed a new trial in which the guarantees of due process of law are ensured' and that the state 'adopt the appropriate measures to amend those laws that this judgment has declared to be in violation of the American Convention'.[32]

Having established the fundamental principle that military tribunals are prohibited from trying civilians because the judges are not independent and impartial and civilians have no military duties, the next line of cases involved civilians who were tried before both military and then civilian courts.

(b) Evidence used in military trials cannot be the basis for a conviction in a subsequent civilian trial and the reliance on an unwritten 'margin of appreciation' The case of Maria Elena Loayza Tamayo involved a Peruvian citizen and professor arrested as a suspected collaborator of the terrorist organisation, the 'Shining Path'. Under the treason statute (Decree Law 25.659), the accused was prohibited from filing a habeas corpus petition to challenge the legality of her detention.

Ms Loayza was tried by a series of military tribunals. First, the Special Naval Court, composed of 'faceless' military judges, acquitted her of

31 *Castillo-Petruzzi* v. *Peru*, at [128]. The doctrine of the restricted scope of military jurisdiction was first set forth by the Inter-American Court in the *Durand and Ugarte* case. *Durand & Ugarte* v. *Peru* [2000] Inter-Am Court HR (ser. C) No. 68, at [117].

32 *Castillo-Petruzzi* v. *Peru*, at [226 (13) and (14)].

treason on 5 March 1993. She was then convicted by the Special Naval Court Martial on 2 April 1993. The Special Tribunal of the Supreme Council of Military Justice, in its judgment of 11 August 1993, rejected a requested nullification of the sentence and acquitted her of treason. It ordered the case to be remitted to the civilian courts so that she could be tried for the crime of terrorism. The Assistant Special Attorney General petitioned for special review of the sentence before the Full Chamber of the Special Supreme Military Tribunal, which culminated in a judgment affirming her acquittal on 24 September 1993.[33]

Ms Loayza Tamayo then was tried in various civilian courts under the terrorism statute (Decree Law 25.475). She filed a *res judicata* objection based on the principle of *non bis in idem* or double jeopardy. On 10 October 1994, the 'faceless' special tribunal of the civilian courts dismissed her objection and sentenced her to twenty years' imprisonment on the basis of the same cause.[34]

In addition to finding that the military and civilian courts under Decree Laws 25.475 and 25.659 violated the due process provisions of Article 8(1) of the American Convention for failing to provide a 'competent, independent and impartial tribunal', the Inter-American Court also held that Peru had violated Article 8(4) of the American Convention, which provides that '[A]n accused person acquitted by a nonappealable judgment shall not be subjected to a new trial for the same cause'. The Court found a violation of Article 8(4) as the civilian trial was based on the same evidence used in the military trial in which she had been acquitted. The Court ordered Peru to release Ms. Loayza Tamayo and within a month after the judgment was delivered she was released.

The Commission and Court considered a number of additional 'terrorism' cases before civilian courts, but since they involved civilian and not military tribunals they do not concern our subject matter. The case of Lori Berenson, however, deserves mention since the Court devised what could be termed an unwritten 'margin of appreciation' in favour of the Peruvian Government in this case. Lori Berenson, a US national, was tried and convicted of treason under Decree Law 12.659 by a 'faceless' military court and, on 11 January 1996, sentenced to life imprisonment for having been a leader of the Movimiento Revolucionario Túpac Amaru (MRTA), a terrorist group.[35] Her lawyer filed an appeal for annulment of the conviction, which was denied in 1996. He filed again

[33] *Loayza Tamayo* v. *Peru* at [3(e)]. [34] Ibid., at [66]–[77] and especially [77].
[35] *Lori Berenson Meijía* v. *Peru*, at [88(26)] and [88(30) and (31)].

in 1999, and it was admitted on 13 January 2000. On 18 August 2000, the Supreme Council of Military Justice, based on intelligence obtained during the MRTA's seizure of the residence of the Japanese Ambassador, decided that Ms. Berenson was not a leader of the MRTA, which meant that she could not be guilty of the criminal conduct of which she had been accused and convicted,[36] and stated that 'an evident error has been made that must be rectified'.[37] Her conviction was annulled and the file transferred to ordinary criminal jurisdiction

On 28 August 2000, the same day the file was transferred, the Provincial Prosecutor *ad hoc* for crimes of terrorism accused Lori Berenson of being a member of the MRTA and of a series of acts of collaboration.[38] The pre-trial civilian proceedings were held in the Chorillos Women's Prison and the plenary took place in the Trial Chamber in the Lurigancho Prison. On 20 June 2001 the National Terrorism Chamber convicted Lori Berenson of being a 'perpetrator of acts of terrorism' under paragraphs (a) and (d) of Article 4 of Decree Law No. 25.475, characterised by acts of collaboration, and sentenced her to twenty years' imprisonment.[39] Inexplicably, after the military courts had convicted her of being a 'leader' of the MRTA, the 'civilian' court (i.e. the National Terrorism Chamber) decided that there was insufficient evidence to conclude that she had even been a 'member' of the MRTA.[40] The Peruvian Supreme Court affirmed the conviction.

The civilian court proceedings against Ms. Berenson were carried out pursuant to Decree Law 25.475, which was criticised by both the Inter-American Court and expert witnesses who appeared in subsequent cases for failure to provide the due process guarantees in the American Convention. For example:

> 73(4) In accordance with Decree Law No. 25.475 promulgated on 5 May 1992, trials for crimes of terrorism were characterised, *inter alia*, by: the possibility of ordering the absolute incommunicado [detention] of those detained for the maximum time defined by law; the restriction of the defense lawyers' participation until after the person detained had made a statement; the inadmissibility of parole for the defendant during the pre-trial proceedings; the prohibition to offer as a witness anyone who had intervened, because of his functions, in the preparation of the police deposition; the obligation of the Superior Prosecutor to formulate a charge 'under his own responsibility';

[36] Ibid., at [88(43)]. [37] Ibid. [38] Ibid., at [88(46)]. [39] Ibid., at [88(69)].
[40] Ibid., at [88(67)].

the holding of the trial in private hearings; the inadmissibility of raising objections to any of the judges and judicial agents intervening in the trial; the participation of unidentified judges and prosecutors; and continuous solitary confinement during the first year of the resulting prison sentence.[41]

In turn, Decree-Law No. 25.475 did not guarantee due process of law, as it delegated the criminal investigation to the police, and restricted the participation of the Public Prosecutor's Office. In addition, the decree 'restricts the participation of the defense counsel, bars release during the preliminary investigation proceedings except for unconditional release, and does not allow police officers who took part in the police investigation to give testimony as witnesses'.[42]

The Inter-American Court, however, found no violation of the fair trial guarantee in Article 8(1) in the civilian proceedings conducted against Ms. Berenson. Only Judge Cecilia Medina, in dissent, was willing to recognise that Article 8 of the American Convention had been violated in this case because the state allowed the evidence from the military court proceedings to become the basis for the conviction in the civilian proceedings.[43] It appears that the Court felt compelled to grant Peru an undeclared margin of appreciation in this case.[44] Ms. Berenson contributed to her own notoriety as a publicly vilified 'terrorist' and the Court opted for a margin of appreciation in favour of the Government of Peru and thereby saved it from a popular uproar had it ordered Ms. Berenson's release. In addition, the political context in Peru had changed dramatically. President Alberto Fujimori had fled Peru for Japan in November 2000 and Mr Valentin Paniagua, a professor of constitutional law, was elected interim president. One of President Paniagua's first acts was to return Peru to the American Convention on Human Rights and to the compulsory jurisdiction of the Inter-American Court.[45]

[41] *De la Cruz Flores* v. *Peru*, at [73(4)].

[42] *Garcia Asto et al.* v. *Peru*, at [86], Expert Evidence of Mario Pablo Rodríguez-Hurtado, attorney-at-law.

[43] *Lori Berenson Mejía* v. *Peru*, at [XVIII]: Dissenting opinion of Judge Medina Quiroga.

[44] The term 'margin of appreciation' refers to the doctrine of the European Court of Human Rights which allows the state a certain measure of discretion, subject to European supervision, when it takes legislative, administrative or judicial action in the area of a Convention right. See David Harris, Michael O'Boyle, Edward Bates and Carla Buckley, *Law of the European Convention on Human Rights*, 2nd edn (Oxford University Press, 2009), p. 11.

[45] On 9 July 1999, the Peruvian Government of President Fujimori had presented an instrument to the General Secretariat of the OAS wherein it advised that it was withdrawing its declaration consenting to the optional clause in the American Convention recognising the contentious jurisdiction of the Court. See *Ivcher Bronstein Case* at [28]. See also Christina M. Cerna, 'Questions of International Law Raised by Peru's

Affirming the actions of the civilian terrorism court had popular political support in Peru. The Court in the Berenson judgment pointed out that Mr Javier Perez de Cuellar, who was Minister of Foreign Affairs during the government of President Paniagua (November 2000–July 2001), noted (in his affidavit) that:

> during his mandate, he did not receive any formal protests from the US Government or from human rights organizations concerning the trial and conviction of Ms. Berenson by the civilian courts. He recalled that local and international public opinion was able to observe the conditions in which the trial was held, because the court authorized the presence of the press, and the hearings were filmed and broadcast live.[46]

Former president Paniagua also stated (by affidavit):

> No formal protests were received owing to the result of this [the Lori Berenson] case. He knew about two official statements made by the US State Department, which confirmed that the US Government was observing the conditions in which the trial was held and the final ruling of the Supreme Court, and considered that the basic standards of due process of law had been respected. The local human rights community shared this opinion.[47]

2 Cases involving retired military officials

The prohibition on military courts trying civilians was extended to include retired military defendants. The Court held in the 1999 case of *Cesti Hurtado* v. *Peru* that a retired military official is a civilian.[48] In that case, a retired military official, who was a private contractor providing security for the military, was charged with fraud (together with some active duty colleagues) and detained in a military prison. His lawyer obtained an order for his release by filing a writ of habeas corpus in an ordinary court. The writ was granted, but the military refused to release him. He sought redress before the inter-American system that found a violation of his right to be heard by a competent tribunal (art 8(1)) and held that the military proceedings must be annulled and that he was entitled to reparations for the violation of his rights.[49]

"Withdrawal" from the Inter-American Court of Human Rights' in Sergio Antonio Fabris (ed.), *Trends in the International Law of Human Rights* [Liber Amicorum Cançado Trindade], vol. II (Porto Alegre, SA Fabris, 2005).

46 *Lori Berenson Mejía* v. *Peru*, at [75(a)]: Testimony (affidavit) of Javier Perez de Cuellar.

47 Ibid., at [75(d)]: Testimony (affidavit) of former President Valentin Paniagua.

48 *Cesti Hurtado* v. *Peru* [1999] Inter-Am Court HR (ser. C) No. 49, at [151].

49 Ibid., at [195]–[198]. See also *Cesti Hurtado* v. *Peru* [2001] Inter-Am Court HR (ser. C) No. 86.

In the 2005 case of *Palamara-Iribarne* v. *Chile*, a retired Chilean Naval officer, hired as a civilian contractor by the Navy, was criminally prosecuted and convicted by a military court for self-publishing a thousand copies of his book, *Ethics and Intelligence Services*, in which he criticised military intelligence issues from an ethical point of view.[50] The State sought to prohibit the publication of the book and seized all copies, including the computer text, before they could be sold. The Chilean military system brought two criminal proceedings against Mr Palamara-Iribarne, one for the criminal offences of disobedience and breach of military duties and the other for the criminal offence of contempt of authority.

The Inter-American Court concluded that Chile had violated Article 8(1) of the American Convention as Mr Palamara-Iribarne had been tried by a court not competent to do so, and ordered Chile 'to bring its domestic law in line with the international standards on military criminal jurisdiction'. The Court noted that 'should the State consider that having military criminal courts is in fact necessary, their jurisdiction should be restricted to cases concerning crimes of a strictly military nature committed by military personnel in active service only'.[51] On 30 December 2010, Chile published Law No. 20.477, which explicitly excluded civilians and minors from the jurisdiction of military tribunals.

3 Human rights violations committed by military officials are not offences committed in the line of duty and cannot be tried in military courts

A second, more prevalent, group of cases in the hemisphere involved military proceedings, or the lack thereof, against military officials charged with crimes that constituted human rights violations.[52] These are the

[50] *Palamara-Iribarne* v. *Chile* [2005] Inter-Am Court HR (ser. C) No. 135.

[51] Ibid., at [256].

[52] *El Amparo* v. *Venezuela* [1995] Inter-Am Court HR (ser. C) No. 19; *Caballero Delgado and Santana* v. *Colombia* [1995] Inter-Am Court HR (ser. C) No. 22; *Genie Lacayo* v. *Nicaragua* [1997] Inter-Am Court HR (ser. C) No. 30; *Durand y Ugarte* v. *Peru* [2000] Inter-Am Court HR (ser. C) No. 68; *Cantoral Benavides* v. *Peru* [2000] Inter-Am Court HR (ser. C) No. 69; *19 Merchants* v. *Colombia* [2004] Inter-Am Court HR (ser. C) No. 109; *Mapiripán Massacre* v. *Colombia* [2005] Inter-Am Court HR (ser. C) No. 134; *Pueblo Bello Massacre* v. *Colombia* [2006] Inter-Am Court HR (ser. C) No. 140; *Almonacid Arellano* v. *Chile* [2006] Inter-Am Court HR (ser. C) No. 154; *La Rochela Massacre* v. *Colombia* [2007] Inter-Am Court HR (ser. C) No. 163; *Escué-Zapata* v. *Colombia* [2007] Inter-Am Court HR (ser. C) No. 165; *Tiu-Tojín* v. *Guatemala* [2008] Inter-Am Court HR (ser. C) No. 190.

'impunity' cases, where the military courts failed to investigate or prosecute serious human rights violations committed by military officials. In response, the Commission developed a doctrine that gross human rights violations carried out by members of the security forces (military or police) cannot be considered military offences committed in the line of duty (*delitos de función*).

A number of these cases have involved Mexico.[53] Despite Mexico's constitutional prohibition on military jurisdiction extending beyond 'the crimes and offenses against military discipline', Article 57 of the Mexican Code of Military Justice extended military jurisdiction to cover crimes of ordinary jurisdiction when they were committed by members of the military.[54] Despite the supremacy of the Constitution over other laws in the Mexican legal system, civilian courts routinely ceded jurisdiction to military courts when a member of the military was the accused.

Radilla Pacheco v. *Mexico* was the first case concerning Mexico's expansion of military jurisdiction to be heard by the Inter-American Court. On 25 August 1974 Mr Rosendo Radilla Pacheco was arrested and forcibly disappeared by the Mexican army in the militarised state of Guerrero. Given the lack of response to the formal complaints filed by his family denouncing his disappearance before state and federal authorities, the Mexican Commission for the Defense and Promotion of Human Rights and the Association of Relatives of Disappeared Detainees and Victims of Violations of Human Rights in Mexico presented a complaint against Mexico before the Commission alleging that Mexico had failed to conduct an effective investigation to establish Radilla Pacheco's whereabouts or to punish those responsible.

In 2005, the Federal District Court of Guerrero ordered the arrest of Lt. Col. Francisco Quiroz Hermosillo, who was in charge of the militarised area when Radilla Pacheco was arrested. That court, however, ceded jurisdiction to a military court, characterising the offence as one of military discipline, in accordance with Article 57 of the Code of Military Justice. Radilla Pacheco's family challenged the transfer of jurisdiction,

[53] *Radilla-Pacheco* v. *Mexico* [2009] Inter-Am Court HR, Case 777/01, Report No. 65/05; *Fernandez Ortega* v. *Mexico* [2010] Inter-Am Court HR, Case 540-04, Report No. 94/06; *Valentina Rosendo Cantú* v. *Mexico* [2010] Inter-Am Court HR, Case 972-03, Report No. 93/06.

[54] Article 13 of the Mexican Constitution states that 'The military jurisdiction subsists for the crimes and offenses against military discipline'. Article 57 of the Mexican Code of Military Justice defines 'crimes against military discipline' to include crimes 'committed by soldiers'.

but were not successful. On 29 November 2006, the military court dismissed the case owing to the extinction of the criminal action following the death of the defendant on 19 November 2006. In July 2005 the Commission issued its decision, holding Mexico responsible for violating the rights to life, personal liberty, humane treatment, fair trial and judicial protection of the American Convention.

The Mexican government failed to comply with the Commission's recommendations and consequently the Commission submitted the case to the Inter-American Court. The Court ruled that the forced disappearance of the victim at the hands of the Mexican military and the transfer of the investigation from civilian to military jurisdiction violated Articles 8 and 25 of the American Convention. The Court found that 'upon expanding the competence of the military jurisdiction to crimes that are not strictly related to military discipline or with juridical rights characteristic of the military realm', the state had violated the rights of the next of kin to a competent tribunal and to effective recourse for contesting the exercise of military jurisdiction.[55] To prevent repetition of this violation, the Court ordered Mexico to 'adopt, within a reasonable period of time, the appropriate legislative reforms in order to make Article 57 of the Code of Military Justice compatible with the international standards in this subject and the American Convention'.[56]

In 2010, the Inter-American Court issued two further judgments involving human rights crimes committed by members of the Mexican Armed Forces.[57] In the cases of *Ines Fernandez Ortega* and *Valentina Rosendo Cantu* two indigenous women had been raped, in separate incidents, by soldiers in 2002. Mexico acknowledged its international responsibility before the Court for violating Articles 8 and 25 of the American Convention for failing to submit the criminal investigation of the rape to the appropriate civilian authorities. This violation was especially serious since the investigation had remained within the military justice system even after the Court gave judgment in the *Radilla Pacheco* case, in which it held this practice to be incompatible with the state's obligations under the American Convention.

[55] *Radilla-Pacheco* v. *Mexico*, at [313]. [56] Ibid., at [392(10)].

[57] *Fernandez Ortega* v. *Mexico* and *Valentina Rosendo Cantú* v. *Mexico* (above n. 53). An unprecedented 1230 complaints were filed before the (Mexican) National Human Rights Commission against the army during 2008. The violations included illegal invasions of residences, arbitrary detentions, rape and sexual abuse, and torture. In 28 cases the presumed human rights violations resulted in the death of the victims.

On 6 July 2011, the Mexican Supreme Court opined that Mexican courts were required to comply with the Inter-American Court's judgment in *Radilla Pacheco*. The Mexican government also stated that it would respect the Supreme Court's ruling. The *Radilla Pacheco* judgment had been issued on 23 November 2009, but the two further judgments issued in 2010, involving grave human rights violations against civilians by members of Mexico's military, gave added impetus to the Supreme Court's opinion. On 12 August 2011, the Prosecutor's Office notified Ines Fernandez Ortega and Valentina Rosendo Cantu that the rape and torture investigations had been handed over to the Attorney-General's office and the federal prosecutors took control of the cases. Mexico subsequently adopted an *amparo* law that made it possible to challenge the application of military jurisdiction. The Inter-American Court affirmed that Mexico had carried out the appropriate legal reforms.[58]

4 Does military jurisdiction violate international human rights standards?

(a) The abolition of military jurisdiction – *Rodolfo Correa Belisle* v. *Argentina* Arguably the most interesting cases regarding military jurisdiction have concerned the question whether military jurisdiction, as a separate justice system, should exist at all. The cases of *Rodolfo Correa Belisle* v. *Argentina* and *Hugo Oscar Arguelles et al.* v. *Argentina* led to the abolition of military jurisdiction in Argentina, not just for civilians but, more interestingly, also for members of the military.[59] In an attempt to resolve both cases by means of a 'friendly settlement' rather than a merits decision of the Commission or a judgment by the Court, Argentina repealed its Code of Military Justice.

In *Correa Belisle*, the alleged victim, a captain in the Argentine Army was ordered to conduct a search for the body of a private, named Carrasco, who had disappeared. The body was found and Captain Rodolfo Correa Belisle was summoned to testify before a civilian court about the details. During the course of the hearing, his military superior was offended by his statements, including that he had 'heard even General Balza lie about the Carrasco case'. In response, General Balza

[58] Inter–Am Court HR, Resolución de la Corte Interamericana de Derechos Humanos de 17 de abril de 2015, *Casos Radilla Pacheco, Fernández Ortega y Otros y Rosendo Cantú y otra v. México*, Supervisión de Cumplimiento de Sentencia.

[59] *Rodolfo Correa Belisle* v. *Argentina* [2010] Inter-Am Court HR, Report No. 15/10, Petition 11.758, Friendly Settlement. Available on the Commission's website, above n. 10.

initiated criminal proceedings before a military criminal court against Correa Belisle on the charge of 'disrespect'. Captain Correa Belisle sought to have the case dismissed for lack of jurisdiction, alleging infringement of the right to a competent judge. He argued that the case belonged in the ordinary civilian courts as the only criminal conduct involved was defamation, an offence over which the federal civilian courts had jurisdiction. The motion for dismissal was denied on 18 December 1996 by the federal judge of Neuquen, who found that 'disrespect' was an essentially military offence in light of the military status of the accused and the legally protected interest of military discipline. Consequently, only military tribunals had competence to pass judgment. Correa Belisle was eventually sentenced to three months' imprisonment for the military offence of 'disrespect' as provided in Article 665 of the Argentine Code of Military Justice.

Captain Correa Belisle was not permitted judicial review of the military tribunal's judgment and appealed to the Inter-American Commission alleging violations of the rights of due process and access to justice. He had not been permitted to choose his own lawyer during the proceedings and had been impeded in exercising his right of defence. The State accepted its international responsibility for violations of the American Convention in this case, and proposed the repeal of the Code of Military Justice. The Code was replaced with a system enabling crimes committed by members of the military to be prosecuted by ordinary courts. The new Code of Military Justice came into force on 27 February 2009, eliminating military jurisdiction in times of peace and abolishing the death penalty, which had continued to exist in Argentina in the Code of Military Justice.

(b) ***Arguelles et al.* v. *Argentina*** The case of Hugo Arguelles involved twenty-one members of the Argentine Air Force who were prosecuted for military fraud and connected crimes in proceedings initiated during the military dictatorship in September 1980.[60] The Commission held that the right to a fair trial (Article 8 of the American Convention) had been violated in the course of military court proceedings against members of the military for military fraud.[61] What distinguished this case from earlier cases is that the petitioners requested the Commission to determine whether military court proceedings against military officials for military

[60] Argentina returned to a democratic government in December 1983 when President Raul Alfonsin assumed power.

[61] See Inter-Am Court HR, *Press Release* (15 June 2012).

crimes met the standards provided in the American Convention. Earlier cases had challenged the use of military jurisdiction in the prosecution of members of the military for human rights crimes or in the prosecution of civilians, but did not question whether military jurisdiction, used for the purposes for which it was created (to try members of the military for military crimes), was compatible with the state's obligations pursuant to the American Convention.

The Commission concluded that the Code of Military Justice included certain provisions that *prima facie* constituted an infringement of the right to a fair trial and access to justice.[62] The Code of Military Justice had been repealed in the framework of a friendly settlement in this case together with the *Correa Belisle* case. The *Correa Belisle* case ended in a friendly settlement, but an agreement could not be reached in the *Arguelles et al.* case on the issue of reparations. *Arguelles et al.* was sent to the Inter-American Court on 29 May 2012. The Inter-American Court held that there were violations of the rights to personal liberty, to a defence lawyer, and to a trial within a reasonable time.[63] However, the petitioners had failed to raise the question whether military jurisdiction complied with human rights before the domestic courts. They also had a right to appeal to the civilian courts in Argentina. Consequently, the Inter-American Court found that Argentina did not violate the rights to due process or access to justice.

IV Conclusion

The trend in international human rights law is to narrow the scope of military jurisdiction whereby it applies only to military officials who have committed military crimes and offences in the line of duty. This accords with the United Nations Principles Governing the Administration of Justice through Military Tribunals, which state in Principle 9, 'Trial of persons accused of serious human rights violations':

> In all circumstances, the jurisdiction of military courts should be set aside in favor of the jurisdiction of the ordinary courts to conduct inquiries into serious human rights violations such as extrajudicial executions, enforced disappearances and torture, and to prosecute and try persons accused of such crimes.

The trend of states in the Americas, however, is not all in one direction. President Alan Garcia, the former president of Peru, issued four decrees on

[62] Ibid. [63] *Argüelles et al v Argentina* [2014] Inter-Am Court HR (ser. C) No 294.

1 September 2010 by which he attempted to modify the military justice system. Article 27 of Decree 1095 sought to subject 'illicit conduct allegedly committed by military personnel' to military jurisdiction. By establishing that any 'illicit conduct' carried out by military personnel would be subject to military jurisdiction, Decree 1095 could be used to prevent civilian courts from trying human rights violations by military personnel against civilians. Despite outcry by civil society and international human rights bodies, Decree 1095 has not been repealed.[64] Similarly, in July 2015 the Colombian Congress approved Law No. 1765 which expands military jurisdiction. It extends military jurisdiction to civilians who serve in positions in police and criminal military justice and to retired members of the military who carry out the same functions. It also recognises crimes distinct from those inherent in military service. This law is being challenged before the Colombian Constitutional Court.[65]

It is too early to tell whether the emerging trend towards the abolition of military jurisdiction in the Americas will be replicated in other countries in the region or whether it will generate a push-back from the militaries to restore their prerogatives. There is clearly a trend away from forced recruitment in favour of voluntary service and towards the civilianisation of the military, although conscription still exists in a number of countries in the region. Whatever the motives for enlisting in the armed forces in the Americas today, recruits are driven by civilian opportunities such as regular and paid employment, and benefits such as access to higher education and medical care, as well as service to country. It is not surprising that the need to attract volunteers to the military has also opened the door to the demand for recognition of human rights, such as the right to due process. In a region that as recently as thirty-five years ago was dominated by military dictatorships, the increasing recognition of respect for human rights, including the human rights of military personnel, is a development worth following.

[64] See Human Rights Watch, *World Report 2013: Peru* (31 January 2013). In a 2015 judgment the Peruvian Constitutional Court interpreted the term 'illicit conduct' subject to military jurisdiction to include only such conduct that comprises a military and not a human rights crime: Tribunal Constitucional Sentencia Exp. No 00022–2011–PI/TC.

[65] *Ante la Corte fue demandada la ley que reforma la Justicia Penal Militar*, 24 November 2015, El País.com.co; *Víctimas, organizaciones y congresistas demandan la ley que reestructuró fuero penal militar*, Lunes 23 de noviembre de 2015, por Prensa – Colectivo: http://www.colectivodeabogados.org/Victimas-organizaciones-y-congresistas-demandan-la-ley-que-reestructuro-fuero.

17

The future of military summary trials in the modern age

AIFHELI ENOS TSHIVHASE

I Introduction

Military justice systems around the world have faced attacks from courts, scholars and civil society. Most of these challenges have been directed to the constitution and judicial independence of courts martial or military courts. Military summary trials have not been the primary target of the onslaught but serious questions are now emerging about the future of such trials. The jurisprudence of the European Court of Human Rights, which is the most comprehensive of all international courts on issues of military justice, suggests that summary military justice may face many doctrinal problems.

This chapter examines the possible future of military summary trials from a global perspective. It considers questions about the jurisdiction, independence and process of military summary trials.[1] The chapter explains the role and purpose of summary trials before considering these forums in a comparative context. It will be shown that summary military trials across jurisdictions possess several common features. The chapter also argues that summary trials are an important aspect of military justice that should be retained, although subject to reform. The chapter concludes that the future of military summary trials in their current form is uncertain unless targeted steps are taken to preserve them.

II The role and purpose of military summary trials

Summary trials are a critical part of the military justice system. They are designed to provide speedy justice where the nature of the offence and the circumstances in which it was committed are best addressed quickly. In

[1] In this chapter, the phrases military summary trials, summary courts martial and summary trials are used interchangeably.

Canada the formal purpose of summary proceedings 'is to provide prompt but fair justice in respect of minor service offences and to contribute to the maintenance of military discipline and efficiency ... in time of peace or armed conflict'.[2] Similarly, Chris Griggs states in the context of New Zealand that 'the purpose of summary trials is to provide commanders with a method of dealing expeditiously and simply with less serious disciplinary infractions, whether they be in New Zealand, at sea or in an overseas operation'.[3] Michael Gilbert puts it even more crisply when he says that 'the summary court-martial ... is valuable when a military member needs to be taught a swift lesson that will serve as a message to others about to fall off the precipice of good order and discipline.'[4] These and other explanations stress the importance of some military offences being resolved quickly and that a failure to do so can hamper the order and operation of military forces. It is clear that expeditious and swift enforcement of discipline is a key attribute of summary trials, something that can hardly be said of a fully-fledged military court staffed by lawyers.

III Summary trials in comparative military justice

A comparative overview of the status and nature of summary trials is important for purposes of identifying the common and divergent features of these forums in a number of jurisdictions. The countries chosen for comparison are from five different continents, namely Africa, Europe, North America, Asia and the Asia-Pacific region. These are: South Africa, India, the United States, the United Kingdom, New Zealand and Canada.[5] The latter is generally considered as the leader in the reform of military justice following that country's Supreme Court ruling in *R* v. *Généreux*.[6] The countries selected provide a useful comparison because

[2] Queen's Regulations and Orders for the Canadian Forces, vol. II, ch. 108, r. 108.2.

[3] Chris Griggs, 'A New Military Justice System for New Zealand' (2006) 6 *New Zealand Armed Forces Law Review*, p. 62, at 66.

[4] Michael Gilbert, 'Summary Courts-Martial: Rediscovering the Spumoni of Military Justice' (1996) 39 *Armed Forces Law Review*, p. 119.

[5] Australia was omitted because temporary summary proceedings existed at the time of writing, after the Australian Military Court was declared unconstitutional: *Lane* v. *Morrison* (2009) 239 CLR 230.

[6] [1992] 1 SCR 259. See Eugene Fidell, 'International Developments in Military Law' (2012) 17 *Canadian Criminal Law Review*, p. 83, at 84 expressing similar sentiments. For a description of summary trials in Canada and a brief critique of such trials followed by a call for reform see Michel Drapeau, 'Military Summary Trials: A Victorian System of Justice' (2010) 17(9) *Esprit de Corps*, p. 16, at 18.

they have recently reviewed their military justice systems and have similar legal traditions rooted in common law and democratic values. The survey will assess aspects of summary trials with respect to their status, composition, the right to legal representation, and jurisdiction in respect of persons and penalties.

The survey shows that summary trials enjoy many similarities in the six countries under consideration. In three countries, summary trials are not formally referred to as 'courts martial' or at least the word 'court' is not used in reference to these trials.[7] In the United States, summary courts martial are part of the hierarchy of military courts,[8] as is the case in South Africa. In South Africa, the relevant Act classifies a summary trial (formally known as the Commanding Officer's Disciplinary Hearing (CODH)) as part of the hierarchy of the military court system.[9] It is at the lowest level of military courts. In the Indian Army, there are four kinds of courts martial.[10] Summary courts martial are the lowest level of courts martial too.[11] In contrast, in the Indian Navy, there is no summary court martial in a formal sense but a commanding officer is empowered to summarily try and punish any person other than an officer for a non-capital offence.[12] Although the Indian Navy Act does not use the phrase 'summary court martial' with reference to the powers of the commanding officer, it could be argued that due to the nature of the powers and the manner in which such powers are exercised, the summary trial by the commanding officer is an equivalent of a summary court martial in the Indian Army Act. Similarly, the Air Force Act makes no provision for the summary court martial.[13]

[7] These are the United Kingdom, Canada and New Zealand.

[8] Uniform Code of Military Justice, 10 USC § 816 art. 16 (2010), which lists summary courts martial alongside general courts martial and special courts martial. The latter two courts have wide powers and are presided over by military judges. Summary courts martial must be distinguished from non-judicial punishment which may be imposed by a commanding officer on any military personnel including officers. The latter appears less formal compared to summary courts martial. See § 815, art. 15 for detail about non-judicial punishment.

[9] Military Discipline Supplementary Measures Act 1999 (South Africa) s. 6(1)(d).

[10] Army Act, 1950 s. 108 (Indian Army Act).

[11] Other courts martial are general courts martial, district courts martial, and summary general courts martial. India has retained the old British model of a separate military justice system for each arm of service (Air Force; Navy; and the Army). In the Air Force only three types of courts martial are provided for. The differences between the services in India are explained in Umesh Jha (ed.), *The Military Justice System in India: An Analysis* (Nagpur, LexisNexis Butterworth Wadhwa, 2009), pp. 280–82. See also Chapter 9.

[12] See Navy Act, 1950 s. 93(2).

[13] See Airforce Act, 1950 s. 109.

Nevertheless, in all the countries studied, summary trials are essentially the sole domain of commanding officers because they act as both prosecutors and judges. This blurring of roles (in which a person is both prosecutor and judge) is normally prohibited in civilian law because it contravenes requirements of fairness and rules against bias. Some blurring of function may be desirable. Decision makers, including civilian and military judges, are better informed if they have experience in the matters in which they preside. In *R (Carroll)* v. *Secretary of State for the Home Department*[14] Lord Rodger accepted that the professional experience of decision makers could inform their functions without affecting their impartiality. His Lordship suggested that similar reasoning applied to 'the realities of life in many organisations' such as schools, prisons and the military, where senior officials administered discipline but impartiality would not be possible if officials were called upon to adjudicate upon decisions in which they were involved.[15] Military justice systems have generally not confronted this issue, although New Zealand has introduced an additional element to the composition of summary trials to increase impartiality, that is, the 'presenting officer' who assists the commanding officer in the presentation of a case.[16] Other countries may have informal arrangements to this effect, but it is not indicated in their primary military laws.

With respect to jurisdiction of summary trials, almost all of the countries considered impose restrictions concerning persons that may be tried and penalties that may be imposed upon a finding of guilty. Each of these countries permits a sentence of detention at a summary hearing. Periods of detention range from thirty days to ninety days; but only India permits its commanding officers to impose a sentence of imprisonment at a summary trial. Thus, Indian summary courts martial have the most powers of all jurisdictions investigated. They may pass any sentence which may be passed under the Indian Army Act with the exception of the following: a sentence of death or transportation, or of imprisonment

[14] [2005] 1 All ER 927. [15] Ibid., at [11].

[16] Armed Forces Discipline Amendment Act (No 2) 2007 (NZ) s. 115. New Zealand is one of the latest countries to have 'voluntarily' overhauled its military justice system – including summary trials. There has not been any major challenge to New Zealand's military justice system but Griggs suggested that the recent reforms to New Zealand's military justice system were made, partly at least, in anticipation of possible challenges: Griggs, above n. 3, at 62–64. However, a deliberate policy stance has been taken not to introduce any major changes to the core elements of summary trials by commanding officers. See, again, Griggs, above n. 3, at 69.

for a term exceeding three months or one year depending on the rank of the officer holding the hearing.[17] Given the pressure exerted on the Indian military justice system and events elsewhere in the world, it is unlikely that commanding officers will retain their power to impose a sentence of imprisonment in the event that there is broad reform of the military justice system. In his analysis of India's summary court martial, Umesh Jha points out that a sentence imposed at a summary trial is a non-judicial punishment because the officer conducting the proceedings is not a court and the trial is by a summary proceeding.[18] In the light of several peculiar procedural inadequacies, including lack of access to defence counsel or the right to elect to be heard by a court martial, and the arbitrary nature of the way in which summary trials are conducted in India, Jha urges the abolition of summary courts martial. At the same time, however, Jha acknowledges the importance of summary trials and to an extent supports the reform of summary trials elsewhere in his work.[19]

New Zealand breaks with tradition by subjecting *all* its officers to the jurisdiction of summary trials.[20] This is unprecedented but both the United Kingdom and Canada have taken a step in a similar direction by subjecting certain officer ranks to the jurisdiction of summary trials, against the norm that summary trials are generally used to discipline non-commissioned officers.[21]

Each of the countries does give a choice to elect trial by a court martial, albeit that this choice is discretionary (on the part of the commanding officer) in the case of New Zealand in certain circumstances.[22] Placing this decision within the discretion of commanders arguably amplifies the powers of commanders because it enables them to indirectly determine the scope of punishments defendants may face.

Finally, none of the countries studied provides for the right to legal representation at a summary hearing as a general rule. Only the United States provides for this right in exceptional circumstances.[23] Lawyers are

[17] Army Act, 1950 s. 120(4). [18] Jha, above n. 11, p. 178. [19] See ibid., p. 299.

[20] See Armed Forces Discipline Amendment Act (No 2) 2007 (NZ) pt. 5 in particular.

[21] The Armed Forces Act 2006 (UK) c. 52, s. 52(3) provides that an officer below the rank of commander, lieutenant-colonel or wing commander may be heard summarily. In Canada, officers from the rank of lieutenant-colonel may be tried summarily provided certain requirements are satisfied: National Defence Act RSC 1985, c. N-5, ss. 163(1) and (3), 164(1)(a) and 164(3) (Canada's National Defence Act).

[22] Armed Forces Discipline Amendment Act (No 2) 2007 (NZ) s. 117L(1)(2).

[23] See Rule 1301(e) of the Rules for Courts-Martial. In terms of the Rule, the accused may be permitted to be represented by a qualified civilian counsel 'if such appearance will not unreasonably delay the proceedings and military exigencies do not preclude it'.

deliberately kept out of summary trials in order that summary trials can be a swift disciplinary tool for commanders. The presence of lawyers could frustrate that key purpose because their involvement usually leads to longer and more complex hearings.[24] However, in New Zealand,[25] Canada[26] and the United Kingdom[27] there has been a trend to strengthen the assistance available to the accused at a summary hearing. Such changes reflect an increasing demand for summary trials to be fairer in the modern age. Some countries have even created specialist appeal courts for summary trials which may help deal with some of the excesses of these forums.[28] The addition of an appeal court specifically for summary trials is novel.

IV The application of the rights to be tried by an independent and impartial tribunal to military summary trials

The right to a fair trial in human rights law requires a hearing by an independent and impartial tribunal. In the past two decades there has been some general acceptance that the right to a fair trial applies to fully-fledged military courts, even though most international human rights instruments do not directly address the status of military tribunals.[29] However, there has been very little commentary on the application of the

[24] Lawyers are said to 'juridify' hearings: M. Loughlin, 'The Underside of the Law: Judicial Review and the Prison Disciplinary System' (1993) 46(2) *Current Legal Problems*, p. 23, at 39.

[25] The accused before a summary hearing must be assigned a defending officer to assist him or her in the preparation and presentation of his or her case and to act on behalf of the accused, and this officer must not be a lawyer: Armed Forces Discipline Amendment Act (No 2) 2007 (NZ) s. 114.

[26] The accused can be assisted by the so-called 'assisting officer' appointed by or under the authority of the commanding officer in order to assist him or her at the hearing. Queen's Regulations and Orders for the Canadian Forces, vol. II, ch. 108, r. 108.14. In certain circumstances, the rules allow defendants to be assisted by an officer of their choosing. This assistance includes speaking for the accused during the trial, something unique among the jurisdictions considered here.

[27] The regulations under the previous Act (Armed Forces Act 1996 (UK)) made provision for the accused to take legal advice before electing to be heard by a commanding officer and to have access to the so-called accused's adviser.

[28] For example, the United Kingdom has established the Summary Appeal Court to which an accused may appeal against findings or punishments: Armed Forces Act 2006 (UK) c. 52, s. 141.

[29] See Aifheli Enos Tshivhase, 'Military Courts in a Democratic South Africa: An Assessment of their Independence' (2006) 6 *New Zealand Armed Forces Law Review*, p. 96, at 97–102 where this author discusses the application of the right to a fair trial to military courts (excluding summary trials).

same right to military summary trials. The situation of summary trials in most jurisdictions is peculiar because they only deal with disciplinary offences. The applicability of the right to be tried by an independent and impartial tribunal to summary military trials raises questions about the future of these forums in their current form. This question was raised sharply in *Bell* v. *United Kingdom*,[30] *Thompson* v. *United Kingdom*[31] and to some extent *Hood* v. *United Kingdom*.[32] In these cases the European Court of Human Rights held that British summary trials (as constituted before 2006) contravened arts 6(1) and (3) of the European Convention on Human Rights. The most relevant part of that article for our purposes is art. 6(1), which provides that 'in the determination . . . of any criminal charge against him, everyone is entitled to a fair and public hearing . . . by an independent and impartial tribunal established by law'.[33]

The Court reached its conclusion by application of a two-fold criterion developed in the earlier cases of the Court, most notably in *Engel* v. *Netherlands*.[34] The starting point of the enquiry is whether the offence charged belongs, according to the legal system of the state concerned, to criminal law, disciplinary law or both.[35] In many jurisdictions, proceedings before summary trials arguably assume both a criminal and disciplinary character because the principles of liability are those applied in criminal law and the sentencing processes assume a criminal law character but with a strong emphasis on discipline. Consequently the first criterion would be met with respect to summary trials of most countries at least according to the logic of the jurisprudence of the European Court of Human Rights.[36]

The supervision of the Court goes further and takes into consideration the severity of the penalty, including the maximum potential penalty, that the person concerned risks incurring. In *Bell* v. *United Kingdom*, the Court considered a sentence of detention for a period of twenty-eight

[30] (2007) 45 EHRR 24. (*Bell*) [31] (2005) 40 EHRR 11. (*Thompson*)

[32] (1999) 26 EHRR 365.

[33] Convention for the Protection of Human Rights and Fundamental Freedoms, 4 November 1950, in force 3 September 1953, 213 UNTS 221, art. 6. (ECHR) art. 6(1).

[34] (1979) 1 EHRR 647.

[35] Ibid., at [82]. See also *Bell* v. *United Kingdom* (2007) 45 EHRR 24.

[36] This approach is not unlike that developed in Canadian law, where courts have held that the distinction between criminal and disciplinary offences or proceedings depends largely on the character and consequences of the proceedings in which matters are heard. This distinction means that some offences can be heard in either criminal or disciplinary forums, or both: *R* v. *Wigglesworth* [1987] 2 SCR 541; *Shubley* v. *R* [1990] 1 SCR 3.

days to be a serious enough deprivation of liberty to render the charge against the accused to be of a criminal nature that attracted the application of art. 6 of the ECHR.[37] The criterion developed by the European Court of Human Rights is instructive for the standards applicable to military tribunals. In almost all jurisdictions considered in this chapter, the maximum sentence in respect of deprivation of liberty is detention or confinement to barracks for a period ranging from twenty-one days to ninety days, with India being the only country that permits its commanding officers to impose a sentence of imprisonment at a summary trial. Following the analogy of the European Court of Human Rights, the right to be tried by an independent and impartial tribunal would apply to summary trials in those countries. This conclusion is consistent with some prevailing views in Canada and New Zealand. In Canada, the Office of the Judge Advocate General concluded that 'a summary trial is . . . "by nature" a criminal proceeding' and that '[o]nce the "by nature" test is passed it is irrelevant if the summary trial awards penal sanctions'[38] for purposes of deciding whether the right applies or not. This would mean that the right to a fair trial would apply to a summary trial. New Zealand has decided to adopt a similar policy position regarding the application of the right under consideration, but sees the continued use of summary trials in their current form as a justifiable limitation of the right in question in line with the New Zealand Bill of Rights Act 1990 (NZ).[39]

V Options for preserving military summary trials in the modern age

The above discussion shows that military summary trials are at a cross-road or at least approaching a cross-road in some jurisdictions. There is a

[37] (2007) 45 EHRR [41]–[42]. In that judgment, the Court used the words 'imprisonment' and 'detention' interchangeably even though they are different. It is not entirely clear whether the Court would have arrived at a different conclusion had it properly understood the nature of the sentence of detention given its emphasis on deprivation of liberty. Some states entered a reservation to the effect that art. 6 of the ECHR would not apply to discipline within their armed forces. The UK did not do so, and thus faced challenges to its military justice system based on art. 6. There have been calls in Parliament for the UK to withdraw from the Convention and re-ratify with an appropriate reservation: Peter Rowe, 'A New Court to Protect Human Rights in the Armed Forces of the UK: The Summary Appeal Court' (2003) 8 *Journal of Conflict and Security Law*, p. 201, at 202.

[38] Office of the Judge Advocate General, Canada, *Summary Trial Working Group Report*, vol. I (2 March 1994), p. 51 (referred to in Griggs, above n. 3, at 71).

[39] See Griggs, above n. 3, at 69–72 outlining the policy stance adopted.

need to evaluate their preservation given the demands of the modern era in accordance with the options below.

A Election and waiver option

The right to elect trial by a summary court martial is generally seen as a measure which legitimises summary trials despite their deficiencies. When accused persons elect to be tried by a summary court martial, they are deemed to have waived most rights that come with trial by a court martial. These include the right to be tried by an independent court and the right to legal representation. Most countries considered in this chapter provide an accused with the right to elect not to be heard by a summary trial.[40]

It is generally accepted in law that rights can be waived but not all waivers are valid. According to the European Court of Human Rights, a waiver of a right guaranteed by the ECHR must not run counter to any important public interest, must be established in an unequivocal manner and requires minimum guarantees commensurate to the waiver's importance.[41]

In both *Thompson* v. *United Kingdom*[42] and *Bell* v. *United Kingdom*,[43] the European Court of Human Rights declared the election and waiver option in the context of summary trial vis-à-vis court martial to be invalid due to the circumstances surrounding the waiver.[44] First, the accused was directly subordinate[45] and in close structural proximity to his commanding officer. In essence, the waiver and election option entails that the accused must choose between the commanding officer and a court martial. According to the Court, this factor would have affected the free and unambiguous nature of the choice available.[46] Second, the European Court of Human Rights stated that the accused would have been influenced by the fact that a summary procedure involved a maximum sentence of twenty-eight or sixty days (if extended powers were granted) whereas trial by a court martial could in theory have led to a sentence of up to two

40 The only country where an accused does not at all have a right to elect trial by a court martial is India.

41 *Thompson* v. *United Kingdom* (2005) 40 EHRR 11, at [43]. 42 Ibid., at [43].

43 (2007) 45 EHRR 24.

44 However, in *Bell* v. *The United Kingdom*, Maruste J wrote a dissenting opinion to the effect that defendants who choose to be tried by a summary trial validly waive applicable rights.

45 *Thompson* v. *United Kingdom* (2005) 40 EHRR 11, at [44]. 46 Ibid., at [44].

years' imprisonment. In other words, it could be argued that the choice of the accused was influenced by fear of a possible heavier sentence by a court martial. Third, the applicant, being a lay person, was not in a position to evaluate his legal position with respect to the choice because legal representation was not allowed at the summary hearing when the opportunity to elect was afforded to the accused.[47]

The third reason for declaring the waiver invalid can easily be remedied by ensuring that accused persons have access to legal representation at the time when an opportunity to elect is afforded. However, the first and second reasons go to the very structure of military discipline that cannot be altered without fundamentally tampering with the key tenets of military discipline. One of the key tenets in this instance is that commanding officers should directly retain a measure of control over military discipline, which means they should naturally be part of the process, albeit with limited sentencing powers. This, in my view, renders election and waiver a dead option because there are good reasons for questioning its validity.

B The appeal and review option

The availability of an appeal mechanism against finding and sentence of a summary hearing and the process of automatic review could arguably be relied on as a justification for making use of summary trials in their current form. Almost all the countries surveyed have these mechanisms built into their military justice systems in one form or another.

However, in both *Findlay* v. *United Kingdom*[48] and *Thompson* the European Court of Human Rights held that the structural defects in British military tribunals 'could not be corrected by a subsequent review other than a first instance hearing which met the requirements of Article 6(1) of the Convention.'[49] Regrettably, the Court did not give reasons for

[47] Ibid., at [44]. [48] (1997) 24 EHRR 221.

[49] Ibid., at [79]. See also *Thompson* v. *United Kingdom* (2005) 40 EHRR 11, at [46]. It may be important to point out, however, that *Findlay* was decided in the context of a general court martial where the accused was faced with serious charges classified as criminal under both domestic and Convention law. Whether or not the reasoning in *Findlay* can be applied comfortably with respect to summary trials is a point for debate and arguments could be advanced on both sides. The United Kingdom seems to be relying on the summary appeal court mechanism to compensate for the flaws within summary trials. See The Court Martial and The Summary Appeal Court Guidance (June 2011) at [7.1] issued under the authority of the Judge Advocate General and the Director of the Military Court Service where reliance on this mechanism is made, among others, accessed at www.justice.gov.uk/downloads/courts/judge-advocate-general/procedure-guide-vol-2.pdf.

its ruling on this point but there are two obvious reasons that can be advanced in support of application of its ruling with respect to summary trials. First, the structural defects regarding the independence of summary trials are so glaring that a review or appeal process cannot remedy them. The commanding officer has a direct and vested interest in the maintenance of military discipline within the unit. Second, reliance on judicial review may remedy infringements of the right to be tried by an independent tribunal but does not prevent them.[50] This means that reliance on appeal and review mechanisms as a justification for structural flaws in summary trials may have fundamental problems.

C *The limitation of rights option*

Some countries have a general limitation clause in their constitutions which can be relied on to justify a limitation or an infringement of a right. The Canadian and South African constitutions are prime examples.[51] Section 36 of the South African Constitution provides as follows:

> The rights in the Bill of Rights may be limited only in terms of law of general application to the extent that the limitation is reasonable and justifiable in an open and democratic society based on human dignity, equality and freedom, taking into account all relevant factors, including – (a) the nature of the right; (b) the importance of the purpose of the limitation; (c) the nature and extent of the limitation; (d) the relation between the limitation and its purpose; and (e) less restrictive means to achieve the purpose.

Consequently, the rights in the Bill of Rights may be limited in terms of law of general application to the extent that the limitation is reasonable and justifiable in an open democratic society based on the listed factors. In this respect, the South African and Canadian constitutions differ from many other bills of rights and international human rights instruments.[52]

[50] See Jane Franco and Cathleen Powell, 'The Meaning of Institutional Independence in *Van Rooyen v The State*' (2004) 121 *South African Law Journal*, p. 562, at 564 who make the same argument while critiquing the Constitutional Court of South Africa for sanctioning a lower degree of judicial independence in respect of magistrates' courts because those courts are subject to supervisory review by superior courts.

[51] Section 1 of the Canadian Constitution provides that 'the Canadian Charter of Rights and Freedoms guarantees the rights and freedoms set out in it subject only to such reasonable limits prescribed by law as can be demonstrably justified in a free and democratic society': Canada Act 1982 (UK) c. 11, sch. B pt. I (Canadian Charter of Rights and Freedoms). There is a similar limitation clause in Bill of Rights Act 1990 (NZ) s. 5.

[52] Ian Currie and Johan de Waal (eds.), *The Bill of Rights Handbook*, 6th edn (Cape Town, Juta, 2013), p. 152. These include the United States Constitution and the European

Neither the International Covenant on Civil and Political Rights or the ECHR have a general limitation clause; but certain rights have internal qualifiers. In both instruments, the provisions dealing with the right to a fair trial by an independent and impartial tribunal do not have such qualifiers. This means that an infringement of such rights cannot be justified.

Nevertheless, the South African limitation clause provides a case study of the way in which arguments for justifying the utilisation of summary trials in their current form could proceed. The analysis 'involves the weighing up of competing values, and ultimately an assessment based on proportionality . . . which calls for the balancing of different interests.'[53] It is to the limitation analysis that attention will now turn[54] as it is a possible option for preserving military summary trials, if available, to those seeking reform of military justice.[55]

An enquiry under s. 36 of the South African Constitution has two stages.[56] The first is whether a right in the Bill of Rights has been infringed or limited by law or conduct of the respondent. This is essentially a matter of interpretation of the right in question as already attempted above. The second stage, the justification enquiry, often involves an assessment of factual evidence. The minimum requirement for a limitation is that the limiting law must be of general application in that it must be sufficiently clear, accessible and precise[57] – and also that it must equally apply to all people similarly situated and must not be arbitrary in its application.[58]

There is no doubt that the South African Military Discipline Supplementary Measures Act is a law of general application and therefore easily qualifies for purposes of s. 36(1) of the Bill of Rights. A positive answer to the first question leads us to the second question – whether the limitation of the right to be tried by an independent court can be justified

Convention on Human Rights. The ECHR does not have a general limitation clause but some rights have internal qualifiers. This means that an infringement of a right which does not have an internal qualifier such as art. 6 cannot be justified under the ECHR.

53 *S* v. *Makwanyane and Another* 1995 (3) SA 391 (Constitutional Court), at [104].

54 In this section I draw heavily from the work of Currie and de Waal, above n. 52, pp. 150–75 regarding the jurisprudence of the Constitutional Court of South Africa on the limitation clause in the South African Constitution.

55 The author recognises that this analysis may prove unhelpful to those countries involved in the reform of military justice systems that do not have a general limitation clause.

56 Ibid.

57 *Dawood* v. *Minister of Home Affairs* 2000 (3) SA 936 (Constitutional Court), at [47].

58 See Currie and de Waal, above n. 52, p. 153.

(the second stage of the analysis). The onus of proving that the limitation is justifiable rests on the party relying on the limitation (usually the state).

The second stage of the analysis, the proportionality test, focuses on whether the law in question is reasonable and justifiable in an open and democratic society based on human dignity, equality and freedom, taking into account all relevant factors listed in s. 36(1)(a)–(e). In *S* v. *Makwanyane*[59] the Constitutional Court stated that:

> The limitation of constitutional rights for a purpose that is reasonable and necessary in a democratic society involves the weighing up of competing values, and ultimately an assessment based on proportionality ... In the balancing process the relevant considerations will include the nature of the right that is limited and its importance to an open and democratic society based on freedom and equality; the purpose for which the right is limited and the importance of that purpose to such a society; the extent of the limitation, its efficacy and, particularly where the limitation has to be necessary, whether the desired ends could reasonably be achieved through other means less damaging to the right in question.[60]

What follows is an analysis of each of the factors involved in the proportionality enquiry in the light of the paragraph quoted above. The starting point is s. 36(1)(a) dealing with the nature of the right limited by the law in question – the right to a public trial before an ordinary (independent) court which is part of the right to a fair trial.[61] Although this is a procedural right, it is clearly important in ensuring that the interests of the accused are protected, and also crucial in making sure that people have confidence in the justice system. Moreover, independent courts and tribunals are better placed to ensure fairness and curb abuse of authority.[62]

The requirement of reasonableness requires that the limitation of a right serve some purpose, and justifiability requires that purpose to be worthwhile and important in a constitutional democracy.[63] The purpose of summary trials is to ensure the swift enforcement of military

[59] 1995 (3) SA 391 (Constitutional Court), at [104].

[60] *S* v. *Makwanyane and Another* 1995 (3) SA 391 (Constitutional Court), at [104]. Although the Court was referring to the limitation clause in the Interim Constitution, its views apply with equal force to the interpretation of s. 36 because this provision is substantially similar to the limitation clause in the Interim Constitution.

[61] This is how the right is phrased in the Constitution of the Republic of South Africa Act 1996 (South Africa) s. 35(3)(c).

[62] The Constitutional Court of South Africa expressed similar sentiments in *De Lange* v. *Smuts* 1998 (3) SA 785 (Constitutional Court), at [63].

[63] Currie and de Waal, above n. 52, p. 166.

discipline. In South Africa, the importance of maintenance of military discipline is a constitutional imperative as highlighted in s. 200(1) of the Constitution, which provides that '[t]he defence force must be structured and managed as a disciplined military force'. Kriegler J, in *Minister of Defence* v. *Potsane*,[64] stated that military discipline 'is about having an effective force capable and ready to protect the territorial integrity of the country and the freedom of its people'.[65] The level of discipline of any military force can mean the difference between life and death, and has an international dimension given that the UN relies on defence forces of Member states for peace enforcement measures. In South Africa, it is the 'primary object of the defence force to defend and protect the Republic, its territorial integrity and its people . . .'[66] Only a disciplined force can do so effectively. This means that the importance of the purpose of the limitation cannot be questioned in a constitutional democracy.

Let us now consider the nature and extent of the limitation (s. 36(1)(c)). What is required is an assessment of the way in which the limitation affects the rights concerned.[67] The question that is usually asked is whether the limitation is a serious or relatively minor infringement of the right.[68] On the face of it, the infringement of the right in the present case is serious, as an accused is tried not by a forum which is a court or another independent tribunal, but by the commanding officer or nominee and a member of the executive branch of the military (the military command).

However, a number of factors may compensate for the extent of the infringement. First, the damage that may be caused as a result of trial by the CODH or summary trial is reparable because 'every finding of guilty, any sentence imposed and every order made by a military court shall be subject to the process of review'.[69] This process happens automatically although the flaw with the automatic review process in South Africa is that it is not conducted by a court of law.[70] Section 34(5) of the South

[64] 2002 (1) SA 1 (Constitutional Court) at [38] (*Potsane*). This case dealt with the constitutional validity of the military prosecution authority operating independently from the National Prosecuting Authority of South Africa.

[65] *Minister of Defence* v. *Potsane* 2002 (1) SA 1 (Constitutional Court), at [38].

[66] Constitution of the Republic of South Africa Act 1996 (South Africa) s. 200(2).

[67] Currie and de Waal, above n. 52, p. 168. [68] Ibid.

[69] Military Discipline Supplementary Measures Act 1999 (South Africa) s. 34(1).

[70] The review is conducted by the Review Authority headed by the Director Military Judicial Reviews: Military Discipline Supplementary Measures Act 1999 (South Africa) ss. 25, 26(3)(b).

African Military Discipline Supplementary Measures Act provides that '[a]n offender may within the time limits and in the manner prescribed in a rule of the Code, apply for the review of the proceedings of his or her case by a Court of Military Appeals.' This arguably compensates for the flaw with regard to the automatic review process. Second, an accused has the right to elect to be tried by a military court instead of the CODH. This means that the accused can be understood to have waived certain rights provided the waiver could be considered valid (as discussed). Viewed cumulatively, it could be argued that all these factors suggest that the nature and the extent of the infringement are not that serious because there are checks and balances built into the system.[71] Nevertheless, the waiver and election, and the appeal and review arguments, are questionable. This means that in the context of South Africa, it is difficult to reach a firm conclusion on the extent of infringement of the right concerned.

The next factor that falls for consideration is the relationship between the limitation and its purpose (s. 36(1)(d)). It requires that the law must serve the purpose that it is designed to serve.[72] A law which does not do this or which only marginally contributes to achieving its purpose cannot be an acceptable justification for a limitation of a right. A summary trial by a commanding officer contributes significantly to a swift maintenance of discipline, as they can enforce discipline more visibly and effectively than any other authority. They are the central pillar of military discipline.

The last factor (s. 36(e)) asks the question whether a less restrictive means exists to achieve the purpose, in this case swift military discipline. A legitimate limitation must achieve benefits which are proportionate to the costs of the limitation.[73] Most limitation arguments stand or fall on whether or not less restrictive means exist to achieve the same purpose. [74] In the military context, the potentially less restrictive means for swift maintenance of discipline would be to make use only of fully fledged military courts, assuming that these courts are sufficiently independent.[75]

[71] Rowe's analysis of summary trials in the United Kingdom appears to favour similar safeguards in the conduct of summary trials by commanding officers. See Rowe, above n. 37, pp. 214–15.

[72] Currie and de Waal, above n. 52, p. 169. [73] Ibid., p. 170. [74] Ibid., p. 171.

[75] In a PhD thesis entitled 'Military Courts in a Democratic South Africa: In Search of their Judicial Independence' (PhD Thesis, University of Cape Town, 2012, available at https://open.uct.ac.za/handle/11427/11662), this author concluded that South African military courts did not currently meet the basic requirements of judicial independence. Of course, these courts are far better than summary trials. See, further, AifheliEnos Tshivhase 'Institutionalising a military judicial office and improving security of tenure of military judges in South Africa' (2015) 19 Law, Democracy & Development 79.

However, it is questionable whether military courts can achieve swift military discipline in the same manner as commanding officers. The main problem with the courts option is that these are generally associated with delays in finalising cases. Wade and Forsyth put it well when they state that '[t]he process of the courts of law is elaborate, slow and costly'[76] in comparison with administrative or similar tribunals which generally follow a relatively simple procedure. Delays in court processes cannot be attributed to a single factor, but to a combination of factors whose influence will vary according to the circumstances of each case.[77] Two factors that are commonly associated with delays in military court proceedings are the lack of availability of witnesses and sometimes even that of accused persons (sometimes for operational or administrative reasons) and the need for the accused to obtain private legal representation. In addition, court rolls are usually full – the situation is likely to be exacerbated if commanders are to be stripped of their disciplinary powers. This means that swift maintenance of military discipline would not be guaranteed, which would be at odds with South Africa's Constitution which requires the defence force to be structured and managed as a disciplined military force. Sometimes delays can be caused by lack of availability or shortage of court personnel. It could be argued that these challenges could be addressed with proper planning, management and hiring of a far greater number of judges and court personnel to fill the gap that may be left by the disbandment of the CODH (summary trial). However, it is unrealistic to expect that the South African government would direct more resources towards this effort, given the challenges the country faces regarding its civilian criminal justice system, which deals with a far greater number of people – let alone the socio-economic situation in the country arising from the legacy of apartheid.

Another reason against the alternative option is that it is not good military policy for commanders to lose direct control over the formal disciplinary structures of the military completely, because they bear final responsibility for enforcement of discipline in any military force. Commanders have (for good reasons) lost direct control over full-fledged military courts – the CODH or summary trial is the only remaining formal instrument by which they have a direct say in the enforcement of

[76] Cited with approval by the Constitutional Court of South Africa in *Sidumo and Another* v. *Rustenburg Platinum Mine Ltd and Others* 2008 (2) SA 24 (Constitutional Court) at [125].

[77] The factors highlighted here refer to South Africa but it is likely that they could be of general application as military organisations the world over share common attributes.

discipline of those under their command. As James points out and quoted with approval by the Constitutional Court in *Potsane*: 'it is the responsibility of those who command to instil discipline in those who they command'.[78] Similarly, Griggs states that 'as a consequence of the need for officers to directly maintain discipline in their commands, disciplinary offences are heard by those officers rather than courts'.[79] All these are consistent with the principle of command empowerment and the need for expeditious maintenance of military discipline.[80]

Therefore, it would appear that there are no less restrictive means to ensure swift maintenance of discipline for minor transgressions other than using a hearing by commanding officers. However, my analysis regarding the possible defensibility of commanding officer's disciplinary hearing does not suggest that it cannot be improved in order to increase its fairness. Much can be done to ensure that the accused appearing before the commander's hearing is adequately assisted. Furthermore, there could also be greater emphasis on the impartiality of commanders and an improvement in their training.[81]

D *Way forward: reforms*

Reform of military summary trials looks inevitable in the short to medium term but the sensitive nature of the area means serious resistance from military commanders can be expected. Real options for preserving military summary trials in the modern age are limited. As is demonstrated by Jha's analysis with respect to India, summary military trials are sufficiently important that they should be reformed rather than abolished. From the above discussion, the area requiring reform is relatively clear. Commanding officers must be stripped of powers to hear criminal charges or disciplinary charges which are criminal in nature. This means that they should not hear any offences where the penalty involves deprivation of liberty resulting in detention or imprisonment for a significant

[78] *Minister of Defence* v. *Potsane* 2002 (1) SA 1 (Constitutional Court), at [38].

[79] Griggs, above n. 3, at 69. [80] Ibid., at 77.

[81] The study conducted by Rowe, above n. 37, pp. 205–6 in respect of the workings of the United Kingdom's Summary Appeal Court shows that much can be done to improve the fairness and training of commanders regarding their role in summary trials. The study shows that between October 2000 and September 2002, only 14 per cent of commanding officer's decisions were upheld by the Summary Court. Many of the reasons proffered for this phenomenon suggest that there is a need to improve the process of summary trials and the training of commanding officers. Although the study only looked at the UK, it could prove to be instructive to other jurisdictions as well.

period. The reason for this is that, as seen from the jurisprudence of the European Court of Human Rights, trial of offences where the penalty involves detention or imprisonment triggers the application of the rights to be tried by an independent court or tribunal and to legal representation. It is beyond question that military summary trials, as currently constituted, cannot be regarded as independent courts or tribunals. This means that the penal jurisdiction of commanding officers requires some re-configuration to address emerging concerns. In the process of reform, a careful study needs to be undertaken to ascertain the extent to which such reforms may weaken the ability of commanders to swiftly maintain military discipline in their respective units. The reform process may necessitate a review of penal sanctions of some military offences in order to minimise the potential negative impact on discipline arising from necessary reforms.

This chapter examined the future of military summary trials primarily in the light of the jurisprudence of the European Court of Human Rights. It argued that summary trials are an important mechanism for commanders to enforce discipline expeditiously. Options for preserving summary trials must take into account that standards of independence apply to these forums. Out of the four options apparently available, only one of these appears to be the real option in the modern age (reform) – in particular the removal of the commanding officer's powers over criminal offences or serious military offences involving significant deprivation of liberty. But this would be the least favoured option given that summary trials are probably the most sensitive space regarding the enforcement of military discipline. Nevertheless, targeted reforms appear to be inevitable in the light of increasing challenges to military justice.

18

A rose by any other name: how the United States charges its service members for violating the laws of war

CHRIS JENKS

I Introduction

In the early morning of 11 March 2012, a US service-member, Staff Sergeant Robert Bales, slipped undetected from Village Stability Platform Belambai (VSP) about 30 kilometres from Kandahar, Afghanistan. Bales was one of approximately forty US military personnel deployed to VSP Belambai. Their mission was 'to assist the Afghan government in maintaining security, reconstructing the country, training the national police and army, and providing a lawful environment for free and fair elections'.[1] Sergeant Bales, however, was on a very different mission.

Bales, alone and on foot, hiked to two separate Afghan villages where he murdered sixteen women and children, attempted to murder six more, and assaulted others.[2] The victims ranged in age from small children to an elderly grandmother. Bales murdered eleven members of one family, shooting most of them in front of one another, stomped to death at least one victim and set ten victims' bodies on fire. The US Army apprehended Bales as he attempted to return to VSB Belambai. The Army transferred Bales to the United States and military confinement and prosecuted him under the US military's criminal law and procedure, the Uniform Code of Military Justice (UCMJ). At an Army court martial held in June 2013 in the United States, Bales pleaded guilty to sixteen counts of premeditated murder, six counts of attempted murder and six counts of aggravated

Borrowing from Shakespeare's, *Romeo and Juliet*: 'What's in a name? That which we call a rose. By any other name would smell as sweet.'

[1] United States Mission to NATO, *U.S. Policy toward Afghanistan & Pakistan: A Dossier* (2014) United States Mission to NATO http://nato.usmission.gov/afghanistan.html.

[2] *United States* v *Robert Bales*, Charge Sheet (23 March 2012) (redacted). A redacted version of the charge sheet is available at http://i2.cdn.turner.com/cnn/2012/images/03/23/bales.charge.pdf.

assault inflicting grievous bodily injury. A military panel, or jury, sentenced Bales to be dishonourably discharged and to be confined for the duration of his natural life without the possibility of parole.

In so doing, the US Army continued its long-standing policy and practice of asserting jurisdiction over its service members who commit crimes during armed conflict and charging them with enumerated offences of the UCMJ rather than violations of the laws of war, or war crimes. Yet, while not prosecuting its own service members with such crimes, the United States continues to conduct military commissions at Guantanamo Bay, Cuba and to prosecute members of al Qaeda and the Taliban for just such offences, that is, violations of the laws of war.

This chapter examines the US practice of not charging its service members with war crimes. The chapter briefly explains how the United States asserts criminal jurisdiction over its service members before turning to how the US military reports violations of the laws of war. It then sets out the US methodology for charging such violations as applied to its service members, and compares this methodology to that applied to those tried by military commissions. The chapter then discusses the varied meanings of the term 'war crimes' and the way in which the 1949 Geneva Conventions can provide a benchmark against which the elements of offences, and their punishments, can be compared. While the US practice fares adequately in this comparison, the argument for a pragmatic approach to charging over the expressive value of a war crime charge is rendered untenable as a result of the disparate manner in which the United States charges detainees when compared to its own service members.

II US practice

A History of the UCMJ

The UCMJ resulted from the US Congress' desire, following World War II, to establish a 'a code that would apply to all branches of the military and create greater uniformity in the substantive and procedural law governing the administration of military justice'.[3] While the UCMJ dates from 1951, its origins are in and with the founding of the United States during the American Revolutionary War with England. In June 1775, the fledging (and rebellious) Second Continental Congress enacted the Articles of War, which, somewhat ironically were 'generally a copy of

[3] Mynda G. Ohman, 'Integrating Title 18 War Crimes into Title 10: A Proposal to Amend the Uniform Code of Military Justice' (2005) 57 *Air Force Law Review*, p. 1 at 4.

the then-existing code governing England's "ministerial army"'.[4] Following the Revolutionary War, the US Constitution granted the US Congress the power '(1) to make Rules for the Government and Regulation of land and naval Forces'; and '(2) to define and punish ... offenses against the Law of Nations'.[5] Thus, beginning with the 1806 revisions to the Articles of War, US 'military personnel were subject to a code that required them to obey certain laws and customs of war or face trial by court-martial or military tribunal'.[6] In the century that followed, the US Congress updated the Articles of War in 1874 and 1916.[7] The articles were again amended in 1920, with lessons learned from World War I, and in 1949 following World II.[8] The 1951 UCMJ replaced the Articles of War and established 'a single codified system of military law, separate from the criminal justice systems of the various states and of the Article III [federal] courts'.[9] The features of the UCMJ have been described as follows:

> The UCMJ permanently transformed the nature of military law. The UCMJ was more than a structural change to ensure uniformity across all branches of service. It added articles, defined new crimes, and established rules designed to protect the substantive and procedural rights of military personnel. New provisions designed to ensure a fair trial included the right against self-incrimination; equal process for the defense and prosecution to obtain witnesses and depositions; the prohibition on receiving guilty pleas in capital cases; the requirement that both prosecution and defense counsel be legally trained; the right for an enlisted accused to be tried by a panel [military jury] that included enlisted members; the requirement that the law officer (now the military judge) instruct the panel members on the record regarding the elements of the offense, presumption of innocence, and burden of proof; the provision mandating that voting on findings and sentencing be conducted by secret ballot; and an automatic review of the trial record.[10]

One of the advantages of the UCMJ is its broad jurisdictional scope.

[4] Judge Advocate General's Corps, US Army, *The Army Lawyer: A History of the Judge Advocate General's Corps, 1775–1975* (Washington, DC, Government Printing Office, 1975), p. 7. The following month the Congress elected William Tudor as the first Judge Advocate General of the Army.

[5] United States Constitution art. 1 § 8 cl. 14. See also Tara Lee, 'American Courts-Martial for Enemy War Crimes' (2003) 33 *University of Baltimore Law Review*, p. 49 at 52–53.

[6] Eric Talbot Jensen and James J Teixeira Jr, 'Prosecuting Members of the U.S. Military for Wartime Environmental Crimes' (2005) 17 *Georgetown International Environmental Law Review*, p. 651 at 658.

[7] Ohman, above n. 3, at 4. [8] Ibid. [9] Lee, above n. 5, at 52–53.

[10] Ohman, above n. 3, at 9–10.

> The UCMJ applies to all [US] service members regardless of whether the offense can be tied to military discipline and effectiveness. The UCMJ is applicable both in the United States and in foreign countries. Because the UCMJ applies worldwide, a court-martial convened under the UCMJ may be held anywhere in the world. This flexibility allows for the prosecution to take place near the situs of the crime, presumably near the location of any relevant witnesses. This makes the prosecution of a crime that occurs during the conduct of military operations, such as in Iraq [or Afghanistan], easier than it would be if the case had to be heard in a Federal District Court or before an international body convened at the Hague or some other site distant from the court's location.[11]

For the UCMJ to have personal jurisdiction over US service-members regardless of where in the world the service-member is or whether they were on or off duty is one of the strengths of the system. But the manner in which the system charges US service members for crimes blunts the efficacy, either real or perceived, of the UCMJ as an accountability mechanism.

B Charging violations of the laws of war

As one US Army lawyer noted in a primer for the practitioner of charging war crimes, '[t]he first step in analyzing how to charge the service member is to look for any offenses specifically enumerated in the UCMJ Articles 80 through 132'.[12] These articles address a wide range

[11] Jensen and Teixeira, above n. 6, at 658. Although one of the advantages of the UCMJ is the ability to hold courts martial in a combat theatre such as Iraq or Afghanistan, it is noteworthy that often the US military does not choose this course of action. As discussed in the introduction, Staff Sergeant Bales committed his crimes in Afghanistan and against Afghan civilians, but Bales' court martial was held in the United States.

[12] Martin N. Watt, 'Charging War Crimes: A Primer for the Practitioner' (February 2006) *Army Lawyer*, p. 2. As Watt explains, '[t]he [service lawyer prosecutor] should begin with this analysis due to the preemption doctrine'. The preemption doctrine 'prohibits application of Article 134 to conduct covered in Articles 80 through 132'. *Id.* Article 134 is for misconduct not addressed in the enumerated punitive section of the UCMJ. Article 134 of the UCMJ, among other things, allows for the incorporation of federal offences as a military charge. But under the preemption doctrine, a prosecutor may not incorporate a federal charge to address conduct an enumerated article of the UCMJ covers. For example, Article 118 of the UCMJ criminalises murder. The US Code, in Title 18 § 1111 also criminalises murder. Therefore a military prosecutor would need to charge the murder offence under Article 118; he or she could not incorporate the federal murder offence through Article 134. However, unlike the UCMJ, the US Code specifically criminalises war crimes as such, in Title 18 § 2441. This raises the question of whether a military prosecutor could incorporate the federal statute under Article 134 and thus charge a US service member with war crimes. The answer where the underlying conduct

of criminal conduct, and include both completed and inchoate offences. The crimes listed in the UCMJ include common offences such as larceny, assault, rape and murder and arcane offences, such as abusing a public animal and jumping from a vessel to the water. There is no enumerated offence for violating the laws of war. Yet the UCMJ itself acknowledges that '[t]o the extent permitted by the [US] Constitution, courts-martial may try any offense under the code, and in the case of a general courts-martial, the law of war'.[13]

In explaining how to allege offences, the current US *Manual for Court-Martial* states that '[a] charge states the article of the code, law of war, or local penal law of an occupied territory which the accused is alleged to have violated'.[14] Not only does this indicate the possibility of a law of war charge, the accompanying discussion details that '[i]n the case of a person subject to trial by general court-martial for violations of the law of war, the charge should be: "Violation of the Law of War"'.[15] But that discussion concludes with the guidance that '[o]rdinarily persons subject to the code [a category which includes US service members] should be charged with a specific violation of the code rather than a violation of the law of war'.[16] Likewise, the Department of the Army's field manual, *The Law of Land Warfare*, in a section entitled Persons Charged with War Crimes, states that 'The United States normally punishes war crimes as such only if they are committed by enemy nationals or by persons serving the interests of the enemy State. Violations of the law of war committed by persons subject to the military law of the United States will usually

is reflected in a punitive article is unclear. For example, if a military prosecutor incorporated the federal war crimes statute and charged a grave breach of the Geneva Conventions, the unlawful killing of a protected person, the defence would challenge such a charge under the preemption doctrine, arguing that Article 118 of the UCMJ already addresses unlawful killing. But to the extent the underlying conduct is not reflected in a punitive article of the UCMJ, charging the conduct as a war crime through Article 134 and the federal statute appears a possibility. The challenge is to identify acts which constitute a grave breach of the Geneva Conventions or violate Common Article 3 and which are not already reflected in a punitive article of the UCMJ.

13 *Manual for Courts-Martial*, Rules for Courts-Martial r. 202 (2012). See also Uniform Code of Military Justice, 10 USC § 818 art. 18 (2010).

14 *Manual for Courts-Martial*, Rules for Courts-Martial r. 307(c)(2) (2012).

15 Ibid., Discussion (D).

16 Ibid. The analysis of that rule, also contained in the *Manual for Courts-Martial*, adds little clarity. The appendix to the 1969 *Manual for Courts-Martial* merely states that '[i]n the case of a person subject to trial by general court-martial by the law of war . . ., the Charge should be: "Violation of the Law of War"': *Manual for Courts-Martial* (1969) Appendix 6a at [12]. That same manual lists as a source of military jurisdiction, international law, which it states includes the laws of war.

constitute violations of the Uniform Code of Military Justice and, if so, will be prosecuted under that law.'[17]

That guidance, while not styled as an absolute requirement, has proved to be one in US practice. For example, the US charged Lieutenant Calley with violating Article 118, Murder, of the UCMJ, for his role in the Mei Lai massacre during the Vietnam War. There is considerable similarity between the charges against Calley and Bales. Calley was charged as follows:

> In that First Lieutenant William L. Calley, Jr . . . did, at My Lai 4, Quang Ngai Province, Republic of South Viet-Nam, on or about 16 March 1968, with premeditation, murder an unknown number, not less than seventy, Oriental human beings, males and females of various ages, whose names are unknown, occupants of the village of My Lai 4, by means of shooting them with a rifle.[18]

Bales was charged as follows: '[i]n that Staff Sergeant (E-6) Robert Bales, U.S. Army, did, at or near Belambay, Afghanistan, on or about 11 March 2012, with premeditation, murder a female of apparent Afghan descent known as [redacted] by means of shooting her with a firearm'.[19]

The historian for the US Army Judge Advocate Generals' Corps claims that the United States has never charged a US service member with a law of war violation as such.[20] But one commentator, Professor (and former Army lawyer) Jordan Paust, claims that the United States charged a service member during the Vietnam War with 'cutting off an ear from the body of an unknown dead Viet Cong soldier, which conduct was of a nature to bring discredit upon the Armed Forces of the United States as a violation of the Law of War'.[21]

The legislative intent behind Rule for Court Martial 307, or the commentary, provides no clarification. Noted Army legal scholars, and

[17] Department of the Army Field Manual FM 27–10 *The Law of Land Warfare* (July 1956) at [507].

[18] *United States* v. *First Lieutenant William L Calley, Jr*, Charge Sheet (5 September 1969) Specification 1. Similar action was taken with respect to Calley's Company Commander, Captain Medina. 'In keeping with United States policy, Captain Medina was not charged with violations of the law of war, but rather, was charged with violations of the UCMJ.' Michael L. Smidt, 'Yamashita, Medina, and Beyond: Command Responsibility in Contemporary Military Operations' (2000) 164 *Military Law Review*, p. 155, at 194.

[19] *United States* v. *Robert Bales*, Charge Sheet (23 March 2012) (redacted) Charge I, Specification 1.

[20] Email from Fred Borch to author, 6 November 2012.

[21] Jordan Paust, 'My Lai and Vietnam: Norms, Myths and Leader Responsibility' (1972) 57 *Military Law Review*, p. 99, at 118 (referring to *United States* v. *Passantino*, Hq. 1st Inf. Div. Special Court-Martial Or-der No. 11, 11 February 1968).

military justice practitioners, claim that, as stated in the *Manual for Courts-Martial*, the United States may court-martial a US service member for a violation of the law of war.[22] The US Congress has also failed to provide an answer, although it briefly discussed the issue in 1996. During the debate on the War Crimes Act, members of Congress discussed the potential for US service members to be court-martialled for violating the law of war and determined that it 'was not a viable option'.[23]

C *Commissions*

The US military's internal practice stands in stark contrast to that of the military commissions, the stated purpose of which is to 'try alien unprivileged enemy belligerents for violations of the law of war'.[24] The Military Commissions Act of 2009 lists a host of law of war violations, including murder of a protected person, attacking civilian objects and property, pillaging and the denial of quarter.[25] In its zeal to charge law of war offences in the commissions, the United States added the qualifier 'in violation of the law of war' to other charges, such as murder and destruction of property, when no such crimes exist, at least in the traditional, international, conception of the law.[26] But before the US approach can be evaluated and discussed, clarifications to the terminology are warranted.

III War crimes

A common misconception is that any violation of the Geneva Conventions is a war crime.[27] First, the Conventions do not utilise the term war crimes. Instead, each of the four Conventions details violations

22 Jan E. Aldykiewicz and Geoffrey S. Corn, 'Authority to Court-Martial Non-U.S. Military Personnel for Serious Violations of International Humanitarian Law Committed During Internal Armed Conflicts' (2001) 167 *Military Law Review*, 74, at 76.

23 Ibid. 24 Military Commissions Act of 2009, 10 USC § 948b(a) (2009).

25 Ibid., § 950t(1). Given the US' opposition to the ICC, the similarities between criminal offences under the Rome Statute and the Military Commissions Act of 2009 are interesting. That a US citizen could not be subject to prosecution for such offences by military commission reinforces a common US stereotype: the United States holds itself to a lower standard than that it claims others should meet under international law.

26 See John Dehn, 'The Hamdan Case and the Application of a Municipal Offence: The Common Law Origins of "Murder in Violation of the Law of War"' (2009) 7(1) *Journal of International Criminal Justice*, p. 63.

27 The US Army's own field manual on the Law of Land Warfare is, at least in part, to blame. It states, that '[t]he term "war crime" is the technical expression for a violation of the law of war by any person or persons, military or civilian. Every violation of the law of war is a

that constitute a 'grave breach' of the particular Convention. For those violations, States Parties have agreed to enact legislation to provide 'effective penal sanction'.[28] The Conventions refer to lesser violations as 'other than grave breaches', for which States Parties agree to 'take measures necessary for the suppression' of such acts.[29]

A *International law*

In its study of international humanitarian law, the International Committee of the Red Cross (ICRC) attempted to identify the customary international law principles of international humanitarian law. Rule 156 of the study states that 'serious violations of international humanitarian law constitute war crimes'.[30] In response, the legal advisers to the United States Departments of Defense and State wrote a letter to the ICRC claiming that the term war crimes 'is an amorphous term used in different contexts to mean different things'.[31] The United States stated that:

> The national legislation cited in the commentary to Rule 157 employs a variety of definitions of 'war crimes', only a few of which closely parallel the definition apparently employed by the Study, and none that matches it exactly. Much of the legislation cited does not precisely define 'war crimes' ... Although the military manuals of Croatia, Hungary, and Switzerland, among others, appear to define 'war crimes' as 'grave breaches', the lack of specificity leaves the intended meaning ambiguous. Even among the few States that employ a definition of 'war crimes' similar to that in Rule 156, no State definition mirrors the Study's definition precisely.[32]

Part of the difficulty stems from what constitutes 'serious'. This is then compounded by the definition of international humanitarian law. US

war crime': Department of the Army Field Manual 27–10 *The Law of Land Warfare* (1956) at [499].

28 Geneva Convention Relative to the Treatment of Prisoners of War, 12 August 1949, in force 21 October 1950, 75 UNTS 135 art. 129 (Geneva Convention III).

29 Ibid.

30 Jean-Marie Henckaerts, 'Study on Customary International Humanitarian Law: A Contribution to the Understanding and Respect for the Rule of Law in Armed Conflict' (2005) 87(857) *International Review of the Red Cross: Customary Law*, p. 175 at 211, r. 156 ('ICRC Study').

31 John B. Bellinger III and William J. Haynes II, 'A US Government Response to the International Committee of the Red Cross Study Customary International Humanitarian Law' (2007) 89(866) *International Review of the Red Cross*, p. 443, at 467. Rule 157 provides that 'States have the right to vest universal jurisdiction in their national courts over war crimes.'

32 Ibid.

federal law and the Rome Statute of the International Criminal Court provide similar definitions which serve as a starting point for a comparison to their counterpart under the UCMJ.

US federal law provides that '[w]hoever, whether inside or outside the United States, commits a war crime ... shall be fined under this title or imprisoned for life or any term of years, or both, and if death results to the victim, shall also be subject to the penalty of death'.[33] Pursuant to this approach, a war crime includes grave breaches of any of the 1949 Geneva Conventions, certain articles from the 1907 Hague Convention IV, grave breaches of article 3 common to each of the 1949 Geneva Conventions and certain violations of Protocol II of the Convention on Certain Conventional Weapons, the Protocol on Prohibitions or Restrictions on the Use of Mines, Booby-Traps and Other Devices.

The Rome Statute defines war crimes as grave breaches of the 1949 Geneva Conventions, 'serious violations of the laws and customs' applicable to international and other than international armed conflict, and serious violations of article 3 common to each of the 1949 Geneva Conventions.[34]

IV Elements comparison

How then do the elements (and punishments) of Rome Statute war crimes compare to an analogous charge under the UCMJ? This section compares the following offences: wilful killing, committing outrages

[33] War Crimes Act of 1996, 18 USC § 2441 (1996). Under the federal law, the term 'war crime' means any conduct:

(1) defined as a grave breach in any of the international conventions signed at Geneva 12 August 1949, or any protocol to such convention to which the United States is a party;
(2) prohibited by Article 23, 25, 27, or 28 of the Annex to the Hague Convention IV, Respecting the Laws and Customs of War on Land, signed 18 October 1907;
(3) which constitutes a grave breach of common Article 3 (as defined in subsection (d)) when committed in the context of and in association with an armed conflict not of an international character; or
(4) of a person who, in relation to an armed conflict and contrary to the provisions of the Protocol on Prohibitions or Restrictions on the Use of Mines, Booby-Traps and Other Devices as amended at Geneva on 3 May 1996 (Protocol II as amended on 3 May 1996), when the United States is a party to such Protocol, willfully kills or causes serious injury to civilians.

[34] Rome Statute of the International Criminal Court, 17 July 1998, in force 1 July 2002, 2187 UNTS 90 art. 8 (Rome Statute).

against personal dignity, wilfully causing great suffering or serious injury, and extensive destruction of property.

The elements for each war crime under the Rome Statute include that the conduct took place 'in the context of and was associated with' an armed conflict and that the accused was aware of that conflict. Yet the introduction to the elements explains that:

> There is no requirement for a legal evaluation by the perpetrator as to the existence of an armed conflict or its character as international or non-international;
>
> In that context there is no requirement for awareness by the perpetrator of the facts that established the character of the conflict as international or non-international;
>
> There is only a requirement for the awareness of the factual circumstances that established the existence of an armed conflict that is implicit in the terms 'took place in the context of and was associated with'.[35]

A Wilful killing

Article 8(2)(a)(i) of the Rome Statute provides the following elements for the crime of wilful killing to be committed in an international armed conflict:

1. The perpetrator killed one or more persons.
2. Such person or persons were protected under one or more of the Geneva Conventions of 1949.
3. The perpetrator was aware of the factual circumstances that established that protected status.
4. The conduct took place in the context of and was associated with an international armed conflict.
5. The perpetrator was aware of factual circumstances that established the existence of an armed conflict.[36]

Article 118 of the UCMJ provides as follows:

1. That a certain named or described person is dead.
2. That the death resulted from the act or omission of the accused.
3. That the killing was unlawful.

[35] International Criminal Court, *Elements of Crimes*, Doc No. ICC-ASP/1/3 (part II-B) (adopted 9 September 2002) art. 8 (*Elements of Crimes*).

[36] Ibid., art. 8(2)(a)(i).

4. That, at the time of the killing, the accused had a premeditated design to kill.[37]

The maximum punishment under the UCMJ is death. There is a mandatory minimum of imprisonment for life with eligibility for parole. For the ICC crimes, the maximum punishment for war crimes is 'life imprisonment when justified by the extreme gravity of the crime and the individual circumstances of the convicted person'.[38]

Facially, the differences between the UCMJ and the ICC Statute are a higher *mens rea* in case of the UCMJ (premeditation) and the fact that wilful killing under the ICC requires proving both the protected status of the victim and the underlying existence of an armed conflict. Qualitatively wilful killing is a more circumspect offence, proscribing a rule not against any wilful killing, but the wilful killing of a certain class of victims – protected persons.

Could Staff Sergeant Bales be charged with wilful killing? Even with the expansion of protected person status to include ethnicity and not just nationality,[39] the alleged victims were not protected persons for the purposes of the Geneva Conventions. They were Afghan nationals, allegedly killed in Afghanistan by a member of the US military when the US military was neither fighting against nor occupying Afghanistan, but instead aiding the government of Afghanistan in its counter-insurgency efforts. Thus, while the offence of wilful killing is uniquely tailored to armed conflict, it proves less useful in certain conflict based settings than the more general murder charge under the UCMJ.

B Maltreatment of persons

Article 8(2)(c)(ii) of the *Elements of Crimes* outlines the elements of the crime 'outrages upon personal dignity' as follows:

1. The perpetrator humiliated, degraded or otherwise violated the dignity of one or more persons.
2. The severity of the humiliation, degradation or other violation was of such degree as to be generally recognized as an outrage upon personal dignity.

[37] Uniform Code of Military Justice, 10 USC § 918 art. 118 (2010).
[38] Rome Statute, above n. 34, art. 77 (1).
[39] *Prosecutor* v. *Tihomir Blaskic* (International Criminal Tribunal for the former Yugoslavia, Appeals Chamber, Case No IT-95-14-T, 3 March 2000) at 3.

3. The conduct took place in the context of and was associated with an international armed conflict.
4. The perpetrator was aware of factual circumstances that established the existence of an armed conflict.

In article 93 of the UCMJ 'cruelty and maltreatment' is defined as:

1. That a certain person was subject to the orders of the accused.
2. That the accused was cruel toward, or oppressed, or maltreated that person.

In the UCMJ the maximum punishment is dishonourable discharge, forfeiture of all pay and allowances, and confinement for one year. Once more the Rome Statute provides for a maximum term of thirty years or life in particularly grave circumstances. Attention is immediately drawn to the brevity of the UCMJ charge (it contains only two elements) as well as the disparity between possible punishments: one year compared to thirty years. Arguably the UCMJ charge is not analogous to the ICC offence, or certainly not a complete equivalent. The UCMJ charge requires that the victim be subject to the orders of the accused. While being subject to orders is broadly defined, it is nonetheless a significant limitation on the application of the charge. Finally, under the UCMJ offence the victim must be alive. By comparison, an outrage against personal dignity better lends itself to the misconduct that occurs during armed conflict, particularly towards corpses.[40] For outrages against personal dignity, the *Elements of Crimes* provides that '"persons" can include dead persons. It is understood that the victim need not personally be aware of the existence of the humiliation or degradation or other violation. This element takes into account relevant aspects of the cultural background of the victim.'[41]

[40] For example, some of the actions US service members have taken in recent years in Afghanistan, including urinating on, or burning, corpses; videotaping and photographing themselves with corpses and cutting off body parts as trophies could fall within this crime. In Iraq, the Abu Ghraib abuses could constitute such violations. As the detainees were subject to the orders of the US military guards cruelty and maltreatment could (and did) apply. In such situations, the question becomes whether a maximum sentence of one year confinement is adequate.

[41] *Elements of Crimes*, above n. 35, art. 8(2)(c)(ii).

C *Wilfully causing great suffering or serious injury*

Article 8(2)(a)(iii) provides that the crime of wilfully causing great suffering or serious injury to body or health occurs when:

1. The perpetrator caused great physical or mental pain or suffering to, or serious injury to body or health of, one or more persons.
2. Such person or persons were protected under one or more of the Geneva Conventions of 1949.
3. The perpetrator was aware of the factual circumstances that established that protected status.
4. The conduct took place in the context of and was associated with an international armed conflict.
5. The perpetrator was aware of factual circumstances that established the existence of an armed conflict.[42]

According to Article 128 of the UCMJ aggravated assault occurs in the following circumstances:

1. That the accused attempted to do, offered to do, or did bodily harm to a certain person;
2. That the accused did so with a certain weapon, means, or force;
3. That the attempt, offer, or bodily harm was done with unlawful force or violence; and
4. That the weapon, means, or force was used in a manner likely to produce death or grievous bodily harm.[43]

There are a number of subsets of this offence, including when a firearm is used and when it is committed against a child under the age of sixteen years. Absent one of those qualifiers, the maximum punishment is a dishonourable discharge, forfeiture of all pay and allowances, and confinement for three years.

Of the offences being compared, these two (wilfully causing great suffering and aggravated assault) may be the most similar. Interestingly the UCMJ version applies to attempts and completed acts, while the ICC offence only applies to the completed acts. The ICC offence encompasses mental pain or suffering while the UCMJ version is limited to bodily harm. Again disparity between the possible punishments arises: the ICC crime yields a sentence range up to thirty years while the UCMJ is generally limited to three years. Even when the qualifiers are considered, the UCMJ

[42] Ibid., art. 8(2)(a)(iii).

[43] Uniform Code of Military Justice, 10 USC § 928 art. 128 (2010).

punishment only increases to five years for a child victim and eight years when a firearm is used.

D Destruction of property

The crime of extensive destruction and appropriation of property is defined in the Rome Statute as occurring when:

1. The perpetrator destroyed or appropriated certain property.
2. The destruction or appropriation was not justified by military necessity.
3. The destruction or appropriation was extensive and carried out wantonly.
4. Such property was protected under one or more of the Geneva Conventions of 1949.
5. The perpetrator was aware of the factual circumstances that established that protected status.
6. The conduct took place in the context of and was associated with an international armed conflict.
7. The perpetrator was aware of factual circumstances that established the existence of an armed conflict.[44]

Article 103 of the UCMJ provides that the crime of looting or pillaging captured or abandoned property occurs in the following circumstances:

1. That the accused engaged in looting, pillaging, or looting and pillaging by unlawfully seizing or appropriating certain public or private property.
2. That this property was located in enemy or occupied territory, or that it was on board a seized or captured vessel.
3. That this property was
   (i) left behind, owned by, or in the custody of the enemy, an occupied state, an inhabitant of an occupied state, or a person under the protection of the enemy or occupied state, or who, immediately prior to the occupation of the place where the act occurred, was under the protection of the enemy or occupied state; or
   (ii) part of the equipment of a seized or captured vessel; or

[44] Rome Statute, above n. 34, art. 8(2)(a)(iv).

(iii) owned by, or in the custody of the officers, crew, or passengers on board a seized or captured vessel.[45]

The maximum punishment is 'any punishment, other than death, that a court-martial may direct'.[46]

The striking feature of the UCMJ charge is that it represents a rare US military offence – one that only applies to armed conflict or during times of military occupation. Although anachronistic, this offence nonetheless demonstrates the potential for broader offences unique to armed conflict to apply to US service members.

V Conclusion

The above discussion demonstrates that in some ways the crimes in the UCMJ and the Rome Statute are analogous, but in other ways they are not. The enumerated UCMJ offences are more generalised, allowing for application both during peacetime garrison settings and during armed conflict. But in that generalisation, it can be claimed that something is lost. Is the same offence in a garrison setting really the same as when it is committed in an armed conflict? For intra-military offences, for example one service member assaulting another, the answer may be yes. But where the victim of the offence is not American and the armed forces are deployed in an armed conflict environment the answer would appear to be negative. The question becomes whether the various intrinsic and extrinsic values of the US military justice system – designed to promote, protect, and defend – operate in a domestic setting in the same manner as they do in an armed conflict.

One senior US military prosecutor has commented that charging decisions ultimately reflect the narrative the prosecutor wants to convey to a jury. It is difficult to envision a case where adding elements, including the existence of armed conflict or of a protected person, would render that endeavour easier. A pragmatic approach to prosecutions is not unique to the United States.[47] The differences may be explained by degrees – a domestic military charge would apply to a lower ranking

45 Uniform Code of Military Justice, 10 USC § 903 art. 103 (2010). 46 Ibid.

47 Interview with Beth Van Schaack, Deputy Chief of the US Office of Global Criminal Justice describing actions by ICTY prosecutors to employ charges that obviate the need for conflict classification and the use of joint criminal enterprise as a more effective modality than traditional forms of command responsibility.

individual, whereas a 'war criminal' must be an authority figure. Or, it could be argued that property destruction is appropriately addressed by the UCMJ, and that a war crime act of the same conduct would, or should, constitute a graver crime.

Yet the US approach rings hollow, maybe not in an absolute sense but certainly in a relative one. The United States has been involved in armed conflict for over ten years and claims to be in an era of 'persistent conflict'[48] which it believes will exist for 'the next several decades'.[49] This negates an argument that armed conflicts are not long enough to warrant unique military charges.[50] Nor is the argument that specific offences should only exist when they occur with some degree of frequency particularly persuasive given the presence in the UCMJ of offences such as abusing a public animal and hazarding a vessel. But fatally problematic for the US pragmatism argument is that law of war offences are detailed and employed against detainees subject to US military commissions.[51] For either reason, and certainly for both reasons, the United States should modify the charges employed against its own service members.

[48] Pete Geren and George W. Casey Jr, *A Statement on the Posture of the United States Army 2009 Submitted by The Honorable Pete Geren and General George W Casey JR to the Committees and Subcommittees of the United States Senate and the House of Representatives 1st Session, 111th Congress* (Washington, DC, May 2009) (introduction).

[49] See also Mary L. Dudziak, *War Time: An Idea, Its History, Its Consequences* (Oxford, Oxford University Press, 2012) arguing that war is not an exceptional state but the unfortunate status quo.

[50] Moreover, as discussed above, the US military manual for courts martial has for some time contained a few conflict specific offences.

[51] This inconsistent approach to the way in which the United States charges its service members versus the enemy is not new. During World War II, the US Army court-martialled its own service members for killing enemy prisoners of war for murder, while prosecuting Germans who committed similar acts against US POWs for violations of the laws and customs of war. See US011 Case No. 6–24 (*US* v. *Valentin Bersin et al.*).

19

Military justice in operational settings, peacekeeping missions and situations of transitional justice

MICHAEL GIBSON

Public attention to military justice systems in many states is often characterised by long periods of neglect or indifference, with sporadic bouts of intense interest by governments in reaction to high-profile cases that may suggest systemic deficiencies.[1] This pattern of reactive change to military justice is common throughout the world but it should be avoided, as military justice systems are too important to sustain a pattern of neglect followed by sudden and potentially ill-advised changes. It would be far better to pursue a course of regular reviews and adjustments on a principled basis.[2] Despite the frequent public neglect of military justice, there is an international discourse about military justice, much of which is currently sponsored by the International Society for Military Law and the Law of War.[3] This chapter aims to contribute to that discourse in three specific areas, which may not be well understood by audiences in many Western democracies: military justice in operational settings, peacekeeping missions and situations of transitional justice. The chapter will first discuss some general principles of military justice systems, before moving to specific consideration of these areas. The chapter concludes with suggestions as to how adopting and maintaining military justice systems as accountability mechanisms can benefit the armed forces of all states.

I have previously discussed some of these issues in an opinion piece: Michael Gibson, 'Canada's Military Justice System' (2012) 12 *Canadian Military Journal*, p. 61.

1 For example, the recent focus in the US on how the military justice system deals with allegations of sexual assault.

2 For example, the regular independent reviews of the Canadian military justice system now prescribed by Parliament in the *National Defence Act* RSC 1985 c. N-5.

3 The Society publishes much of that scholarship in its journal, *The Military Law and the Law of War Review*.

I Why separate military justice systems?

Separate military justice systems exist because of the needs of armed forces to effectively fulfil their mission of defending the state and their parent societies.[4] A classic articulation of this theme was provided by the Supreme Court of Canada in its seminal 1992 decision in *R* v. *Généreux*.[5] Although the Court identified some significant constitutional problems with elements of the structure of courts martial as they existed at that time, it did not doubt the need for a separate system of military justice. The Court explained:

> The purpose of a separate system of military tribunals is to allow the Armed Forces to deal with matters that pertain directly to the discipline, efficiency and morale of the military. The safety and well-being of Canadians depends considerably on the willingness and readiness of a force of men and women to defend against threats to the nation's security. To maintain the Armed Forces in a state of readiness, the military must be in a position to enforce internal discipline effectively and efficiently. Breaches of military discipline must be dealt with speedily and, frequently, punished more severely than would be the case if a civilian engaged in such conduct. As a result, the military has its own Code of Service Discipline to allow it to meet its particular disciplinary needs. In addition, special service tribunals, rather than the ordinary courts, have been given jurisdiction to punish breaches of the Code of Service Discipline. Recourse to the ordinary criminal courts would, as a general rule, be inadequate to serve the particular disciplinary needs of the military. There is thus a need for separate tribunals to enforce special disciplinary standards in the military.[6]

Such reasoning is a modern expression of a long-standing principle. The paramount need to maintain discipline in a state's armed forces has been recognised since ancient times.[7] But in the popular imagination, this recognition is often accompanied by an unreflective prejudice that military justice systems give scant regard to fairness or justice in order to maintain discipline.[8] This need not be so. The ends of discipline and

[4] Michael Gibson, 'Military Tribunals' in Rudiger Wolfrum (ed.), *The Max Planck Encyclopedia of Public International Law* (Oxford, Oxford University Press, 2012).

[5] *R* v. *Généreux* [1992] 1 SCR 259. [6] Ibid., at 293.

[7] The importance of discipline to the refashioned military that arose after the English civil war, and upon which military justice in the common law world was originally based, is made clear in Charles M. Clode, *The Administration of Justice under Military and Martial Law*, 2nd edn, (London, John Murray, 1872), ch. 2.

On the nature and history of authority in the military, see also N. Keijzer, *Military Obedience* (Alphen aan den Rijn, Sijthof & Noordhoff, 1978).

[8] As reflected in the widely cited and now somewhat tired maxim attributed to the French prime minister Georges Clemenceau that 'military justice is to justice what military music is to music'.

justice are not mutually exclusive. The authority of commanders and the military itself depends upon the obedience, loyalty and trust of its members. Discipline and justice are not competing or mutually exclusive concepts, but are different elements in the same structure. The inherent connection between the two was recognised by the Powell Report of 1960, which reviewed elements of the American *Uniform Code of Military Justice*. The Powell Report recognised that:

> Discipline – a state of mind which leads to a willingness to obey an order no matter how unpleasant or dangerous the task to be performed – is not a characteristic of a civilian community. Development of this state of mind among soldiers is a command responsibility and a necessity. In the development of discipline, correction of individuals is indispensable; in correction, fairness or justice is indispensable. Thus, it is a mistake to talk of balancing discipline and justice – the two are inseparable.[9]

Any examination of military justice systems should proceed on the understanding that notions of discipline and fairness are not competing concepts. Any consideration of reform should not therefore be guided by questions of whether the level of discipline or fairness should be raised or lowered. Rather than becoming entrenched in rigid positions that reflect ideological predispositions about military justice, the question that should be posed is: what is it that a particular country, as a state, needs its military justice system to do? Once the answer to this key question is ascertained, the next question is: what functional attributes does such a system need to possess in order to effectively accomplish these ends? Once this analysis is undertaken, it is possible to determine what the ambit of the jurisdiction of the military justice system should be in terms of offences, persons, territory and time, and what differences in procedure from civilian criminal justice systems may be required.

The Canadian military justice system provides useful illustrations of these issues. The Canadian system has experienced extensive scrutiny and reform in recent years, including independent reviews conducted by senior retired members of the civilian judiciary.[10] The Canadian military

9 United States Department of Defense, *Report to the Honourable Wilber M. Brucker, Secretary of the Army, by Committee on the Uniform Code of Military Justice, Good Order and Discipline in the Army (Powell Report)* (OCLC 31702839)(18 January 1960), at 11, www.loc.gov/rr/frd/Military_Law/pdf/Powell_report.pdf. The report is known as the Powell Report because it was chaired by Lt Gen Herbert Powell.

10 One is known as the 'Lamer Report', which is *The First Independent Review by the Right Honourable Antonio Lamer PC, CC, CD of the provisions and operation of Bill C-25, An Act to amend the National Defence Act and to make consequential amendments to other*

justice system is now accepted to have two fundamental purposes. The first is to promote the operational effectiveness of the Canadian forces by contributing to the maintenance of discipline, efficiency and morale of military personnel. The second is to contribute to respect for the law and the maintenance of a just, peaceful and safe society. The system thus serves the ends of both discipline and justice.[11]

These purposes are stated in the statutory articulation of purposes, principles and objectives of sentencing in the military justice system, now found in the National Defence Act[12] by virtue of the amendments recently made to it by Bill C-15.[13] Those new stated purposes include the two fundamental objectives of promoting operational effectiveness of the armed forces by 'contributing to the maintenance of discipline, efficiency and morale' and also 'respect for the law and the maintenance of a just, peaceful and safe society'.[14] The other wider social and military legislative objectives of sentencing in Canadian military justice include the promotion of a habit of obedience to lawful commands, the maintenance of public trust in the Canadian armed forces as a disciplined entity, the denunciation of unlawful conduct, the promotion of a sense of responsibility in offenders, deterrence and the possible reintegration of offenders into the armed forces' functions.[15] This statutory list recognises that it is in the process of sentencing that the following question is most acute: what is the purpose of trying a person in the military justice system? It is against that background that one can fully appreciate the remarks of the sentencing judge in a case delivered prior to the enactment of this statutory list. In the case of *R* v. *R.A. Semrau*,[16] in which a soldier was found to have shot a wounded person while on patrol in Afghanistan, the court stressed the wider social and legal values of Canada upon which

Acts, as required under section 96 of the Statutes of Canada 1998, c.35 (2003). The other is known as the 'Le Sage Report', namely the *Report of the Second Independent Review Authority to the Honourable Peter G. Mackay, Minister of National Defence* (2011). There will be further such reviews as the Minister for Defence is now required to call for an independent review of key elements of defence legislation at seven-year intervals: National Defence Act, RS 1985 c. N-5, s. 273.601.

11 It is also arguable that the system, although directed to the armed forces and its personnel, serves a wider national function. That possibility is alluded to in the short title of an Act to amend the National Defence Act and to make consequential amendments to other Acts, which is the Strengthening Military Justice in the Defence of Canada Act SC 2013, c. 24.

12 National Defence Act, RS 1985, c. N-5. s. 203.1(1)(a).

13 Strengthening Military Justice in the Defence of Canada Act SC 2013, c. 24, cl. 62.

14 National Defence Act, RS 1985, c. N-5. 203.1(1).

15 Ibid., s. 203.1(2).

16 [2010] CM 4010 (*Semrau*).

that nation's armed forces and their justice system were based. The judge then explained that:

> Canadian soldiers become role models for their ... counterparts through the application of our doctrine, our training, our code of conduct and our rules of engagement. A disciplined approach to war that adheres to our lawful orders and our doctrine ensures the success of the mission.[17]

The synthesis of the classic criminal law sentencing objectives of denunciation, specific and general deterrence, rehabilitation and restitution, with those targeted at specifically military objectives, such as promoting a habit of obedience to lawful commands and orders and the maintenance in a democratic state of public trust in the military, illustrates that military law has a more positive purpose than the general criminal law in seeking to mould and modify behaviour to the requirements of military service. Simply put, an effective military justice system, guided by the correct principles, is a prerequisite for the effective functioning of the armed forces of a modern democratic state governed by the rule of law.[18] It is also crucial to ensuring the compliance of states and their armed forces with the normative requirements of international human rights law and international humanitarian law.

II Functional attributes

In order to accomplish these fundamental purposes, service tribunals must possess certain functional attributes. These include the requisite jurisdiction to deal with matters pertaining to the maintenance of discipline and operational effectiveness; that those possessing the powers of adjudication must possess an understanding of the necessity for, the role of and the requirements of discipline; they must operate in a legally fair manner and be perceived to be fair. This final attribute arises both from the need to maintain societal support in a democratic society and the fact that, in all-volunteer armed forces, soldiers, sailors and airmen and airwomen will not long abide by a system they feel to be fundamentally unfair. Service tribunals must also be compliant with the constitutional law of the state and the international law applicable to

[17] Ibid., at [36].

[18] A compelling case to this effect was made by Mark Martins in his landmark article 'Rules of Engagement for Land Forces: A Matter of Training, Not Lawyering' (1994) 143 *Military Law Review*, p. 1.

that state;[19] and, they must be prompt, portable and flexible.[20] These features account for the design of the two types of service tribunals in the Canadian military justice system; courts martial and summary trials.

The last three attributes require further explanation. Promptness is required in order to fulfil the requirement to maintain discipline. There are also constitutional requirements that criminal offences be tried within a reasonable time.[21] This objective requires that the trial of alleged offences occur sufficiently proximate in time to the commission of the offence. The important purposes of specific and general deterrence are lost if discipline is not administered clearly and as quickly as fairness allows. The maintenance of discipline is not assisted if a trial is held over a year later, thousands of kilometres from the place of commission of the offence. Portability refers to the ability of the military justice system to hold trials in various locations, including extraterritorial deployments in zones of active armed conflict. Flexibility refers to the ability to hold trials at all points along the spectrum of conflict, from peacetime in garrison on the home territory of the state, to zones of active armed conflict. Therefore, military justice must be as flexible as the military itself.

III Military justice in operational settings

The necessity for portability and flexibility of military justice systems arises most acutely in deployed operations, particularly extraterritorial deployments outside the domestic territory of the sending state. When military forces are sent into operational settings, the sending state will have very little recourse to its domestic civilian courts. The ability to hold trials in such circumstances may be regarded as a core attribute, or even

[19] Most prominently reflected in the judicial guarantees found at Article 14 of the International Covenant on Civil and Political Rights, 16 December 1966, in force 23 March 1976, 999 UNTS 171.

[20] For an expanded discussion of these functional attributes, see Michael Gibson, 'International Human Rights Law and the Administration of Justice through Military Tribunals: Preserving Utility While Precluding Impunity' (2008) 4 *Journal of International Law and International Relations*, p. 1.

[21] Those broad requirements arise from s. 11(d) of the Canadian Charter of Rights and Freedoms, which the Supreme Court of Canada has held require trial within a 'reasonable time': *R* v. *Morin* [1992] 1 SCR 771 (*Morin*). The several factors in *Morin* used to determine whether a delay is/is not reasonable are applicable to military justice cases but seem also to provide sufficient flexibility to meet the particular concerns of military justice. See *R* v. *LeGresley* [2008] CMAC 2.

the raison d'être, for military justice systems. Whenever troops are deployed, the need for some form of justice inevitably arises. This point came into focus in the case of *Semrau*, where the accused soldier challenged the decision to convene his court martial in Canada rather than the Kandahar airbase in Afghanistan. The accused argued that his court martial could only be validly conducted in the place where the offence occurred. The General Court Martial rejected the claim, finding that common law concepts governing the appropriate 'venue' of a trial and the military justice notions of 'convening' a court martial essentially governed the issue of where a trial could or should be held. Importantly, the more restrictive rules of the common law could not sensibly apply to military justice. The Court Martial cautioned 'That is not to say that the factors applicable to a change of venue in ordinary criminal courts are irrelevant when the parties seek to change the location of the trial or portions of the trial.'[22] But the Court Martial also made clear that decisions about the venue of a military hearing were ultimately procedural ones that were not subject to review.

Experience has demonstrated that it is possible to describe a range of offences that may occur in operational settings. A broad taxonomy might be described in the following terms. The first category is criminal-type offences against the person. Examples of this might include murder, torture, assault or sexual assault. It is essential that allegations of such offences which arise during operational deployments be promptly, thoroughly and effectively investigated and, where the investigation discloses grounds to lay a charge, be dealt with expeditiously and effectively in the military justice system. Recent controversies concerning allegations of sexual assault in the US armed forces illustrate the importance for the maintenance of discipline, operational effectiveness and public confidence in the armed forces that such cases be dealt with promptly and appropriately.[23] While the right to a speedy trial is widely regarded as an important civil right, in the military it is as important to the institution as it is to the individual defendant.[24]

[22] *R* v. *Semrau* [2010] CM 1003, at [21].

[23] The most notorious modern example in the US defence forces is the so-called Tailhook scandal, which is explained in D. Schlueter, 'Arrest Tail: The Prosecution of Sexual Harassment in the Military' (1994) 140 *Military Law Review*, p. 1. These issues are regarded with such seriousness that the US Department of Defense is required to report annually to Congress on the measures it is taking to detect and prevent sexual assault within the armed forces. See www.sapr.mil/index.php/annual-reports.

[24] A point developed at more length in Chapter 17.

The second category of offences is criminal-type offences against property, such as fraud and theft of material. Deployed zones of operation offer a number of opportunities for fraud and theft, given the many allowances disbursed to deployed personnel and the large stocks of equipment, vehicles, foodstuffs, fuel, computers and other materiel that will likely be present in any major operation. A third category includes the classic disciplinary-type offences such as quarrelling, drunkenness, failure to properly maintain equipment or weapons, and negligent or unintended discharge of weapons. The ever-present necessity to deal promptly and effectively with such offences is only heightened with the stresses and demands of operating in deployed environments, frequently in zones of conflict.

A fourth category of offences is those which might colloquially be described as 'dumb' offences, arising from the boredom or stupidity which inevitably arises in operational settings. The life of a soldier on deployment in an active zone of operations is often described as constituting 90 per cent boredom, and 10 per cent panic. It is essential to maintain discipline and efficiency during the periods of boredom, as incidents that might at first appear to be merely comic or annoying can quickly transition into tragedy. One example of this from Canadian experience is the case of *R* v. *Corporal M.A. Wilcox*.[25] Corporal Wilcox was a Reserve Force soldier whose task on deployment was to be a gate guard at the ISAF base in Kandahar Airfield, Afghanistan. This involved long shifts of routine in an environment where danger potentially constantly lurked. On 6 March 2007, Corporal Wilcox was alleged to have shot and killed one of his tent mates in a game of 'quickdraw' that took place in their tent after the end of a long guard shift. Corporal Wilcox was charged with manslaughter, criminal negligence causing death and negligent performance of a military duty.[26] A General Court Martial found Wilcox guilty of criminal negligence causing death and negligent performance of duty.[27] He was sentenced by the Military Judge to four years' imprisonment, dismissal, a weapons prohibition order for five years following release, and an order to be registered in the federal DNA databank. His appeal to the Court Martial Appeal Court on technical grounds relating to the selection of the panel of the General Court Martial was allowed, and a new trial

[25] [2011] CM 3012.

[26] A claim of self-defence was rejected in the second and final trial: *R* v. *Corporal M.A. Wilcox* [2011] CM 3012, at [132]–[134].

[27] *R* v. *Corporal M.A. Wilcox* [2009] CM 2014.

ordered.[28] On re-trial, he was again convicted of the same offences, and sentenced to the same punishments.[29] The tragic circumstances of the *Wilcox* case illustrate both the necessity of strict maintenance of discipline in what may be boring and routine duties on deployed operations, and the necessity to deal effectively with such breaches of discipline when they occur for reasons of both general and specific deterrence. The charge and resulting sentence no doubt provided a salutary reminder to soldiers and their commanders of the need to guard against lax behaviour and its potentially dangerous consequences.

The fifth category is what might be described as operational offences. Such offences have a special nexus with the operational setting in which they occur. This can be illustrated by the case of *R* v. *Captain R.A. Semrau*.[30] On 19 October 2008, in Helmand Province, Afghanistan, Captain Semrau was a member of the Operational Mentor and Liaison Team (OMLT), one of the most dangerous jobs in the Afghan theatre of operations. On that day he was the leader of a group of four Canadian soldiers acting as mentors to an Afghan Army patrol which was engaged by insurgents. After an Apache helicopter strike was called in, the group came upon a severely wounded Afghan man. The sequence of events that occurred next was the subject of controversy and led to charges of attempted murder, disgraceful conduct and negligent performance of a military duty against Captain Semrau.[31] It was alleged that he dispatched the wounded insurgent with two shots from his rifle as a 'mercy killing'.[32] A General Court Martial found him guilty of disgraceful conduct,[33] and he was sentenced to reduction in rank to Second Lieutenant and dismissal from Her Majesty's Service.

The reasons for sentence of the Military Judge delivered on 5 October 2010 provide a keen insight into the realities of the situation and the underlying importance of states abiding by their obligations under

28 *R* v. *Wilcox* [2011] CMAC 534. 29 *R* v. *Corporal M.A. Wilcox* [2011] CM 3012.

30 [2010] CM 4010.

31 Negligent performance of a military duty is contrary to s. 124 of the Code of Service Discipline contained in the National Defence Act RS 1985 c. N-5.

32 The issue of mercy killing has attracted the attention of Canadian courts, most notably in *Carter* v. *Canada (Attorney General)* [2012] BCSAAC 886. The lengthy decision of the Supreme Court of British Columbia in that case considered mercy killing in the context of physician assisted suicide. The Supreme Court did not cite the *Semrau* case.

33 An offence contrary to s. 93 of the Code of Service Discipline contained in the National Defence Act RS 1985 c. N-5. That section provides that anyone 'who behaves in a cruel or disgraceful manner is guilty of an offence and on conviction is liable to imprisonment for a term not exceeding five years or less punishment'.

international humanitarian law, even under the most difficult of circumstances. The Military Judge explained that:

> Decisions based on personal values cannot prevail over lawful commands . . . you committed a serious breach of discipline. You failed in your role as a leader because you chose to put aside your training and orders . . .
>
> You might have been torn between your personal moral values and your duties as a Canadian soldier when you made your choice; but did you consider the dilemma you were inflicting upon your subordinates? . . .
>
> How can we expect our soldiers to follow the laws of war if their officers do not? . . .
>
> In the military context, you committed a grave breach of discipline because you decided to set aside your orders, training and fundamental principles. As I stated previously, this conduct is deemed disgraceful because it is so fundamentally contrary to our values and training that it is shockingly unacceptable. The profession of arms is synonymous with the management of violence. Officers are ultimately entrusted to lead soldiers and to use weapons systems to put in to effect the will of our government. Our discipline and respect for the rule of law ensures that we remain an effective and efficient armed force that reflects Canadian values and makes Canadians proud of its military force's achievements around the world. You personally failed to abide by one of our most important responsibilities: that of only using force in accordance with lawful orders.[34]

IV Challenges in operational settings

The importance of maintaining discipline and the ability to hold trials in operational settings is quite clear but there may be many practical challenges in putting this into actual practice. The first of these is the perceived administrative burdens of holding courts martial in zones of active military operations. Commanders, who have many other responsibilities, including taking what may be life-and-death decisions, may be reluctant to divert their attention and resources from what they may perceive as more pressing or higher priority tasks. There are very real questions of cost: it is expensive to bring military judges, court reporters and panel members to a theatre of operations. It also requires operational readiness and flexibility on the part of military judges. Procuring witnesses may be a difficult, complex and expensive undertaking. Requiring members of court-martial panels to deploy into theatre inevitably has an opportunity cost in terms of taking them away from their regular duties

[34] *R* v. *Semrau* [2010] CM 4010, at [36], [37]–[38] and [45].

for a (usually uncertain) period of time. Moreover, the complexity of procedures of a court martial compared to a summary trial may seem an awkward luxury in the austere circumstances of a deployed operation in a place such as Afghanistan.

There is some salience to all of these potential impediments to holding trials in deployed theatres of operation. However, there are a number of important considerations in any cost–benefit calculation. The first (as already explained) is the overriding imperative to maintain discipline and operational effectiveness. The second is the necessity to preclude real or perceived impunity for the commission of offences. The third is to uphold the rule of law. The rule of law is now often cited in the context of both national and multinational operations sanctioned by resolutions of the United Nations Security Council as one of the fundamental principles animating and underlying operations.[35] In addition it is also important to consider the rights of soldiers charged with offences. Whatever form a justice system might take when troops are deployed, it cannot deny or significantly diminish the rights of the accused. Either by reason of the seriousness of the alleged offence, or by having made an election to do so, soldiers may have a legal right to trial by a court martial, with the full panoply of legal protections that this implies. Finally, there is the simple but profound imperative of doing justice: justice for the soldiers alleged to have committed offences, justice for the victims, who may include members of the local population, and justice for the broader community of members of the armed forces and civil society. Overall, the expense of holding courts martial in zones of active military operations should be seen as merely part of the cost of doing business for a modern military bound by legal obligations and determined to uphold the rule of law.

Negative effects of not trying cases in theatres of operation may also be readily identified. These include allowing perceptions of impunity to fester and the risk of diminished legitimacy and consequent negative impact upon the reputation of the mission. In many situations, these issues are the very centre of gravity of mission success. There will certainly be a negative impact upon the maintenance of discipline and

[35] A striking Canadian example is the *Statement of Defence Ethics*, which applies to employees of the Canadian Department of National Defence (DND) and the Canadian Armed Forces (CAF). Clause 3.1 provides that 'At all time and in all places, DND employees and CAF members shall uphold Canada's parliamentary democracy and its institutions by respecting the rule of law'. See www.forces.gc.ca/en/about/statement-of-defence-ethics .page.

consequently the operational effectiveness of the force. Finally, as a general precept of law and societal values, justice for victims of offences committed by soldiers on deployed operations must not only be done, but be seen to be done.

V Peacekeeping operations

The application of these precepts seems fairly clear in the context of national operations. They are also very important in considering peacekeeping missions created by or in association with the United Nations. One of the great embarrassments for the international community over the past decades has been the prevalence of sexual abuse and exploitation and black marketing by military and civilian members of UN contingents.[36] A prominent example is that of forces deployed under the aegis of the United Nations in the Democratic Republic of the Congo. These issues have led to a number of responses being taken. One is the creation of Conduct and Discipline Units within the Department of Field Support and within UN Department of Peacekeeping Operations (DPKO) missions.[37] Another is the creation of a Draft Convention on criminal accountability of UN officials and experts on mission, and the adoption by the United Nations General Assembly of a Resolution on the criminal accountability of United Nations officials and experts on mission.[38] However, both of these measures are of limited utility in the context of UN peacekeeping missions. The bottom line is that military personnel in a peace support operation are under the jurisdiction of their sending state as the UN is unable to exercise criminal jurisdiction. There is no 'UN Court' for DPKO missions, and as Peter Rowe has indicated the likelihood of such an evolution remains a distant dream.[39]

It is also unlikely that the International Criminal Court could be effectively used as a vehicle for enforcement of discipline on UN

[36] See, for example, the *Report of the Secretary-General*, '*Special Measures for Protection from Sexual Exploitation and Sexual Abuse*', 58th Sess, UN Doc A/58/777 (23 April 2004).

[37] It should not be assumed that these problems are limited to international or peacekeeping operations. Similar problems have occurred in Africa when armed forces have been engaged in operations within the borders of their own nation. See, for example, Akachi Odoemene, 'The Nigerian Armed Forces and Sexual Violence in Ogoniland of the Niger Delta Nigeria, 1990–1999' (2012) 38 *Armed Forces and Society*, p. 225.

[38] 6th Comm 67th Sess, UN Doc A/RES/63/119 (15 January 2009).

[39] Peter Rowe, 'Maintaining Discipline in United Nations Peace Support Operations: The Legal Quagmire for Military Contingents' (2000) 5 *Journal Conflict & Security Law*, p. 45.

peacekeeping missions.[40] Such a suggestion ignores the fact that the ICC, in the terms of the *Rome Statute*,[41] is meant to exercise its jurisdiction over only 'the most serious crimes of international concern,'[42] and confuses an aspiration for the future effectiveness of the ICC with the practical reality of resource constraints. It also ignores the basic fact that the ICC is meant to operate on the principle of complementarity with national jurisdictions and is not designed to replace them.

Although it is ultimately the responsibility of sending states to discipline their troops, the application of standard regulations to all personnel is necessary for the effective functioning of a mission. However, violations of UN Codes of Conduct are not subject to disciplinary action without the reinforcement of national criminal law in any event. The reality is that it is for sending states on UN missions to enforce the disciplinary standards of their national contingents. And, notwithstanding the reluctance of some states to enforce at least certain types of offences, such as sexual assault against members of the local population, there is no effective substitute for the ability to hold trials *in situ* in theatres of deployed operations.

This reality is reflected in the assessment and recommendations of the *Zeid Report*, which concluded:

> An on-site court martial for serious offences that are criminal in nature would afford immediate access to witnesses and evidence in the mission area. An on-site court martial would demonstrate to the local community that there is no impunity for acts of sexual exploitation and abuse by members of military contingents . . .
>
> Therefore, all troop-contributing countries should hold on-site courts martial. Those countries which remain committed to participating in peacekeeping operations but whose legislation does not permit on-site courts martial should consider reform of the relevant legislation.[43]

40 For a discussion of the use of the Rome Statute to prosecute sexual abuse by peacekeeping forces, see: Melanie O'Brien, 'Sexual Exploitation and Beyond: Using the Rome Statute of the International Criminal Court to Prosecute UN Peacekeepers for Gender-Based Crimes' (2011) 11 *International Criminal Law Review*, p. 803.

41 Rome Statute of the International Criminal Court, 17 July 1998, in force 1 July 2002, 2187 UNTS 90 (Rome Statute).

42 For a discussion of the problems associated with potential prosecution by the ICC, see Roisin Burke, 'UN Military Peacekeeper Complicity in Sexual Abuse: The ICC or a Tri-Hybrid Court' in Morten Bergsmo (ed.), *Thematic Prosecution of International Sex Crimes* (Beijing, Torkel Opsahl Academic EPublisher, 2012), p. 317.

43 *A Comprehensive Strategy to Eliminate Future Sexual Exploitation and Abuse in UN Peacekeeping Operations* 59th Sess UN Doc A/59/710 (24 March 2005) (*Zeid Report*).

The consequence of all of these considerations is that states should undertake to structure and resource their justice systems to provide for an ability to hold trials *in situ* for their national military and civilian personnel on deployed operations.

VI Transitional justice and capacity-building

In states recovering from protracted periods of conflict, in which much or most of the human resources and physical infrastructure necessary to run an effective justice system have been dissipated or destroyed, military justice systems may well constitute the only near-term possibility of achieving justice in many cases. Although there may be limited enthusiasm for this proposition on the part of some in the international human rights community, its salience has been recognised by the United Nations Security Council. For example, paragraph 12 of UN Security Council Resolution 1925 regarding MONUSCO, the United Nations Mission in the Democratic Republic of Congo, provided that the mandate of the mission includes:

> (m) Assist[ing] the Government, along with international and bilateral partners, in strengthening its military capacity, including military justice and military police . . . support military justice institutions and mobilize donors to provide equipment and other required resources.

Such a perspective reflects a very clear-sighted recognition of both practical realities and principle.

As demonstrated in the case of the Democratic Republic of Congo (DRC), Security Sector Reform (SSR) is often one of the key objectives of UN peacekeeping missions in countries in transition. This recognises the reality that in many such countries, the security sector is not designed to protect the population. There is often a clear correlation between armed conflict and crime. Military forces such as the Congolese Armed Forces (FARDC) may use the abuse of the population as a military tactic. There are often situations of entrenched corruption and exploitation as well as a cycle of impunity. The goal of the international community should be to put an end to the cycle of impunity and transition the security sector in such countries from being an abuser of the population, to being its protector. The armed forces would then fulfil their appropriate mission of defending the population and its territory, and being a symbol of pride and unity for the people of a state, rather than one of terror.

Why does military justice in countries such as the DRC ultimately matter? First, as recognised in successive UN Security Council Resolutions, strengthening the military justice system in the DRC is imperative because in its own right, the military justice system is a primary vehicle for promoting the rule of law and human rights.[44] It is the main legal tool and accountability mechanism within the FARDC for ending the culture of impunity amongst its members. Second, reforming and strengthening the capacity of the military justice system is also an essential prerequisite for security sector reform. The level of individual and institutional discipline in the FARDC is low, and thus its operational effectiveness and ability to defend the DRC and its people is low. Improving the effectiveness of the DRC military justice system is an essential prerequisite for improving the discipline and operational effectiveness of the FARDC, and thus its ability to fulfil its constitutional mission of protecting the DRC, in a manner that is consonant with its obligations under international law, including respect for human rights and international humanitarian law.[45] This proposition is one that may readily be transferrable to situations of transitional justice in other countries.

VII Self-interest of armed forces in accountability

It may be cogently argued that armed forces have a clear self-interest in any country in accountability and in developing a military justice system as a mechanism to achieve this goal. There are many reasons why this is so. Encouraging recognition of this, and appropriate resource allocation, by developing states to give effect to this goal, may make a significant contribution to improving the quality of justice in those states.

The first of these reasons relates to the reality (discussed above) that an effective military justice system is essential for the operational effectiveness of the armed forces, and for promoting its constituent elements of discipline, cohesion and morale. The existence of an operationally effective armed force is ultimately one of the primary reasons that states invest their human and financial capital in such forces. Second, military justice systems serve to do justice, both for the members of the armed forces themselves, and for others with whom they come into contact, both domestically and internationally. Third, properly constituted and operated, military justice systems serve to

44 For example, SC Res 1925, 6324 mtg, UN Doc S/RES/1925 (28 May 2010), at [12(d)].

45 See discussion at Monusco United National Organization Stabilization Mission in the DR Congo http://monusco.unmissions.org. The author contributed his views in this regard during his deployment with the Rule of Law Unit of MONUC.

protect the rights of soldiers whom the state and its people ask to undertake dangerous and essential risks and tasks. Fourth, such systems uphold the rule of law as a key value. Fifth, they enhance the prospect of broader societal support, which is important for recruitment, the allocation of resources by the government (particularly in times of budget stringency, when there may be many other competing demands), and legitimacy of the armed forces within society. Sixth, it enhances internal support within the armed forces, which is important for morale and retention of trained service members. Next, it has a direct impact on the perceptions of legitimacy of the armed forces, which can have a direct and crucial impact on mission accomplishment. Moreover, self-regulation is often seen as a hallmark of professionalism. The 'Profession of Arms' would in this case partake of the same principle as other professions such as medicine, law, engineering and others. Ninth, the creation and operation of an effective and fair military justice system is a key element in precluding impunity for the commission of crimes. Tenth, in situations of transitional justice, military justice systems can play a key role in societal transformation and security sector reform. Finally, professionalisation of the armed forces is one of the core attributes of mature and stable states, and can constitute a key element to progress in creating just, stable and sustainable societies.

VIII Conclusion

Military justice systems are important because they possess unique functions and qualities which set them apart from the wider legal systems in which they operate. Military justice can be better understood if greater attention is paid to the unusual circumstances in which the military must operate. The increasing importance of operational deployments, UN peacekeeping missions and situations of transitional justice in developing states recovering from periods of protracted armed conflict make such circumstances ideal for further analysis of military justice. While these and other missions sometimes operate far from the eyes of domestic audiences, they now constitute a crucial element of military operations. International peacekeeping missions and deployments in developing states during periods of transitional justice cannot be regarded as isolated or novel forms of military activity. Every aspect of the military must adjust to these circumstances. States should undertake a clear-eyed analysis and provide their military justice systems with the appropriate legal jurisdiction and practical resources to enable them to fulfil their responsibilities in these vital areas.

AUTHOR INDEX

INDEX